**Going
Underground**

Going Underground

LARA LANGER COHEN

RACE, SPACE, AND
THE SUBTERRANEAN IN
THE NINETEENTH-CENTURY
UNITED STATES

DUKE UNIVERSITY PRESS *Durham and London* 2023

© 2023 DUKE UNIVERSITY PRESS
All rights reserved
Project editor: Ihsan Taylor
Designed by Matthew Tauch
Typeset in Adobe Jenson Pro by
Westchester Publishing Services

Library of Congress Cataloging-in-Publication Data
Names: Cohen, Lara Langer, author.
Title: Going underground : race, space, and the subterranean in the nineteenth-century United States / Lara Langer Cohen.
Description: Durham : Duke University Press, 2023. | Includes bibliographical references and index.
Identifiers: LCCN 2022029781 (print)
LCCN 2022029782 (ebook)
ISBN 9781478016847 (hardcover)
ISBN 9781478019480 (paperback)
ISBN 9781478024125 (ebook)
Subjects: LCSH: American literature—African American authors—History and criticism. | American literature—19th century—History and criticism. | African Americans—Intellectual life—19th century. | Literature and society—United States—History—19th century. | Politics and literature—United States—History—19th century. | African Americans—Race identity. | African Americans—History—19th century. | United States—Race relations—History—19th century. | BISAC: LITERARY CRITICISM / Modern / 19th Century | LITERARY CRITICISM / American / General
Classification: LCC PS153.B53 C644 2023 (print) | LCC PS153.B53 (ebook) | DDC 810.9/003—dc23/eng/20220927
LC record available at https://lccn.loc.gov/2022029781
LC ebook record available at https://lccn.loc.gov/2022029782

Cover art: Thomas Wallace Knox, *Underground, or Life Below the Surface*, frontispiece, 1873. Courtesy of the Library Company of Philadelphia.

Contents

ACKNOWLEDGMENTS   vii

Introduction: A Basement Shut Off and Forgotten during the Nineteenth Century   1

1   The "Blackness of Darkness" in Mammoth Cave   25

2   Early Black Radical Undergrounds   46

3   The Underground Railroad's Undergrounds   74

4   The Depths of Astonishment: City Mysteries and Subterranean Unknowability   104

5   "To Drop beneath the Floors of the Outer World": Paschal Beverly Randolph's Occult Undergrounds   133

6   Subterranean Fire: Anarchist Visions of the Underground   166

Epilogue: Staying Underground   198

NOTES   205
BIBLIOGRAPHY   245
INDEX   267

Acknowledgments

So many people contributed so much to this book in the long time it took me to write it, and it's a pleasure to get to thank them in print. A National Endowment for the Humanities Fellowship at the American Antiquarian Society supported early research on this project, and I am grateful to all the librarians and staff at the AAS. Thank you especially to Paul Erickson for sharing his vast knowledge of city mysteries, asking key questions, driving me to the emergency room, and making me laugh until I thought I would truly die. An American Council of Learned Societies Frederick Burkhardt Fellowship gave me time away from teaching for writing, as did a George Becker Faculty Fellowship from Swarthmore College. I thank Tania Johnson and David Foreman in Swarthmore's Office of Sponsored Programs for their help with the application process, as well as Marcia Brown in the Provost's Office and Denise Risoli in the Controller's Office for facilitating all the financial aspects.

Many people read drafts, talked over ideas with me, and offered suggestions, provocations, and encouragement. Thank you to David Anderson, Paula Austin, Nancy Bentley, Hester Blum, R. J. Boutelle, Daphne Brooks, Gina Marie Caison, Brian Connolly, Peter Coviello, Jonathan Eburne, Sari Edelstein, Paul Erickson, Jonathan Flatley, P. Gabrielle Foreman, Travis Foster, Kara French, Aston Gonzalez, Miles Grier, Colin Hogan, Gordon Hutner, Brian Kane, Danny Kroha, Trish Loughran, Geo Maher, Bakirathi Mani, Meredith McGill, Lloyd Pratt, Lindsay Reckson, Tyler Roeger, Britt Rusert, Susan Ryan (especially for the Mammoth Cave trip!), Kyla Schuller, Yumi Shiroma, Derrick Spires, Gus Stadler, Patricia White, Ed Whitley, Kidada Williams, and Lisa Ze Winters. Years ago, Laura Heffernan gently suggested to me that everything I was writing at the time was about unrecognizability; that recognition clarified so much. Conversations with Holly Jackson have fueled this project from the beginning, and her warm and insightful reading of the final chapters brought it all together.

I've been lucky to test out many of the ideas in this book in talks, and those invitations and the conversations that came out of them proved crucial. Thank you to interlocutors at the American Literature Working Group at the University of Pennsylvania, Penn State University, the Black Sound in the Archive Workshop at Yale University, the Faculty Working Group in American Studies at Haverford College, the Second Book Project Symposium at University of Illinois at Urbana-Champaign, the Workshop in the History of Material Texts, the Rutgers Americanist Colloquium, Columbia University, Lehigh University, and the University of Louisville.

At Duke University Press, Ken Wissoker's understanding of what I wanted to do in this project was almost uncanny. He believed before I did that a book about nineteenth-century undergrounds could speak to the present, and I am immensely grateful for his support. Two anonymous readers offered vital feedback that brought the book into focus, and I can't thank them enough for their suggestions and encouragement. One of those readers turned out to be Britt Rusert, which means that her brilliant thinking has shaped the project at nearly every stage. Ihsan Taylor deftly steered the manuscript through editing and production, Barbie Halaby copyedited it with patience and care, and Ryan Kendall made everything go smoothly. Kurt Newman not only expertly indexed this book but also helped me make a thematic playlist.

The Swarthmore English Department is full of scholars I admire who also happen to be generous colleagues and good friends. Thank you especially to Rachel Buurma, Anthony Foy, Nora Johnson, Bakirathi Mani, Gina Patnaik, and Eric Song. Nina Johnson and BuYun Chen and I never talk about writing, which is one reason among many I treasure their friendship. I am grateful to my students, too, for their sharp thinking and their commitment to make what we do in the classroom matter outside of it. The endnotes tell a fuller story of some of their contributions.

My intensely cerebral mother, Michele Langer, developed Alzheimer's as I was writing this book. I've never known anyone who enjoyed the pleasure of thinking—of revolving an idea until it caught new light—the way she did. I miss those conversations so much. I could not have written the book without Yanique Brown, who has cared for my mother with extraordinary insight and dedication and who has taught me a great deal about staying close to the unknowable. I am lucky to get to live in the same city as my father, Alan Cohen, and our closeness has been the joy of these years. Sacha Langer is the nearest thing I have to a sister, and I'm so glad. There are no words adequate to thank John Pat Leary for upending his career for mine. But I can say that there is nobody with whom I'd rather talk about anything, and the example of his own writing inspires me always. He line-edited many sentences in this book, hashed out ideas, and insisted I go big. I've been working on this book for Louisa Leary's entire life. Her ebullience and tenderheartedness lifted me that whole time, and both her notes of encouragement and her suggestion that we throw the work in the trash helped me finish at last.

Finally, thank you to my three writing groups; without them this book would definitely not exist. Both writing and taking breaks from writing are worlds better with Asali Solomon and Linda Kim. Bakirathi Mani and Patricia White read countless chapter drafts and offered incisive advice and the enormous gift of their faith in the project. Paula Austin, Kidada Williams, and Lisa Ze Winters make virtual camaraderie feel immediate and sustaining. The wisdom they bestowed on this book and everything beyond it has been invaluable.

Introduction

A BASEMENT SHUT OFF AND FORGOTTEN DURING THE NINETEENTH CENTURY

> I wish I was a mole in the ground,
> Yes, I wish I was a mole in the ground,
> If I was a mole in the ground, I'd root that mountain down,
> And I wish I was a mole in the ground.
>
> **"I Wish I Was a Mole in the Ground," first recorded by Fred Moody, 1921**

At the end of Ralph Ellison's *Invisible Man*, the unnamed narrator, running from three drunken white men, falls into an open coal chute. After "whirling on in the blackness" for a time that "might have been days, weeks," he famously decides to "take up residence underground." Making his home below "a building rented strictly to whites, in a section of the basement that was shut off and forgotten during the nineteenth century," he adopts a way of life that is also figuratively underground: he fights a "battle" against the resonantly named Monopolated Light & Power by stealing electricity and learns to speak in a subterranean register he calls "the lower frequencies."[1] *Going Underground* takes his descent as a provocation to ask what other undergrounds were "shut off and forgotten during the nineteenth century" and what possibilities they may yet hold.

Practices of collective subversion, resistance, refusal, and insurrection have existed as long as practices of domination. But the idea of the underground as a site of clandestine, unruly activity is an invention of the nineteenth century. First popularized as a metaphor by newspaper coverage of the Underground Railroad in the 1840s, the underground gave people new language and imagery to envision possibilities for living otherwise. In order to discern these visions, *Going Underground* excavates a vibrant world of nineteenth-century subterranean literature, including Black radical manifestos, anarchist periodicals, exposés of the urban underworld, manuals for sex magic, and the initiation rites of secret societies. I also seek out the underground obsessions of more familiar literature from the period— one whose emblematic text, *Moby-Dick*, after all, begins with the voice of the "Sub-Sub Librarian," a "painstaking burrower and grub-worm."[2] This study of early undergrounds is not simply antiquarian; it also has designs on the present. By mining past ideas of the underground, what forgotten modes of political imagination might we reanimate for today?

Before Subculture

To address this question, it is useful to distinguish *underground* from what is now often seen as its synonym, *subculture*. But *subculture* is a later invention, first defined over one hundred years after *underground*, and the two terms name historically specific, conceptually distinct formations.[3] In some ways nineteenth-century undergrounds—and, for that matter, various earlier unorthodox forms of social activity—prefigure what would crystallize into twentieth-century subculture, but in many other ways they elude its definition. These divergences, opacities, and losses are what occupy me most in this book. Although I am interested in the long history of subculture, I am even more interested in seeking out versions of the underground that were never incorporated into it. Let me highlight some key differences between these early versions of the underground and the concept of subculture that would supersede them.

One, the concept of subculture enters culture top-down, as a subject of scholarly inquiry, beginning with the Chicago school of sociology's urban ethnographies in the 1930s and continuing, in different veins, through the research on youth cultures at the University of Birmingham's Centre for Contemporary Cultural Studies in the 1970s and work on punk, hip-hop, techno, heavy metal, and other music scenes; drag cultures; tattoo enthusiasts; manga; early internet communities; and more in the decades that followed.⁴ But the idea of the underground emerges bottom-up. It takes shape in the pages of popular print culture—"popular" in the sense of vernacular, if not always widely read—including the newspapers, pamphlets, cheap fiction, songbooks, and so on that form the archive of this book. Accordingly, while *subculture* constitutes an attempt to define social life, *underground* addresses itself to no such task. As an idea, it comes into being by gradually accreting and constellating meanings rather than by methodically assigning them.

In fact, for much of the nineteenth century, *underground* names something indefinite and even undefinable—a "mystery," to borrow a word often associated with undergrounds. This presents a second difference from subculture. It would be impossible to construct a typology of nineteenth-century undergrounds, as Dick Hebdige famously did for postwar British youth subcultures in *Subculture: The Meaning of Style*. Such indefinability is partly a function of the idea's newness. But even once the figurative meaning of *underground* became a familiar description of subversive organizations—a shift I chart over the course of this book—these groups remained more recessive than "spectacular," as Hebdige describes subcultures, less concerned with recognition than with the affordances of opacity.⁵ This aversion to visibility endures in the use of *underground* today as a synonym for *secret*, as in underground movements, underground newspapers, or underground venues. But the undergrounds I explore theorize a more capacious, less instrumentalized understanding of opacity than *secrecy* conveys. Scandalous as they were, the occultist movement built by clairvoyant/sex magician/political activist/Freedmen's Bureau teacher Paschal Beverly Randolph (chapter 5) and the Chicago anarchist movement in the 1880s (chapter 6) were undergrounds not just out of necessity—that is, not just to do things that otherwise could not be done—but also because they understood the underground as a good in itself, which would be not only hidden from the world above but fundamentally out of keeping with it.

Three, the underground exceeds subculture's oppositional relation to dominant culture. Nineteenth-century undergrounds often have an autonomy from, or simply non-adhesion to, the world above ground that subculture's reactive model cannot encompass. While they are built below the surface, they are not bound to it, either through determination or rejection. At times going underground is an effect of subjugation, but at other times it is an act of refusal. Some undergrounds are sites to carve out other worlds, like the cave studio of the fugitive artist Bernice in William J. Wilson's newspaper serial "Afric-American Picture Gallery" (chapter 2), and some are sites to prepare the destruction of this world, like Detroit's militant antislavery secret society the African-American Mysteries (chapter 3). Undergrounds may oppose what lies above, but they may also ignore, reject, or nullify this bifurcation and forge different configurations. Because they are not locked into a countervailing relation with dominant culture, undergrounds can take us beyond a familiar political analysis that restricts minoritized cultural production to a secondary, reactive role. Chapter 1's discussion of literature about Mammoth Cave offers one example: I argue that the racialization of the cave as Black was not organically created by white visitors and unilaterally imposed upon the cave and the enslaved guides; rather, it was a response to the Black intellectual and imaginative work already taking place there.

A fourth conceptual difference between *subculture* and *underground* may be indexed by a semantic difference: *underground*, used in this sense, is a metaphor. Since it signifies what it does not explicitly name, it can enfold an array of meanings; it can even reference disparate meanings simultaneously. The clearest and most consequential example of the underground's early multiplicity is the long entanglement of its figurative meaning with its literal meaning, which I will discuss further shortly. Its expression as a metaphor allowed the concept of the underground to move promiscuously in the nineteenth century. It did not designate a single meaning so much as it summoned a repertoire of them, each of which imparted something of itself to the concepts of difference, noncompliance, and subversion the underground was coming to express. In short, the underground meant *more* in the nineteenth century than it does now. One way to understand the development of the concept of subculture in the twentieth century, then, might be as the regulation of these earlier ideas of the underground.

Two Genealogies of the Underground: Space and Race

As the concept of the underground emerged in the nineteenth century, I argue that it was mediated by two other formations: actual underground spaces and ideas about race. Ellison calls back to this triangulation in *Invisible Man*'s combined literal and figurative underground, rediscovered by a Black man who accesses it through a coal chute and then "whirl[s] on in the blackness." But the roles of space and race in the making of the underground have mostly slipped out of view, part of the "basement that was shut off and forgotten during the nineteenth century." One aim of this book is to recover their influence.

Whether in traditional nation-based literary criticism or in revisionary transnational frameworks, the spatial imaginaries of literary study have tended toward the planar. But before the word *pioneer* referred to settler colonists, Peter Stallybrass has shown, it meant "digger," as Karl Marx well knew when, in *The Eighteenth Brumaire of Louis Bonaparte* (1852), he quoted *Hamlet* to picture revolution as an "old mole," that "worthy pioneer."[6] Turning to these subterranean "pioneers" allows us to access a spatial imaginary that runs athwart the familiar frontiers of literary history. We might see the New Madrid earthquakes—which rocked the middle Mississippi Valley from December 1811 to February 1812, causing shakes, strange sounds and smells, and weird bodily sensations from Georgia to Connecticut—as announcing the unprecedented role of the underground in the nineteenth-century United States.[7] Cities grew down as well as up and out, as rapid urbanization led to the construction of subterranean infrastructures to convey water and sewage.[8] Mining for coal, gold, copper, lead, and other minerals exploded, and in 1859 the drilling of the first commercial oil well in Pennsylvania established petroleum as a major industry. These ventures below the earth's surface markedly reorganized life above it. Underground, Americans found a record of the earth's ceaseless activity and the vastness of its history, which dwarfed humans' almost infinitesimally brief tenure on it. Yet Dana Luciano argues that the dizzying abyss of "deep time," which "offered space for a radical rethinking of the place of the human in the order of nature," tended instead to elicit compensatory modes of thought that worked "to shore up extant human institutions and to extend human agency."[9] Specifically, as Kathryn Yusoff shows, geology—a science that arose in tandem with mining in the Americas that initiated the Atlantic slave trade—enabled a logic of white humanity through a logic of Black inhumanity created by "the traffic between *the inhuman as matter* and *the inhuman as race*."[10] For this reason, Yusoff urges us to understand geology as "a category and praxis of dispossession" and the objectification of Blackness, in turn, as "a geologic proposition."[11] Only through knowledge of this "grammar of geology," she contends, is it possible to forge an "insurgent geology" that "embraces its intimacies with the inhuman" as "a relation, no longer an appendage of fungibility."[12]

Like geology, the development of archaeology made the underground an object of growing intellectual inquiry, which circulated through a broad exhibition and print culture picturing the wonders that lay below readers' feet. The rise of archaeology, whose focus on excavation departed from earlier modes of antiquarianism, was propelled by discoveries like the "Kentucky Mummy" (supposedly found in Mammoth Cave, actually in nearby Short Cave) in 1815 and the excavation of massive ancient earthworks in the Ohio and Mississippi River valleys, built by Native Americans but often attributed to a lost non-Native civilization preceding them. Archaeology's underground revelations, like those of geology, were both ideologically charged and contradictory. On the one hand, the project of finding traces of Indigenous life underground facilitated settlers' possession of the land above by relegating Indigenous people to the buried past. On the other hand, the image of the earth as Indigenous beneath the surface sometimes rebounded in the prospect of an Indigenous underground engulfing settlers or bursting forth in their midst. An exploration of Indigenous ideas about the subterranean awaits another study by a more knowledgeable writer, but a few examples suggest that nineteenth-century Native Americans mobilized the subterranean in resistance to colonialism in ways that may have amplified settlers' misgivings about the relation between Indigeneity and the underground. Consider Nick Estes's observation that "during his campaign against US military invasion, to protect himself Crazy Horse collected fresh dirt from mole mounds"; consider, too, the visions of Crazy Horse's fellow Lakota Short Bull, who saw the ground swallowing US soldiers, and Kicking Bear, who saw all white people buried in a thick new layer of soil blanketing the earth.[13]

Literal undergrounds like those I discuss above were important to the emergent figurative meaning of the underground not just because *underground* was used in both these senses, as it is today, but also because for many years people understood these senses to be connected. A thick, lavishly illustrated 1873 volume by journalist Thomas Wallace Knox, titled *Underground, or Life Below the Surface: Incidents and Accidents Beyond the Light of Day; Startling Adventures in All Parts of the World; Mines and the Mode of Working Them; Under-Currents of Society; Gambling and Its Horrors; Caverns and Their Mysteries; The Dark Ways of Wickedness; Prisons and Their Secrets; Down in the Depths of the Sea; Strange Stories of the Detection of Crime*, illustrates the correlation (figure I.1). At almost a thousand pages, the book testifies to contemporaneous readers' interest in subterranean life. At the same time, the very range of *Underground* suggests how inchoate the idea of an underground was. As the impressive subtitle indicates, the book interweaves undergrounds of all kinds,

I.1 Frontispiece, Thomas Wallace Knox, *Underground, or Life Below the Surface* (1873). Courtesy of the Library Company of Philadelphia.

framing them all in lurid diction that Knox borrows from city mysteries and urban exposés, literary genres dedicated to representing the underground (and the subject of chapter 4). He explains in the preface that the book aims to "describe the life, not only of the miner, but of all who work under ground—whether literally or metaphorically."[14] He is unconcerned about what today we might take to be the irrelevance of these two modes of underground life to one another. Instead, he blithely jumbles chapters on "Explosions in Mines," "The Underground Railroad," "Vesuvius and Its Eruptions," "Underground in the Metropolis," "Animals Underground," "The Mammoth Cave," "Underground in Politics," "Guano and the Coolie Trade," and more into what one admiring reviewer called a veritable "encyclopedia of subterranean wonders."[15]

To observe the long and fitful disembedding of figurative from literal undergrounds is not to claim that every sewer or mine was synonymous with subversion in the nineteenth century. (Though as Marx reminded readers in 1844, the word *radical*—in German as in English—comes from "root": "To be radical is to grasp matters at the root."[16]) But it can help us discern versions of subversion that do not readily appear to us today. I am especially interested in how the residual spatiality of the underground *emplaces* subversion. What are the political affordances of visualizing insubordination as a space where one could dwell? To address this question, I examine figurations of cultural or political undergrounds that retain an oddly spatial dimension, such as the art studio in a cave that also turns out to be the site of vigilante antislavery praxis in Wilson's "Afric-American Picture Gallery" (chapter 1), the recurrent representations of the Underground Railroad as an actual subterranean train in the 1840s and 1850s (chapter 3), and the depictions of subversive elements gathering in tunnels, caverns, and tombs in city mysteries (chapter 4).

While literal undergrounds have some relation to figurative undergrounds, however extraneous that connection may appear from our perspective, racial thought has no obvious connection to the underground. Yet the chapters that follow will make the case that nineteenth-century ideas of the underground were often racialized, and most often, they were racialized as Black. This racialization of the underground proceeded from images of literal undergrounds and from there became a key vector for the emergence of the underground's figurative meaning. Moreover, because race is not a fixed biological category but a shifting cluster of concepts for producing hierarchies among humans (specifically, as Sylvia Wynter teaches us, by sorting their claims to humanity), this process also worked in reverse.[17] Even as ideas of racialized Blackness shaped ideas of the underground, ideas of the underground shaped ideas of racialized Blackness, so that the racialization of the underground takes place alongside what we might describe as the subterranization of Blackness. This intertwined genealogy elucidates how racialization takes place on ground that was never solid.

Associations between the underground and racialized Blackness took disparate forms and served disparate ends. Because categories of Blackness and Indigeneity have often been co-constitutive, as scholars including Frank Wilderson, Shona Jackson, Tiya Miles, and Tiffany Lethabo King have shown, associations between the underground and racialized Blackness emerged alongside and sometimes in explicit relation to associations between the underground and Indigeneity; chapters 1 and 2 offer examples of how different writers understood this relation. Some associations between the underground and racialized Blackness, especially from white writers, drew on predictable comparisons between subterranean darkness and the darkness of skin, like the analogies that white visitors to Kentucky's Mammoth Cave made between the Black guides and the cave itself. Some hinged, as Yusoff argues, on the intertwined histories of slavery and mining, and on the conflation of enslaved people with the inhuman, extractable matter they mined—an association perhaps haunted by the growing geological knowledge that rocks do move, sometimes with catastrophic results for those above. In other instances, associations between the underground and racialized Blackness render topographically the subjugation of African Americans in a white supremacist society. In still other instances, they emphasize how that society rests upon such subjugation. The most infamous example of this racialized subterranean imaginary may be South Carolina senator James Henry Hammond's "mudsill theory," a reference to the framing timbers of a building that are embedded underground, supporting what lies above. In an 1858 speech before the Senate, Hammond argued that all societies require a class that "constitutes the very mud-sill of society and of political government" and that the South has "found a race adapted to that purpose to her hand."[18] Hammond uses the metaphor of the mudsill to justify slavery, while indicting the North for using the white working class as *its* mudsill, which he considers "a degradation" rather than a natural disposition.

What became known as "mudsill theory" speaks to a contradictory logic underlying the racialization of the underground: on the one hand, the exclusion of Black life from the terrain of the world; on the other hand, the reliance *upon* Black life for that anti-Black world's coherence. By this second point

I mean both modern capitalism's dependency on Black labor, which Hammond acknowledges, and a deeper point, which he does not acknowledge but that lies at the heart of Cedric Robinson's concept of racial capitalism: modern capitalism's dependency on racism for its development. For Robinson, capitalism emerged as an "opportunistic strata" on a racialized social order, "willfully adaptive to the new conditions and possibilities offered by the times."[19] As capitalism developed, it continued (contrary to Marx's predictions) "not to homogenize but to differentiate—to exaggerate regional, subcultural, and dialectical differences into 'racial' ones."[20] Yet it is precisely by doing so that capitalism presents itself as what Robinson terms "an objective system"—a distinct order unto itself rather than an expansion of a racial order.[21] Hammond's mudsill metaphor is more telling than he realized. It not only images the construction of capitalism on a racialized hierarchy; its subterranean character also illustrates how racialized Blackness nonetheless *cannot be recognized* as foundational, the basis for capitalism's "opportunistic strata," to return to Robinson's words. As a constitutive element of capitalism, racialized Blackness must be submerged, like a mudsill, beneath the surface.

But if the underground figures racist hierarchies, it also conjures the specter of such hierarchies' upheaval. For when writers represent the underground, it is almost never as a static space but as one of unseen growth, movement, concealment, and other activity. Consider the widespread nineteenth-century trope of slavery as a "slumbering volcano" that might erupt on an enslaving nation at any moment. Once a fairly common expression for instability, starting in the early part of the century "slumbering volcano" became used more specifically as a metaphor for the inevitability of enslaved people's uprising. This usage seems to have derived from the Count of Mirabeau's warning in the early days of the Haitian Revolution that the colonists in Saint-Domingue "slept on the edge of Vesuvius," a phrase English-speaking writers from James McCune Smith to Harriet Martineau quoted in their accounts of the revolution.[22] But antislavery activists extended the metaphor to evoke the unacknowledged energies of enslaved people in the United States. In his 1827 prospectus for the short-lived magazine the *African Observer*, Quaker abolitionist Enoch Lewis envisioned every enslaved person "sunk and degraded below the proper level of humanity" as a volcano unto themself, full of "dormant passions" roiling unseen, "for the slumbering volcano retains its fires, and those who occupy its smoking verge themselves become the victims of the devouring element."[23] The same year, the first Black newspaper in the United States,

Freedom's Journal, envisioned these subterranean fires on a far wider scale. Urging readers, "Remember Egypt—remember St. Domingo," the paper warned, "The elements of combustion are gathering in frightful masses—the earth beneath us already trembles with the labours of the heaving volcano—we are on the very verge of its opening chasm—and without great exertions, a tremendous eruption will soon convince us that it will be impossible to escape the vortex of inevitable destruction."[24] Over the next several decades, writers continued to call on the image of the slumbering volcano until the Civil War opened its own "vortex of inevitable destruction."

In chapter 2, I discuss Frederick Douglass's remarkable riff on this trope in his speech "Slavery, the Slumbering Volcano" (1849), as well as Martin Delany's staging of it in his serialized novel *Blake; or, the Huts of America* (1859, 1861–62). For now, I just note several features of its general use. First, the slumbering volcano pictures the gathering forces of rebellion as a physical underground, in the conjunction of literal and figurative that I have proposed characterizes early ideas of the underground. Second, because the slumbering volcano belongs to what Marlene Daut calls the transatlantic "tropics of Haiti"—"symbols of the epistemological uncertainty" produced by the Haitian Revolution—its image of subterranean fires that might burst forth at any moment also summons the image of Haiti's revolutionary energies exploding *north* at any moment.[25] It maps the topography of the underground onto the geography of the hemisphere. Third, this image of the underground not only figures the latent dangers of race-based slavery but also is itself often racialized, so that Lewis describes enslaved people themselves as "sunk and degraded below the proper level of humanity" but fomenting revolution nonetheless. Fourth, it is precisely the subterranean depths of the slumbering volcano that make it active. "Sunken" is here not a synonym for abjection but for proximity to unseen fires, a promise of inevitable eruption. Fifth, the slumbering volcano exemplifies a very different narrative of subterranean activity than subculture's reactive model. Where subculture is a secondary phenomenon that results from or responds to a dominant culture, the underground forces figured by the slumbering volcano are undetermined by what lies above.

Going Underground explores various examples of the racialization of the underground, but it foregrounds Black authors who used the underground to imagine Black life within unfreedom. Some use the underground as a means to consider the ongoing negation of Black life in a society that nevertheless rests on its existence. They examine subjection by comparison to submersion, enslavement by comparison to entombment. Others use the underground to envision scenes of escape, covert organization, insurgency, and proximity to another world. Often, authors do some combination of this work. We find their theorizing in diverse and sometimes unexpected places: in the maps and tours of Stephen Bishop, an enslaved guide in Mammoth Cave (chapter 1); in Douglass's extension of the "slumbering volcano" metaphor (chapter 2); in the Underground Railroad ballads of songwriter Joshua McCarter Simpson (chapter 3); in Paschal Beverly Randolph's visions of the underground as the threshold of the cosmos; and in Pauline Hopkins's novel *Of One Blood*, in which an occultist medical student seemingly based on Randolph learns that he is king of a hidden Ethiopian city accessible only through underground passages (chapter 5). I posit that their work established an enduring intellectual tradition that later Black writers and artists would mine and renew (and that also prefigured crucial frameworks in Black studies, as I describe in chapter 2). This introduction began with perhaps the most famous example, Ellison's *Invisible Man* (1952). A very partial list would also include W. E. B. Du Bois's short story "The Comet" (1920), which centers on a bank messenger who survives the destruction of New York City when his boss sends him on a menial errand to "the lower vaults," "down into the blackness and silence beneath that lowest cavern . . . in the bowels of the earth, under the world"; Richard Wright's novel-turned-short story "The Man Who Lived Underground" (1942), which prefigures *Invisible Man* in its portrayal of a protagonist who "triumphed over the aboveground"; Curtis Mayfield's song "Underground" (1971), which envisions a refuge from earthly destruction that will also become a place of sensory transformation, cultivating "long-range sight for an eternal night" even as "there will be no light so there can be no sight"; Martin Puryear's sculpture *Old Mole* (1985), which materializes Marx's citation of *Hamlet* in *The Eighteenth Brumaire of Louis Bonaparte* as a beaked shape woven of strips of wood, suggesting a continuity between the subterranean and the aerial; Toni Morrison's novel *Beloved* (1987), which recounts how forty-six men, imprisoned in cells built into ditches, escape together by diving down through the mud during a storm; Suzan-Lori Parks's *The America Play* (1995), which revolves around a gravedigger who turns his skills to creating a replica of an amusement park called the Great Hole of History; and Evie Shockley's poem "ode to my blackness" (2012), which analogizes Blackness to "the tunnel john henry died / to carve":

> i dig down deep and there you are   at the root of my blues
> you're all thick and dark, enveloping   the root of my blues
> seems like it's so hard to let you go   when i got nothing to lose[26]

The list goes on: it also includes Kiese Laymon's novel *Long Division* (2013), whose characters drop beneath the red clay of Mississippi to travel through time; Jordan Peele's film *Get Out* (2017), which envisions a realm of Black abjection called the Sunken Place; and its follow-up, *Us* (2019), which centers on subterranean doppelgangers plotting an uprising against their counterparts on the surface; and Alexis Pauline Gumbs's poetry collection *M Archive* (2018), which depicts a postapocalyptic future when Black people have abandoned the surface of the earth to build a life underground, in "the archive of our failure."[27] Readers can certainly add more instances. The variation among these examples, whose undergrounds range from horrifying to liberatory, reflects not only the creativity of the writers and artists but also the underground's unsettled character, contested history, and expansive possibilities.

Subterranean Method

Not surprisingly, the undergrounds of the nineteenth century can be hard to find. This is partly an archival predicament familiar to anyone who works with marginalized or subversive materials. Underground movements tend to leave few written traces, and those they do leave are less likely to be preserved. For example, aside from a few cryptic references in personal correspondence, the only written traces left by the militant Detroit antislavery secret society the African-American Mysteries, which I discuss in chapter 3, are two newspaper interviews the organizers gave decades after the group had disbanded. Some underground texts are deliberately suppressed because of their perceived danger: copies of David Walker's 1829 manifesto *Appeal to the Coloured Citizens of the World*, for instance, which I examine in chapter 2, were confiscated throughout the US South, and those suspected of distributing it were arrested, sentenced to hard labor, or sold.[28] At other times the problem is less archival scarcity than distortion: mainstream texts represent undergrounds in wildly exaggerated form, like the paranoid reports of the Underground Railroad that filled newspapers in the 1840s (chapter 3) or city mysteries' suggestions that all manner of undergrounds teemed beneath most major cities and many small ones (chapter 4).

Yet if finding nineteenth-century undergrounds presents one challenge, a still greater one is recognizing the presence of the underground when we find it. Because nineteenth-century ideas of the underground do not necessarily resemble the later shapes into which the idea settled, their early manifestations are difficult to discern in retrospect. Moreover, even in the nineteenth century, the idea of the underground was not fully fledged: its meanings were diverse and fluid, and they did not necessarily travel under the word *underground*. The indeterminacy of early undergrounds does not diminish their theoretical power, interest, or relevance; to the contrary, one premise of this book is that it increases them. But that indeterminacy does make it harder to locate the object of study. How do we devise ways of reading for an idea that has not yet been expressed as such and whose features we may no longer know even when we see them? How do we attempt the historiographical work Michel Foucault called "archaeology" on the underground itself, if the underground presents no "regularity of a discursive practice" to "uncover"?[29]

Such is the challenge of studying an emergent idea, to use Raymond Williams's endlessly useful term. Williams defines the emergent as the "new meanings and values, new practices, new relationships, and kinds of relationship" that develop as "substantially alternative or oppositional" to "dominant culture."[30] Earlier I questioned how well the underground fits the model of opposition to dominant culture. But one advantage of Williams's analysis is that it conceives of cultural dominance not as "a system or a structure" but as a "process" of hegemony that "has continually to be renewed, recreated, defended, and modified," while it is "continually resisted, limited, altered, challenged by pressures not at all its own."[31] Of these pressures, emergent elements of a culture are particularly hard to identify. They are subject to incorporation, especially when they are perceived as threatening, which makes for an analytical paradox: to understand emergent cultural elements clearly, we need to see them before they become clear. "What we have to observe is in effect a *pre-emergence*, active and pressing but not yet fully articulated, rather than the evident emergence which could be more confidently named," Williams explains.[32] Thus, while I take the introduction of the figurative sense of *underground* as a kind of bellwether for this project, I follow Williams in supposing that the idea of the underground actually begins to take shape before such naming. The earliest texts I discuss precede the figurative use of the word, some texts never mention it at all, and even the naming of the underground does not fully fix the idea in place. As a result, the preemergent and emergent ideas of the underground in the nineteenth century are various, sometimes even incommensurate. The resonance between the terms *preemergent* and *underground*, which both name something that has not surfaced, indicates one of the more disorienting (but I hope also interesting) features of this project: it seeks an underground that is *itself* underground, historically and conceptually.

To write this book then, I have had to go underground, too. Often I undertake a kind of archival burrowing that leads me toward texts that seem slight, eccentric, or ephemeral. Moreover, the underground rarely comes into focus as a main subject (and when it does, as we will see, a narrative often crumbles or comes to a sudden halt), so I tend to burrow *in* texts, seeking out undergrounds in backgrounds, tropes, and allusions. I also burrow between seemingly incongruous versions of the underground, seeking out connections that may not be visible from the surface or "fully articulated," in Williams's words. In chapter 2, for example, I begin my reading of Walker's *Appeal* from the observation that Walker laces his call for Black people to rise up against their subjugation by white people with a motif of Black people forced to labor as miners "three or four hundred feet under ground."[33] From there, I notice how these visions of a gathering Black revolutionary force and this motif of Black miners unfold over pages marked by Walker's increasingly energetic use of footnotes, where he often places his most militant statements. Over the course of the *Appeal*, the footnotes multiply and lengthen, threatening to overtake the page from below. Even if Walker never describes his goal as mustering a Black radical underground (although we might), I argue that by associating his call for Black revolutionary organizing with the image of Black people working underground, Walker helps build a nascent figurative sense of the underground while staging subterranean power compositionally. Striking combinations like these register the emergence of the underground as an idea. More than that, they demonstrate some of the affordances of the underground as an emergent idea, whose apparent incoherence was also a source of amplitude and power.

As an interpretive method, burrowing does not presume a singular object, a locatable object, or an object that can be brought to light. Rather, it is an action of tunneling patiently, of submersion without a known destination, of study that honors its subject's elusiveness. But the search for (pre-)emergent ideas of the underground also creates an unresolved tension in *Going Underground*, as it oscillates between an impulse toward recuperation and recognition that this task is impossible. More than being impossible, the task of recuperation may even be unfaithful to the underground, invested as it is in remaining below the surface. If one of the challenges of this book is to devise methods for understanding early undergrounds, then another is to devise methods for *not* understanding early undergrounds, at least not fully. This, too, is an act of burrowing, of immersing myself in undergrounds without exactly trying to bring them to light. Instead I try to find a way to linger critically with their indeterminacy, to study them while honoring their elusiveness.

In doing so, I take guidance from the work of scholars in Black studies who have confronted archival erasures and distortions and elaborated powerful alternative methods for thinking historically. Carla Peterson's account of Black feminist "acts of speculation" and Saidiya Hartman's concept of "critical fabulation," a practice that seeks "both to tell an impossible story and to amplify the impossibility of its telling," have been especially formative in this body of thought.[34] More recently, Peterson's and Hartman's work has been fruitfully extended in books like Tina Campt's *Listening to Images* (2017); Ada Ferrer's *Freedom's Mirror: Cuba and Haiti in the Age of Revolution* (2014); Marisa Fuentes's *Dispossessed Lives: Enslaved Women, Violence, and the Archive* (2016); David Kazanjian's *The Brink of Freedom: Improvising Life in the Nineteenth-Century Atlantic World* (2016); Britt Rusert's *Fugitive Science: Empiricism and Freedom in Early African American Culture* (2017); and Christina Sharpe's *In the Wake: On Blackness and Being* (2016). All model how a commitment to marginalized historical subjects can lead us away from belief in or desire for archival recovery toward more open-ended modes of inquiry. As Sara E. Johnson explains, such "informed speculation" may employ "a certain interpretive and writerly mode" that "allows for possibilities," or make a "recurring gesture toward what might have been," or create a mood of "yearning" in order "to productively move beyond the impasse of that which we cannot know or understand with certainty."[35] While scholars working in this speculative mode demonstrate how one may exceed available epistemologies, I am also indebted to Scott Herring's determination, in *Queering the Underworld: Slumming, Literature, and the Undoing of Lesbian and Gay History* (2007), to thwart them: to "spoil" the expectations of revelation that scholars, like other disciplinarians, have brought to bear on "underworld sexual knowledge."[36] Herring's call for a mode of reading that respects the hiddenness of queer underworlds resonates with the undergrounds that were arguably their predecessors and that were not only hidden but indeterminate.

In addition to being inspired by these recent scholarly interventions, I have returned repeatedly to an older term for the value of non-empirical thinking: *mystery*. *Mystery* appears frequently in the archives of the underground, from Martin R. Delany's short-lived newspaper the *Mystery* to the African-American Mysteries secret society to the midcentury literary genre known as city mysteries. We tend now to define a mystery as a puzzle to solve, but in the nineteenth century the term still carried more of its earlier theological meaning of an idea beyond comprehension—*mystery* as in the mystery cults of ancient Egypt, Greece, and Rome or in the medieval Christian sense as synonymous with *miracle*. This sense of mystery, as we will see, pervades representations of the underground. For all the time I spent researching nineteenth-century undergrounds, I often felt that I did not get any closer to understanding them. But I have tried to learn something from the idea of mystery these undergrounds thematize about the value of study that cannot arrive at a solution. The participle of the book's title attempts to capture something of this approach. The underground is not a place one gets to: one is always *going* there, one is sometimes there before one knows it, and there are always further depths to go.

Chapter Overview

This book tracks how various nineteenth-century thinkers used the concept of the underground to imagine how to break open an unjust world and live anew within it. The chapters are roughly chronological, since to a certain extent they tell a story about change over time. But the underground, as I will argue, does not mark just a distinct kind of space but also a distinct kind of time, and its temporality is not quite linear. Subterranean time stretches and stills, offers passage from the present to the past and future; and one of the aims of this book is to explore these temporalities. They also shape the book's own itinerary: some chapters jump forward in time or backward; some texts loop in and out.

The first four chapters show a burst of interest in the underground in the 1840s and 1850s, when the term's figurative usage first gained currency. But while the idea of an underground fascinated readers and writers, it had not achieved definitional stability. Rather, the texts I examine proliferate different versions of the underground that clustered in proximity to one another, a loose assemblage of disparate subterraneities. The book begins with the most famous underground in the early nineteenth-century United States: Kentucky's Mammoth Cave, the longest cave in the world, which generated a host of newspaper reports, travel narratives, fiction, and poetry after it opened to the public as a tourist attraction in the late 1830s. Chapter 1, "The 'Blackness of Darkness' in Mammoth Cave," shows that the cave's fame derived in part from the fact that its guides were all enslaved men, who guided visitors through miles of tunnels by lamplight. The white-authored literature of Mammoth Cave often describes visitors' disordered senses of themselves and their surroundings in terms unconnected to the actual hazards of their journeys; instead, I argue, they fearfully conflate the power of the cave and its guides. In doing so, they reinvent the guides' knowledge of the cave as affinity with it, identifying subterranean darkness with racialized Blackness. Including Mammoth Cave in the history of the underground may seem willfully literal-minded. But it illuminates how the racialization of the underground becomes a vector for the emergence of its figurative meaning, as the literature of Mammoth Cave repeatedly conjures strange realms of Black sovereignty. At the same time, I ask what we can glean from the literature of Mammoth Cave about the body of Black thought it sought to disavow: the alternative relations between race and the underground that the guides theorized through their own subterranean explorations.

Chapter 2, "Early Black Radical Undergrounds," turns to four texts that develop the radical political potential of images of the Black underground: David Walker's fiery pamphlet *Appeal to the Coloured Citizens of the World* (1829), Frederick Douglass's anticolonizationist speech "Slavery, the Slumbering Volcano" (1849), Martin R. Delany's novel of hemispheric Black revolution, *Blake; or, the Huts of America* (1859, 1861–62), and William J. Wilson's imaginary museum tour/adventure story "Afric-American Picture Gallery" (1859). I analyze these texts' fascination with subterranean spaces, like mines, volcanoes, and caves, as well as spaces that are not actually subterranean but subterranized, like footnotes on a page, a ship's hold, and the positions of Haiti and Cuba latitudinally "underneath" the United States. These works, I argue, use the underground both to theorize the negation of Black life in a society that nevertheless rests on its existence and to imagine modes of Black life impossible aboveground. They anticipate important twentieth- and twenty-first-century intellectual frameworks in Black studies, like Édouard Glissant's "abyss," Sylvia Wynter's "underlife," Stefano Harney and Fred Moten's "undercommons," or Frantz Fanon's "zone of nonbeing," a "descent into a real hell" that is also "where authentic upheaval can be born." But they also hold theoretical possibilities of their own. By following the metaphorization of the underground, I demonstrate how nineteenth-century Black writers wrest resources for world-building from analyses of anti-Blackness and place this transformation among what Cedric Robinson felicitously calls the "roots" of the Black radical tradition.

At the beginning of the introduction, I noted that the metaphorical use of "underground" in the United States was popularized by the lively media coverage of the Underground Railroad in the 1840s. Today, the Underground Railroad has been institutionalized in celebratory narratives of national history, but chapter 3, "The Underground Railroad's Undergrounds," argues that contemporaneous representations envisioned undergrounds far in excess of these stories. One of the most vivid fantasies was that of the Underground Railroad as an actual subterranean train. The first part of the chapter examines this fantasy through antebellum newspaper reports, engravings, poetry, and song, showing how it evinced desires less for escape north than for a space beyond the world's planar coordinates. The chapter hypothesizes that the extravagant discourse of the Underground Railroad in turn inspired antislavery undergrounds beyond its arrangements. Piecing together the faint evidence of letters and memoirs, I excavate the subterranean strategies—rhetorical and paramilitary—of clandestine organizations including Detroit's African-American Mysteries, Boston's Anti-Man-Hunting League, and John Brown and his comrades, whose raid on Harpers Ferry was preceded by an unrealized plan to invade the South called the Subterranean Pass Way. Finally, in the last part of the chapter, I jump forward in time to postbellum writer Pauline Hopkins's play *Peculiar Sam; or, the Underground Railroad* (1879) and her novella *Winona* (1902), a fictionalized account of John Brown's Kansas campaign. In these works, I show, Hopkins seeks out possibilities for freedom that antebellum undergrounds might continue to harbor after legal—but never actual—emancipation.

Chapter 4, "The Depths of Astonishment: City Mysteries and Subterranean Unknowability," studies a midcentury literary genre dedicated to the secretive collectivities and insurgent activities Americans were beginning to refer to as undergrounds. Wildly popular, city mysteries were cheap, sensational novels chronicling the underbelly of urban life. The undergrounds they depict consistently have one feature in common: they are located physically underground. This chapter pursues the convergence of literal and figurative undergrounds in the city mysteries toward two readings in tension with one another. On the one hand, I argue that the "mystery" these authors find underground becomes the basis for powerful critiques of capitalism and visions of its upheaval. Here, the underground educates the reader in the pleasures of and possibilities of unknown worlds. On the other hand, I demonstrate that the white authors of city mysteries derive the unfathomable mystery of the underground from the association with racialized Blackness that I traced in the previous three chapters. In the nineteenth century and arguably beyond, the underground is never not a racialized trope. The chapter's conclusion reflects on the city mysteries' topographical obsessions as a useful vantage point for understanding demystification as a critical practice. Analyzing Marx and Engels's account of city mysteries in *The Holy Family* (1844) and Marx's famous image of the "old mole" in *The Eighteenth Brumaire of Louis Bonaparte* (1852), I outline a version of demystification that does not attempt to dispel mystery but preserves a dialectical relation to it.

Where the first four chapters of *Going Underground* focus on the production of the underground as a concept in the early to mid-nineteenth-century United States, in the final two chapters I turn to the late nineteenth century and to writing *from* the underground—that is, writing by people who understood themselves to be participating in insurgent movements. Chapters 5 and 6 consider two very different examples of such movements, although I will show that they have more in common than we might expect: occultism and anarchism. Chapter 5, "'To Drop beneath the Floors of the Outer World': Paschal Beverly Randolph's Occult Undergrounds," departs from the juxtapositional approaches of the previous chapters to focus on a single author: the occultist/sex magician/political activist/educator Paschal Beverly Randolph. The child of a Black mother and a white father, Randolph struggled against racism his whole life. But he contended that his experience of alienation cultivated spiritual sensitivities that allowed him to access an unseen universe, while his "mixed identity" gave him the power to channel other souls in addition to his own. In the first half of the chapter, I examine Randolph's creation of what Jonathan Eburne, in his book, *Outsider Theory: Intellectual Histories of Unorthodox Ideas*, calls "a theory of outsider theory."[37] In handbooks, pamphlets, novels, newspaper articles, manifestos, historiography, and a memoir, as well as printed "private letters" and handwritten manuscripts he circulated covertly, Randolph sought to mobilize an occult underground that would use sex, drugs, and study to connect with extraterrestrial spirits. The second half of the chapter draws out the political dimensions of Randolph's thought by focusing on the writing he produced while a teacher and advocate for the Freedmen's Bureau in Louisiana. Highlighting the oddly topical digressions that often disrupt his occult instruction, I show how, as Randolph grew increasingly despondent over the prospects of Reconstruction, he came to envision the underground as a portal to the cosmos, whose forces might be brought to transform the order of things on earth. Finally, I return to Pauline Hopkins, whose final novel, *Of One Blood* (1902–3), centers on a character I hypothesize is based on Randolph, who finds himself transported via subterranean tunnels to a mystical, ancient Ethiopian civilization. In *Of One Blood*, Hopkins both extends her earlier explorations of the underground through Randolph's occult thought and ultimately confronts the idea that it may offer no way back to the world above.

Chapter 6, "Subterranean Fire: Anarchist Visions of the Underground," takes up a more obviously political underground movement: the anarchist International Working People's Association. The IWPA flourished briefly in the 1880s before the Haymarket bombing in 1886 and the notoriously unjust trial of eight members, at which defendant August Spies, upon receiving his death sentence, described the movement as a "subterranean fire" that could not be extinguished or even grasped. This chapter explores the ramifications of the IWPA's underground imaginary. While chapter 5 read for the politics of Paschal Beverly Randolph's occult thought, here I draw out the supernatural qualities of the IWPA's political thought. Analyzing reporting, poetry, and short fiction in the IWPA's Chicago-based English-language newspaper, the *Alarm*, I show how contributors built an anarchist underground through visions of the dead as buried but not stilled. I trace the dispersion of this vision into several other striking motifs that theorize the buried dead's galvanizing influence: of dynamite as an image of latent force, of tramps as the living dead, and of anarchism as the revival of abolition's unfinished work. The chapter's conclusion considers the influence of Haymarket on Herman Melville's novella about suspected conspiracy and the injustice of law: *Billy Budd, Sailor*, which Melville drafted during the trial and its aftermath. The relation between Haymarket and *Billy Budd* has gone almost unnoticed by critics, but it flashes into view when we notice how Melville borrows August Spies's famous words to describe the master-at-arms Claggart's tumultuous feelings for Billy Budd as a "subterranean fire." I argue that Melville's relocation of anarchism's underground to Claggart's heart indexes the beginning of the underground's transformation into "an inside narrative," in the words of *Billy Budd*'s subtitle—a figure for interiority that would reach its fullest expression in emerging theories of the unconscious.

Finally, a brief epilogue, "Staying Underground," considers the fate of nineteenth-century ideas of the underground by examining a recent burst of literature and visual art about the Underground Railroad. Rather than recapitulate the stories familiar from textbooks and historical sites, these works cultivate a deep strangeness much closer to mid-nineteenth-century representations of the Underground Railroad. I focus on Colson Whitehead's critically acclaimed, best-selling 2016 novel *The Underground Railroad*, which takes as its premise the literalization of the Underground Railroad that so enthralled antebellum readers. Like the Chicago anarchists' invocations of radical abolitionism, Whitehead's vision of the Underground Railroad suggests the continuing pull of the subterranean in and on the present. The novel ultimately leaves the underground behind for the West. But Whitehead's account of going underground raises the indelible question of what it would mean to find a way to stay there.

Nineteenth-Century Undergrounds Now

To some extent, this book's story of the emergence of the underground pieces together the strange history of a now-familiar idea. I hope it will interest readers drawn to the odd, restive, or little-known corners of nineteenth-century American literature: to unruly thinkers, obscure texts, idiosyncratic theories, and all the other elements that make the period at once fascinating and unfathomable for us today. I especially hope the project will interest readers who come to it from their own immersion in undergrounds of one kind or another—that it will illuminate how this formation came to be and why it continues to beckon to us. But if the underground's past has something to offer its present, I think it lies less in the path to the idea as we know it than in a glimpse of what got left behind along the way, which might yet be recovered and reimagined. Today the concept of a cultural or political underground has become so familiar that we no longer refer it to hollow earth theories, the habits of a mole, the space of a cave, or the world of the dead—all key images of the underground I discuss in the chapters that follow. But what resources for living otherwise might we find if we did?

In her luminous recent book *Black Utopias: Speculative Life and the Music of Other Worlds,* Jayna Brown recalls José Esteban Muñoz's statement in *Cruising Utopia* that "queerness is a structuring and educated mode of desiring that allows us to see and feel beyond the quagmire of the present." Brown responds to Muñoz by suggesting that we direct our utopian thinking not only toward the future but toward the "synchronic layering" of the here and now. "I think that the present is actually dimensional and the place of great improvisations," Brown writes. "I suggest that we descend into the quagmire, for it holds great depth."[38] Brown's phrasing recuperates the metaphor of the quagmire, which for Muñoz signifies the predicament of being fatally stuck, as an unseen space of possibility and movement. *Going Underground* explores the long history of similar lines of thought, which look underground to find new dimensions to the present. Following Brown, I hypothesize that to think about nineteenth-century undergrounds now is to crack open what we mean by *now*.

The hope that drives this project is that the history of the underground could help us multiply the possibilities for being in but not of a rotten world. In particular, I hope that through the nineteenth-century underground's unfamiliar forms, we might expand our models of political agitation outside the customary oppositional frameworks of dissent and resistance. Of course, I am not (as it were) against dissent and resistance. But there are so many kinds of imaginative and lived activity that their rational, reactive, circumscribed nature doesn't quite describe. *Going Underground* seeks to join recent work exploring modes of recalcitrance outside their frame, including Kevin Quashie's *quiet*, Audra Simpson's and Tina Campt's versions of *refusal*, Ashon Crawley's *otherwise*, Avery Gordon's *in-difference*, and the extensive scholarship on *fugitivity*.[39] The nineteenth-century undergrounds I explore suggest some new—which is to say old—modes of world-making and world-breaking for a time when this world feels untenable. In doing so, I seek both to follow Ellison's narrator in reopening the "shut off and forgotten" undergrounds of the nineteenth century and to ask how we too might use them to build spaces for ourselves and to dream, as he does, of descending even further into their depths, to a "lower level" and a "still lower level."[40]

1 The "Blackness of Darkness" in Mammoth Cave

In the late 1830s, the underground became famous in the United States. A lawyer named Franklin Gorin purchased Kentucky's Mammoth Cave, the longest known cave in the world, in 1838 and began to transform it into a major tourist attraction. Inside the cave, Gorin offered tours led by an eighteen-year-old he enslaved named Stephen Bishop; above, he offered visitors food and lodging at a hotel. The following year, Gorin sold both Bishop and the cave to John Croghan, a Louisville doctor who continued to develop the site, leasing two more enslaved men, Materson Bransford and Nicholas Bransford, from a neighbor to conduct additional tours. By this time, Mammoth Cave already had a long history of exploration. Early Woodland people had harvested gypsum and other minerals from its walls. Later, Shawnee and Cherokee hunters took shelter there, and during the War of 1812, scores of enslaved people mined saltpeter in the cave for use in gunpowder. But over the next three decades, the "monarch of caves" became an international sensation, attracting tens of thousands of visitors and generating a host of travel accounts, magazine illustrations, panoramas, poetry, stereographs, a waltz, newspaper articles, and fiction.[1]

This chapter considers Mammoth Cave as an unlikely but crucial site for nineteenth-century theorizations of the underground. Central to Mammoth Cave's fame, and central to my argument, is the fact that until the Civil War, the cave's guides were all enslaved men.[2] Visitors seem to have found the guides nearly as captivating as the cave itself. The literature of Mammoth Cave—all, to my knowledge, by white writers—dwells on their persons and performances at length. More than that, these writers persistently identified the racialized bodies of the guides with the space of the cave. Underground and in the hands of Black men, white visitors believed they saw "the Blackness of Darkness," as Reverend B. F. Crary titled his account.[3] This chapter traces the logic of the cave's racialization back to its causes and forward to its effects. I argue that when white visitors conflated the cave with the guides, they reframed—strategically or reflexively—the guides' knowledge of the cave and their production of its space. But I also show that writers' racialization of Mammoth Cave tended to slip out of their control. As they associated the cave's spatial darkness with racialized Blackness, the literal underground of Mammoth Cave flickered into something more than literal—a mysterious black formation, of unguessed dimensions and certain danger, beneath the world as they knew it. Throughout the chapter, I ask how the guides themselves might have conceived of the cave and their positions within it. In this inquiry, I tack between delving deep into the literature of Mammoth Cave and trying to look beyond its limits—specifically, by speculating that the guides took the cave as a site for their own speculative activity. Finally, returning to the example of *Invisible Man*, which in the introduction I suggest reopens a truncated nineteenth-century history of the underground, I propose that Ellison's depictions of the underground can help us think about the countervailing relations between racialized Blackness and the underground that the guides theorized through their experience.

Black Geographies of Mammoth Cave

What did white tourists think as they descended into Mammoth Cave behind Stephen Bishop, Materson Bransford, or Nicholas Bransford, squeezed along ledges after them, and followed them to the edges of yawning pits? In an indispensable essay, "Trying the Dark: Mammoth Cave and the Racial Imagination," Peter West posits that white tourists were drawn to "the contained reversal of traditional racial roles" inside the cave. Surveying a wide array of Mammoth Cave literature, West shows how its writers used the cave "to articulate white anxieties about the instability of racial distinctions, to enact melodramatic fantasies of white supremacy, and to envision apocalyptic nightmares of racial revolution." West argues that they did so "by treating Mammoth Cave as a stage, complete with costumes, music, props, and illusions," which allowed them to present "the underground specter of black authority as an entertaining, but ultimately fleeting unreality."[4] To the types of racializing play that West locates in the cave, we might add the racial masochism Frantz Fanon attributes to white men in the United States—a tendency toward self-punishment that, as Amber Musser elaborates, "does not occur at any social cost to the white man; the actual burden is felt by the black man."[5] (Visitors' frequent grumblings about the ugly mustard-colored flannel costumes the guides provided for use in the cave, for instance, move out of the background if we read for possible attachment to that humiliation.[6]) In these readings, the presence of the Black guides increases the cave's attractiveness to white visitors by adding to its natural wonders the opportunity to engage in self-affirming racial theatrics.

Reading for the ways white writers played out temporary inversions of authority illuminates the alternating experiences of subjugation and aggression we will see them narrating frequently inside the cave. But it is important to note that while the visitors' experiences of the cave were inevitably overdetermined by the social order outside of it, they were also overdetermined by the guides' productions of the space. The visitors depended on the guides to light their way in absolute darkness; to explain what they dimly saw; to lead them across the cave's pits, its treacherous pathways, and its water crossings; and to find its exits. Moreover, the stagecraft of Mammoth Cave was not solely or even primarily the invention of the visitors. It was the guides who provided the "costumes, music, props, and illusions," and while the visitors were performing, the guides were performing, too. In the expeditions they choreographed, which typically lasted from early morning until dusk, they conducted visitors along the narrow paths, presented each cavern, directed visitors where to look, explained the cave's geological features, executed dramatic lighting effects, rowed visitors across the subterranean rivers, sang them songs, told them stories, and occasionally played tricks on them. Their performances may have been partly directed by Gorin and Croghan, or molded to the visitors' desires, but they were enacted by Bishop, Bransford, and Bransford—and given the variations visitors reported between tours with different guides, the exigencies of cave exploration and the frequent improvisation it required, and the reputation of Bishop, in particular, for volubility and showmanship, the guides seem not to have stuck closely to a script. In considering how white visitors looked for ways to manage their racial anxieties in Mammoth Cave, we need not assume they successfully found them—or that theirs were the only desires and imaginations at work there.

Centering the guides' investigative, imaginative, and interpretive labor in Mammoth Cave unfolds other dimensions to the negotiations of racial identities that transpired there. It allows us to see that the writers' accounts of the underground, with all their variously phobic and fetishizing anti-Blackness, had their own underground in the guides' productions of space. Even as Mammoth Cave catered to the pleasures of white tourists, it was built on what Katherine McKittrick has theorized as "black geographies": spatial practices built on Black people's "knowledges, negotiations, and experiences."[7] Black geographies call into question the "secure and unwavering" appearance of "geographies of domination," which "unjustly organize human hierarchies *in place*," McKittrick explains.[8] Working "alongside and beyond traditional geographies," they "site a terrain of struggle" in seemingly "transparent space."[9] If we understand Bishop, Bransford, and Bransford as producing Black geographies in Mammoth Cave, we can see their thought as both enabling the cave's commodification for tourists and exceeding it. We can begin to perceive that when white visitors to Mammoth Cave played out racial fantasies on the model of "human hierarchies," they did so on ground that was not as "secure and unwavering" as they believed.

Stephen Bishop's work offers the clearest example of Black geographies in Mammoth Cave. Before Bishop's arrival at Mammoth Cave, human exploration had stopped at a vast chasm known as the Bottomless Pit. But by crossing the pit on a ladder, Bishop discovered miles of new rooms and passages, geological formations, underground streams, and the eyeless fish that swam through those waters. He drew an extraordinarily accurate and detailed map incorporating these discoveries, which revealed the cave to be far larger than anyone had previously guessed; it was included as a foldout insert in Alexander Clark Bullitt's book *Rambles in the Mammoth Cave, during the Year 1844* (figure 1.1). British visitor Marianne Finch marveled that he "seems more like the high-priest and expounder of [the cave's] mysteries, than a hired guide, much less a slave," a description that disconnects him from bondage, from commerce, and even from the constraints of earthly logic.[10] In a much-reprinted essay, the renowned writer and abolitionist Lydia Maria Child called Bishop "the presiding genius of Mammoth Cave." She observed admiringly,

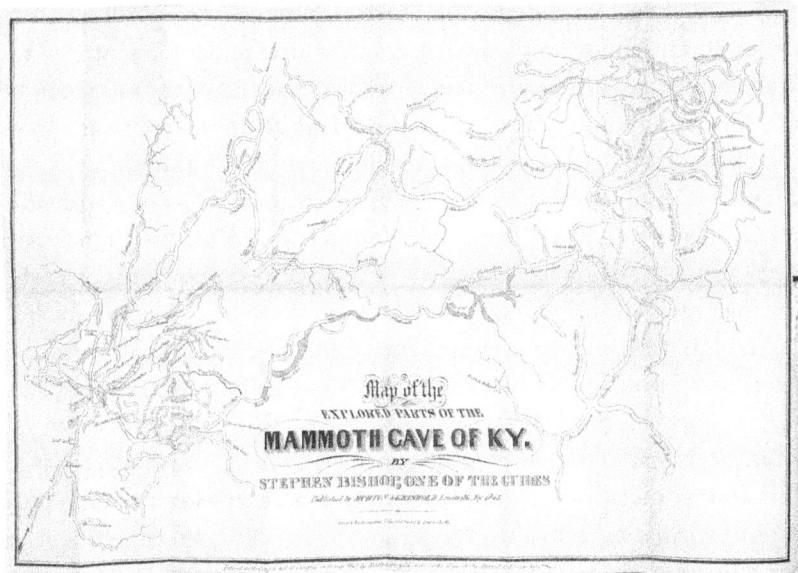

1.1 Map of Mammoth Cave by Stephen Bishop, from Alexander Clark Bullitt, *Rambles in the Mammoth Cave, during the Year 1844* (1845). Courtesy of the Library Company of Philadelphia.

A large proportion of the discoveries are the result of his courage, intelligence, and untiring zeal. His vocation has brought him into contact with many intelligent and scientific men, and as he has great quickness of perception and a prodigious memory, he has profited much by intercourse with superior minds. He can recollect everybody that ever visited the cave, and all the terms of geology and mineralogy are at his tongue's end.[11]

A self-taught natural scientist who artfully extracted from visitors what he could not learn alone, Bishop practiced what Britt Rusert calls "fugitive science," a tradition of antebellum Black scientific investigation that "provided a rich speculative terrain" beyond the ken of racist science by "transform[ing] the spaces of the everyday into laboratories of knowledge and experimentation."[12] In Mammoth Cave—an extraordinary space for visitors but an everyday one for Bishop—he taught himself to read and write by closely observing visitors write their names on the cave walls with smoke from their torches, turning their possessive gestures into resources for his own education.[13] His knowledge competed with the more conventional authority of visitors to the cave, who found him, as one put it, "uncommonly smart" and seem to have squirmed a little under his scrutiny. "He was conversant with many of the scientific terms for the various [geological] formations and made me rack my brains of their Greek knowledge to answer some of his questions," recalled a writer for the *Knickerbocker* somewhat testily, and when Yale chemist Benjamin Silliman Jr. visited in 1851, he discovered that his atmospheric observations had been anticipated by Bishop's "remarkable powers."[14] (Silliman is best known for discovering that "rock oil," or petroleum, could be an illuminant, helping catalyze the capitalization of the underground in the nineteenth century, so this encounter with Bishop wonderfully stages two emergent versions of subterranean power facing off with one another.) To the editor of *Peterson's Magazine*, Charles J. Peterson, who spent two days touring the cave in 1852, Bishop was "most remarkable for his readiness at repartee and his amplitude of words," an ambiguous compliment that hints Bishop did not let the tourists' speech go unanswered.[15] In the exasperation and faint praise of his guests, we can hear Bishop's Black geographies as they quite literally "speak back to the geographies of modernity, transatlantic slavery, and colonialism," in McKittrick's words.[16]

Racialization and Its Echoes Underground

Most white writers, however, represented Bishop, Bransford, and Bransford's deep knowledge of the cave as a personal connection it. For instance, Horace Martin's *Pictorial Guide to the Mammoth Cave* erroneously states that Bishop actually lived in the cave and had "begun to fancy it would be impossible to quit it."[17] Consequently, when reports circulated in the 1850s that Bishop had been emancipated and was preparing to embark for Liberia, several writers refused to believe them. As one demurred, "He has some idea of emigrating to Liberia, but his attachment to this cave and its surroundings is so great that I doubt whether he can ever be induced to be separated from it."[18] W. E. Surtees, an English traveler, reported asking Bishop "if he would, when in Africa, often think of the Mammoth Cave. He answered, in a voice of much feeling, 'often.'" Surtees then presents a poem "suggested by these incidents," "Stephen's Adieu to the Echo of the Mammoth Cave," which riffs on Bishop's routine of "wak[ing] up the echoes" in the cave by singing in the large caverns.[19] Written from Bishop's point of view, the poem recounts how he awakened a personified Echo who had been "ages bound" there, becoming her "first fond love." This narrative transforms Bishop's forced labor in the cave into a romantic interest, transfers bondage from Bishop to Echo, makes Bishop her liberator, and frames Bishop's trip to Liberia as compulsion: "Now I must seek far Afric's land," he laments. Still, the poem's first rhyme, the subterranean pair "grave" and "cave," summons the absent rhyme of "slave" like a ghost.[20]

The anecdote about Bishop's feelings for the cave may have been as much the author's invention as the poem, or it may have been true. No one seems to have known the cave better than Bishop did, and one can only guess what a contradictory space it was for him, where he was compelled to work, on the one hand, but exercised unusual degrees of authority and mobility, on the other. Behind white writers' interpretations of the guides' attachments to the cave, then, we can also imagine the guides' own, different understandings of that relation. Consider the account of Union soldier J. F. Rusling, who visited the cave in 1864. He reported that he invited Materson Bransford to return to Nashville with him and "be free at once" but that Bransford had replied that he couldn't leave the cave: "It seems most like a child now, you know, we've been togedder so long."[21] Bransford would have had many reasons to decline a white stranger's offer of freedom, but maybe he did call the cave kin. Three of his four children were sold away from him; would this have made him more likely to find a child in the nonhuman world? Or would knowing so acutely what it means to have and lose a child have made the notion of seeing the cave as another one preposterous, obscene?

The white writers who dwelled on the guides' attachments to the cave did not speculate on the nature of these attachments. Instead, they took for granted that they were based on affinity—not only liking but likeness. Here Lydia Maria Child's description of Bishop as "the presiding genius of Mammoth Cave" is significant, for as Gustavus Stadler has shown, *genius* was a remarkably unstable word in the mid-nineteenth century, which shifted between the modern sense of exceptional mental powers and the older sense of embodying the character of a place.[22] When Child calls Bishop the "genius of Mammoth Cave," she both recognizes his knowledge and pictures him as personifying the cave himself. Bishop was, as another white writer, Carlton Holmes Rogers, explained, "so closely identified with the cave and its associations"—a remark that connects Bishop and the cave not by circumstance (because he is its most famous guide, or because they are both legally the property of John Croghan) but because he shares the cave's "associations."[23] Rogers does not specify these associations. But his account, and those by other white writers, suggest that what Crary called the "Blackness of Darkness" in Mammoth Cave was always a racialized Blackness.

J. F. Rusling's suggestion of a family resemblance between Materson Bransford and the cave he loved "like a child" provides one example of how white writers identified the cave and the guides. A more indirect example can be found in visitors' repeated attributions of Indigenous ancestry or simply Indigenous "looks" to Stephen Bishop.[24] Whether true or untrue, the frequency of these statements should be read in light of the much-publicized Indigenous history of the cave itself. Early tourist interest in Mammoth Cave was stoked by the discovery and subsequent exhibition of mummified bodies, as well as pottery, tools, petroglyphs, pictographs, cloth, and other remnants of Indigenous people's long use of the cave. When visitors described Bishop, too, as "Indian," they extended the cave's history to him. They never specify a particular tribal affiliation or heritage. Instead, within an archaeological discourse that framed living Native Americans as relics of the past, their comments suggest that he belongs to the cave itself.

Whether purposeful or not, visitors' identification of the guides with the cave proceeds from white supremacist habits. Such habits impelled them to disavow and reimagine the guides' knowledge of the cave, and to do so by positing a resemblance between the all-too-knowing guides and a form of nature that was not only nonhuman but inanimate. But the analogy between the guides and the cave, which rested on reified notions of Blackness, itself proved volatile. Although it enters the literature of Mammoth Cave as a disavowal of the power of Black geographical thought and action, it echoes back in the cave with its meaning transfigured. For the cave was not only dark but also unknown, indefinitely enormous, at once beautiful and terrifying: a subterranean manifestation of the sublime. As Child observed, "The vastness, the gloom, the impossibility of taking in the boundaries by the light of lamps,—all these produce a deep sensation of awe and wonder."[25] Racializing the cave, then, introduces a manifestation of Blackness likewise vast, formidable, and impenetrable. In short, it threatens to transform the literal underground of Mammoth Cave into a Black underground in the figurative sense.

Consider what happens in a few instances when writers' identifications of the space of the cave with the bodies of the guides bounce back unsettlingly. When N. P. Willis writes that his party was "twelve hours in the hands of darkness and Stephen" in Mammoth Cave, his correlation of "darkness and Stephen" personifies the cave by extending Stephen's hands to it, and he envisions himself as subjugated by this alliance.[26] In Charles J. Peterson's article "Two Days in Mammoth Cave," we can hear the echo between the cave and the guides as it reverberates ever more wildly. Recall that Peterson is the writer who commented on Stephen Bishop's "amplitude of words," a description that pictures the magnitude of Mammoth Cave recurring in Bishop's own mouth, or Mammoth Cave as a manifestation of Bishop's voice. In fact, Peterson analogizes Bishop and the cave explicitly, calling him "as great a wonder almost as the Cave."[27] This apparently admiring comparison also attempts to manage Bishop's "wondrous" powers: it objectifies him by likening him to a feature of the landscape and presents his expertise as a curiosity and (to the extent that the cave was a "wonder" in the sense of a tourist spectacle) a commodity for the entertainment of others.

But Peterson's comparison between Bishop and the cave grows considerably more fearful as the article settles into its theme, a feverish reckoning of the cave's darkness, which, as quickly becomes clear, is also to say its racialized Blackness. In a torrent of mixed metaphors, Peterson depicts his terror inside the cave: "It is a labyrinth groping blindly through primeval gloom, for hundreds of miles under ground; and the darkness that fills it is palpable, enveloping you like black waters." Peterson's analogy between Bishop and the cave haunts this personified "labyrinth" as well as his dread of the cave's "palpable" "darkness," whose physicality seems inseparable from Bishop's own. Peterson's account swells into full-blown horror as he pictures the cave's embodied darkness ruling over him: "In those silent depths night reigns eternal and supreme.... There darkness sits devouring his prey from everlasting to everlasting."[28] The analogy between Bishop and the cave quickly escalates here into a far more troubling conflation. It may trouble us to the extent that it confuses a person and a geological formation, the fear of darkness with the fear of racialized Blackness, but it troubles Peterson to the extent that it turns a dangerous natural landscape into a confrontation with Black power.

The racialized fear of the dark that visitors experienced inside Mammoth Cave could precipitate a crisis of whiteness. This threat snapped into focus when Bishop played his most famous trick. Extinguishing the visitors' lamps, he would lead them down a pathway in total darkness. A writer in the *Knickerbocker* who signed himself Barnwell struggled to explain its intensity: "Enclose yourself in the darkest room, and you will still have a glimmer of light, an indefinite idea of distinction between the white wall and the dark furniture," he writes. But in the cave "white and black were, as some philosophers prove, all the same."²⁹ What frightens Barnwell is not just the darkness itself, it turns out, but its erasure of distinction between "white and black." While this initially seems to be a matter of color perception (the "distinction between the white wall and the dark furniture"), it quickly transforms into a matter of ontology ("white and black were ... all the same").³⁰ And in the next sentences, Barnwell's fears about the disappearance of color distinctions come to rest on Bishop. He recalls the terror that settled on him when the guide blew out the lamps: "The feeling of unknown, unavoidable, invisible danger!—utter inability to defend one's-self, entire subjection to those who possess this invaluable gift!" Note how the focus of Barnwell's fear abruptly shifts again, from the "unknown, unavoidable, invisible danger" of total darkness to his "entire subjection to those who possess [the] invaluable gift" of "defend[ing] one's-self"—presumably the guides. Note too how he reframes the guides' scientific knowledge in militant political language, as a capacity for self-defense. (In reality, the guides needed to defend themselves less against the darkness than against the visitors, who regularly targeted them in ways that seem retaliatory for upended racial hierarchies. Barnwell himself recounts alarming Bishop while he was paddling the group down a stream by repeating the guide's own echo trick and shooting a revolver around him, making the report ricochet around the cave.³¹ In the *Rutgers Literary Miscellany*, James C. Zabriskie, who would go on to minor fame for a speech advocating the extension of slavery to the entire United States, concluded his report on Mammoth Cave by recounting how his companion danced in the boat to make Bishop fall out, only "succeeding, after several efforts, in reaching the shore, much to his gratification and our amusement."³²)

After Bishop had left the visitors in total darkness for a bit, he would lead them into a cavern called the Star Chamber, relight the lamps, and instruct them to look up (figure 1.2). When the lamplight reflected off gypsum crystals on the cave's ceiling, it looked like a night sky filled with stars. (Emerson readers may recall a version of this scene from the beginning of the essay "Illusions," where Emerson recounts both his awe and his annoyance at being manipulated by "this theatrical trick."³³) At this point, Barnwell recounts, he "immediately began searching for the North-star."³⁴ Scrambling to reorient himself after the crisis of whiteness he experienced in the dark, ironically, he only exacerbates it, as he seeks to place himself using a coordinate that in 1849, at the time of writing, was indelibly associated with fugitives from slavery. (Frederick Douglass's newspaper the *North Star*, for example, ran from 1847 to 1851.) Students of blackface

1.2 The Star Chamber, from Alexander Clark Bullitt, *Rambles in the Mammoth Cave, during the Year 1844* (1845). Courtesy of the Library Company of Philadelphia.

minstrelsy will anticipate how this crisis gets resolved: when, leaving the Star Chamber, Barnwell's group meets two other tour groups, they cheer, wave handkerchiefs, and "immediately struck up a negro song"—that is, a minstrel song. Barnwell recalls, "Some twenty voices bore the notes far into the deepest of those vaults." Their performance chases away the specter of a subterranean Blackness with the reassuring act of making it fodder for their amusement.

Notably, the visitors' impromptu blackface performance restages a scene of the guides' own making. As I mentioned earlier, when Bishop rowed visitors across the cave's rivers, he would sing "a negro song," which would then get "echoed and reechoed back."[35] (Bishop named a branch of one of the cave's subterranean rivers that he discovered Echo River for this reason, an invention that irked N. P. Willis, who found it, ironically, "a needless multiplying of names."[36]) Materson Bransford, too, would reportedly sing "a negro melody" while beating the water in time with his paddle, leading visitors to believe "a voice hails us from the darkness."[37] By 1861 Mammoth Cave was so associated with Black music that a writer for *All the Year Round* built an article on the cave around a racist caricature of a guide breaking into song at every turn.³⁸ Whether the tourists' recapitulation of these scenes made their blackface reprise more or less effective at restoring racial hierarchies—whether they were appropriating Blackness or possessed by it—is an open question. But what recurs in this archive is the image of the guides' subterranean singing creating a chorus of phantom Black voices in the cave, staging what one writer described as "an answer from another and unseen world."³⁹

Madge Vertner: Black Female Sexuality Underground

I want to follow the racialization of Mammoth Cave as it "echoed and re-echoed" one step further by looking at one of its most striking literary appearances: in Mattie Griffith's abolitionist novel *Madge Vertner*, where the cave appears as something between a setting and a character. Griffith, a white antislavery and feminist activist born to a family of enslavers in Kentucky, is best known for her 1857 pseudo slave narrative, *Autobiography of a Female Slave*. *Madge Vertner*, her second and final novel, which was serialized in the *National Anti-Slavery Standard* from 1859 to 1860, tells a seemingly familiar story of an angelic, petted white Southern girl's realization of the evil of slavery. Madge's misgivings begin on her family's plantation, but it is a trip to Mammoth Cave that "did truly open new worlds to her."⁴⁰ Outside her hotel window, Madge overhears a conversation between two enslaved guides, Stephen and Matt (presumably based on Stephen Bishop and Materson Bransford, often called Mat), who discuss slavery, the brutality of their enslaver, and the possibility of freedom. Their conversation deeply affects Madge, perhaps because it reiterates an earlier conversation she overheard beneath her window at home between two enslaved people planning to run away. Griffith never comments on the parallel, but it at once pictures Mammoth Cave as a site of freedom dreams and connects those dreams with the freedom dreams of enslaved people elsewhere. The next day, when Madge and her family tour the cave, Madge notices with surprise that her usually haughty mother converses easily with Matt, who is guiding them, and even tells him that he "ought to be free." Griffith claims that this is not unusual. "A fact it is that the most aristocratic ladies and gentlemen who visit the Cave seem to forget for a time those unnatural distinctions of race and caste, and associate with the colored guides in the most familiar manner." Mrs. Vertner's subterranean transformation prompts Griffith to proclaim, "Truly, the Mammoth Cave should be the temple of abolitionism."⁴¹

Here, the significance of *Madge Vertner*'s otherwise unexplained detour to Mammoth Cave becomes clear. A subterranean island of antislavery principles in the midst of Kentucky, Mammoth Cave is an environmental counterpart of Madge, herself consistently depicted as "a child of nature."[42] Together, they hold out the promise that antislavery principles naturally belong to the land and pro-slavery politics are but superimposed on it. Yet the parallel between Madge and Mammoth Cave, which seems designed to catalyze change, does not. It turns out that the resemblance runs all too deep. Madge learns that she shares not only the cave's "natural" abolitionism but also its underground Blackness: she is the daughter of an enslaved woman, the victim of one of her father's youthful "follies."[43] And this revelation brings the novel to an abrupt halt. Soon after learning of her parentage, Madge falls ill and dies. What is worse, from the point of view of the sentimental reformism the novel seems to embrace, her death fails to redeem any other characters. When she tells her supposedly abolitionist fiancé of her history, he deserts her, and although she exacts a deathbed promise from her doting father to free his human property, Griffith concludes by tersely observing that he never fulfilled it. Thus, while Madge initially seems poised to be another Little Eva, her trajectory as an abolitionist heroine runs aground on the revelation of her racial identity. In Hortense Spillers's formulation, Blackness ungenders Madge, disqualifying her from her roles as beloved daughter and romantic interest and thereby scuttling the sentimental genre logic on which the novel depends.[44]

The parallel between Madge and Mammoth Cave suggests that, in addition to being quite explicitly racialized, Mammoth Cave may also have been less perceptibly gendered, even as Madge's own embodiment of Black femininity proves impossible for the novel to sustain. In this respect, *Madge Vertner* indicates a pattern we will see repeatedly in the literature of the underground: while underground actors are largely depicted as men, the space of the underground itself is often feminized. (The feminization of Mammoth Cave in the novel likewise seems to indicate a pattern in literary representations of Black femininity, in which its alienation from *people* enables its availability to conceptualize other things.) It does not take much imagination to feminize Mammoth Cave, a vast hole flowing with subterranean streams, which both attracted countless explorers and threatened them; recall the figure of Echo, the embodied spirit of Mammoth Cave in Surtees's poem "Stephen's Adieu to the Echo of the Mammoth Cave." But the unraveling of *Madge Vertner* indicates that the feminization of Mammoth Cave, like its racialization and specifically in tandem with it, introduces imaginative possibilities that exceed their authors' grasp. Mammoth Cave becomes a kind of black hole that swallows up the novel's sentimental abolitionist narrative—or, more specifically, a "Black (w)hole," if we follow Evelynn Hammonds's use of this phrase as a trope for Black female sexuality. Hammonds's influential essay "Black (W)holes and the Geometry of Black Female Sexuality" invokes Michelle Wallace's observation that the invisibility of Black feminist creativity makes it a kind of intellectual "black hole," but Hammonds reframes this figure of negation as a figure of abundance. Although a black hole cannot be seen, Hammonds—a historian of science—points out that it is "not empty; it is a dense and full place in space" that manifests its "energy" through "distorting and productive effects" on the bodies around it.[45] Hammonds's trope resonates strikingly in Mammoth Cave, raising the possibility that this subterranean black (w)hole images a similar configuration of Black female sexuality. To my knowledge, outside of *Madge Vertner*, the literature of Mammoth Cave never addresses the potent intersection between the cave's racial and gendered imaginaries. But Hammonds's work allows us to understand this silence precisely as marking the "energy" of this intersection rather than its "emptiness." When Griffith introduces an analogy between the cave and Madge in *Madge Vertner*, and when it sends the novel into disarray, perhaps we can infer an occluded dimension to other representations of Mammoth Cave's power. Perhaps these accounts, too, summon a vision of Black female sexuality that they cannot name or face.

Speculative Fictions of "Lower America"

I have been arguing that white writers who visited Mammoth Cave persistently identified the cave with its guides, positing an analogy between subterranean darkness and racialized Blackness. But this analogy summoned unbidden visions of a Black underground in the figurative sense, a mysterious, dangerous formation of Black collectivity. The political implications of the racialization of the world's longest cave system become clear in writers' depictions of Mammoth Cave as its own society.

When Mattie Griffith pictures Mammoth Cave as a "new world," a realm ungoverned by prevailing laws, whose very climate was antislavery, she participates in a broader pattern of writing about the cave. Lydia Maria Child described it as "a subterranean world, containing within itself territories extensive enough for half a score of German principalities."[46] To Alexander Clark Bullitt and Carlton Holmes Rogers, it seemed like somewhere closer to home but made strange: Bullitt touted it as "large enough, if not populous enough, for admission into the Union as an independent State," and Rogers likewise envisioned it as "a small subterranean state of itself, which might almost claim to be admitted separately into the Union, if it had any population save 'rats, bats, and eyeless fish,' to legislate and enjoy the rights of suffrage."[47] For Bayard Taylor, the cave belonged to another world entirely: being in the cave was like being on "Uranus or Neptune, or some planet still more deeply buried in the frontier darkness of our solar system," with Bishop as the "chief ruler" of this extraterrestrial "realm."[48] Taylor's comment ties his sense of Mammoth Cave as an autonomous domain to its Black rulers. N. P. Willis adopts a similar logic when he frames Bishop's work in Mammoth Cave as a dress rehearsal for political office in famous sites of Black freedom, predicting that he was "likely to be heard of, some day, as President of Liberia or Ambassador from St. Domingo."[49]

In more or less oblique terms, these visions ruminate on the sovereignty of a Black underground. Does it properly belong to the United States, to another country, or to another planet entirely? Jokes about Mammoth Cave's eligibility for admission into the Union play on the controversies over whether new states would allow or disallow slavery that led to the passage of the Kansas-Nebraska Act in 1854. But images of the cave as an "independent State" also summon sites of Black liberation and autonomy in the Americas. They connect Mammoth Cave to Haiti (notice that Willis imagines Bishop as ambassador *from* St. Domingo, not to it), as well as realized and unrealized rebellions by enslaved people in Louisiana along the Mississippi River (1811); Charleston, South Carolina (1822); Southampton, Virginia (1831); Matanzas, Cuba (1843); and more. Significantly, two of the best-known travel narratives of Mammoth Cave, Willis's 1853 *Health Trip to the Tropics* and Rogers's 1862 *Incidents of Travel in the Southern States and Cuba, with a Description of Mammoth Cave*, include it on Caribbean itineraries, linking it to sites with majority-Black populations and histories of antislavery and anticolonial resistance. The impenetrability of Mammoth Cave also evokes the maroon communities scattered throughout the Americas, where fugitives from slavery built autonomous societies within the borders of state authority but out of its view—most famously, the Great Dismal Swamp, so closely associated with Nat Turner's 1831 rebellion. (Newspapers at the time reported that Turner either recruited fugitives from the swamp to be revolutionaries or planned to retreat there after the uprising, although as Sylviane Diouf shows, neither was true; in fact, Turner hid in caves that he dug himself.⁵⁰) Like Mammoth Cave, the Great Dismal Swamp eludes planar geographies: its low-lying, unreliable ground and downward suck evince a kind of kinship with the subterranean. And as Monique Allewaert has shown, colonials in the Americas saw swamps in general as understood by and hospitable to Black people but threatening to white ones—a racialized geography that Mammoth Cave may have recalled as well.⁵¹ Visitors often commented how separate Mammoth Cave felt from the world above it; inside, Willis imagined himself as an "emigrant from Above-ground" who had left its familiar "clocks and jurisdiction" and traveled into a place of "underground freedom."⁵² Willis is being coy, as usual, but other writers' visions of Mammoth Cave's subterranean sovereignty suggest that they saw much more politicized, racialized, and potentially revolutionary times and spaces of "underground freedom" there.⁵³

While travel writers pictured Mammoth Cave as a submerged "realm" ruled by the enslaved guides, more fantasy-minded writers imagined Mammoth Cave as a portal to another world entirely. The earliest, Montgomery E. Letcher's *Wonderful Discovery! Being an Account of a Recent Exploration of the Celebrated Mammoth Cave* (1839), unearths blue-eyed residents who have "skin clear and fair as the whitest of our own country" and cannot comprehend the dark skin of the enslaved men who accompany the white scientists; the cave dwellers "rub their skins hard, as if they expected to find the black color of their faces was merely a species of paint."⁵⁴ But as Mammoth Cave's reputation became entwined with that of its guides, it came to open upon lost Black civilizations. An 1850 tale titled "New Wonders of the Mammoth Cave," by the eccentric Massachusetts clergyman Henry Webster Parker, begins as a group of explorers in Mammoth Cave, led by a guide named Stephen, discover a new cavern. When they break through its far wall, they find a "race of winged and scaly men" populating "a busy continent beneath the one we tread upon," which the narrator denominates "Lower America."⁵⁵ Stephen initiates contact with this people, whom the explorers name Anthropoptera (winged men), and the bulk of the tale admiringly details their physical appearance, customs, political arrangements, history, artistic accomplishments, and so on.

At first the narrator hypothesizes that the Anthropoptera descend from the Aztecs. But the story concludes with the discovery of a set of ancient "hieroglyphics"—a picture of a human body with a group of figures running across it—that suggest otherwise. The narrator realizes the body is a map, which reveals a now-vanished land route through the Global

South that once connected Africa (the head, "surrounded with stars, the dark or night-like color of the Ethiopean") to the Caribbean and South America (the torso). It reveals that Anthropoptera originated in Africa and traveled to the Americas prior to Native Americans, before being trapped underground by an earthquake.[56] Much as the singing tourists in Barnwell's *Knickerbocker* article try to put Mammoth Cave's Black power to work for whiteness, in making the Anthropoptera "the first inhabitants of this continent," Parker leverages Mammoth Cave's Black underground in the service of settler colonialism to displace Indigenous land claims.[57] Foreclosing the connection between the genocide and dispossession of Native Americans and the establishment of African slavery—and with it, what Aileen Moreton-Robinson calls "the question of how anyone came to be white or black in the United States"—Parker's Black underground naturalizes white national identity.[58] Indeed, he notes that the Anthropoptera ultimately lost all trace of their African origins, having become "of an almost colorless transparency."[59]

But the process by which they have done so scrambles the guarantees of white identity and strikingly heightens the power of subterranean Blackness. The narrator attributes the change in the Anthropoptera's appearance to their collective "imagination dwelling on" the cave's famous colorless fish, which "form their exclusive diet." The Anthropoptera likewise develop wings, he speculates, from thinking about the bats in the cave, which together with the fish are "the only living things, but themselves, these beings could contemplate."[60] This hypothesis borrows from eighteenth-century theories of what Katy Chiles calls "transformable race" but inverts their environmental basis, locating the determinants of racial identity in the deepest recesses of the mind instead: the Anthropoptera alter their physical appearance not through *eating* the fish but by *contemplating* the fish they eat (and the bats)—a collectivity bodily transformed by Black thought.[61] (And here the hieroglyphics' image of Africa as a head, circled by stars, resonates.)

This explanation is fascinating for a number of reasons. One is that it seems to engage the contemporaneous theories about the fish being advanced by Parker's Boston neighbor, Harvard professor Louis Agassiz, at the same time that he was also propagating his influential theories of polygenesis. Agassiz believed the development of the eyeless fish was "one of the most important questions to settle in Natural History." A strong antagonist of evolutionary theory, Agassiz argued that the fish had eyes in embryo, as related species did, but they disappeared as the fish matured, because they were "created under the circumstances in which they now live"—that is, they were divinely designed for the cave's darkness.[62] Where Agassiz attributes the fishes' physical appearance to God's hand, Parker attributes the Anthropoptera's physical appearance to the power of their own minds, a theory that rejects both creationism and evolution while offering a staggering rejoinder to Agassiz's scientific racism, which argued for the intellectual inferiority of African-descended people. And while Agassiz denies Black people's humanity by claiming they came *from* separate origins, Parker pictures Black people transforming themselves *into* new beings beyond the human. My point here is not that "New Wonders of Mammoth Cave" is antiracist; its racial politics are too messy to support such a reading. Rather, I submit that, purposely or not, Parker's vision of the metamorphic effects of the Anthropoptera's imaginations fleetingly wonders about the Black study actually happening in Mammoth Cave. In particular, it wonders about the cave as a site of transformative Black speculation.

What did Bishop and the other guides' "imaginations dwell . . . upon," to borrow Parker's words, during their long hours in the cave? What did they think about being underground? Because the question here surely isn't "Did the guides think about being underground?" but "How could they not?" To consider the thinking the guides did in Mammoth Cave alongside the writing white people did about it is to look in the cave for what Miles Grier calls "the wonderful concurrent logic of *meanwhile*: White people are doing what they do, meanwhile . . ."[63] How did the guides relate the power they built in Mammoth Cave to their enslavement? Did they talk about their guests once the last group of the day had left, as they rested their legs, or hung up the costumes visitors wore in the cave, or repaired the boats, or turned back into the cave's passages to explore further? Did they laugh at the resemblance between the eyeless white fish and the cave's benighted white visitors? Did the correlation between the fishes' whiteness and their life in total darkness spark discussions among the guides about the sources and consequences of human pigmentation? What parts of the cave did they enjoy, what parts bored them, what parts did they dread? How did they describe it to those close to them, and did they ever slip their own families or friends inside? Bishop reportedly "took a newspaper"; did he read any accounts of Mammoth Cave there?[64]

We cannot read the unwritten Black geographies of Mammoth Cave as we can the written accounts they made possible. But one subject we know Bishop did study while working there was freedom. In his 1852 book

Observations on American Slavery, British antislavery activist Russell Lant Carpenter recounts how he took three cave trips with Bishop while on a yearlong observational tour of the Southern states. He pronounced Bishop "the most intelligent slave that I ever met." Unlike most visitors, who toured Mammoth Cave in groups, Carpenter made his excursions with Bishop alone, and these unusual circumstances may have influenced the conversations they had. Bishop told Carpenter that his owner frequently sent him to explore other caves, though none above the 36°30′ line, "but he hopes, when he is free," to explore further and to come visit English caves. Carpenter added, "He was interested in hearing that F. Douglass had been my guest, and we had a good deal of conversation on slavery."[65] Carpenter says no more about what they discussed. But we learn from his narrative that Frederick Douglass was a familiar name to Bishop, that Bishop was "interested" in him, and that he, too, was contemplating his freedom. When John Croghan died in 1849, he stipulated in his will that Bishop, his wife Charlotte, and their child Thomas were to be emancipated in seven years, meaning that Bishop lived the period from 1849 to 1856 suspended between his present enslavement and the promise of (legal) freedom.[66] The stories about Bishop's emigration to Liberia had begun circulating by 1851, suggesting that Bishop studied this plan for a long time. In those years of anticipating his life in Liberia, did he begin to "improvise freedom," as David Kazanjian describes Black colonists in Liberia doing?[67] Did he practice something like those colonists' "action toward" freedom in Mammoth Cave, where, as an explorer in bondage, to-be-free but not-yet-free, he might have recognized something of "the continuing possibility of freedom, at once radically ungiven and recursively bound to the ways and fashions of unfreedom," theorized by those he hoped to join in Liberia?[68] In the cave, before his manumission and after it, was Bishop, in Saidiya Hartman's words, "trying to live as if [he] were free"?[69]

Ultimately, Bishop abandoned the plan to emigrate to Liberia. Instead, after he was finally emancipated, he bought seventy-five acres of land near Mammoth Cave. He died the following summer. Perhaps Bishop was already ill when he made the purchase and the trip to Liberia no longer seemed feasible. Perhaps he had soured on the colonization scheme. Perhaps, as Carlton Holmes Rogers predicted, he stayed because of his "attachment to the cave and his surroundings." But while Rogers and other writers explain that attachment as identification with the cave, we might consider other explanations. Above, I read Henry Webster Parker's tale "New Wonders of Mammoth Cave" as an example of a sci-fi-ish subgenre of Mammoth Cave literature that pictured the cave as a portal to another world. Bishop may also have worked in that genre. One of the furthest passages of the cave was known as Symmes Pit Branch, which ended in Symmes Pit, a deep hole. The name alludes to John Cleves Symmes's theory, first advanced in 1818, that the earth was hollow and habitable and that its inside could be accessed through openings in the poles. For several years Symmes and his followers petitioned Congress to sponsor an expedition in search of the earth's inner worlds, which Symmes predicted were "warm and rich land, stocked with thrifty vegetables and animals if not men."[70] The petitions were unsuccessful and garnered considerable derision in the early nineteenth-century press, but Symmes's theory also inspired an enduring strand of utopian fiction envisioning another, better world inside this one.[71] The naming of Symmes Pit and Symmes Pit Branch predates Bishop's arrival at Mammoth Cave, and perhaps because of the section's remoteness, it does not seem to have been a regular stop on Bishop's and the other guides' tours.[72] Still, Bishop knew and considered the names: he included Symmes Pit and Symmes Pit Branch on his 1844 map. What if we understand Symmes Pit as a contribution in two words to the genre of speculative fiction about Mammoth Cave, and Bishop as one of its primary readers and interpreters? From this perspective, Mammoth Cave represents less Bishop's failure to reach Liberia than the point of entry to a different freedom dream, below Kentucky instead of across the Atlantic, which by delving inside the earth seeks another world altogether.

The "Blackness of Blackness" in Mammoth Cave

I began this book by proposing nineteenth-century undergrounds like Mammoth Cave as intertexts for *Invisible Man*'s underground, which help us understand its potent combination of literal and figurative subterraneity. I want to end by proposing that, read transversely, *Invisible Man* also becomes a useful intertext for Mammoth Cave. For if the literature of Mammoth Cave tells us something about the racialization of the underground, *Invisible Man* points toward a relation between Blackness and the underground that eludes the limits of the literature of Mammoth Cave but may inhere in the unwritten theories and practices of the guides. When Ellison's narrator listens to Louis Armstrong's "What Did I Do to Be So Black and Blue" underground, he recounts, "I not only entered the music but descended, like Dante, into its depths." In his dreamlike trip through the music, the narrator finds "a slower tempo and a cave . . . and beneath that lay a still lower level . . . and below that I found a lower level."[73] There he hears the call-and-response of a preacher delivering a sermon on "The Blackness of Blackness"—a pointed rewriting of "the Blackness of Darkness," the phrase from Jude 1:13 that Reverend B. F. Crary applied to Mammoth Cave. Where "the Blackness of Darkness" takes "Blackness" as a known, fixed concept in order to explain "Darkness," the circular construction of "the Blackness of Blackness" refuses to pin down Blackness.

This scene limns a relation between racialized Blackness and the underground that stands in contrast to the literature of Mammoth Cave. Here, racialized Blackness and the underground are proximate but not identical. Ellison's novel allows us to imagine an alternative analytic for racialized Blackness inside Mammoth Cave—an analytic in which the subterranean opens toward the antifoundational. It allows us to speculate that even as the guides were compelled to commodify the cave for white visitors, the cave may have offered a reprieve from the killing constructions of Blackness that organized those visitors' accounts. The narrator of *Invisible Man* finally determines to leave his underground, in an epilogue that Fred Moten cuttingly describes as "a frightened attempt to retreat into the etiolated metaphysics of America."[74] But perhaps in Mammoth Cave the guides made the underground into a more sustaining place, one that allowed them to move in and out of this world indefinitely. In the next chapter, I trace the lasting mark of the Black underground that the entangled imaginations of Stephen Bishop, Materson Bransford, Nicholas Bransford, and their visitors co-created, exploring how later nineteenth-century Black writers extended and politicized it in ways Mammoth Cave's white visitors hardly dared to imagine.

2 Early Black Radical Undergrounds

In his monumental study *Black Marxism: The Making of the Black Radical Tradition*, Cedric Robinson profiles three major Black radical thinkers: W. E. B. Du Bois, C. L. R. James, and Richard Wright. But while these representatives of the Black radical tradition belong to the twentieth century, Robinson makes clear that the Black radical tradition itself does not. "The Black Radical Tradition was an accretion, over generations, of collective intelligence gathered from struggle," he writes.[1] For centuries, millions of people across the African diaspora waged the struggle against enslavement, the racial order it intensified, and the dehumanization that both proceeded from and justified it. Their resistance took forms ranging from marronage to outright rebellion and, as Saidiya Hartman adds, from sexual recalcitrance to infanticide.[2] Yet the scale of the struggle did not guarantee it would be apprehensible. Later thinkers like Du Bois, James, and Wright had to "rediscover" the Black radical tradition from "a Black historical experience nearly grounded under the intellectual weight and authority of the official European version of the past." This would be "the foundation upon which they stood."[3] Notice Robinson's topographical language: how the Black radical tradition that had been "grounded under" became the "foundation" on which later thinkers would stand—this in a section of *Black Marxism* called "The Roots of Radicalism." His "grounded under" replaces the more expected "ground under," supplanting the fatality of being crushed (i.e., "ground," the past tense of "grind") with a more ambiguous fate of being buried.

This chapter responds to Robinson's call to understand the Black radical tradition as predating the thinkers we usually refer to as Black radicals. Furthermore, it considers Robinson's subterranean phrasing itself as a vital part of the Black radical tradition. I analyze four texts that center images of the underground: David Walker's militant pamphlet *Appeal to the Coloured Citizens of the World*; Frederick Douglass's anticolonizationist speech "Slavery, the Slumbering Volcano"; Martin Delany's novel of Black revolutionary organizing, *Blake*; and William J. Wilson's imaginary museum tour–turned–adventure story, "Afric-American Picture Gallery." Like the literature of Mammoth Cave, these texts all figure the underground as a racialized space. But where the white visitors to Mammoth Cave recognize the political potential of a Black underground only fitfully and fearfully, these four authors work to elaborate and activate it.

The undergrounds Walker, Douglass, Delany, and Wilson envision are disparate, even incommensurable. They can be difficult to recognize *as* undergrounds today. They take shape in a range of genres, from Walker's manifesto and Douglass's speech to Delany's and Wilson's extravagant fictions. They include physical places like caves and mines, compositional spaces like footnotes on a page, geographies that join sites below the ground and south of the equator, political movements like insurrections, and acts of refusal and withdrawal. And they not only differ between texts; each text assembles multiple, seemingly unrelated undergrounds, which resonate with each other insistently even as they remain unarticulated explicitly. I am interested in how these undergrounds, presented appositionally, nonetheless impart meaning to one another. Walker never links his call for Black revolution with the footnotes that increasingly threaten to overwhelm the pages of his manifesto, for example, nor does Douglass connect the trope of slavery's "slumbering volcano" with his antipathy to "the ground" of colonizationist ideology. Yet as these iterations of the underground gather in each text, they echo one another, associate, and accumulate a new conceptual density. Certain iterations of the undergrounds also reappear from text to text, creating, if not quite patterns, then passages between them. By following those passages, I show how the underground becomes an overlooked site of nineteenth-century Black radical thought.

Taking seriously what Robinson calls the "the roots of Black radicalism" throws into relief a rich body of underground imagery that twentieth- and twenty-first-century Black studies scholars have used to theorize both anti-Blackness and Black world-making. One keynote here is Frantz Fanon's influential description, in *Black Skin, White Masks*, of Black life entombed in a "zone of nonbeing, an extraordinary sterile and arid region, an utterly naked declivity."[4] Nelson Maldonado-Torres, amplifying Fanon's topographical trope, explains the zone of nonbeing as "what lies below being," in a relation of "sub-ontological difference."[5] However, Fanon adds that if one is willing to attempt the "descent into a real hell," the zone of nonbeing is also "where an authentic upheaval can be born."[6] Imaging both negation and revolution, the subterranean metaphors of *Black Skin, White Masks* help us hear the very different inflections the title of *The Wretched of the Earth*, published nine years after, bears in its original French, *Les damnés de la terre* (a quotation from "L'Internationale"). There the seeming abjection of the English "wretched" carries the demonic power of the *damnés*, while the "earth," prone to abstraction in English, retains the actual earthiness of the *terre*.[7]

Images of the underground have proven particularly generative for scholars thinking about slavery's regimes of racial violence and terror alongside the modes of knowledge, imagination, and culture that enslaved people fashioned. While Fanon theorizes the subontology of *les damnés de la terre*, Édouard Glissant calls on a more watery realm of the subterranean to describe "the abyss" of the Middle Passage. The abyss, for Glissant, encompasses the "unknown" of the ship's hold, the ocean's depths, and what lies at "the edges of a nonworld that no ancestor will haunt."[8] But crucially, he adds, the "absolute unknown" of the abyss "in the end became knowledge. Not just a specific knowledge, appetite, suffering, and delight of one particular people, not only that, but knowledge of the Whole, greater from having been at the abyss."[9] Glissant's abyss is the condition of possibility for turning death into life, void into totality, alienation into comprehension. These transformations do not entail moving beyond the abyss but instead "quicken[ing]" it into material for world-building.[10] Its chasms prove generative, Glissant asserts; "we gamble on the unknown."[11] Sylvia Wynter finds similar possibilities in what she calls the "underlife," the "counterstruggle" of the "plantation subproletariat" that endures into nominal freedom.[12] As Nijah Cunningham explains, Wynter's underlife is not just a resistant force but a wholly different concept of life. It includes both lived experience and as-yet-unrealized modes of existence; it "can be seen as a gathering of potentialities and the site of the unfolding of nascent modes of sociality."[13] Much as Fanon's hell harbors both suffering and revolution, Glissant's abyss and Wynter's underlife traverse fatality and vitality.

More recent scholars have used metaphors of the underground to describe their own critical practices in what Saidiya Hartman calls the "afterlife of slavery" and Christina Sharpe terms its long "wake."[14] Hartman and Simon Gikandi invoke the subterranean to convey the problem of historical recovery. Gikandi compares the history of transatlantic slavery to a "crypt" within "modern subjectivity" and explains, "My goal is to find a language for reading what lies buried there."[15] Hartman likewise argues that slavery occupies "the underground ... of discourse," but she is less convinced of the possibility of retrieval from an archive that is itself "a tomb, a display of the violated body, an inventory of property, a medical treatise on gonorrhea, a few lines about a whore's life, an asterisk in the grand narrative of history."[16] Hartman argues that scholars of slavery should not seek to excavate a "truer picture" of slavery (whose truths will never be those of the enslaved) but rather engage in the speculative, provisional writing she calls "critical fabulation," which embraces "the impossibility that conditions our knowledge of the past and animates our desire for a liberated future."[17] While Hartman and Gikandi picture the history of slavery as locked underground, even as we live in its "afterlife," others have asked what it would mean for Black scholars to "stay in the hold of the ship," as Frank Wilderson puts it.[18] Wilderson drops this explosive phrase into the acknowledgments to his book *Red, White, and Black: Cinema and the Structure of U.S. Antagonisms* and lets it burn, but Christina Sharpe and Fred Moten have taken it up and unfolded its meanings. In *In the Wake: On Blackness and Being,* Sharpe draws on the work of Hortense Spillers, Dionne Brand, and Omise'eke Natasha Tinsley to theorize the hold as both the "immi/a/nent death" that suffocates Black life and, potentially, as a space to "enact a beholden-ness to each other, laterally."[19] Moten insists, against the contrast Wilderson draws between "staying in the hold" and "fantasies of flight," that these two do not exclude each other. "There are flights of fantasy in the hold of the ship," he maintains, and he takes this "fantasy in the hold" as descriptive of Blackness.[20] Perhaps more than any other contemporary thinker, Moten has made figures of the underground fundamental to his work, from his Fanonian characterization of Blackness as "ontology's underground" to his corresponding characterization of Black studies as a project that attunes itself to "how the underground operates out in, and as, the open," to his influential account, with Stefano

Harney, of "the downlow lowdown maroon community" they name "the undercommons."[21]

This survey of Black studies scholars' subterranean imagery, brief and incomplete as it is, hints at the enduring importance of the underground to Black radical thought. The pages that follow will posit the undergrounds of Walker, Douglass, Delany, and Wilson as submerged prehistories to this work. But I am especially interested in how these nineteenth-century writers not only lay the groundwork for theorizing to come but themselves theorize the underground in ways that might yet extend later scholars' ideas. The undergrounds they theorize do not have their successors' precision. They are undisciplined because they are (pre)emergent: inchoate and scattered, at once partial and too much. This chapter, too, takes a somewhat undisciplined approach, as it departs from linear argument to map the undergrounds that proliferate in each text. But it is because the (pre)emergent metaphor of the underground is so anarchic, I suggest, that it proves fruitful for Walker, Douglass, Delany, and Wilson. It allows them to transcode racialized subjection as subterraneity and, in doing so, to imagine various ways that subterranized Blackness might elude or even destroy the world above it.

"Three or Four Hundred Feet Underground" in Walker's *Appeal*

David Walker's 1829 pamphlet *Appeal to the Coloured Citizens of the World* must be one of the most famous underground texts of the nineteenth century—in all the contemporary senses of "underground" and then some. A searing missive from Fanon's zone of nonbeing ("For what is the use of living, when in fact I am dead?" Walker demands), the *Appeal* also broadcasts "Black life insisted from death," in Christina Sharpe's words.[22] Walker privately published the *Appeal* in Boston and covertly distributed it, giving copies to sailors headed south to circulate there and mailing other parcels, unsolicited, to free Black people with instructions to sell it to those who could pay and give it to those who could not.[23] Local authorities immediately recognized the insurrectionary character of the pamphlet and took extraordinary steps to suppress it, including petitions to the mayor of Boston, an emergency legislative session in Virginia, and the imprisonment of Walker's agents in Charleston, South Carolina, and Wilmington, North Carolina.

Walker calls his readers to arms against slavery and racism with blazing militancy. "Never make an attempt to gain our freedom or *natural* right, from under our cruel oppressors and murderers, until you see your way clear," he writes but adds in a footnote, "It is not to be understood here, that I mean for us to wait until God shall take us by the hair of our heads and drag us out of abject wretchedness and slavery" (13). Instead, Walker awaits a divinely mandated version of what Lenin would call a "revolutionary situation": "[W]hen that hour arrives and you move, be not afraid or dismayed; for be you assured that Jesus Christ the King of heaven and of earth who is the God of justice and of armies, will surely go before you" (13–14).[24] Unlike the "white Christians of America" he derides throughout the *Appeal*, Walker invokes Christ not to smother rebellion but to incite it. His Christ is "the God of justice and armies," and his way is revolutionary violence. "[I]f you commence, make sure work—do not trifle, for they will not trifle with you—they want us for their slaves, and think nothing of murdering us in order to subject us to that wretched condition—therefore, if there is an *attempt* made by us, kill or be killed" (28).

Walker's rallying cry for a Black revolutionary underground waiting on God's signal to "move" remains breathtakingly distinct today. But I argue that other aspects of the *Appeal* that may not register to us as subcultural also belong to its underground vision. One of these is its invocation of actual subterranean spaces, particularly in the *Appeal*'s culminating section, article IV, "Our Wretchedness in Consequence of the Colonizing Plan." There Walker writes of "the enlightened Christians of America": "They keep us three or four hundred feet under ground working in their mines, night and day to dig up gold and silver to enrich them and their children" (68). He repeats the phrase "to dig up gold and silver" throughout the section to explain why white Americans enslave Black people (53, 55, 62, 71). Walker probably does not mean this as a literal description of contemporary slavery in the United States; although some enslaved people worked in mines, they were far more likely to mine coal than gold or silver, and the vast majority of enslaved labor in the 1820s was agricultural and domestic. Instead, Walker's figure maps contemporary slavery in the United States onto earlier regimes of Indigenous and African slavery in South America, which primarily focused on gold and silver mining. It was this mining, Kathryn Yusoff reminds us, that "initially instigated" the slavery and anti-Blackness that are the subject of the *Appeal*, as European colonists, having decimated Indigenous populations, turned their sights on Africa to replace the lost labor.²⁵ "Gold and silver" may have been severed from these histories of extraction to become a metonym for money in the burgeoning capitalist economy of the late 1820s United States, but Walker's anachronistic image rewrites the progress narratives of "the enlightened Christians of America" in the "letters of blood and fire" that Marx famously ascribes to the history of primitive accumulation—or, as Marx restates it a few chapters later, "blood and dirt."²⁶ In this respect, the phrase exemplifies Walker's resolutely materialist analysis of slavery in the *Appeal*, where he speaks less of the Southern states than of the United States as a slaveholding nation, and where he often seems strategically uninterested in observing a difference between those who are legally enslaved and those who are nominally free. (Notice how the statement "They keep *us* three or four hundred feet under ground" includes Walker among the enslaved.)

Beyond its implicit critique of capitalist progress narratives, Walker's motif of Black miners "three or four hundred feet under ground" presents a vivid figuration of anti-Blackness. His image of people trapped hundreds of feet beneath the surface of the earth pictures slavery as a kind of hell; more literally, it renders racial subjugation as a process of making subterranean. Colonization schemes in particular, which would transport Black people off US soil, serve to bury them beneath it. Walker elaborates this idea through a motif of Black sunkenness, almost two hundred years before Jordan Peele's indelible vision of the Sunken Place in *Get Out*. Walker's descriptions of Black sunkenness constitute a kind of refrain through article IV. Like his images of subterranean Black miners, these images pointedly group nominally free people with legally enslaved ones. Colonizationists aim to "get those free people and sink them into wretchedness" (51), "sinking . . . our children into ignorance" as well (54), just as they "sink us into miseries and wretchedness by making slaves of us" (52). The "enlightened Christians of America," for their part, "keep us sunk in ignorance" (68), "sunk in the most profound ignorance and stupidity" (55), and "sunk in the most barbarous wretchedness" (71). In these figures of submersion, anti-Blackness engulfs Black people like quicksand. Yet Walker fears that white people cultivate an "ignorance," like "a mist," that keeps Black people from recognizing their position "low down into the very dark and almost impenetrable abyss in which, our fathers for many centuries have been plunged" (21). One goal of the *Appeal*, then, is to inform Black people of their underground condition.²⁷

This is key because Walker's images of an underground filled with Black people also carry insurgent possibilities. They implicitly assert that slavery and anti-Blackness have already hollowed out the ground beneath white Americans and that oppression is nothing less than training for uprising. Given the right conditions—given a hearing of the *Appeal*, say—these subterranean people could "move" (14) and "tyrants quake and tremble on their sandy foundation" (34). While Walker summons this underground through his subterranean imagery, he also materializes it compositionally, in the footnotes that increasingly troop over the pages of the *Appeal*. In reading the *Appeal*'s footnotes for their visual drama, I take my cue from Marcy Dinius's remarkable analysis of its typography, which she describes as "a graphic riot of italics, small and full capitals, exclamation points, and pointing index fingers."[28] Dinius reminds us how arduous it was to compose type by hand and how much extra work—moving between cases, inserting additional punctuation—the *Appeal* demanded. Such labor-intensive typography suggests that Walker conceived the *Appeal* visually as well as textually and gave the printer instructions accordingly. Reading the pamphlet's extravagant footnotes in light of Dinius's reading of its typography allows us to see their presence, too, as a crucial visual element of the *Appeal* rather than as an afterthought. Plenty of texts use footnotes, of course, but few compare to the *Appeal* in terms of either quantity or disposition. At the beginning of the pamphlet, Walker often uses citational footnotes, but as it goes on the footnotes grow in length and frequency, agitating the text from below. By article IV, discursive footnotes appear on nearly every page. Sometimes these subterranean texts grow so extensive that they impinge on the body of the text (figure 2.1). Just as Walker summons a Black revolutionary underground, both explicitly and in the image of Black extractive industries, the footnotes conjure its graphic counterpart: a voice rising from the depths, swarming over the page, threatening to overtake the main text.[29]

At the same time, the footnotes embody what cannot easily be said aloud, either physically or socially. Walker explains that the *Appeal* is designed to be an oral text as well as a written one: "It is expected that all coloured men, women, and children, of every nation, language and tongue under heaven, will try to procure a copy of this Appeal and read it, or get some one to read it to them, for it is designed more particularly for them," he writes (2). Dinius argues that its typography signals readers "how to properly voice the appeal aloud and spread its affect for others."[30] How, then, to read the footnotes, which do not fit comfortably into the flow of oral performance? Does a speaker stop speaking, signal a footnote, read it, and then return to the main text? What happens when the footnotes come that some of you, (whites) on the continent of America, will yet curse the day that you ever were born. You want slaves, and want us for your slaves!!! My colour will yet, root some of you out of the very face of the earth!!!!!! You may doubt it if you please. I know that thousands will doubt—they think they have us so well secured in wretchedness, to them and their children, that it is impossible for such things to occur.* So did the antideluvians doubt

---

* Why do the Slave-holders or Tyrants of America and their advocates fight so hard to keep my brethren from receiving and reading my Book of Appeal to them?—Is it because they treat us so well?—Is it because we are satisfied to rest in Slavery to them and their children?—Is is because they are treating us like men, by compensating us all over this free country!! for our labours?—But why are the Americans so very fearfully terrified respecting my Book?—Why do they search vessels, &c. when entering the harbours of tyrannical States, to see if any of my Books can be found, for fear that my brethren will get them to read. Why, I thought the Americans proclaimed to the world that they are a happy, enlightened, humane and Christian people, all the inhabitants of the country enjoy equal Rights!! America is the Asylum for the oppressed of all nations!!!

Now I ask the Americans to see the fearful terror they labor under for fear that my brethren will get my Book and read it—and tell me if their declaration is true—viz. if the United States of America is a Republican Government?—Is this not the most tyrannical, unmerciful, and cruel government under Heaven—not excepting the Algerines, Turks and Arabs?—I believe if any candid person would take the trouble to go through the Southern and Western sections of this country, and could have the heart to see the cruelties inflicted by these *Christians* on us, he would say, that the Algerines, Turks and Arabs treat their dogs a thousand times better than we are treated by the *Christians.*—But perhaps the Americans do their very best to keep my Brethren from receiving and reading my "Appeal" for fear they will find in it an extract which I made from their Declaration of Independence, which says, " we hold these truths to be self-evident, that all men are created equal," &c. &c. &c.—If the above are not the causes of the alarm among the Americans, respecting my Book, I do not know what to impute it to, unless they are possessed of the same spirit with which Demetrius the Silversmith was possessed—however, that they may judge whether they are of the same avaricious and ungodly spirit with that man, I will give here an extract from the Acts of the Apostles, chapter xix.—verses 23, 24, 25, 26, 27.

" And the same time there arose no small stir about that way. For a cer-
" tain *man* named Demetrius, a silversmith, which made silver shrines for
" Diana, brought no small gain unto the craftsmen; whom he called together
" with the workmen of like occupation, and said, Sirs, ye know that by this
" craft we have our wealth: moreover, ye see and hear, that not alone at
" Ephesus, but almost throughout all Asia, this Paul hath persuaded and turn-
" ed away much people, saying, that they be no gods which are made with
" hands: so that not only this our craft is in danger to be set at nought; but
" also that the temple of the great goddess Diana should be despised, and her
" magnificence should be destroyed, whom all Asia and the world worship-
" peth."

I pray you Americans of North and South America, together with the whole European inhabitants of the world, (I mean Slave-holders and their advocates) to read and ponder over the above verses in your minds, and judge whether or not you are of the infernal spirit with that Heathen Demetrius, the Silversmith: In fine I beg you to read the whole chapter through carefully.

thick and fast? Different speakers likely handled the footnotes differently, but in all cases they remain a problem built into the text, which presents itself for oral performance while including a subterranean level of text that resists being spoken. The footnotes' challenge to enunciation is especially arresting because they contain so many of the *Appeal*'s most incendiary statements. These include the critique of nonviolence quoted earlier ("It is not to be understood here, that I mean for us to wait until God shall take us by the hair of our heads and drag us out of abject wretchedness and slavery"); a wager that a fraction of the Black population of Virginia—"(let them be well equipt for war)"—could overthrow "every white person on the whole continent of America" (66); and the blunt statement "You are not astonished at my saying we hate you, for if we are men, we cannot but hate you, while you are treating us like dogs" (73).[31] Radical subterranean texts that defy utterance, the *Appeal*'s footnotes provide a mise en abyme of its underground ethos.

One further motif in the *Appeal* instantiates what will become a rich vein of nineteenth-century subterranean writing: the image of the underground as a double of the world above it. This doubling restages familiar sights out of place, flaunting the incongruity. It critically mirrors the known world, rendering it unstable and provisional. But its effect is visionary as well as negating; when the certainty of the known world trembles, other possible worlds may come into view. In enacting manifest impossibilities, subterranean doubling invites us into a speculative mode. Versions of this doubling will recur throughout this book, from the Underground Railroad's ironically mechanical language of depots, cars, and tracks to the city mysteries' images of "twin cities" lying beneath familiar streets. In Walker's *Appeal*, it appears not as an image but as a literary technique: an uncanny citation of US nationalist texts.

This practice of citation begins in the very form of the *Appeal*. Organized into a "Preamble" followed by four "Articles," it unmistakably signifies on the US Constitution. The repetition is at once ironic, a critique of the original document's hypocrisies, and prophetic, a founding document for a more just world to come. (Walker similarly reopens the Declaration of Independence at the end of the *Appeal*, duplicating its famous opening paragraphs and demanding whether Americans "understand your own language" [78].) Still more disorienting is Walker's reiteration of Thomas Jefferson's *Notes on the State of Virginia*, a text whose arguments for Black inferiority he eviscerates at length. He marvels how Jefferson's assertions have been "swallowed by millions of the whites" (16), and he predicts the white nationalism they subtend will have a violent recoil:

> But when I reflect that God is just, and that millions of my wretched brethren would meet death with glory—yea, more, would plunge into the very mouths of cannons and be torn into particles as minute as the atoms which compose the elements of the earth, in preference to a mean submission to the lash of tyrants, I am with streaming eyes, compelled to shrink back into nothingness before my Maker, and exclaim again, thy will be done, O Lord God Almighty. (30)

What makes Walker's vision of divinely mandated, apocalyptic Black revolution especially arresting is that it repurposes Jefferson's own famous vision of slavery's end in *Notes*: "Indeed I tremble for my country when I reflect that God is just: that his justice cannot sleep forever: that considering numbers, nature, and natural means only, a revolution of the wheel of fortune, an exchange of situation, is among possible events: that it may become probable by supernatural interference!"[32] Simultaneously excoriating and ventriloquizing Jefferson, Walker turns the *Appeal* into a counterfactual double of Jefferson's *Notes*—one "refreshed . . . with the blood of patriots and tyrants," to follow Walker's own example of mustering Jefferson's words against him.[33]

As an aesthetic practice, Walker's counterfactual doubling stages its own kind of insurrection by occupying the nation's foundational texts. In doing so, Walker presses on a politics beyond them—perhaps the "world" he looks toward when he addresses the *Appeal* "to the coloured citizens of the world," as the full title states. Although Walker focuses on African Americans, here we can understand him mustering an African diasporic identity or solidarity among people of color broadly. (Pequot minister and activist William Apess, for one, seems to have read the *Appeal* and seen its significance to "black or red skins or any other skin of color": his 1833 essay "An Indian's Looking-Glass for the White Man" conspicuously borrows some of Walker's phrasing and echoes many of Walker's arguments, replacing Thomas Jefferson with Andrew Jackson.[34]) Yet it also seems important that in the eyes of the law, there is no such citizenship. For that matter, the enslaved people in the United States who constituted Walker's target audience were refused citizenship of any kind. Walker's proleptic "citizens" seems less like a bid for any official form of citizenship than for what Eddie S. Glaude Jr., in his discussion of ideas of nationhood among Black writers in the early nineteenth-century United States, calls "an ambiguously rich notion of 'we-ness.'"³⁵ Read in this context, we can see the address of the *Appeal* as advancing the possibility that, as Walker puts it, "the world in which we live does not exist" (22). Instead, it speaks to the immanence—and imminence—of another world entirely, one augured by the fact that, as Apess points out, God "made fifteen colored people to one white and placed them here upon this earth."³⁶ Walker pledges his allegiance not to what, throughout the *Appeal*, he calls "*these* United States" (a formulation whose substitution of the demonstrative "these" for the direct "the" suggests the ephemerality of the nation as we know it) but to some other possible formation, as yet unrealized.

The Topographies of Douglass's "Slavery, the Slumbering Volcano"

Walker's warning that revolution inevitably awaited a slaveholding nation assumed explicit subterranean form in the popular nineteenth-century trope of the "slumbering volcano." In the introduction I examined several examples of its usage, but it was Frederick Douglass who gave perhaps the most extended meditation on it, at an April 23, 1849, meeting of 1,200 Black opponents of the American Colonization Society (ACS). There Douglass turned the phrase "slumbering volcano" into the keynote for a speech that folds this subterranean imagery over and over on itself. His stunningly layered underground motif analyzes racism as giving white people the *ground*—the world and its premises—while placing Black people below it.

Widely reprinted in antislavery newspapers, Douglass's speech denounced the ACS's recent efforts to establish English auxiliaries, "plant[ing] themselves" above the "honored graves" of recently deceased abolitionists like William Wilberforce and Thomas Clarkson.³⁷ Douglass contrasts the colonizationists' arrogation of this sacred ground with their efforts "to drive us from our home and country" (150). He suggests the ACS's simultaneous attempts to place themselves and displace African Americans exemplifies the "fundamental" problem with their colonizationist ideology: "[T]hat it assumes that the coloured people, while they remain in this country, can never stand on an equal footing with the white population of the United States." He continues, "This objection, I say, is a fundamental one; it lies at the very basis of this enterprise, and, as such, I am opposed to it, have ever been opposed to it, and shall, I presume, ever continue to oppose it. It takes the ground that the coloured people of this country can never be free" (151). Just as the colonizationists "plant themselves" where they wish, they "take the ground" that African Americans "cannot stand on an equal footing" with white Americans. That is, the colonizationists believe that African Americans lack the standing to "take the ground" themselves. Political theorist George Ciccariello-Maher has traced a similarly racialized language of standing and ground from Hegel's concepts of *Grund* and *Selbständigkeit* (self-consciousness, literally self-standing-ness), exemplified in the master-slave dialectic, to the Stand Your Ground law, which George Zimmerman invoked to justify his murder of Trayvon Martin. Hegel presumes that master and slave confront one another from "the same universal *Grund*," as Zimmerman claimed that he and Martin did. But Ciccariello-Maher observes that Frantz Fanon's critique of the master-slave dialectic in *Black Skin, White Masks* shows that "Black subjects do not confront white subjects on the smooth plane of reciprocal relation envisioned by Hegel"; instead, they are relegated "beneath the ostensible universality of Ground."[38] When Douglass argues that the ACS believes African Americans "can never stand on equal footing with the white population of the United States" and thus "never be free," he prefigures both Fanon's account of what Maldonado-Torres calls "sub-ontological difference" and its subterranean idiom. But even as Douglass asserts that colonizationist ideology places African Americans beneath the feet of "the white population," he undermines the colonizationists' "footing." If the colonizationists claim the "ground," his own "objection" is "fundamental"; "it lies at the very basis of this enterprise." Douglass's language extends the (by now somewhat dizzying) topographical motif by introducing another space below the colonizationists' "footing"—its foundation or "very basis"—and launching his critique from there. His subterranean wordplay anticipates his more explicit statement in *The Life and Times of Frederick Douglass* that "to *understand*," one must "*stand under*."[39]

Douglass's topographical language prepares the way for the trope of the slumbering volcano, which will destabilize the colonizationists' ground still further. He prefaces it with the declaration that enslaved people, rather than going to Africa, should "remain here and add to the number of those who may yet imitate the example of our fathers of '76"—that is, prepare for revolution.

> I do not mean to say here, my friends, that this result is a desirable one—the result to which I look—but I look to it as an inevitable one, if the nation shall persevere in the enslavement of the coloured people. I have not the slightest doubt but that at this moment, in the Southern

States, there are skillfully-contrived and deeply-laid schemes in the minds at least of the leading thinkers there, for the accomplishment of this very result. The slaveholders are sleeping on slumbering volcanoes, if they did but know it. (151)

By pluralizing *the* slumbering volcano of popular discourse into multiple "slumbering volcanoes," Douglass pictures an explosive underground of "deeply-laid schemes" that extends beyond any single attack on slavery, even the earthshaking Haitian Revolution the trope invokes. Perhaps his pluralization also invites his audience to translate into action his earlier rhetorical effort to explode the "very basis" of white supremacist belief. Certainly, the audience responds enthusiastically to the idea: when Douglass adds that "at least one coloured man in the Union"—meaning himself—"would greet with joy the glad news . . . that an insurrection had broken out in the Southern States," and "it is not impossible that some other black men . . . may have occasion at some time or other, to put this theory into practice," they answer with "great applause" (153). And when Douglass cites the same famous line from Thomas Jefferson that David Walker does—"I tremble for my country when I reflect that God is just, and that his justice cannot sleep forever" (152)—it resonates differently in the shadow of the slumbering volcano. Now sleeping justice seems to take the shape of the slumbering volcano, and it is not just Jefferson but the whole country (which Jefferson, of course, claimed to represent) that trembles as the underground awakens.

In the final section of the speech, Douglass offers an illustration of what the slumbering volcano might look like when it finally erupts on "those who have trampled upon us for the last two hundred years" (152). He tells the story of the 1841 revolt aboard the *Creole* led by Madison Washington, whose history he would later fictionalize in the short story "The Heroic Slave" (1853). As Douglass's language of "trampling" predicts, this example retains and dramatizes the slumbering volcano's image of revolution as literally submerged. When the fugitive Washington is captured and taken on board the *Creole* with nineteen other enslaved people, bound for New Orleans, they are "placed beneath the hatchway" (155). Douglass asks us to picture their imprisonment belowdecks while we watch their captors above: "[T]he slave-dealer—I sometimes think I see him—walking the deck of that ship freighted with human misery, quietly smoking his segar, calmly and coolly calculating the value of the human flesh beneath the hatchway" (155). Although the enslaved captives are not underground exactly, this stacked image—the enslaved entombed in the hold while the slave-dealer strolls above—invites the comparison. And it restages the slumbering volcano in embodied form when, after eight days of "repose," the hold explodes. Washington "had been at work all the while," releasing himself and his fellow captives from their irons. "He leapt from beneath the hatchway, gave a cry like an eagle to his comrades beneath, saying, *we must go through*" (155).[40] Douglass's image of the *Creole*'s insurgent hold realizes the accumulated underground topographies of "Slavery, the Slumbering Volcano," demonstrating the power of the subterranean in action.

Hemispheric Subterraneity: *Blake*'s "Deep Laid Secret Organization"

A kind of secret history of the present, Martin Delany's novel *Blake; or, the Huts of America* grippingly dramatizes Douglass's insistence that "at this moment, in the Southern States, there are . . . deeply-laid schemes." It also suggests how this "slumbering volcano" figured an underground that was inseparable from the United States' hemispheric "underside" in the revolutionary Caribbean. Serialized in part in the *Anglo-African Magazine* in the first half of 1859 and in full in the *Weekly Anglo-African* from November 1861 to May 1862, *Blake* tells the story of Henry Holland, or Blake, or Carolus Henrico Blacus, who was kidnapped from Cuba as a teenager and enslaved on a plantation in Mississippi. Years later, the sale of his wife impels him to escape, and he sets off to foment a transnational Black revolution. The novel follows Blake as he slips through the US South, recruiting other enslaved people, and finally travels to Cuba, where he reunites with his wife and assembles the Army of Emancipation, a secret pan-African revolutionary force. Throughout, Delany works through a series of "seclusions" and "organizations," words he uses less as nouns to describe something already existing (e.g., the seclusion of the forest or the activities of a secret organization) than as nominalized verbs that name activities in progress. Each place he visits, Blake "holds" or "enters into" a seclusion with a trustworthy few in order to "complete" or "effect" a wider organization. The outcome of these activities remains a mystery: no known copies of the issues of the *Weekly Anglo-African* containing the final installments of the novel survive. Yet even if these chapters did survive, and even if they did narrate the outbreak of the revolution, they conclude within five issues, as Jerome McGann shows in his recent edition.[41] Since the *Weekly Anglo-African* ran one to four chapters per issue, this is a small portion of the novel compared to the seventy-four chapters that precede it. In other words, revolution may be the climax to *Blake*, but it does not really seem to be the point. Rather, *Blake* rejects a conventional linear narrative in favor of a kind of panorama of subterranean revolutionary strategy.

In doing so, *Blake* transforms the story of its titular character into that of a revolutionary Black underground, or what the *Anglo-African Magazine*'s advertisement for the novel called "a deep laid secret organization."[42] John Ernest has shown that *Blake*'s "secret organization" reflects Delany's own long-standing involvement with Prince Hall Freemasonry.[43] In his 1853 pamphlet *The Origins and Objects of Ancient Freemasonry*, Delany argued that even white Masons participated in a historically Black tradition: "To Africa is the world indebted for its knowledge of the mysteries of Ancient Freemasonry," and to "the Egyptian *slave*—may I not add, the *fugitive* slave," is the world indebted for the transmission of those Masonic traditions.[44] White Masons might try to deny those origins, but for African Americans, "the mysteries of Ancient Freemasonry" provided a powerful resource for life in the present. When Delany named the newspaper he founded in 1843 *The Mystery*, despite the fact that it had no explicit connection to Freemasonry, he announced the relevance of both Masonic ritual and the Egyptian past to contemporary Black community. Years later, in *Blake*, this conviction deepened into a vision of a Black secret organization that would transform these subterranean traditions into a means of insurrection.

While the novel initially seems to be structured around Blake's visionary leadership—"I have laid a scheme, and matured a plan for a general insurrection of the slaves in every state, and the successful overthrow of slavery!" he announces early on—Delany quickly undercuts Blake's singularity.[45] Instead of having one name, which would distinguish him, Blake takes on multiple ones. His seeming individuality becomes something like an embodied collectivity, and the eventual revelation of his original surname, Blacus, telegraphs his representative Blackness. Despite his messianic appearance, Blake is synonymous, as the subtitle's "or" indicates, with "the huts of America," a Black underground that persistently precedes and exceeds his conscription. Each person Blake meets seems to anticipate his arrival, they already have communication networks, and they apprehend the plan as soon as it comes out of his mouth, if not sooner. The first time Blake gathers a group of confidants and "imparted to them the secrets of his organization," they cannot believe that they did not guess it before. "What fools we was that we didn't know it long ago!" one man exclaims (40). Blake's role turns out not to be to organize enslaved people so much as it is to show that they are already organized, by activating what the advertisement for the novel described as "the formidable understanding among the slaves throughout the United States and Cuba."[46] As Fred Moten writes, glossing Cedric Robinson in *The Terms of Order*, "the one who is said to have given the call is really an effect of a response that had anticipated him."[47] Thus as the Army of Emancipation's plans for an uprising ripen, the collaborators' conversations fall into a peculiar pattern:

> "I hope much from tomorrow," suggested Placido.
> "We must make much of tomorrow!" replied Blake.
> "We can if we will!" added Placido.
> "Then we will!" decisively concluded Blake. (241)

Or:

> "And if we say it shall, it will be so!" added Madame Cordora.
> "Then it shall be so!" declared Blake.
> "Then," concluded the Madame, "it will be so!" (263)

Or:

> "That's the word of God," said Placido.
> "I'm sure God's word is His will," added the Madame.
> "We would what God wills," responded Placido.
> "Then let God's will be done," said Blake. (285)

In these almost incantatory exchanges, each participant's contribution actualizes an idea immanent in the previous one, finally arriving collaboratively at a declaration. Their language performatively renders the novel's vision of underground organization as a collective realization of something already there—secret preparations that unlock knowledge secreted inside their participants. Importantly, we never learn the scheme itself. Perhaps *Blake*'s commitment to secrecy extends to its own disclosures. Perhaps the scheme itself is simply less important to the novel than the subterranean network that it calls into action.[48] Perhaps Delany's readers, like the members of the Army of Emancipation or David Walker's audience, will simply realize when they are ready.

Delany's focus on "deep laid secret organization," along with Blake's cryptic instruction that the Army of Emancipation's surroundings themselves will "illustrate" their plan and "keep it constantly before their eyes and in their memory" (39), suggestively reframes other aspects of the novel, too, as manifestations of subterranean forces. First, like Douglass's "Slavery, the Slumbering Volcano," *Blake* presents a slave ship's hold as a kind of underground, both literal and figurative. As part of the Army of Emancipation's plan, Blake enlists on the *Vulture*, a ship making an illegal kidnapping expedition to the Gulf of Guinea. On the return trip, the captives, pent up in the hold, become increasingly restive. Simultaneously, a storm begins to gather, "but nothing in comparison with the angry threatening of the dusky faces below" (232). By the time the storm erupts, Delany has driven home the analogy between the "black and frowning skies and raging hurricane above; the black and frowning slaves with raging passions below" (234) so energetically that the reader expects mutiny immediately. But then Delany unexpectedly pulls back: "Suddenly the winds changed, the clouds began to disperse, the thunder and lightning ceased to be seen and heard" (236). Delany stokes the readers' anticipation of an uprising only to keep the action in the hold. This reversal creates suspense and, to some extent, advances the plot, as it allows word of the near-insurrection to spread, depreciating the captives' market value and allowing agents of the Army of Emancipation to purchase them. Yet as much as the events on the *Vulture* serve any narrative purpose, dwelling on the image of the rebellious hold builds out the motif of the subterranean and signals the novel's commitment to mystery and possibility. Here, as in *Blake*'s larger narrative, Delany centers the underground rather than the uprising, the ongoing threat rather than its anticipated climax.

Second, Blake's determination to make Cuba the source of the revolution that will spread north frames Cuba as a kind of geographic underground to the United States. I noted in the introduction that the trope of the slumbering volcano in the mid-nineteenth-century United States was animated by a conflation of topography and hemispheric geography. It inescapably summoned the Haitian Revolution, given both the phrase's initial reference to it and the portentousness of Haiti's example. The volcano's image of a fiery underground ready to burst to the surface was thus also the image of the revolutionary history of Haiti ready to erupt north into the United States. In *Blake*, Delany extends the idea of Haiti as the United States' underground to Cuba, whose colonists, too, are living "on the brow of a volcano" (305), by suggesting that the island's recent history of insurrectionary plotting motivates Blake's decision to hatch the revolution there.[49] In 1844, after a series of risings by enslaved people in Matanzas, Cuban colonial authorities, inflamed by fears of the island's growing Black population, claimed they had uncovered a plan for a vast insurrection, which came to be known as the Conspiración de la Escalera.[50] The plans of the Army of Emancipation rewrite the conspiracy as the first act of a hemispheric revolution. The prospect of enslaved people in Cuba inciting a revolution in the United States makes it, in Judith Madera's words, a "literary counter-mapping of U.S. expansionist maps" that represented Cuba as ideally situated for annexation, which Southern enslavers and their allies saw as key to maintaining their power.[51] *Blake* creates an alternate geographic logic, which would make Cuba not the means to expand US slavery from the North to the South but the means to destroy it from the South to the North.

In reality, Cuban colonial authorities crushed the suspected revolt through a brutal campaign of repression. But Delany's depiction of Cuban rebels continuing to conspire "below" the United States animates a third underground by resurrecting the rebel dead. Many readers of the *Anglo-African Magazine* would have recognized Blake's Cuban second-in-command and long-lost cousin, Placido, "the distinguished poet of Cuba" (192), as one of the alleged leaders of the 1844 rebellion, the subject of tributes by Delany, John Greenleaf Whittier, and Henry Highland Garnet, among others.[52] This recognition would likely come as a surprise, since the real-life poet Plácido had been executed in 1844, nine years before Blake's arrival. This anachronism "reanimates a potential for allied Afro–New World revolt that had, in fact, been severely undercut," as Eric Sundquist observes.[53] John Patrick Leary points out that it does so by playing US imperialist discourse against itself: while expansionists represented Cuba as "a site of belatedness," Delany reinterprets this as a capacity "to restage the 'would-have-been.'"[54] Having presented Cuba as the United States' underground in a cartographic and political sense, then, Delany deepens its subterranean character by making it a place of access to people and possibilities presumed buried.

"That Place of Mysteries": The Underground Art of the "Afric-American Picture Gallery"

So far I have argued that Walker's *Appeal*, Douglass's "Slavery, the Slumbering Volcano," and Delany's *Blake* articulate their visions of Black revolution by proliferating images of the underground. Some of these images clearly represent undergrounds, like Walker's references to Black people trapped "three or four hundred feet under ground," or Douglass's figure of slavery's "slumbering volcano"; others, like Walker's footnotes or Delany's mirror images of the seething hold of a slave ship and an insurgent Cuba churning below the United States, evoke the underground more obliquely. But in the accumulation and unexplained clustering of these images, we can trace the emergence of the underground as a key trope for articulating Black radical thought. Rather than crystallizing into a single definition, the undergrounds that gather in these texts promiscuously absorb meaning from each other, constellating into a loose and dynamic assemblage of underground-ness.

In this last section, I turn to a text in which the underground becomes a space less of revolutionary activity than of thrillingly arcane modes of defiance: William J. Wilson's serial "Afric-American Picture Gallery," which ran alongside *Blake* in the *Anglo-African Magazine*.[55] Wilson began his writing career in the early 1850s as the Brooklyn correspondent for *Frederick Douglass' Paper*, where he contributed witty, acerbic sketches of Black life in New York under the pseudonym Ethiop.[56] As Radiclani Clytus has shown, Wilson's newspaper columns critiqued the distorting lenses the white press brought to bear on Black culture and encouraged Black readers to look at each other through what he termed "a glass of our own."[57] To do so, Clytus explains, Wilson drew on "urban spectatorial literature" to give Ethiop the persona of a flaneur, while rejecting that genre's propensity to make Black city dwellers objects of "surveillance and ridicule." Instead, Ethiop's sketches "make it possible for Black New Yorkers to see themselves" in images that affirm them.[58] Notably, Clytus connects Ethiop's "vision-centered epistemologies" with the physically "elevated perspective" he employs in his letters, which afford him a "panoramic gaze" on the city below.[59] Where other correspondents for *Frederick Douglass' Paper* give only their city in their datelines, Wilson reports from the resonant neighborhood of Brooklyn Heights—and as Clytus notes, when Wilson relocates, he moves to what he calls "a snug little nook on the top of Washington Park," where he commands "a fine, mental bird's eye view."[60] Four years later, however, "Afric-American Picture Gallery" would question this elevated point of view, and the commitments to the political utility of visibility and representation it entails, by setting the turning point of the story in the underground studio of a mysterious artist.

Wilson's "Afric-American Picture Gallery" extends the visual project of Ethiop's newspaper sketches by imagining a museum of Black art. Not only does the museum not exist, but no illustrations accompany the text. Instead, Wilson vividly renders a series of fictional artworks in print, providing description, evaluation, and analysis of each one. "Afric-American

Picture Gallery" thus serves as a kind of imagined laboratory to test out the theories about Black visuality that Ethiop developed in his earlier writing. As the story begins, Ethiop recalls how, in the course of his "rambles" about the city, he "stumbled over" an "almost unknown Gallery" of works by Black artists.⁶¹ The museum contains portraits of people of African descent, both famous and obscure, including Phillis Wheatley; Toussaint L'Ouverture; a *"beautiful colored girl*, with a hideous monster of a white-faced doll in her arms"; and the editor of the *Anglo-African Magazine*, Thomas Hamilton, with Samuel Cornish, the recently deceased editor of *Freedom's Journal*, peering over his shoulder. It also contains landscape paintings of scenes from the Black diaspora, including a slave ship, the Underground Railroad, the 1830 Colored Convention in Philadelphia, and Abeokuta, Martin Delany's planned site for an African American colony in the Niger Valley.⁶² Ivy Wilson argues that Ethiop's tour of the gallery seeks to "foment a subversive political sensibility" among readers by shifting the way they literally view Black culture.⁶³ His interpretive practice, which tends to focus on a picture's apparent details rather than its focal point, undermines given modes of seeing and "necessitate[s] attention to the margins, the outside, and the Other."⁶⁴ Ethiop's efforts to use visual representation to transform subjectivity clearly align with the work Clytus shows him pursuing in his newspaper sketches. But as the story unfolds, Ethiop seems increasingly doubtful of the political efficacy of the project, and the story turns its attention from what Ivy Wilson describes as a "black counter-public" to the mysteries of the underground.⁶⁵

To understand this shift, it is useful to chart the sequence of events that narratively leads Ethiop out of the museum and to the underground. Initially, Ethiop cherishes the gallery as a "hiding-place" from "the blast and chill of the world," and in his description we can recognize Christina Sharpe's formulation of anti-Blackness as "the weather" of Black life.⁶⁶ But this haven does not last. In Ethiop's deeply meta-serial narrative, the publication of the first installment induces curious visitors to seek out the gallery, and halfway through the second installment, "after sundry searchings and pryings [they] have found *our secret*."⁶⁷ The new visitors' criticisms of the gallery, and Ethiop's increasingly exasperated attempts to defend it, overtake the rest of the installment. After the visitors leave, he runs out the door, instructing the gallery's attendant, Tom Onward, "to bar it against all further intruders."⁶⁸ Although Ethiop returns to the gallery in the next installment, he does not stay for long. In a bewildering sequence of events, he takes up a painting labeled as the Black Forest, drawn to the "air of profound mystery that seemed to pervade it," only to find that his gaze keeps returning to a portrait of Tom. Suddenly, Tom himself enters with an anonymous invitation to visit the Black Forest, along with directions, without which "the keenest mind could not by any process penetrate even the recesses of the Black Forest, much less the exact spot in question."[69] Suffice to say that this Black Forest is not the German one. After two days' harrowing journey, first by stagecoach with a Virginian enslaver and kidnapper, who are pursuing fugitives, and then by foot, Ethiop reaches the Black Forest and finds his host, who turns out to be a self-emancipated artist named Bernice.

Up until this point, "Afric-American Picture Gallery" more or less abides by the realist genre conventions of the newspaper sketch. But once Ethiop reaches the Black Forest, the narrative veers sharply into what Leif Eckstrom and Britt Rusert, in the introduction to their digital edition of the story, describe as "counterfactual terrain."[70] In fact, the strangeness of these scenes has everything to do with their terrain—or rather, their subterraneity. When Bernice leads Ethiop outside his house, Ethiop is stunned to discover that a "huge stone laying almost in [the] pathway covered the mouth of a famous cave." To readers in 1859 (and hopefully for readers of the previous chapter), Wilson's "famous cave" would likely have conjured Kentucky's Mammoth Cave, whose possible undiscovered entrances were a topic of frequent speculation.

> At a slight touch from the old man's hand this stone rolled away as if by magic, and revealed a deep dark *Cavern*. With a firm step he began to descend a ladder and I followed. Down, down, down we went. Down, down, down; and long was it ere we reached the bottom; and when we did so, we were brought upon a massive door which like the stone above, yielded to the touch of the old man's hand.[71]

This is an indisputably surprising scene, but for Ethiop, it is a challenge to his worldview. In contrast to the high perch he customarily enjoyed in *Frederick Douglass' Paper*, he goes deep within the earth, and not his discerning gaze but Bernice's magic touch possesses revelatory powers. And the revelations are extraordinary. Inside, Bernice presents the nineteenth-century forerunner of Ellison's electrified underground in *Invisible Man*: a lamp-lit subterranean artist's studio, filled with finished pieces, materials, and works in progress. "In this place, far from man's baseness, and man's vile injustice, have I labored," Bernice tells Ethiop.[72]

Bernice's studio may be "two days journey" from the gallery, but as his emphasis on its distance from "man" suggests, it also seems to belong to another realm entirely. Its actual location is unknown: Ethiop declines to give the "precise locality of the Black Forest, nor fully the manner of the people dwelling there, nor yet wholly their doings."[73] But more than unknown, Ethiop suggests the Black Forest is *unknowable*, at least by ordinary means. Noting Ethiop's description of its "wild sublimity," Derrick Spires observes that the Black Forest embodies the sublime's ability to "tap . . . into that part of us that allows us to think about that which we cannot know/comprehend through established channels of understanding, ultimately opening new imaginative vistas, new senses of power, and objects of desire."[74] With a name that references a real-life location that it conspicuously is not, Black Forest shuns recognized geographies. It is a place of "profound mystery," Ethiop says. *Mystery* is a word we will see in frequent company with nineteenth-century undergrounds (note here how the adjective "profound," which expresses intensity as depth, instantiates the affiliation), and as I will show at greater length in chapters 3 and 4, it connotes an inexplicability that exceeds secrecy's binary of concealment and exposure. (By contrast, the "secret" Afric-American Picture Gallery is quickly revealed.) Ethiop insists that "I could not if I would" represent his conversations with Bernice, and even his own experiences defy documentation: "A faithful recital of what I heard and what I saw, lengthened out in a dozen carefully collated and closely written volumes, would scarcely do justice to my three days' stay in that place of mysteries," he maintains.[75]

Yet despite its distance from the Afric-American Picture Gallery, part of what makes Bernice's "Grotto Home" so confounding is that there is something oddly familiar about it.[76] Consider how the "profusion" of artworks in the studio, including a "bust, statues, statuettes; landscapes, portraits, fancy pieces," recapitulates the variety and "unstudied arrangement" of artworks in the gallery; it even contains a duplicate of the gallery's portrait of Tom, the attendant.[77] Wilson also embeds the Black Forest within the gallery formally, by presenting its sights with the standard label he uses for each picture in the gallery's collection, so that "PICTURE NO. XIII.—A PICTURE OUTSIDE OF THE GALLERY" introduces the forest, and "PICTURE NO. XIV.—PORTRAIT OF A MAN" introduces Bernice.[78] He embeds the Black Forest within the gallery visually as well, by hanging its image "in beautiful miniature" on the gallery walls. This picture serves as a kind of portal that opens to the forest narratively: recall that the invitation to visit the Black Forest appears when Ethiop is looking at the painting of it in the gallery. These unexplained repetitions suggest that while the cave may be two days' journey from the gallery, and seems much further, it is also, in some weirder way, much closer. The cave's mirroring of the gallery recalls the doubling that runs through David Walker's *Appeal*, where Walker's unmarked quotations of US nationalist texts both mock their authority and imagine worlds beyond it. In my discussion of Walker, I linked this doubling to the *Appeal*'s representations of undergrounds, from its motif of mines to the graphic subterraneity of its copious footnotes. In "Afric-American Picture Gallery," Wilson makes explicit the relation between doubling and the underground by depicting an actual subterranean space that uncannily restages a familiar site above. This estrangement in proximity signals that the literal underground of Bernice's cave is also staging a figurative sense of the underground, as a realm of activity that cannot be assimilated to the order of things upstairs.

As Ethiop explores Bernice's underground studio, he discovers indications that the Black Forest not only stands apart from the world as we know it, but that it is fundamentally unsynchronized with it. Among Bernice's works he finds a stone tablet headed "Year 4,000. The Amecans, or Milk-White Race," which chronicles the history of chattel slavery and the eventual extinction of white Americans in twenty-five verses written in forty-one "singular, new and beautiful characters." Adopting the inflections of both scripture and settler-colonial historiography, complete with the pseudo-indigenizing truncation of "Americans" to "Amecans" (rhymes with "Mohicans," as in "last of the"), the tablet recounts how white Americans "wrapped themselves up in their ease and luxury in hopeful security" until "great physical and mental weakness came over them" and "yea as a cloud did they vanish from off the face of the whole land."[79] Ethiop wonders, "Is it fiction, is it history, is it prophecy?" But these distinctions do not hold in the underground's "place of mysteries," and he concludes, "Who can tell?"[80] The presence of this artifact from the future suggests that, like Cuba in *Blake*, Bernice's cave somehow harbors temporalities unlike those that govern above. Such nonlinear temporalities will recur frequently as a feature of nineteenth-century undergrounds in this book.

As the tablet's promise that racism will literally be the death of white Americans demonstrates, when "Afric-American Picture Gallery" goes underground, the mode of the narrative shifts, from realistic to speculative; its tone also shifts, from musing and ironic to something much fiercer. In the gallery, Ethiop mocks the arrogance of white visitors ("not Anglo-African, but Anglo-Saxon, or Anglo-American or something of that sort; botheration,

I could never get the hang of these Angloes!"), but Bernice confronts white supremacy more directly.[81] He predicts to Ethiop that his subterranean art "will yet not only see the light, but command the just approbation of even the enemies of my race" after he is dead. "I say it not in a boastful spirit," he adds, and I hear it less as a boast than a threat. Bernice's militant language does not suggest that he desires the approval of white people; they remain "the enemies of my race," and they give their respect for his art only under "command." Rather, while Ethiop's earlier newspaper sketches envision visual culture as a means of transforming Black subjectivity, Bernice suggests that he makes art to use as a weapon against anti-Blackness.

If my analysis of Bernice's philosophy of art seems to over-read his bellicose figures of speech, consider the next sight he shows Ethiop. Again opening a door with the touch of his hand, Bernice guides Ethiop through further "subterraneous windings" and then magically opens yet another door to reveal a cell. Inside is a wasted, shrieking white man chained to a wall. Bernice explains that the man once held him in bondage, murdered his son, and sold his wife. We now realize that Bernice is a fugitive from slavery, and the Black Forest a maroon community of one. "I made my resolve and came hither," he explains tersely. "He was brought hither, by what means I need not say." Since then, Bernice has reversed their positions, holding his enslaver captive and reminding him that everything he now does, the enslaver once did to him. When Ethiop ventures to say "something about the law, redress, justice, &c.," Bernice retorts, "*Laws!!* what laws, what justice is there for the oppressed of our *class*? What laws except to oppress them harder?" Like Walker quoting Thomas Jefferson, Bernice ventriloquizes white supremacy against itself, quoting Chief Justice Roger B. Taney's infamous line from the *Dred Scott* decision: "He plead earnestly for his rights. I told him he had no rights that I was bound to respect." Then he calmly explains he will keep the man there until he dies, at which point he will throw his body to the vultures.[82]

Though Ethiop initially seems shocked by Bernice's rough justice, ultimately he is persuaded. Wilson's readers, for their part, would have encountered Bernice's actions in an intertextual frame that may have inclined them likewise. This installment of "Afric-American Picture Gallery" ran in the June issue of the *Anglo-African Magazine* following chapters 17 to 20 of *Blake*, in which Blake seeks out an elderly man reputed to have killed his former overseer ("Then *he's* the very man I want to see!" [79]) and continues through Louisiana and Texas, "sowing the seeds of future devastation and ruin to the master and redemption to the slave" (83). *Blake* was followed in turn by Liberian colonist Edward Wilmot Blyden's "A Chapter in the History of the African Slave Trade," which concludes by proposing that slavery's "hideous and menacing roars" are signs of "his dying paroxysms," presaging its "supervening enervation and overwhelming overthrow."[83] Readers of this issue of the *Anglo-African Magazine* might well have connected Blyden's personification of slavery as a man raging frantically against his impending death to the "wild and loud imprecations" of Bernice's shattered former enslaver a few pages before. Bookended by *Blake*'s connection between the "ruin" of the enslaver and the "redemption" of the enslaved and Blyden's depiction of slavery as a ruined tyrant ripe for "overthrow," Bernice's scheme of violent retribution assumes a strong relation to the destruction of slavery as a system, although the nature of the relation remains unexplained. And in our last glimpse of Bernice, he hints that the cave contains still further surprises. As he leads Ethiop out of the enslaver's cell, he tells him, "My son, thou hast as yet seen but little of this place."[84]

After Ethiop leaves the cave, he returns to the gallery, but it is no longer what it once was to him. Having begun as a fantasy of a "black counterpublic sphere," in Ivy Wilson's words, "Afric-American Picture Gallery" grows increasingly skeptical about that fantasy, coming to manifest what Britt Rusert describes as "the problem of the public and of publicity itself for Black art."[85] Ethiop's quiet contemplation is interrupted by another flock of visitors, causing him "such a storm of choleric feelings as will serve for all of life to come."[86] And in the next and final installment, Ethiop rejects the narrative's earlier ekphrastic format. Unlike the other installments, this one is not labeled as a "picture"; it simply reads "The Early Days of the Underground Railroad." Instead of describing and analyzing a work of art with his usual rich detail, Ethiop recalls an episode from the "earlier days of the Afric-American Picture Gallery, when its quiet was seldom disturbed by visitors of any kind": his encounter with a fugitive from slavery named Bill, who enters the gallery "in a towering rage" because he has just seen the man who claims to own him on the street.[87] The rest of the installment consists of Bill's backstory. We do not learn that it corresponds to a work of art until the last sentence, when Ethiop briefly points out "the portrait of our sable hero" hanging on the wall.[88] Even then, the portrait format seems inapposite to Bill's history of fugitivity and resistance, which would not be legible in a portrait. Worse, with his enslaver searching for him outside, Bill's life could be endangered by it. By these final installments, "Afric-American Picture Gallery" seems far less confident than when it began about the emancipatory possibilities of visual representation.

It is Ethiop's discovery of the underground, I think, that shatters his fantasy of the counterpublic. What he finds in Bernice's cave is an alternative formation of Black culture. While counterpublics constitute "parallel discursive arenas" to the bourgeois public sphere, as Nancy Fraser writes in her foundational account, Bernice's cave both mirrors the gallery and operates according to a wildly different logic.[89] It stands not only outside the gallery but also on another stratum entirely, an oblique rather than parallel space. And while counterpublics are "by definition not enclaves," Bernice's cave, secluded in the Black Forest and buried beneath the earth, could not be more of one.[90] Notably, Wilson's turn away from the model of a counterpublic and the promise of visibility that undergirds it coincides with a return to the underground—this time, the Underground Railroad, the ostensible subject of the final installment's picture. As it transpires, the Underground Railroad per se barely figures in Bill's story; Ethiop notes that Bill initially attempted to escape by way of the Underground Railroad before being caught, yet he never mentions it again, and his second, successful escape is unrelated. But at the same time as "The Early Days of the Underground Railroad" stays relatively silent about the Underground Railroad, it evokes the story's other underground, Bernice's cave. Bill's history recalls Bernice's: both are fugitives from slavery, and much as Bernice has taken his former enslaver's life into his own hands, Bill kills two kidnappers and vows to do the same for the man who claims to own him. "Afric-American Gallery" thus ends with a haunting echo of the subterranean story to which Ethiop earlier warned he "could scarcely do justice" in a dozen books.

More than that, much as Bernice's cave doubles the Afric-American Picture Gallery, and Bill's experience doubles Bernice's, so too does Bill's experience double Ethiop's. Bill's self-defense against the two kidnappers restages the moment when Ethiop, en route to the Black Forest, finds himself sharing a stagecoach with an enslaver and a kidnapper who mistake him for a fugitive and "prepare[s] . . . to make summary work with them."[91] And the installment's title, "The Early Days of the Underground Railroad," echoes its opening lines, which set it "in the earlier days of the Afric-American Picture Gallery," creating a parallel between the Underground Railroad and the Afric-American Picture Gallery. If the doubling between the Underground Railroad and Bernice's cave connects these two undergrounds *as* undergrounds, the way they both come to double the Afric-American Picture Gallery demonstrates the implacable pull of the underground on the story. Their triangulation suggests a fantasy that the story does not itself realize: that the Afric-American Picture Gallery might itself become yet another manifestation of the underground. In the next chapter, I take up more directly the Underground Railroad's presence in antebellum media culture. Its simultaneous prevalence and elusiveness in "Afric-American Picture Gallery," I will suggest, indexes how antebellum representations of the Underground Railroad often exceed their reference to an escape route from slavery and theorize more expansive modes of subterraneity.

3 The Underground Railroad's Undergrounds

The portrait of the fugitive Bill titled "The Early Days of the Underground Railroad" is not the only appearance the Underground Railroad makes in William J. Wilson's "Afric-American Picture Gallery." A pair of other pictures in the gallery depicts "the Southern and Northern portions of that mysterious road." The former shows the legs and feet of a group of fugitives hurrying along "a dark road leading through a darker forest"; the latter shows their faces after they arrive in Canada.[1] The outsize presence of the Underground Railroad in the Afric-American Picture Gallery is not surprising. The Underground Railroad was the subject of extensive media coverage in the 1840s and 1850s; as I noted in the introduction, these accounts first popularized the figurative use of "underground" to describe a subversive political or cultural formation. Yet if representations of the Underground Railroad were common, what distinguishes the paired pictures for Ethiop is that they capture its "undefined and undefinable" character: "that air of mystery which envelopes" it, "the mysterious manner in which those feet and legs move bodies towards freedom."[2] While these pictures seem to bear a closer relation to the Underground Railroad than the portrait of Bill does, their representations are almost impossible to comprehend. They defy visualization: Ethiop explains that they focus tightly on the fugitives' feet and faces, respectively, but they also include landscape details that should be out of view from this perspective (the North Star in the first picture, a lake in the foreground of the second).[3] Their fantastically torqued point of view bends the pictures' famous subject toward something much harder to imagine.

The Underground Railroad of classrooms, historical markers, and popular culture—that network of hiding places and lantern-lit routes leading to safety in Canada—is nowhere to be seen here. But if it is difficult to recognize in "Afric-American Picture Gallery" the Underground Railroad as we have come to know it, the story has a great deal to tell us about a version of the Underground Railroad—and a version of the underground—that we have come to forget. For decades, historians have been challenging the stories of "intrepid abolitionists sending multitudes of passengers over a well-organized transportation system to the Promised Land of freedom," as Larry Gara put it in his foundational study, *The Liberty Line: The Legend of the Underground Railroad* (1961).[4] Gara showed that this mythology was largely the invention of post–Civil War historians of abolitionism, who painted a romanticized, whitewashed picture of the movement.[5] Since Gara's study, scholars have given us a much fuller picture of the practices that actually constituted the Underground Railroad, as well as other practices of resistance our focus on the Underground Railroad has eclipsed.[6] They have demonstrated that what was called the Underground Railroad consisted of ad hoc arrangements rather than an organized conspiracy; that the vast majority of fugitives were self-emancipated and had to invent the means of their escape; that when fugitives did receive assistance, they primarily did so from other Black people; that the majority of fugitives did not go to Canada; that even there, "freedom" was always nominal; and that many who never permanently escaped slavery practiced temporary forms of fugitivity, such as lying out and absconding.

While these recent histories of the Underground Railroad have done remarkable work to sift its facts from its fictions, this chapter does the opposite. My aim is to recover less the material reality of the Underground Railroad than the extraordinary fantasies it animated. I want to try to see it as Wilson did, as a richly strange site for theorizing subterraneity. To do so, this chapter explores the representations of the Underground Railroad that circulated in antebellum print culture, including newspaper reports, illustrations, and poetry. Earnest or joking, nervous or wishful, these representations imagined undergrounds far in excess of the Underground Railroad's actual operations or, for that matter, the stories we tell about it today. In particular, I focus on the work of Black radical songwriter Joshua

McCarter Simpson, whose extraordinary body of songs about the Underground Railroad depicts it less as a path to freedom than as an alternate dimension of freedom. I examine how such fantasies of the Underground Railroad came to inspire subterranean practices of militant abolitionism, glimpsed in letters, petitions, memoirs, constitutions, and initiation rites, which we might think of as the Underground Railroad's undergrounds. Finally, I explore how the prolific author, editor, and performer Pauline Hopkins returned to the memory of the Underground Railroad after the Civil War in order to revive potentialities of Black freedom that legal emancipation did not bring. Reframed by this history, the familiar narratives of the Underground Railroad appear not only as misrepresentations but as attempts to manage the Underground Railroad's insurgent antebellum energies and to replace this version of the underground with a more palatable one. The aim of this chapter is to shed some of these historical accretions so that the earlier character of the Underground Railroad may once again come into view.

Literalization as Fantasy

The first use of the phrase *Underground Railroad* that scholars have found appears in September 1842 in the *Tocsin of Liberty*, an Albany newspaper edited by white radical antislavery activist Charles Turner Torrey. It is a taunt from Torrey's Black colleague Thomas Smallwood, who worked with his wife, Elizabeth Smallwood, and Torrey to help "about 400" fugitives in the Washington, DC, area escape slavery in the 1840s.[7] Referring to Smallwood by the pseudonym under which he often wrote for the *Tocsin of Liberty*, Samuel Weller, Torrey writes, "Sam Weller requested to tell the slave-holders that we passed twenty-six prime slaves to the land of freedom last week, and several more this week thus far. Don't know what the end of the week will foot up.—All went by 'the underground railroad.'" The squib apparently caught the imagination of readers, as it was quickly reprinted in regional and antislavery papers.[8] The phrase *underground railroad* traveled even more widely, propelled by what Meredith McGill calls the "culture of reprinting" and what Ryan Cordell describes as the generally "viral" tendencies of antebellum periodical culture.[9] Antislavery newspapers regularly published reports, statistics, poetry, and narratives about the Underground Railroad; proslavery newspapers broadcast warnings about it luring away enslaved people. Writers used the term *underground railroad* to describe an ever-expanding range of activities, including unaided escapes; improvised acts of assistance; guidance and shelter from practiced activists; and the work of vigilance committees, organizations that formed in Northern cities to defend Black residents against kidnappers, help fugitives, and generally pursue what David Ruggles, founder of the New York Committee of Vigilance, called "practical abolitionism."[10] This indiscriminate usage may well reflect white writers' inability to conceive of Black self-emancipation, but it also inadvertently magnified the Underground Railroad's power to astonishing proportions and garnered it even greater renown. By 1845, Frederick Douglass declared that the Underground Railroad "has been made most emphatically the *upperground railroad*."[11]

As a rhetorical construction, the Underground Railroad took on a life of its own, which often bore little resemblance to fugitives' actual modes of escape. Perhaps the most widespread example of this transformation was the literalization of the Underground Railroad as an actual train running beneath the earth. Some Southerners reportedly believed this to be true, but more often it was Northern antislavery newspapers and activists who pictured the Underground Railroad as a real subterranean train. These accounts reimagined an underground movement as actual *underground movement*. They routinely referred to "agents," "conductors," "passengers," "cars," "tracks," "stations," and "stockholders" with an enthusiasm that seemingly outstrips this language's strategic usefulness, despite now-familiar descriptions of it as a "code." In 1844, for example, Illinois minister and radical antislavery activist John Cross published what the *Liberator* called a "flaring handbill" promoting the Underground Railroad that pictured "the train just plunging under the earth." The advertisement, which Cross ran in the Chicago *Western Citizen*, invited "Gentleman and Ladies, who may wish to improve their health or circumstances, by a northern tour," to take passage on the "Liberty Line," traveling on "improved and splendid Locomotives" (figure 3.1). To reach the railroad, Cross advised, prospective passengers should simply look beneath their feet, and "for seats apply at any of the trap doors."[12] Several years later, when three enslaved people from Brazil vanished from a New York City jail, the *Springfield Gazette* reported that they had taken "a profound dive into obscurity" on the Underground Railroad, which "runs directly under the prison," having "let themselves down through a stone trap-door into one of the peculiar cars which regularly pass over this mysterious thoroughfare."[13] Facetious as it is, the article, like Cross's advertisement, invites readers to imagine a "peculiar," "mysterious" world just beneath the most oppressive institutions of this one.

3.1 John Cross's advertisement for the Liberty Line, from the Chicago *Western Citizen* (1844). Courtesy of Chicago History Museum, ICHi-061416.

Late nineteenth-century historians took up this railroad imagery—most influentially, Wilbur H. Siebert, who created a set of detailed maps that claimed to show the "routes" and "stations" of "the Underground Railroad system" for his sweeping study *The Underground Railroad from Slavery to Freedom* (1898)—and it continues to figure prominently in stories of the Underground Railroad. Such analogies between the Underground Railroad and an actual railroad help present it as a well-established and efficient system. They inscribe a division of labor that attributes the work of emancipation to white abolitionist "conductors," while assigning self-emancipated fugitives the roles of mere "passengers." At the same time, focusing on the significance of "railroad" risks obscuring the destabilizing effects of the "underground" that precedes it, especially because we retrospectively normalize that modifier in two ways. One, today the ubiquity of subways (first built in the late nineteenth and early twentieth centuries) has made the notion of an underground railroad unremarkable. But in a time before subway travel, the image of fugitives quietly dropping into invisible subterranean cars gave the Underground Railroad the air of the fantastic.[14] Two, we now easily read the "underground" in "Underground

Railroad" as synonymous with "secret." But in the 1840s and 1850s, when the figurative meaning of "underground" was still emergent, commentators more often described it as "mysterious." As I suggested in the previous chapter, the difference between the words is significant: while *secrecy* indicates undisclosed knowledge, *mystery*, in midcentury usage, emphasizes disorientation and perplexity, without the promise that these could be surmounted. The combination of these historical factors—*underground* was not yet clearly metaphorical, nor was a literal underground railroad yet real—made the Underground Railroad much stranger than it appears to us today.

To recuperate the weirdness of the literalized Underground Railroad, consider one example of the widespread newspaper poetry about it: "Underground Railroad," by a Detroit correspondent named A. S. Myrick, which appeared in the *Liberator* in 1853. The poem begins:

> Oh, know ye the path of the silent train,
> For the hunted negro found,
> Who fleeth fast from his galling chain,
> The railway under ground?
>
> Softly along the track it rolls,
> And its bell gives back no sound
> For it beareth a freight of living souls,
> Deep, deep beneath the ground.[15]

It soon becomes clear that the answer to the poem's opening query, "know ye the path of the silent train," must be no. The train is "silent," muffled in the earth, and the "keenest scent" of the "grim bloodhound" "must lose its power, / Deep, deep beneath the ground." In Myrick's poem, the Underground Railroad is not so much secret as beyond apprehension, inaccessible to those on the surface.

If the Underground Railroad defies apprehension in the world "high above," the poem's final lines suggest that this is because its tie is to a world beyond it:

> For though our railroad's stock is low,
> And its bonds are laughed to scorn,
> 'Twill pay a thousand fold, we know,
> On the resurrection morn.

In the interval between the poem's beginning and its end, Myrick peels off the Underground Railroad from empirical knowledge and connects it, instead, to supernatural belief. Eluding the "stocks" and "bonds" that govern popular opinion, the Underground Railroad looks toward a different set of speculative returns, those of the "resurrection morn." This messianic epistemology insists that the Underground Railroad only becomes intelligible in the future anterior; the poem asks us to imagine what it *will have meant* after we are dead. Crucially, "Underground Railroad" ushers the reader, too, into the underground, asking them to imagine being buried and awaiting Judgment Day.[16] From this subterranean perspective, death is neither still nor final but a preparation for something else. "The Underground Railroad" urges readers to redeem this world by inviting them to desire its end.

Underground Music: Joshua McCarter Simpson's *The Emancipation Car*

While A. S. Myrick saw the Underground Railroad as a "silent train" in this world that speaks to the next, Joshua McCarter Simpson envisioned it as full of music.[17] Simpson (figure 3.2), whose contributions to antebellum Black print culture, performance, and politics deserve more attention than they have yet received, self-published two songbooks focused on the Underground Railroad, the pamphlet *Original Anti-Slavery Songs* (1852) and the book-length collection, *The Emancipation Car, Being an Original Composition of Anti-Slavery Ballads, Composed Exclusively for the Underground Railroad* (1854, reprinted 1874). His songs also circulated as broadsheets; in newspapers; in the pages of Martin R. Delany's *Blake*, where Henry Blake's band of fugitive revolutionaries sings them; and in Simpson's own musical performances.[18] He was active in Ohio's Colored Conventions movement, where he prepared music to be sung at each session, as well as in an enigmatic "U.G.R.R. Convention" consisting of secret antislavery organizations, which illustrates the Underground Railroad's tendency to seed undergrounds in excess of itself.[19] There Simpson drafted a platform charging "the colored men of Ohio" to "commence a war with the Great Dragon" "by associating ourselves in such fraternal organizations as will give us an EYE that shall see in the dark, where no *white* man's eye can see."[20] I will return to the U.G.R.R. Convention shortly, but for now, notice how Simpson pictures underground organizing as a sensory experience that surpasses ordinary sight, or at least the "*white* man's eye."

3.2 Joshua McCarter Simpson. Courtesy of Ohio History Connection.

Simpson's image of a mysterious Black collective "EYE that shall see in the dark" remarkably anticipates the mode of Black critical perception and imagination that Fred Moten calls "black optics": a "night vision given in and through voices that shadow legitimate discourse from below, breaking its ground up into broken air; scenes rendered otherwise by undertones that are overheard, but barely."[21] (The title of Moten's essay, "Black Op," refers at once to these "black optics" and to "black operations" and "black optimism"—linked forms of Black study that "embrace the underprivilege of being sentenced to the gift of constant escape."[22]) Crucially, Moten notes that "black optics is an auditory affair," a synesthetic configuration he demonstrates through the "phonoptic" language quoted above.[23] Moten's emphasis on the significance of sound to "black optics" can help us understand the relation music might have had to Simpson's efforts to "see in the dark." What's more, Moten's description of "black optics" as "voices that shadow legitimate discourse from below" illuminates how Simpson might be theorizing and making something we could call underground music, if we use an anachronistically ample sense of that term.

In the preface to *The Emancipation Car*, Simpson suggests that music possesses inherently underground properties. When he was growing up in Ohio, Simpson recalls, "my mind was queerly impressed with the awful condition of my Nation as slaves in the south," but he dared not speak about it. But one day "something seemed to say, 'Write and sing about it— you can sing what would be death to speak.'"[24] Simpson presents singing here as a subterranean alternative to speech, whose "undertones," to return to Moten's term in "Black Op," can baffle a murderous public sphere. While Simpson conceived of music as an underground channel of expression, his composition practices sound further "undertones" by setting antislavery lyrics to popular tunes, including many blackface minstrelsy hits. As Simpson explains in the preface to *Original Anti-Slavery Songs* (and repeats in the preface to *The Emancipation Car*), his practice of resetting words to music aims both to improve on the originals and to undermine them: "To kill [their] degrading influence," as he puts it, "and change the flow."[25] Once he is done, one will never be able to hear "Dandy Jim" again without also hearing "The Fugitive in Montreal," "Come to the Old Gum Tree" without hearing "Old Liberia Is Not the Place for Me," "America" without hearing "Song of the Aliened American," and so on.

Antebellum songbooks routinely put new words to familiar tunes, and abolitionists and other activists were fond of using this practice to ironize the noble sentiments of patriotic songs or Christian hymns. (Think of the parody of "Heavenly Union" with which Frederick Douglass ends his 1845 *Narrative*.) But Simpson enacts particularly artful, surprising transformations of the originals—beginning with the fact that the titles of both of his songbooks refer to *his* songs as "originals," untethering the self-evidence of the ones that came before. At times Simpson satirizes these antecedents: "Song of the Aliened American," for example, turns the opening lines of "America"—"My country 'tis of thee, / Sweet land of liberty / of thee I sing"—into "My Country 'tis of thee, / Dark land of Slavery, / In thee we groan."[26] At times he corrects their distorted pictures, as in "The Slaveholder's Rest," sung to the tune of Stephen Foster's "Uncle Ned." Foster's song describes an enslaver heartbroken over the title character's death, but Simpson reassigns the death to the enslaver while dispensing with all the misplaced sentiment; the enslaved speaker exults, "I tell you now I laughed to myself, when I was told / That the old man's spirit had fled."[27] At still other times, Simpson's songs reframe their musical antecedents as unwittingly prophetic of futures they cannot acknowledge. "To the White People of America," which rewrites another Stephen Foster song, "Massa's in the Cold, Cold Ground," puts Foster's misty-eyed fans on notice by presenting the title's event as a portent of the deaths of all enslavers, proclaiming: "Hear ye that mourning? / 'Tis your brothers' cry! / O! Ye wicked men take warning, / The day will come when you must die."[28] And when Simpson sets "The Voice of the Six Hundred Thousand, Nominally Free" to the tune of "La Marseillaise," he creates a kind of sonic fantasy of Black liberation in the United States reenacting the French Revolution.[29] These songs push aside midcentury popular music's quotidian anti-Blackness (or even, in Simpson's words, "kill" it) and replace it with indicted or barely thinkable scenes: Black anger, retribution, revolution.

Earlier I said that Simpson's songs center on the Underground Railroad, and now I want to return to its place there. My sense is not that he creates what I have been calling underground music in order to sing about the Underground Railroad but that both of these ideas of the underground—the "undertones" he sounds in his songs and his representations of the Underground Railroad—mutually constitute one another. Specifically, Simpson conceives of both music and the Underground Railroad as capable of opening up unseen, unsayable realms of possibility within a scene we already inhabit. His song "The Final Adieu" dramatizes this possibility. It begins with the singer gathering "all my brethren" around and announcing that they have heard a spirit voice, like the one that prompts Simpson to make music, urging them to run away. In the chorus, another singer joins the first, both in song and in flight; after the first sings "I'm bound to run all night," the second responds, "I'm bound to sleep all day." Then, after two more verses, Simpson unexpectedly introduces a third voice: "a low but distinct tone from the kitchen cellar, uttered by an old house servant," who interjects, "If you get there before I do, / ... Look out for me I'm coming too."[30] This third voice is "low" in the sense of "quiet," but its location in the cellar means that it is also "low" in the sense of subterranean. As it rises up without warning, it connects the song's narrative of fugitivity to the experience of being literally underground.

As the voice from the cellar in "The Final Adieu" suggests, the popular literalization of the Underground Railroad is key to Simpson's depictions of it. In those images, the Underground Railroad tunnels out a space underneath the United States, much as Simpson pictures his songs "flowing" beneath the surface of the originals. Simpson returns to the image of the Underground Railroad as an actual train repeatedly in his work. "The Underground Railroad," for instance, begins with the question, "Don't you hear the steam cars? / Don't you hear them hum?" before explaining, "The Underground Railroad / Is a queer machine / It carries many passengers / And never has been seen."[31] (And notice here how Simpson depicts the Underground Railroad as eluding the eye but apprehensible by the ear.) In "A Consistent Slaveholder's Sermon," the title character prays that the people he enslaves will "not fall into the wicked and ungodly hands of the Abolitionists, nor into the cars of the Under-Ground Railroad"; meanwhile, Simpson invites them aboard by ending *Original Anti-Slavery Songs* with a stock illustration of a train.[32] Simpson seems to have been especially drawn to the figure of the "emancipation car," a common euphemism for the Underground Railroad. He pictures it in a song of that name steaming down a track, bell ringing, its engine "new and bright," and when he collected his songs into a book, he titled it *The Emancipation Car*.[33] It is not the car *for* emancipation or even the car *of* emancipation; rather, "emancipation" simply modifies "car." Perhaps in the figure of the "emancipation car," Simpson sounds a possibility embedded in the literalization of the Underground Railroad: that it might not just be a vehicle for freedom but itself instantiate a kind of freedom.

Simpson maps out just such a coincident, rather than linear, relationship between the Underground Railroad and freedom in the song "They Are Still Traveling North":

> We defy the master's power,
> We have robbed him of his might,
> We were freemen from that hour,
> That we took our Northern flight.[34]

The speakers' declaration, "We were freemen from that hour, / That we took our Northern flight" revises the usual association of freedom with Canada and locates it in the act of flight instead. In this respect, the song refuses not only slavery but also the available notions of freedom authorized by national laws and borders, which would understand it as the absence of legal slavery only. Likewise, the song rejects the teleological narratives those terrestrial notions of freedom underwrite, which, in Katherine McKittrick's words, "render violence a past act and liberation achieved."[35] In song after song, including "The Emancipation Car," "Away to Canada," "The Little Maid on Her Way," "Just Before the Day Was Breaking," and "The Fugitive's Dream," Simpson returns to the moment of mid-flight he sings of in "They Are Still Traveling North." Dwelling in that underground interval, dilating it and filling it with music, he composes a "counterdiscourse of freedom," in Saidiya Hartman's words, uncoupled from McKittrick's "seeable territoriality" of Canada and remade as unseeable subterraneity.[36] So perhaps the title "They Are Still Travelling North" refers to the ongoing flow of fugitives from the US South to Canada, but perhaps it describes an ongoingness of flight itself, in which the fugitives might still (always) be traveling to an elusive "north" that cannot be mapped onto any existing geographical or political determinations.[37] As the fugitives' language of "robbing" and "taking" suggests, this is an ungiven freedom, which does not just "defy" the master but defies "the master's power" more broadly. This freedom is itself fugitive, traveling under the name of the Underground Railroad but always escaping it.

The subtitle of *The Emancipation Car* specifies that it is "Composed Exclusively for the Underground Railroad," but the difference between Simpson's representations of the Underground Railroad and its actual operations highlights the ambiguity and downright strangeness of that provision. *The Emancipation Car* is "for the Underground Railroad" in the sense of being about it (though interestingly, not all the songs obviously are about it), and it is "for the Underground Railroad" in the sense of being committed to its purposes. But what purposes are those? The songs' focalization through fugitives' perspectives is largely a fantasy: it is unlikely that

Simpson actually distributed copies of his songs to fugitives in mid-flight. Rather, *The Emancipation Car* seems to be "for" an Underground Railroad that does not exist—for this Underground Railroad in the sense of moving toward it, beckoning it into being. Simpson explains in the introduction to *The Emancipation Car* that the songs had their origins in dreams, which contained "flashes of prophecies, pointing to events which came to pass, and which passed before my mind while writing them, but I did not comprehend their exact meaning, but used them as poetic figures, though they seemed to me to be facts."[38] His vision of the Underground Railroad may be one such "flash of prophecy," a "poetic figure" that speaks to an otherwise imperceptible "fact." In light of Simpson's prophetic method, the phrase "for the Underground Railroad" reads like an invocation, in which the act of singing these songs summons an Underground Railroad below and beyond the Underground Railroad as we know it.

Below and Beyond the Underground Railroad

I have been arguing that fantastical imagery of the Underground Railroad animated ideas of Black freedom untethered to its material reality. But that does not mean that its work was purely notional. In this section, I gather fragmentary records of several clandestine organizations working in the 1850s in order to propose that the Underground Railroad also influenced the creation of startlingly militant antislavery undergrounds. This hypothesis challenges the more familiar interpretation of the Underground Railroad as "the safety-valve for the institution of slavery," as George Washington Williams influentially argued in his 1882 *History of the Negro Race in America*. There he posits, "As soon as leaders arose among the slaves, refusing to endure the yoke, they came North. Had they remained, the direful scenes of St. Domingo would have been enacted."[39] Wilbur H. Siebert and even W. E. B. Du Bois would take up this description as well.[40] But not only does the "safety valve" theory overlook the circumstances that unevenly determined people's chances to escape, the acts of resistance pursued by those still enslaved, and the ultimate mobilization of Du Bois's "general strike"; it also ignores the fact the Underground Railroad itself seems to have influenced schemes that sought to approach the "direful scenes of St. Domingo." Some of the participants in these schemes identified their work with the Underground Railroad and others did not. But I propose that we understand their organizing in the context of media fantasies of the Underground Railroad that envisioned a shadowy movement fighting slavery from below. Necessarily obscure in their own moment, these undergrounds largely elude recovery today. We cannot really know whether they succeeded or failed, or even how we could reckon their success or failure. To consider how these organizations enacted the underground as praxis demands that we attend less to what did happen than to what could have happened. In part, this reflects the limitations of a meager archive; in part, it reflects the uninhibited sense of possibility that characterized the underground itself.

To glimpse the Underground Railroad's undergrounds, let us return to the scene of the Second U.G.R.R. Convention for the State of Ohio, which met in Zanesville from January 6 to 8, 1858, with Joshua McCarter Simpson as first vice president and one of a small committee on "permanent organization." Earlier I cited Simpson's platform there, and it is worth quoting more fully now: "Whereas, the spirit of Radical Abolitionism among our white friends ... has measurably died out," Simpson resolved, "we hold these sentiments to be just and advisable, that we, the colored men of Ohio, commence a war with the Great Dragon, that shall not hear the voice of peace, nor see the flag of truce, until every yoke shall be broken and every limb shall be unfettered."[41] Not surprisingly, the convention minutes reveal few specifics about tactics to be used against the "Great Dragon." But an inventory of resources in each of the communities represented by the delegates includes, among painters, farmers, millwrights, schools, farms, and Masonic lodges, what appear to be two secret antislavery societies: the American Mysteries Secret U.G.R.R. Society in Sandusky, with thirty-one members, and "the Camp of Israel, a secret U.G.R.R. Society," in Zanesville.[42] In fact, these two entries mark the only times the minutes of the Second U.G.R.R. Convention actually mention the Underground Railroad, an omission that suggests its concern may not be the Underground Railroad in itself. Rather, the Second U.G.R.R. Convention seems to call upon the Underground Railroad to authorize the organization of more radical antislavery undergrounds.

The American Mysteries Secret U.G.R.R. Society and the Camp of Israel may have been outliers in the antislavery movement, but they were almost certainly not alone. In 1855, a Pittsburgh newspaper reported the existence of "a regularly organized association of blacks in the city bound together by the most solemn oaths ... whose object is the abduction of Negro servants traveling with their masters."[43] The item might reflect paranoia, like the anonymous pamphlet novel from sensationalist Philadelphia publisher E. E. Barclay that purported to expose the Slaves Masonic

League, a secret antislavery organization that hides a group of fugitives (where else?) in a cave accessed through a trapdoor.[44] But it also tallies with other evidence of Black antislavery undergrounds, especially in the Midwest. If anything, this item may underestimate their radicalism. According to Black abolitionist Moses Dickson, for example, in St. Louis in 1846, he and eleven other men "who were ready to enter into any plan that would assure freedom to the African race" founded a "secret organized body" called the Order of Twelve, which planned to train for ten years and then "open battle for freedom." Dickson's biographer recounted, "These men, with their aides, formed organizations in all the Slave States, except Missouri and Texas. Silently, like the falling of Autumn leaves, the organizations multiplied, until, in 1856, the army of true and trusty men numbered forty-seven thousand, two hundred and forty Knights of Liberty." Only the war, Dickson asserted, prevented them from making "public history."[45]

Meanwhile, in Detroit during the 1850s, two well-known Black activists, George DeBaptiste and William Lambert, founded an organization variously called the African-American Mysteries, Order of the Men of Oppression, or Order of Emigration, which aimed to seed secret societies throughout the North. DeBaptiste and Lambert conceived of the organization as a branch of the Underground Railroad, but like the Second U.G.R.R. Convention, their notion of the Underground Railroad was extraordinarily expansive. Candidates for initiation underwent a series of challenges and ceremonies. In 1886, Lambert showed a *Detroit Tribune* reporter a handwritten copy of "the ritual, the names of the degrees, the test words, grips, descriptions of emblems and lessons," which he kept in a desk drawer alongside a copy of David Walker's *Appeal*.[46] After reaching the first degree, "Captive," a candidate became a "Conductor" to fugitives from slavery. To become fully initiated, however, members had to attain the next degree, "Redeemed," and proceed to the final degree, "Chosen." At this degree, the program intensified from assisting fugitives to full-scale revolution: its highest stage, "Knight of St. Domingo," required "a ritual of great length dealing with the principles of freedom and the authorities on revolution, revolt, rebellion, government." It was only upon becoming Knight of St. Domingo that "the full intention of the Order was first learned. The general plan was freedom."[47]

The specifics of this plan are unclear, though both DeBaptiste and Lambert later attested that the African-American Mysteries planned to join forces with John Brown. Historian Katherine DuPre Lumpkin, who pieced together much of the history of the African-American Mysteries through interviews that Lambert and DeBaptiste gave Detroit newspapers after the Civil War, questions how substantive this alliance was. But Lambert did attend the May 1858 convention of radical abolitionists Brown convened in Chatham, Canada West, and he and DeBaptiste both met and strategized with Brown at a secret meeting held with Black Detroiters in March 1859, where DeBaptiste startled Brown by suggesting they arrange to blow up fifteen Southern churches on a single Sunday.[48] DeBaptiste showed the reporter who interviewed him the key to a telegraphic cipher he said the organization used to communicate with Brown, and a memorandum of a letter Brown sent to DeBaptiste in July 1859 survives (though unfortunately the letter itself does not).[49] According to Lambert, a key figure in the African-American Mysteries was blacksmith George J. Reynolds, who also attended the Chatham Convention. In May 1858, fellow Chatham Convention member George R. Gill recorded in his diary going to Sandusky, Ohio, where Reynolds had moved, to meet with him "in regard to a military organization which, I had understood, was in existence among the colored people." There, "under pledge of secrecy which we gave each other at the Chatham Convention," Reynolds showed Gill the Sandusky organization's meeting place and arsenal, "a fine collection of arms."[50] Reynolds was a delegate to the Ohio Second U.G.R.R. Convention, where Joshua McCarter Simpson spoke, so Gill's account links him to the "American Mysteries Secret U.G.R.R. Society" of Sandusky noted in the convention minutes.[51] Through Reynolds, then, we can trace some connection between Detroit's African-American Mysteries and Sandusky's American Mysteries Secret U.G.R.R. Society. Moreover, Reynolds seems to have told the American Mysteries Secret U.G.R.R. Society of John Brown's plans. In May 1858, another of Brown's associates, Richard Realf, wrote to Brown that he had heard that "a certain Mr. Reynolds (colored) who attended our convention has disclosed its objects to the members of a secret society (colored) called 'The American Mysteries' or some other confounded humbug."[52]

Intriguing as the connections between these Black radical secret societies and John Brown are, we should not allow them to overshadow an even more significant fact: their organizing preexisted their members' discovery of Brown's plans. It seems to have outlived Brown, too. On the day of Brown's death, William Lambert convened "a densely crowded meeting of colored citizens" in Detroit. After a series of prayers and songs, the meeting "assumed a more deliberative and revolutionary character."

Lambert presented a "declaration of sentiments and resolves" on behalf of the Old Capt. John Brown Liberty League. Thanks to the efforts of "Almighty God" and "secret abolition movements"—a cryptic phrase Lambert does not explain to his audience, perhaps because he does not need to do so—Black Detroiters have been able "partially to obtain our liberty." They resolve, therefore, "to concentrate our efforts in keeping the Old Brown liberty-ball in motion and thereby continue to kindle the fires of liberty upon the altar of every determined heart among men and continue to fan the same until the proper time, when a revolutionary blast from liberty's trump shall summon them simultaneously to unite for victorious and triumphant battle."[53] The newly founded league then voted to send the proceedings of the meeting, with its unmistakable call to arms, to local and antislavery papers for publication.

While the Order of Twelve, the African-American Mysteries, and the American Mysteries Secret U.G.R.R. Society developed secret societies to prepare members for war, two offshoots of the Boston Vigilance Committee used immediate guerrilla action to confront enslavers and their supporters. Their militancy may have been heightened by the largely white committee's attitude of genteel intransigence; as member Thomas Wentworth Higginson recalled years later, "It is impossible to conceive of a set of men, personally admirable, yet less fitted on the whole than this committee to undertake any positive action in the direction of forcible resistance to authorities."[54] But the examples of local Black activists, as well as the high-profile armed rescue of fugitive Shadrach Minkins from a Boston courtroom and the failed rescues of Thomas Sims and Anthony Burns, radicalized some members of the committee, and a more militant wing emerged. As Higginson recalls, the split came during an 1854 meeting called in response to Anthony Burns's capture, when one member suggested they "go out and gaze" angrily at the kidnappers when they passed by, "as if Southern slave catchers were to be combated by such weapons." But the departure of the gazers left those "who were willing to act personally in forcible resistance" in like-minded company.[55] Immediately after Burns's reenslavement, committee member Henry Ingersoll Bowditch organized the Anti-Man-Hunting League, a secret society that intended to turn the tables by capturing kidnappers. As Bowditch later recounted, they planned to gather in the common rooms of a kidnapper's hotel and then, "at a signal from the chief of the committee, his five companions were to seize the legs, arms, and head of the hunter," while the other members of the league "were to form a body around the committee, and while apparently astonished and indignant at the struggle going on, and pretending to be trying to rescue the victim, would indirectly help the committee by keeping off all strangers or opponents."[56] Although the Boston Anti-Man-Hunting League never executed its plan, its members armed themselves with leaded billy clubs, drilled regularly for several months, and kept coded records of their activities distributed in multiple books, "so that if any or even all of our books should be seized by the law officers, they would be utterly incomprehensible."[57]

While the Anti-Man-Hunting League was planning to ambush slave-hunters in their hotels, the Boston Vigilance Committee's doorkeeper, Austin Bearse, joined forces with local Black workers to take the fight to sea. With funding from several other Vigilance Committee members, Bearse purchased a yacht that he hired for "pleasure parties or fishing excursions in the harbor," complete with optional catering services, according to the advertisement he took out in the June 18, 1852, *Liberator*. The "well-known and popular caterer" in question was Joshua Bowen Smith, one of the Vigilance Committee's few Black members. Two years earlier, in a meeting of the "colored citizens of Boston" held just after the passage of the Fugitive Slave Law, Smith had "advised every fugitive to arm himself with a revolver—if he could not buy one otherwise to sell his coat for that purpose" and "made a demonstration of one mode of defence" by showing how to stab an antagonist with a knife.[58] On the boat with Bearse, Smith put his plans for armed confrontation into action. The boat's use for "pleasure parties" was a cover story for its real purpose: when Black longshoremen heard that a ship carrying an enslaved person was in the harbor, they would alert Bearse, who would sail alongside and, pirate-style, demand that the crew relinquish the captive. At times Smith and others joined Bearse in the raid; when working alone, Bearse attached "a dozen old hats and coats" to the side of the boat, "which gave me the appearance of having so many men."[59] Once the party reached land again, a carriage would meet them and carry the liberated person to a series of safe houses and on to Canada. The members of this maritime underground named their renegade yacht the *Moby Dick* after a novel that had appeared the previous year, to little acclaim (figure 3.3).

We might understand Bearse and his associates' decision to name the boat after Melville's novel as speaking on its own kind of underground register.[60] The parallel it draws between the yacht *Moby Dick* and the whale Moby-Dick hints that, despite the *Moby Dick*'s reputation as a "pleasure boat," it is a fearsome adversary. It also points beyond the vigilante actions

3.3 The *Moby Dick*, from Austin Bearse, *Reminiscences of Fugitive-Slave Law Days in Boston*. Courtesy of the Library Company of Philadelphia.

the crew takes to a violence that precedes and far exceeds them, for as Starbuck vainly tells Ahab, "Moby Dick seeks thee not. It is thou, thou, that madly seekest him!"[61] And in the early years of the Fugitive Slave Law, it presages an ending in which the hunted brings down the hunter, destroying from underneath. Perhaps, too, Bearse and his associates identified the yacht *Moby Dick* with the novel itself, recognizing an underground kinship with a book introduced by the Sub-Sub-Librarian and narrated by a former "stone-mason, and also a great digger of ditches, canals and wells, wine-vaults, cellars, and cisterns of all sorts."[62] They may even have seen in *Moby-Dick* the radical critiques of slavery and racism toward which the text itself periodically reaches, without ever quite realizing.[63] Perhaps these attenuated critiques called to Bearse and his own crew, who gave them a material form and a political project in their sub-sub-variation on the Underground Railroad.

In the next section, I turn to a better-known antislavery underground—that associated with John Brown. Yet just as the Underground Railroad of this chapter is neither the Underground Railroad of later legend nor that of fact so much as a vision of freedom that outstrips both, I am less interested in what Brown did than in what he dreamed of doing. Furthermore, I read these not as the dreams of a singular visionary but as variations on an idea of the underground that grew out of the Underground Railroad and circulated more widely than Brown's exceptional reputation admits. At times, as with the African-American Mysteries and the American Mysteries Secret U.G.R.R. Society, we can trace Brown's connection to this underground tradition through face-to-face encounters. At other times, we can only discern a shared subterranean logic, which envisioned the underground as an organization one might build in this world in order to break it. But to see Brown in this way requires us to try to inhabit an alternate world ourselves, so that we may hold in abeyance the outcome of his plans, including his posthumous exaltation, in order to discern what might have been.

From the Underground Railroad to the Subterranean Pass Way

When media fantasies of the Underground Railroad inspired new political figurations of the underground as a shadowy site of resistance to slavery, perhaps no one embraced its possibilities as fully as Brown. For many years, Brown assisted fugitives from slavery, and after the passage of the Fugitive Slave Law, he organized a secret mutual defense group among fugitives in Springfield, Massachusetts, called the League of Gileadites. (His advice to the league in the event of an arrest: "Stand by one another and by your friends, while a drop of blood remains; and be hanged, if you must, but tell no tales out of school."[64]) But Brown's most ambitious reinterpretation of the Underground Railroad was the Subterranean Pass Way: a plan for what Brown described to Thomas Wentworth Higginson as "Rail Road business on a *somewhat extended* scale," which would become the basis for the raid on Harpers Ferry.[65] The Subterranean Pass Way inverted the goal of the Underground Railroad: rather than helping fugitives escape the South, the Subterranean Pass Way was designed to invade it. Brown envisioned organizing twenty-five men into armed cells and sending them into the Allegheny Mountains of Virginia, which he believed God had created as a site of antislavery resistance, to establish a series of bases. From there they would conduct periodic raids on nearby plantations, "gradually and unaccountably drawing off the slaves to the mountains," as Brown explained to Frederick Douglass, and establishing growing maroon communities.[66] As W. E. B. Du Bois serenely observed in his biography of Brown, "The exact details of Brown's plan will never be fully known."[67] But Martin Delany, a close ally, described it to his biographer, Frances Anne

Rollin, as "a movement in behalf of human liberty, the most sublime in conception, and mysterious in its accomplishment, written of in modern times."[68] According to Brown's associate Richard Josiah Hinton, Brown's second-in-command, John Henry Kagi, told him that after they seized Harpers Ferry, "the arms in the arsenal were to be taken to the mountains, with such slaves as joined. The telegraph wires were to be cut and railroad tracks torn up in all directions. As fast as possible, other bands besides the original one were to be formed, and a continuous chain of posts established in the mountains."[69] In other words, Brown's final goal was not the raid on Harpers Ferry but the opening of a vast underground campaign to destroy slavery.

Yet the underground movements Brown participated in and contemplated during his lifetime have been largely eclipsed by narratives of his apotheosis. Since he was condemned to death by the state of Virginia, Brown's reputation, at least among those who celebrate him, has largely rested on understanding him as a martyr who sacrificed himself so that the country would end slavery. For many of Brown's supporters, the narrative of martyrdom offered the only imaginable rejoinder to the widespread belief that he must have been insane—or, worse, the painful question asked by Frederick Douglass in a speech twenty-two years later: "Did John Brown fail?" Douglass believed the answer was "a thousand times, No!" Although Brown's plan was foiled, "the hour of his defeat was the hour of his triumph, the moment of his capture was the crowning victory of his life."[70] But after Harpers Ferry, Brown himself believed that he had "failed" by causing "our disaster."[71] It was only in his very last days that he adopted the narrative of his martyrdom already circulating in the press and began to see his "failure" as the greatest possible victory, assuring his family, "in no other possible way could I be used to so much advantage to the cause of God and humanity."[72] It is this Brown who lives on in a literary tradition focused as much, if not more, on his death as on his life—in William E. Channing's "The Burial of John Brown" ("he who lived—to die"); in Henry David Thoreau's "A Plea for Captain John Brown" ("I *almost fear* that I may yet hear of his deliverance"); in Louisa May Alcott's "With a Rose, That Bloomed on the Day of John Brown's Martyrdom" ("the gallows only proved to him / a stepping stone to heaven"); and so on.

But the story that Brown martyred himself to shift public opinion obscures his years recruiting, fundraising, planning, and practicing for an uprising; his study of the Haitian Revolution; his history of guerrilla warfare in Kansas; his stockpiling of weapons. (Reading the US newspaper coverage from England, a puzzled Harriet Martineau sensibly wondered, "If he had no intention of running off slaves, why the collection of arms?"[73]). It means taking the tragedy at Harpers Ferry for the endpoint to Brown's plans when, as his collaborator Osborne P. Anderson insisted afterward, "his plans were not consummated."[74] It means making Brown a singular hero while forgetting the collective nature of his thinking and fighting. It means seeing him as acting within existing legal frameworks—deliberately breaking the law in order to reap the fatal consequences—rather than defying them with an entirely different vision of justice.

If we break our focus on John Brown's apotheosis, we can begin to perceive the significance the underground held for his work. He and his collaborators built an actually existing underground movement dedicated to inventing still further undergrounds. In the Subterranean Pass Way, Brown envisioned a kind of maroon community in the Alleghenies, "which would carve out for the locality of its jurisdiction all that mountainous region in which the blacks were to be established," as associate Richard Realf later testified to a Senate committee.[75] Brown convened the Chatham Convention in May 1858 to discuss his plans for liberation and ratify a constitution. The resulting "Provisional Constitution and Ordinances for the people of the United States" established an alternative "United States" that would exist "within and under the nation," in Holly Jackson's words.[76] William Howard Day, former editor of the Cleveland-based Black newspaper the *Aliened American* (almost certainly either named after fellow Ohioan Joshua McCarter Simpson's poem "Song of the Aliened American" or the other way around), printed the constitution, but because he had to work on it in secret, he could not finish in time for the convention.[77] Only afterward did he complete the job, stitching the pamphlets' binding by hand and omitting any mention of a publisher on the title page—underground literature for an underground polity.[78]

As Brown and his associates readied themselves for the first step in their campaign, they seem to have taken up the language of the underground as a code. In letters among themselves, they refer to their work as "mining" and "prospecting." After Brown moved up the date for the raid, John Brown Jr. worried about the change to their "mining *prospect*." "I had supposed you would not think it best to commence opening the coal banks before spring, unless circumstances should make it imperative," he confided to Kagi, but he still hoped to recruit "some of those old miners of whom I wrote you."[79] Another member of the band, Jeremiah Anderson, used similar terms to apprise his brother of the plan for Harpers Ferry and the actions to follow. "Our mining company will consist of between twenty-five and thirty, well equipped with tools" (i.e., weapons), he wrote. "I expect (when I start again traveling) to start at this place and go through the state of Virginia and on south, just as circumstances require; mining and prospecting, and carrying the ore with us."[80] "Mining and prospecting" served as a cover for the group's real work, of course, but Brown Jr.'s remark about "opening the coal banks" and Anderson's allusion to "carrying the ore with us" suggest that they also used this language metaphorically to describe their plans for recruiting self-emancipated people as they went. The language of coal mining may make a racialized joke, but its meanings seem richer than that. It turns the subjugation of enslaved people, whom Brown once described as "those who are always on the under-hill side," into a prophecy of their combustion.[81] By this light, "prospecting" at once looks down below and out toward a future, forging a connection between these two orientations. Prospecting, in the sense of working underground, becomes prospective, in the sense of envisioning possible worlds.

The undergrounds Brown worked with, enacted, and envisioned largely disappeared with his execution, eclipsed by the mythology of his singular self-sacrifice. But in his 1909 biography, W. E. B. Du Bois tried to restore the underground to Brown's memory by foregrounding the decisive influence of Black revolutionaries on his project, from the historical examples of Toussaint L'Ouverture and Nat Turner to the unknown Black masses. Du Bois pictures them working on Brown as a subterranean force:

> It was not merely moral leadership from above—it was the push of physical and mental pain from beneath;—not simply the cry of the Abolitionist but the up-stretching of the slave. The vision of the damned was stirring the western world and stirring black men as well as white. Something was forcing the issue—call it what you will, the Spirit of God or the spell of Africa. It came like some great grinding ground swell,—vast, indefinite, immeasurable but mighty, like the dark low whispering of some infinite disembodied voice—a riddle of the Sphinx.[82]

In placing Brown in relation to "the push of physical and mental pain from beneath," "the up-stretching of the slave," "the vision of the damned," and "some great grinding ground swell," Du Bois echoes Brown and his associates' own subterranean language of "mining and prospecting." But perhaps he also recognizes more about the influence of the underground on Brown than Brown himself could tell. By identifying as miners, Brown and his associates make themselves the agents of enslaved people's liberation, but Du Bois's vision of the subterranean forces shaping Brown's thought and actions reverses the relation. In Du Bois's account, Brown does not mine a Black underground; a powerful Black underground acts on Brown.

This chapter has followed Du Bois's account by situating Brown within a wider field of largely Black antislavery activism. It has also suggested that Du Bois's subterranean imagery itself embeds a story about the role that the emergent figure of the underground, propagated by the Underground Railroad, played in militant antislavery organizing in the 1840s and 1850s. In the final section, I turn to Du Bois's fellow journalist, editor, and multigenre fiction writer Pauline Hopkins, whose postbellum writing repeatedly revisits antebellum antislavery undergrounds. Mapping the interconnections these undergrounds forge between three very different works—the musical play *Peculiar Sam; or, the Underground Railroad* (1879), the historical romance *Winona: A Tale of Negro Life in the South and Southwest* (1902), and the occult romance *Of One Blood* (1902–3)—I show how Hopkins reopens visions of freedom that legal emancipation did not bring and asks what possibilities might still be found underground.

"By 'the Undergroun'—": Pauline Hopkins's Truncated Undergrounds

The late nineteenth century marked the beginning of a publishing boom for histories and memoirs of antislavery undergrounds, especially the Underground Railroad. These books belong to the period Marcus Wood, riffing on David Brion Davis, calls "the emancipation moment," which celebrated freedom as a "gift" of white abolitionists.[83] Tellingly, it is also the period Rayford Logan famously called "the nadir" of (nominally free) Black experience in the United States.[84] Determinedly triumphant, the late nineteenth-century histories of the Underground Railroad drew a straight line from its successes to the legal freedom of the present. But William Still, who published his massive volume *The Underground Rail Road* in 1872 and revised it in 1879 and 1883, saw the relevance of the Underground Railroad differently. "I am more and more constrained to believe that . . . the necessity of the times requires this testimony," he wrote in the 1879 edition.[85] Where Still's white contemporaries applauded the fulfillment of the Underground Railroad's aims, he cautions that the "times" still "require" it to speak, and his language of constraint sharply belies the achievement of freedom. Accordingly, Still's book is less a history of the Underground

Railroad than an archive; its unstructured form does not commemorate a past so much as it offers a resource for the ongoing project of Black liberation.[86]

The same year Still asserted that "the necessity of the times requires this testimony," a twenty-year-old Pauline Hopkins was also refusing the assimilation of the Underground Railroad to narratives of historical progress. Instead of following the prevailing mode of contented retrospection, her play *Peculiar Sam; or, the Underground Railroad* reopens an antebellum version of the Underground Railroad that exceeds its referent to summon other, odder, more militant forms of subterraneity. *Peculiar Sam* follows Sam, his mother, his sister Juno, and his lover Virginia as they escape to Canada after learning that their enslaver is forcing Virginia to marry a brutal overseer, Jim. The play combines a scathing reminder of the brutality of slavery with music and characterization borrowed from blackface minstrelsy, a volatile mixture that remains difficult to interpret. Its title changed multiple times over its three-year performance history, along with its script and cast, but Hopkins biographer Lois Brown notes that the phrase "Underground Railroad" remained the one constant.[87] Initially, *Peculiar Sam* represents the Underground Railroad in fairly conventional terms. As Sam explains to his family: "Now all ob you kno's dat dars a lot of fellars roun' hyar runnin' off slabes. Dey runs dem to Canidy, an' all 'long de road, de white 'litioners helps 'em deceitfully, an' dey calls dis, de underground railroad."[88] But no white abolitionists appear to help the fugitives in the play. Instead, they escape due to the growing militancy of Sam (who challenges the overseer in a fight, takes him captive, and poisons the slave-catching dogs) and Juno (who gleefully stands guard over the overseer, terrorizing him with a pistol that she learned to shoot by blowing holes in her enslaver's bedstead). Except in one version, Hopkins never mentions the Underground Railroad again until the very last scene. When the fugitives reach the forest hut of Caesar, an elderly enslaved "station master" who joins them, Sam tells him, "I was to come hyar by 'the undergroun'—" before Caesar anxiously cuts him off.[89] But Sam's truncated line is revealing: Hopkins's play does not so much portray the Underground Railroad as it calls to a fuller, stranger underground than actually appears in it, a never-fully-spoken underground as peculiar as Sam himself. We might read Sam's "undergroun'—," too, as signaling the historical abridgment of this version of the Underground Railroad. *Peculiar Sam* aims to recuperate it.

Hopkins does so in part through a kind of unfolding of the word *peculiar*, which Sam adopts as a title. Like the Underground Railroad, it is both central to the play and tantalizingly undefined. Daphne Brooks proposes that Sam's peculiarity refers to his "philosophical deviance," in particular "his vividly fanciful dreams of freedom" and what he calls the "Nat Turner–like 'spirits a movin' in' him," to which he attributes his irrepressible singing and dancing.[90] Like Joshua McCarter Simpson, Sam has prophetic visions, and like Simpson, he channels those "peculiar" visions into song. Brooks and Lois Brown both demonstrate the dramatic significance of Sam's "peculiarity," which is not just a character quirk but a narrative device: his "imaginations and dreams ... drive the play," Brown observes, as Sam "masterfully uses his performance skills to create a path to freedom," in Brooks's words.[91] Another way to describe the propulsive, liberating function of Sam's visionary peculiarity in the play is to say that it parallels the play's portrayal of the Underground Railroad, while constructing a more "peculiar" Underground Railroad than the contemporary historiography recognized. The association explains Sam's odd identification of himself in the final scene as "peculiar Sam of the old underground railroad": Sam may not be *of* the Underground Railroad in any practical sense (he is not a stationmaster like Caesar, for example), but Hopkins elaborates a conceptual kinship between the two that the title of the first and longest version of the play, *Peculiar Sam; or, the Underground Railroad*, telegraphed all along.[92] This kinship, in turn, invests the Underground Railroad with Sam's own prophetic qualities and with the militancy of the "Nat Turner–like 'spirits a movin' in' him." Perhaps we glimpse the outcome of this transfiguration of the Underground Railroad in the startling password Sam gives to Caesar, "de black clouds is risin,'" which seems to frame the family's fugitivity as intimating some wider insurgency.

The year after Hopkins wrote *Peculiar Sam*, she began writing *Winona* as another play, but she put it aside for over twenty years before transforming it into a novel, which was serialized in the *Colored American Magazine* in 1902.[93] As in *Peculiar Sam*, the action in *Winona* runs along the tracks of the Underground Railroad: the protagonist, Judah, who fled slavery with his mother via the Underground Railroad when he was a baby, is reenslaved years later and escapes once more via the Underground Railroad, this time with his adopted sister, Winona. Judah is a kind of successor to Sam, translated out of comedy and into a mix of graver genres. Like Sam, he fights for the freedom of his sister and lover (who are here the same person); like Sam, he sees visions of a world otherwise, including "a cloud of intense blackness" that recalls Sam's evocative Underground Railroad password, "de black clouds is risin.'"[94] In *Winona*, these hints of militancy are realized when Judah and Winona's Underground Railroad escape takes them directly to John Brown's band in Kansas, where Brown is developing a "great scheme for an insurrection among the slaves—an uprising of such magnitude that it should once and for all time settle the question of slavery"—the Subterranean Pass Way (400). Judah joins the campaign as a "special aide" to Brown, and ultimately "his name was heralded with that of Brown as a brave and fearless man bold to recklessness" (376), a remarkable retelling of the campaign that embodies in a fictional Black comrade the influence of unseen Black revolutionaries Du Bois traces on Brown. Judah is a particularly apt companion for Brown because Hopkins links him to another yet underground formation, the slumbering volcano. While he is still enslaved, Judah strikes a deferential attitude that might be "a picture for an artist" of "the Negro passively waiting the verdict of his master," "a living statue of a mighty Vulcan" (323). But Hopkins's allusion ironically undercuts this "picture" of Black submission, since Vulcan is the Roman god of fire from whom the word *volcano* derives. And in fact Judah's actual "latent force" (324) bursts forth soon after this scene, as he escapes with Winona and makes himself "the Lord's instrument to kill" his enslaver (394).

While *Winona*, like *Peculiar Sam*, looks back on antebellum antislavery undergrounds, Hopkins does so without the sense of accomplishment that characterized the historiography of her white contemporaries. As Hazel Carby argues, the novel does not commemorate the past so much as it contends against the present; it is "transparently a call for organized acts of resistance against contemporary persecution displaced to a fictional history."[95] I would add that *Winona* calls for recuperating not only the "organized acts of resistance" of the radical antislavery movement but also the freedom dreams fostered in its visions of the underground, which by Hopkins's time had largely been foreclosed by the false promise of emancipation, stifled by the day-to-day struggle to survive racist violence, and attenuated into fights for political representation and economic advancement. In this respect it is significant that Hopkins's account of John Brown focuses not on the defeat at Harpers Ferry, which had increasingly become assimilated into progressive historical narratives of the antislavery movement, but on the years before it. Like Joshua McCarter Simpson abiding in the interval of fugitivity, Hopkins lingers in this underground moment, declining to narrate "the subsequent fortunes of John Brown and his sons and their trusty followers" or "the happenings of the Civil War." "With these events we are all familiar," she explains (435). Hopkins opts instead for the unfamiliar (the unrecoverable project of the Subterranean Pass Way) and for defamiliarization (the counterfactual history of a Black revolutionary whose name "was heralded with that of Brown"). Accordingly, *Winona* ends by looking toward a future untethered to the present, belatedly introducing a frame narrative in which Aunt Vinnie, a former neighbor of Winona and Judah, tells their story to her neighbors "at intervals" (436). Her chosen form, which parallels Hopkins's serialized novel, resists fulfillment in the present and cultivates anticipation and conjecture instead. Indeed, Vinnie interprets the story as a lesson in prophetic thought: Winona and Judah's "strange fortunes" show that "we's boun' to be free"; the "year of Jubilee" is at hand and "somethin's gwine drap" (436, 437, 436).[96] Her listeners agree, responding with the supernatural signs they, too, have observed. Perhaps Vinnie and her neighbors are predicting the Civil War, but Hopkins's earlier demurral at that subject suggests that their prophecies refer to a freedom beyond legal emancipation.

There is one further underground in *Winona* that is unlike the others but illuminates their operations. After Winona joins John Brown's camp, she finds a "hole in under the bluff" where she hides to dream of the British lawyer-turned-abolitionist Warren Maxwell, who has assisted her and Judah in their escape.

> It was necessary to descend to find it. Presently she was in a tunnel which led into a cavern. She made herself a divan of dried moss and flung herself down at full length to think. Time's divisions were lost on those days when the girl felt that she neglected no duty by hiding herself in her nook. She had come upon the eternal now as she lay in a sweet stupor until forced to arouse herself. (375–76)

Dorri Beam observes that Winona's "nook" becomes a space for her to experience the "passionate ardor" nineteenth-century writers so often denied Black women characters.[97] Hopkins does not connect the literal underground of Winona's cave to the figurative undergrounds that populate the text, at least not at first. Yet the unwonted freedom and desire that Winona finds underground recall, in a different register, the unwonted freedom and desire found in antebellum literalizations of the Underground Railroad; so too does Winona's tunneling away from "time's divisions" and toward an "eternal now" recall the Underground Railroad's divergences from linear time. Moreover, Hopkins soon establishes a more explicit association between Winona's cave and the novel's antislavery undergrounds: as Brown and his associates prepare for their campaign, Winona converts the cave into a storehouse for "provision, ammunition and all other necessaries" for Brown's fighters (403). In making Winona's cave both a refuge for erotic daydreaming and a resource for guerrilla warfare, Hopkins extends the sexual freedom Winona finds there to Brown's visions of freedom, underscoring the imaginative and desirous work of radical antislavery. She politicizes the underground's incitements to fantasy or perhaps simply plays out a more expansive set of dreams the underground already harbored.

In both its reference to radical antislavery and its refusal of linear time, we might see Winona's cave as a precursor to Telassar, the hidden Ethiopian city accessed by "deep underground passages" in Hopkins's final novel, *Of One Blood*.[98] I will return to Telassar later, but for now I propose that it extends a line of thinking about antislavery undergrounds that Hopkins develops in *Peculiar Sam* and *Winona*. Unlike those works, *Of One Blood* is set in Hopkins's present, and antislavery undergrounds do not figure in its story of psychological and occult mystery, slavery's legacies, and Black cultural regeneration in Africa. Still, there are strange narrative continuities between *Of One Blood*, *Peculiar Sam*, and *Winona*. In *Of One Blood*, Reuel's incestuous, tragic love for his sister echoes that of Judah in *Winona*, whose escape from slavery with his sister/lover condenses that of Sam, his sister, and his lover in *Peculiar Sam*; all three characters share a gift for prophetic vision. Moreover, the presence of the past is a central theme of *One Blood*, whose motto might be the words on a sphinx in Telassar's square: "That which hath been, is now; and that which is to be, hath already been; and God requireth that which is past" (552). Carla Peterson has argued that, at a moment of radically attenuated possibilities for Black freedom, Hopkins seeks to "transcend historical time" in order to imagine an alternative future that, as Valerie Rohy puts it, "relies on the return of the past."[99] While Peterson and Rohy refer to the presence of ancient Ethiopia, the more recent past of antislavery undergrounds also flashes up unexpectedly in *Of One Blood*. Reuel's sister/wife, Dianthe Lusk, shares her name with John Brown's first wife, and as Mary Grace Albanese has pointed out, the servant who procures the ticket to the Fisk Jubilee Singers concert where Reuel meets Dianthe is named Redpath, an apparent reference to James Redpath, Brown's biographer and supporter.[100] Hopkins never explains the connection to Brown. Yet she amplifies it in Telassar's setting, which is at once remarkable and strangely familiar:

This city is situated on a forked tributary, which takes its rise from a range of high, rocky mountains, almost perpendicular on their face, from which descend two streams like cataracts, about two miles apart, and form a triangle, which holds the inner city.... The whole area is surrounded by extensive swamps, through which a passage known only to the initiated runs, and forms an impassible barrier to the ingress or egress of strangers. (529)

Like much about Telassar, its topography is astonishing: its mountainous landscape and wide swampy borders lie in the middle of a desert. Telassar does not look much like the part of Ethiopia through which the novel's explorers have traveled. But its swamplands resemble the Great Dismal Swamp, where American maroons famously built hidden civilizations of their own, and the mountains recall John Brown's planned base for the Subterranean Pass Way in the Alleghenies, where he envisioned fugitives from slavery could carve out a home. In particular, Telassar's location at the convergence of "two streams" that descend from the mountains recalls Harpers Ferry's location at the convergence of the Potomac and Shenandoah Rivers, below the Blue Ridge Mountains.[101] When Ai, the prime minister of Telassar, explains, "Here we wait behind the protection of our mountains and swamps" (547), one can hear echoes of Brown's declaration, "The mountains and swamps were intended by the Almighty for a refuge for the slave, and a defence against the oppressor."[102]

It would be a misrepresentation to say that antislavery undergrounds like the Underground Railroad and the Subterranean Pass Way constitute major themes of Hopkins's work. They only obliquely appear in *Of One Blood* and are subordinated to the romance plot of *Winona*. Even *Peculiar Sam*, despite its subtitle, only mentions the Underground Railroad glancingly. Yet even as—and maybe also because—Hopkins does not center these antislavery undergrounds narratively, she revives a sense of the underground they created. During a period of receding hopes for Black freedom in the United States, Hopkins reanimates the mystery, temporal alterity, and untrammeled imagination associated with the antislavery undergrounds of the 1840s and 1850s. And in rejecting "time's divisions" to pursue unrealized versions of freedom, she also enters into the logic of these undergrounds herself, long after they were presumed closed.

4 The Depths of Astonishment

CITY MYSTERIES AND SUBTERRANEAN UNKNOWABILITY

About halfway through George Lippard's *New York: Its Upper Ten and Lower Million* (1853), the narrator extends a dubious invitation to the reader: "Let us descend into the subterranean world, sunken somewhere in the vicinity of Five Points and the Tombs." "Open a scarcely distinguishable door," he instructs.

> Descend a narrow stairway, or rather ladder, which lands you in the darkness, some twenty feet below the level of the street. Then, in the darkness, feel your way along the passage which turns to the right and left, and from left to right again, until your senses are utterly bewildered. At length . . . after groping your way you know not how far, you descend a second ladder, ten feet or more, and find yourself confronted by a door. You are at least two stories under ground, and all is dark around you—the sound of voices strikes your ear; but do not be afraid. Find the latch of the door and push it open. A strange scene confronts you.
> The Black Senate!¹

The Black Senate, we learn, is a sensationalized version of the antislavery vigilance committees discussed in the previous chapter, organized to aid fugitives traveling north and defend them against kidnappers. Its leader,

Old Royal, escaped slavery by getting himself shipped in a box by train to Philadelphia, recapitulating the famous Underground Railroad escape of Henry "Box" Brown.[2] With his characteristic mixture of political radicalism and casual racism, Lippard portrays the Black Senate as both comical and formidable, a shadow government composed of "representatives from all parts of the Union" (117) that metes out justice the official government cannot or will not. A vivid fantasy of the midcentury's antislavery undergrounds, it is all the more striking because its underground character is twofold: as the novel's extended description of its location emphasizes, the Black Senate conducts its subterranean activities "at least two stories under ground."

In the previous chapters, I traced the emergence of the underground as a spatialized, racialized concept, here exemplified in the Black Senate. I argued that the figurative use of "underground" to signify subversive political or cultural movements took shape through images of physical undergrounds—Mammoth Cave, David Walker's gold and silver mines "three or four hundred feet under ground," the geographic "underground" of the Caribbean in Martin Delany's *Blake*, the fantasies of a subterranean railway that overflowed the actual operations of the Underground Railroad, and so on. I tried to discern undergrounds that were not necessarily recognizable as such, in their time or today, by looking for moments when physically subterranean sites produced figurations of power and freedom that exceeded earthly political norms. I turn now to some of the earliest texts to describe what we would now readily recognize as figurative undergrounds: city mysteries, the cheap, lurid novels of urban modernity that exploded in the United States in the wake of Eugène Sue's *Les Mystères de Paris* (1842–43).[3] Sue's serial novel was a hit in Europe, where it spawned several imitators, but the genre caught fire in the United States, and soon most major cities, along with many small towns, could claim mysteries of their own.[4] US city mysteries depicted in shocking terms the undergrounds spawned by rapid urbanization: secret societies, criminal gangs, congeries of sexual deviants, revolutionary organizations, black markets, political conspiracies. And as the Black Senate demonstrates, these groups almost invariably pursue their subversive activities while physically underground. The overlapping literal and figurative undergrounds of the city mysteries raise the question, What was at stake in representing the city's unruly social formations as also spatial ones?

City mysteries are honeycombed with crypts, tunnels, dungeons, sewers, secret basements, subbasements, and sub-subbasements. Most famously, there is Lippard's Monk Hall, the den of iniquity at the center of his 1845 blockbuster *The Quaker City*, with its "three stories above ground and three stories below."[5] (The fact that Monk Hall also has "a printing office on one side and a stereotype foundry on another" makes it a neat figure for the particularly literary alignment of the midcentury underground's literal and figurative registers.) But examples abound. In J. H. Ingraham's *The Dancing Feather, or The Amateur Freebooters* (1842), a gang of self-appointed pirates conducts its "wild bacchanalian orgies" in "a large underground hall" beneath the streets of Boston.[6] In Newton M. Curtis's *The Matricide's Daughter: A Tale of Life in the Great Metropolis* (1850), a counterfeiting operation works out of a secret vault under a tin and copper workshop. Charles Testut's *Les Mysteres de la Nouvelle-Orleans* (1852) takes us into "the underground room of an isolated and silent house" ("le souterrain de [une] maison isolée et silencieuse") to find another counterfeiting operation, "a secret society named: THE FINANCE COMPANY" ("une société secrète qui avait nom: COMPAGNIE DES FINANCES"), which aims to "undermine society" ("flétrit la société").[7] R. T. Wally's *The Cesspool of Crime, or, Important Discoveries and Disclosures in Demolishing the Old Brewery at the Five Points, New York* (1852) reveals the activities of the Grand Lodge of All the Bandits, which meets in a cavern beneath the Old Brewery and is secretly bankrolling Narciso López's filibustering missions to Cuba. The city mysteries' subterranean preoccupations also extend to the seemingly paradoxical variation we might call the rural city mystery, which translated the formulas of its urban counterparts into more remote settings, usually in the western or southern United States. *The Mountain Village: or, Mysteries of the Coal Region* (1849), by "Ralph Rural," juxtaposes the exploitation of Pennsylvania miners with the activities of a secret society called the Chamber of the Moral Order, which meets in the basement of a prominent citizen. George W. L. Bickley's *Adalaska; or the Strange and Mysterious Family of the Cave of Genreva* (1853) introduces a family of exiled European aristocrats living both literally and figuratively underground in Virginia, plotting the 1848 revolutions as well as their continuation in the United States. And the title character of the *Terrible and All Absorbing Narrative and Confession of Edwin Winters* (1854) finds himself transported to a giant underground cavern in Arkansas, where a group of bandits led by a sixteen-year-old girl is planning a revolution that will divide the United States into two empires.

Literal and figurative undergrounds also converge in the popular nonfiction literature that cross-pollinated with city mysteries. The seamy "flash press," which chronicled urban brothels, gossip, theater, and sporting events, reveled in the licentious possibilities of the subterranean: an 1842 cartoon in the *Weekly Rake*, for example, shows a man below a grate looking up between the legs of a woman on the sidewalk above; the woman's own wary glance behind her suggests she is giving him a deliberate show.[8] New York labor radical and nativist Mike Walsh named his paper the *Subterranean* (1843–47) after an incident when his gang/political club, the Spartan Association, got in a dustup with some Whigs and then hid in "the cellars of various dens" in Five Points, as an article in the *New York Times* later recalled; the Whigs "jeeringly denominated them 'the subterranean Democracy,' in allusion to their places of refuge on the occasion, as having reached a lower point than the most radical leveler had ever proposed."[9] As the article's punning suggests, however, part of the appeal of the *Subterranean* as a title lay in its ability to signify multiply: the newspaper's masthead featured a picture of workers toiling below ground, and Walsh referred to its audience as "the subterranean populace of New York."[10] Sensational guides like George G. Foster's *New York by Gas-Light* (1850) and John D. Vose's *Seven Nights in Gotham* (1852) likewise depicted the city's underground spaces as the redoubt of its underworld. Foster shows slumming readers "the lower stratum—the under-ground story—of life in New York" by loitering in subterranean dance halls and all-night basement "oyster saloons," whose shady "customers burrow in their secret holes and dens all day, and only venture out at night."[11] Yet the narrator of *Seven Nights in Gotham* contends that such sites "are nothing to the 'Diving Bell,'" a tavern located in "the lowest part of one of the lowest [streets] in Gotham." His description is not just metaphorical: the Diving Bell, known for interracial dancing and trysting, is "almost *sixty feet under ground*."[12]

Foster and Vose lay it on thick, but it seems that lower Manhattan's underground taverns really were a haven for nonconforming pleasures. The city's bohemians congregated at Pfaff's beer cellar, where they, "as the dead in their graves, are underfoot hidden," as Pfaff's regular Walt Whitman put it in the unfinished poem "The Two Vaults."[13] Henry Clapp, the "King of Bohemia" who was at the center of the Pfaff's circle, was a leading figure in anarchist Stephen Pearl Andrews's short-lived but notorious Free Love League; the actress and writer Adah Isaacs Menken, known for her sexually transgressive performances on- and offstage, also frequented the bar.[14] At Pfaff's Whitman joined the Fred Gray Association, a group of young bachelors who Stephanie M. Blalock has posited were models for the ardent "comrades and lovers" of the "Calamus" poems.[15] And Pfaff's was hardly the only subterranean bar where New Yorkers could enjoy unwonted sexual freedoms. From January through April 1864, the *New York Clipper* devoted a series of articles titled "Broadway below the Sidewalk" to describing the neighborhood's underground establishments, full of "fast boys and fast girls." Part of the attraction of one bar, aptly named the What Is It, was that the difference between these groups might be hard to parse. In a painting near the entrance depicting the scene inside, the writer notes, "one of the 'female clerks' has a very rakish air" and "is dressed somewhat like Queen Mab."[16] The phrase "female clerks" suggests that the "fast girls" of the What Is It are working girls—waiters, selected by the patrons, whose jobs blurred into sex work. But the winking quotation marks, together with this particular worker's "rakish air" and extravagant costume, also play up the feminized reputations of typically male shop clerks to insinuate that the What Is It is particularly an underground destination for transfeminine sex workers and their clients.[17]

City mysteries drew on the city's actual undergrounds; these actual undergrounds may in turn have been shaped by popular literary representations. But if the city's undergrounds often flouted white bourgeois norms in a moment of their consolidation, the politics of the city mysteries' undergrounds are harder to discern. As scholars including Shelley Streeby, Timothy Helwig, Samuel Otter, David Stewart, Matt Cohen, Edlie Wong, and Sari Altschuler have shown, ideologically, city mysteries are maddeningly complicated.[18] As a rule, their authors—all, to my knowledge, white men—struggled to make a living, and class conflict is a hallmark of the genre.[19] But not all novels advance a critique of capitalism, and those that do often get there by viciously racist, xenophobic, misogynist, and otherwise bigoted means. (Recall Radiclani Clytus's argument that William J. Wilson developed his "Ethiop" persona as a counter to "urban spectatorial literature" that pictured Black city dwellers as objects of disgust and ridicule.[20]) City mysteries can exploit economic injustice for cheap thrills in the same breath that they condemn it. As the example of the Black Senate suggests, although city mysteries offer some of the few literary depictions of Black radicalism during the period, these representations are often foreclosed or derisive (or both, in the case of the Black Senate, which makes no further appearance in the novel). Yet Michael Denning's insistence that genuinely "utopian longings" lie in the genre's "paradoxical union of sensational fiction and radical politics" remains hard to dismiss, and indeed the novels' radical politics fascinate precisely to the extent that they are so elusive, so quickly compromised.[21]

Perhaps, too, we have been looking for them in the wrong places. As Christopher Looby's analysis of sensation fiction's "inexorable movement toward eventual affirmation of domestic and political norms" makes clear, the genre's regressive character is largely plot-driven, a function of the romance form.[22] If we go looking for ideas outside the social order, it may make more sense to look for them in elements of the text that do not by definition tend toward resolution—for instance, elements that are spatial rather than temporal. The city mysteries' most radical impulses might be found not in their plots but in their settings.[23] I want to consider the possibility that imaginary spaces might uniquely magnetize their "utopian longings" because setting, unlike the romance plot, does not incline toward the restoration of order. Whereas the city mysteries' plots may critique existing conditions, their settings try to imagine another world. Or more accurately, they try to elicit desire for, and belief in, a world that does not yet exist. By reading for setting in the city mysteries, we may discern different narratives, even different temporalities, beyond those their plots unfold.

Yet to seek out the city mysteries' most utopian desires is not to turn away from the ugliness that often flashes through their radical politics. This chapter questions whether these aspects of the genre are as opposed as we tend to (or want to) believe. Instead I trace a discomfiting dialectic between the two, in which the city mysteries' undergrounds at once appropriate and sublimate the racialized ideas of the underground traced in the previous three chapters. The subterranean resonances of that word, *sublimate*, are to the point here: racialized Blackness goes underground in the city mysteries' depictions of the underground. We can catch glimpses of it in the rare moments when Black characters appear in city mysteries, such as Lippard's depiction of the Black Senate, and perhaps even more revealingly in moments when they reference Black undergrounds without explanation, as in the references to Henry "Box" Brown's famous Underground Railroad escape that crop up in that scene and elsewhere. Most strikingly—and unsettlingly—of all, I show how the city mysteries' sublimation of racialized Blackness shapes their most radical thinking, when they embrace visions of profound otherness—otherness, I argue, ineluctably shaped by ideas of racial difference. (Here it's worth revisiting the underground tavern the What Is It: its name, which telegraphs the gender indeterminacy of its employees, derives from a notorious exhibit at Barnum's Museum that presented a Black actor as, in the words of one advertisement, "a connecting link between the wild native African, and the orang outang."²⁴ In the painting of the "female clerk" at the tavern, the Barnum What Is It peers out from behind her, holding the train of her dress.)

Given its focus on a particular genre, this chapter is the most literary critical in the book. Consequently, in the conclusion I reflect on the interpretive affordances of the city mysteries' topographical ways of seeing. Specifically, I am interested in how the work of demystification appears differently if read through a line of subterranean imagery in Marx's writing that begins with Marx and Engels's analysis of Eugène Sue's *Les Mystères de Paris* in *The Holy Family* (1844). The proposition to consider city mysteries as theoretical texts might not sound promising. Crudely plotted, sloppily written, and derivative, they tend not to impress readers as examples of sophisticated thinking. Moreover, their preoccupation with the city's depths may look particularly artless since the literary critical backlash against practices of "deep reading." But I propose that the subterranean genealogy of demystification challenges familiar understandings of it as a critical practice. Rather than assuming that the purpose of demystification is totalizing disclosure, this genealogy allows us to conceive of demystification as both proceeding from mystery and productive of it.

The Underground's Grotesque-Sublime

When American writers pitted city mysteries with underground spaces, they drew on what I described in the introduction as a growing interest in what lay beneath the surface of the earth, exemplified most famously in Mammoth Cave. Indeed, when Judge Blower, one of the wide-eyed urban explorers in Vose's *Seven Nights in Gotham*, visits the Diving Bell, the literally and figuratively underground tavern in Five Points, he explicitly connects its rowdy multiracial clientele with Kentucky's famous Black underground, concluding that it is "just about as awful a skittish-looking place down there under ground, as can be found in this country. The Mammoth Cave out in Kentucky, not excepted."²⁵ Yet while the city mysteries' representations of the underground may have been sparked by the actual underground spaces with which Americans were increasingly familiar, they are remarkable in part because they are so conspicuously invented. Paris had its catacombs and sewers, which figure prominently in Sue's *Les Mystères de Paris*; Rome, too, had famous catacombs, and by the early 1850s, plans for the London subway were under way.²⁶ But mid-nineteenth-century US cities notably lacked the subterranean infrastructure of their European counterparts. Their characteristic underground spaces were plain basements, which housed either rowdy taverns like the Diving Bell and the What Is It or grim living quarters for the city's poorest residents.[27] City mysteries, however, transformed the city's cramped cellars into vast subterranean networks.

If the city mysteries' expansive undergrounds do not represent actually existing spaces, it is tempting to read them metaphorically. Certainly they evoke a number of ideas integral to the genre: the class stratification of the "upper ten and lower million," for instance, which the novels so often took as their subject; the hidden stories the novels pledge to uncover; and most obviously, the underground movements that drive their plots. Yet this kind of metaphorical reading turns out to be harder than it sounds, if by metaphor we mean the transfer of meaning from an abstract idea to a concrete object. For the city mysteries' figurative undergrounds are not absorbed into their literal undergrounds but brazenly coexist, nested inside them. Moreover, although the city mysteries' underground spaces are literal, they are not therefore concrete. One of the most remarkable spatial features of the city mysteries' undergrounds is that they usually remain uncharted; their boundaries are unseen or even nonexistent. One never fathoms the depths of Monk Hall but rather descends through successive stories before finally reaching a subterranean stream, which in turn flows on indefinitely. Nor does one reach the outer limits of undergrounds like the Dark Vaults of George Thompson's *City Crimes* (1849) or the Twin City of Charles E. Averill's *The Secrets of the Twin Cities; or, the Great Metropolis Unmasked* (1849), which seemingly twist endlessly beneath the city above. The underground is *both* "beneath and beside," in Eve Kosofsky Sedgwick's terms, upsetting the tidier binary logic we tend to associate with "the topos of depth."[28] It is particularly dizzying to read the city mysteries' literal undergrounds as metaphors for cultural undergrounds, even as their contiguity clearly invites analogy, because the cultural underground is itself a metaphor, making the literal underground of the city mysteries a metaphor of a metaphor. The protagonist of *The Secrets of the Twin Cities*, Walter Howard, experiences this uncanny recursivity of the underground on his first visit to the Twin City when, looking into its astonishing depths, he cries out "in the depths of his astonishment."[29] These double undergrounds recall the popular cultural representations of the Underground Railroad, which literalized its operative metaphor; likewise, here vehicle and tenor become images of one another in a kind of subterranean hall of mirrors.

Consequently, while the city mysteries invoke the tropes of surface and depth that recent methodological debates in literary criticism have made so familiar, their topography works in unfamiliar ways. City mysteries may promise to "lift the cover" from the "depths" of urban modernity, as Lippard puts it in the opening pages of *The Quaker City* (4), but it turns out that going underground does not disclose much.[30] Rather, the novels' subterranean perspective registers occlusion without necessarily correcting it. Thompson's *City Crimes* and Averill's *The Secrets of the Twin Cities* illustrate the underground's surprising resistance to the satisfaction of revelation. Both imagine vast cave systems running beneath New York, and both feature dumbfounded bourgeois protagonists who initially take the caves to represent the suppressed truth of the prosperous modern city. After Walter Howard exclaims "in the depths of his astonishment" over the Twin City, he continues: "New York, O New York! with all thy wealth and woe, pride and poverty, magnificence and misery, with all thy proverbial vices, all thy notorious wickedness, the countless thousands who throng thy busy pavements all day long, yet know not one half of thy startling secrets, thy terrible mysteries" (111). Howard's alliterative dichotomies ("wealth and woe, pride and poverty, magnificence and misery") present the Twin City as physically parallel to the city above but socially converse. In this respect, its underground resembles what Michel Foucault, in his influential essay "Of Other Spaces," designates as a heterotopia, a space in which the "real sites that can be found within the culture are simultaneously represented, contested, and inverted." But whereas Foucault's heterotopias enable a visitor "to reconstitute myself there where I am," the Twin City invites profound disorientation.[31] It turns out to be less foreign than it first appears. Once Howard descends into its depths, he finds that it looks quite familiar, complete with "regular rooms cut out of the earth," and "fruit stands, meat shops, bakeries and groceries, which . . . line[d] the subterranean street with places of business" (110–11). The novel's title underscores the disorientation created by the underground by refusing even to recognize the priority of the city above: New York City and the city below are equally "twin cities."

Rather than Foucault's heterotopia, the closer theoretical counterpart to undergrounds like the Twin City may be George Bataille's "base matter." "Base matter" is the low, disgusting, or perverse stuff on which ideals of elevation depend but must disavow. "Base"—in the spatial sense of being foundational as well as in the moral or aesthetic sense of being vile—appears to reify the opposition of high and low, "but this antinomy, more than any other, is thereby immediately deprived of interest and meaning," Bataille writes.[32] Or as Benjamin Noys explains, "Base matter is what makes the very structure of the high/low opposition possible in the first place *and* what ruins it."[33] Thompson's *City Crimes* demonstrates how the underground proves irreconcilable with the world above, refusing to explain its mysteries and frustrating expectations of revelation. Guided by a canny street urchin, the protagonist, Frank Sydney, plunges into a network of caves below the city known as the Dark Vaults. Initially the Dark Vaults, like the Twin City, appears to be a subterranean slum. But deep in the "Infernal Regions," Sydney meets the Jolly Knights of the Round Table, a gang of well-heeled criminals led by a sadist called the Dead Man, who hatch heinous plots below ground while maintaining respectable personas above it.[34] In the Infernal Regions, finally, it seems, the dark underbelly of the city will be exposed. But here, too, the discovery of the underground dialectically negates life on the surface without disclosing a truer picture. The Jolly Knights remain "hideously masked," and with the near exception of the Dead Man and the Doctor, who are known only by those titles, we never learn their identities.[35] Figuratively as well as literally, obscurity is the hallmark of the underground. It deepens the mysteries of the city rather than allowing the reader to get to the bottom of them.

For Bataille, base matter is a mode of political imagination. Embodied by Marx's "old mole" in *The Eighteenth Brumaire of Louis Bonaparte*, who "is still journeying through purgatory" (and to whom I will return at the end of this chapter), base matter tarries "in the bowels of the earth" rather than looking toward more "revolutionary utopias."[36] Bataille envisions the logic of base matter subtending an idiosyncratic version of materialism he calls "base materialism," which, by its "incongruity and by an overwhelming lack of respect, permits the intellect to escape from the constraints of idealism."[37] In *The Quaker City*, George Lippard coins his own term for the underground's untoward potentialities: the "grotesque-sublime." He introduces the term, as Samuel Otter notes, when describing the caretaker of Monk Hall, Devil-Bug, descending "down, down over massive steps of granite, down, down!" (304) into the lowest story of the Pit. By linking the grotesque to Devil-Bug's descent, Otter suggests, "Lippard's narrator conjures the subterranean etymology of the term," which originally referred to the art found in Roman grottoes. Eventually, the word "acquired not only descriptive but also negative connotations and came to be associated with an uneasy mix of horror and humor."[38] It is this uneasiness that Lippard highlights by yoking the grotesque to the sublime. "Our taste is different from yours," he informs the "shallow pated critic," whose "perfumes agree but sorrily with the thick atmosphere of this darkening vault." To Lippard, by contrast, this scene is "full of interest, replete with the grotesque-sublime" (305). Insisting on the "delight" (305) that shelters in the most noisome corners of the underground, Lippard embraces the grotesque without trying to transcend it. Instead, the dyad "grotesque-sublime" holds out the possibility that, as Bataille puts it, "by excavating the fetid ditch of bourgeois culture, perhaps we will see open up in the depths of the earth immense and even sinister caves where force and human liberty will establish themselves, sheltered from the call to order of a heaven that today demands the most imbecilic elevation of any man's spirit."[39] For Bataille, of course, these "immense and sinister caves" are abstractions. But in the work of Lippard and others, they assume material form.

Allegory and "the Wisdom of the Nether World"

If the city mysteries' undergrounds make bad metaphors, stubbornly refusing to illuminate the ideas they evoke, perhaps it makes more sense to approach them as allegories, in Walter Benjamin's unconventional recuperative reading of that term.[40] In *The Origin of German Tragic Drama*, Benjamin contrasts allegories with symbols, which he argues possess a "disinterested self-sufficiency" that "assumes ... meaning" in a "mystical instant" (165). Symbols, in other words, are high-functioning figures of speech. By contrast, allegory produces "a chaotic mess of metaphors" (173) as it "immerses itself into the depths which separate visual being from meaning" (165) and finally "goes away empty-handed" (233). If the parallel between sensationalist nineteenth-century city mystery novels and baroque seventeenth-century drama seems far-fetched, consider the defining characteristics of the *Trauerspiel* (tragedy) in Benjamin's account: its clumsiness; its formulaic quality; its outmodedness (which he connects to its desire "to shock" [183]); its inaccessibility to critical recovery. Even more specifically: its oscillation between earthly concerns and "dreams, ghostly apparitions, the terrors of the end" (134); its predilection for nighttime, especially midnight, scenes (134, 135); its translation of political turmoil into threats to women's "chastity" (74); and most of all, its "enthusiasm for landscape," in which "history merges into the setting" (92).[41] This "enthusiasm for landscape" also infuses Benjamin's account, which renders topographically the distinction between symbol and the *Trauerspiel*'s preferred mode of allegory. Allegory has a subterranean orientation. Whereas symbols elevate the familiar (think of Ralph Waldo Emerson's definition of poetic language, by which objects are "lifted from the ground and afloat before the eye"), Benjamin repeatedly describes allegory's "eruption of images" (173) as operating in the "depths" (165, 166, 183).[42] (Anticipating this description is *City Crimes*, where the Dead Man keeps his child—a stunted, keening, indescribably reptilian creature named "the Image"—locked in a cellar beneath his house.) For Benjamin, allegory's subterranean mode indexes its mood; it is spatially because emotionally depressed. "For all the wisdom of the melancholic is subject to the nether world," he writes, "and it hears nothing of the voice of revelation. Everything saturnine points down into the depths of the earth" (152). Note that Benjamin distinguishes "wisdom" from "revelation," opening the possibility that the "depths of the earth" might contain a different kind of wisdom. Of course, Benjamin is not arguing that the *Trauerspiel*'s settings are subterranean, like those of the city mysteries; rather, he invokes the underground as an allegory of allegory. But even as I pursue a generic comparison between the *Trauerspiel* and the city mystery, I want to attend to Benjamin's subterranean language in order to speculate on a more oblique affinity between allegory and the underground.

What this "wisdom of . . . the nether world" entails lies in Benjamin's interpretation of allegory's historical specificity. Allegory fails to achieve the revelatory transcendence of the symbol not due to the author's incapacity but because it emerges at historical dead ends. As Susan Buck-Morss puts it, "Certain experiences (and thus certain epochs) were allegorical, not certain poets."[43] Benjamin values allegory precisely because it expresses these historical experiences of destruction and decay: "Whereas in the symbol destruction is idealized and the transfigured face of nature is fleetingly revealed in the light of redemption, in allegory the observer is confronted with the *facies hippocratica* of history as a petrified, primordial landscape. Everything about history that, from the very beginning, has been untimely, sorrowful, unsuccessful, is expressed in a face—or rather in a death's head" (166). Allegory is the proper mode for the most devastated periods of history, when the "face of nature" becomes a death's head. Benjamin's description strikingly evokes the city mysteries' grim visions of modernity (and, again, uncannily recalls Thompson's Dead Man, who uses acid to give his face a "death-like appearance" [230]). Insofar as the first sentence of the passage explains allegory's affinity for the wreckage of the present, the second sentence suggests that allegory also testifies to other presents that failed to happen: those that are "untimely, sorrowful, unsuccessful." If allegory captures the worst of history, it likewise captures what never *was* history; if it is a failed rhetorical technique, it is because it is expressive *of* failure. Martin Jay reads Benjamin's attraction to the morbid preoccupations of the *Trauerspiel* as itself a refusal to accept history's outcomes. By fixating on loss, the plays refuse the "allegedly 'healthy' 'working through' of grief" that would "neutralize" the lost object and instead preserve its "intractable otherness"—what Nicolas Abraham and Maria Torok frame as the difference between mourning's "introjection" and melancholy's "incorporation."[44] The significance of melancholic incorporation to Benjamin's theory of allegory becomes even more apparent when Abraham and Torok memorably compare incorporation to the erection of a "crypt" inside the subject, a process that they argue throws linguistic representation into disarray.[45]

City mysteries can seem so painfully dated, so stuck in their own time, that they will not answer to any but the most thoroughly historicized literary criticism. But Benjamin's subterranean-inflected theory of allegory offers one way to recuperate the representational impasses of the city mysteries, helping to explain why they are at once so resonant and so resistant to revelation—and perhaps also why their undergrounds constitute the primary sites of both that resonance and that resistance. Building on Benjamin's account *of* allegory as well as his insistently subterranean language *for* allegory, I read the city mysteries' undergrounds both as signs of the genre's allegorical mode and as especially charged allegories themselves, which do not represent existing cultural undergrounds (as a symbol would) so much as they summon undergrounds too "untimely, sorrowful, unsuccessful" to be represented. Indeed, the kinds of proletarian, often multiracial underground activities one finds in the city mysteries were arguably less prevalent in the actual mid-nineteenth-century United States than in the pages of its novels. Cultural historians have long noted that while the consolidating capitalism of the early nineteenth century galvanized class consciousness, midcentury political, military, and legislative developments threw the burgeoning anticapitalist insurgency into disarray. The story of this foreclosed radicalism has been well told by many scholars, so I will not rehearse it at length here. In brief, however, what Michael Rogin once ironically termed "the American 1848" marks a moment not of class solidarity but of its collapse, as expansionism, combined with the concessions to pro-slavery interests exacted by the Compromise of 1850, shifted the white working class's alliances from class to race.[46] In the undergrounds of the city mysteries—the primary literary genre of antebellum white critiques of capitalism—we can glimpse the "untimely, sorrowful, unsuccessful" project of class struggle, not as it actually existed but as it might have been.

Ironically, the city mysteries' authors saw that vision through the lens of the very racial anxieties that doomed the American 1848. Their subterranean allegories summon the associations between the underground and racialized Blackness described in the previous three chapters, even as they marginalize, exclude, or denigrate Black characters. To return to Thompson's *City Crimes*, for example, the Dead Man tries to force a woman into a sexual relationship by threatening to reveal her affair with a Black servant; when she resists, he rapes her and declares, "Henceforth, I am your master, and you are my slave."[47] Yet even as the Dead Man traffics in white supremacist violence and fantasies of enslavement, he also arrogates to himself subterranean powers of Black antislavery resistance. Like George Lippard's Old Royal, in a pivotal scene the Dead Man reenacts the story of Henry "Box" Brown, whose slave narrative was published the same year as *City Crimes*. Having been imprisoned in Sing Sing, the Dead Man outwits the vigilant "overseer" by packing himself into a wooden box that is being shipped out of the prison's cabinetmaking shop. The box is loaded onto a boat and then, once it reaches New York, transferred to a wagon, where like Brown, the Dead Man bounces down the streets in agony upside down before eventually arriving at a warehouse, where he pries himself out of the box. The Dead Man's pirated escape exploits the image of Brown himself as a dead man made famous by the popular engraving of his "resurrection" from the box; more broadly, it demonstrates how city mysteries sought to capture the subterranean energies of the Underground Railroad in their own undergrounds. The sections that follow will pick up traces of other Black undergrounds in the post-1848 visions of George Lippard's novel *Adonai, the Pilgrim of Eternity* and George W. L. Bickley's *Adalaska; or the Strange and Mysterious Family of the Cave of Genreva*; more speculatively, I will argue that the city mysteries enfold a subterranean racial politics even when they do not address race directly.

Lippard's "Light from the Grave"

George Lippard's 1851 novel *Adonai, the Pilgrim of Eternity*, a kind of messianic-historical variation on the city mystery, extravagantly illustrates a Benjaminian notion of allegory, in which "everything about history that ... has been untimely, sorrowful, unsuccessful" "immerses itself into the depths" in a "chaotic mess of metaphors." An early version of the novel appeared in 1849; Lippard then revised it for *The White Banner*, a short-lived periodical he issued for his mystical socialist secret society, the Brotherhood of the Union. The Brotherhood of the Union in turn incorporated various elements of *Adonai* into its language and rituals, making the novel's otherworldly vision of the underground into a model for a political underground. This luminously strange novel begins in ancient Rome with Lucius the Sybarite, a friend of the emperor, entertaining himself as he stands guard over one hundred poor people imprisoned in a "charnel vault" separated from his room by an iron door.[48] When he opens the door to the cell and finds everyone dead, he immediately converts to Christianity in horror and is almost as quickly himself imprisoned in an underground cell and slated for execution. He falls into a trance only to wake up centuries later, at which point he learns he has a "Two-Fold existence" (25): by returning to "the Subterranean World" (31) periodically, he can move through history, emerging at potential flashpoints for revolt—the Protestant Reformation, the French Revolution, and so on. In search of an answer to "the simple question—'How shall we give to Labor its proper fruits?'" (28)—he surfaces in Paris in 1848. Disappointed with the course of the struggle there, however, he then heads toward the United States. He is so confident that there he will find "a free people, dwelling in Brotherhood, without a single slave to mar their peace, or call down upon their heads the vengeance of God" (42), that his "consciousness of a Two-Fold life" slips away and he becomes "but a Man of the World" (43).

However, soon he arrives at a jail in which enslaved people are held before being sold, which "reminded him of the Iron Door in the Catacombs" (46). His subterranean consciousness reawakens: that night "he traversed the City that was above ground, and also traversed the city that was beneath. And the sights that he saw, and the words that he heard, if written in a book, would not be believed by One man in Ten" (48). Adonai revivifies George Washington from his own subterranean vault for company, and the two set themselves to "surveying the sufferings of the Outcast people of this lower world" (57). What they witness makes them increasingly despondent. In the novel's final scene, they see a vision of the future in which the people rise up across Europe. Adonai and Washington cry out for them to spare their enemies, but a disembodied voice intones, "Whom did these Oppressors spare in the years 1848 and 1849?" Adonai implores the voice whether "peaceful progress" is not possible. But in a novel built around the wild temporalities of the underground, the answer is clearly negative, and the voice replies, "Can peace be kept with tigers hungry for human blood?" (95). *Adonai* ends, abruptly and inconclusively, with a standoff between the spirits of "those, who had in all ages, and in face of all manner of superstition, avarice, and despair," believed "in the *social regeneration of mankind*" and Satan, who announces that he will make his new home in America (97).

Reading Lippard's fantastically overdetermined novel in light of Benjamin's account of allegory's excesses, we could say that *Adonai*'s revolutionary visions—deferred, frustrated, and finally apocalyptic—instantiate the melancholy of a defeated politics. In this reading, its undergrounds would mark the grave of a certain moment of class-based radicalism. Yet here we might recall a motto of Lippard's Brotherhood of the Union, "Light from the Grave," along with Jonathan Flatley's contention that Benjamin's melancholy preoccupation with political failures is not fatalistic:

> Benjamin's counterintuitive contention is that it is precisely by dwelling on loss, the past, and political failures (as opposed to images of a better future) that one may avoid a depressing and cynical relation to the present. What emerges is the picture of a politicizing, splenetic melancholy, where clinging to things from the past *enables* interest and action in the present world and is indeed the very mechanism for that interest.[49]

For Flatley, melancholic thinking "shows one how one's situation is experienced collectively by a community, a heretofore unarticulated community of melancholics" (4). Loss felt as deeply personal (and for Benjamin, of course, the adverb resonates) becomes a means to understand one's coexistence, and perhaps to forge new collectivities as a consequence. Even as it dwells on the past, Benjamin's subterranean untimely projects itself into an unknown future. Building on Flatley's reading, then, we might understand the underground as the beginning of a polity that has not yet come into existence.

So if we return to *Adonai, the Pilgrim of Eternity*, we can reread its ending not only as unfulfilled and unfulfilling but for this reason as gesturing toward unrepresentable futures. We might notice, too, that these possible futures are the province of the underground. The underground here begins literally, as the subterranean vault that moves Adonai (and later Washington) across time. But as the novel goes on, Lippard's imagery draws out a parallel between the regenerative promise of the literal underground represented by Adonai and Washington and the figurative underground of US capitalism—"the subterranean depths of a great city," as Lippard puts it (67). Once Lippard establishes that parallel, the gathering masses of the "subterranean depths" increasingly supersede the subterranean protagonists, who are eclipsed not only by the size of the crowd but also by the limits of their own vision. Lippard enacts that shift quite graphically when, late in the novel, Adonai and Washington traverse an enormous plain to find "a multitude of people, gathered from all the nations and tribes of the earth," representing "all the Poor of the World" (84). One man steps forward, seizes Washington's sword, and wraps it in a cloth stained with "THE BLOOD OF HOLY REVOLUTION!" He identifies it as "THE SWORD OF WASHINGTON, *grasped by the hands of* THE LABORERS OF THE WHOLE WORLD" (89). Washington becomes visibly nervous. By the end of the novel, of course, his and Adonai's vision of "peaceful progress" has been sidelined by the promise of violent revolution by "all the Poor of the World."

In *Adonai*, the literal underground germinates a figurative underground. Its potentialities are never realized in the novel, although rumblings of "holy revolution" are distinctly audible. But in his own life, Lippard materialized *Adonai*'s vision of the underground in the Brotherhood of the Union. Founded in 1848 and continuing at least through the 1970s, the Brotherhood was dedicated to making the United States into "the Palestine of Redeemed Labor."[50] It did not busy itself much with particular political agendas or specific actions. Instead, Lippard assured members, "When all Brothers of the Union are fully indoctrinated with the Truths of the B.G.C. the *general plan of action* will not be difficult to find."[51] In the meantime, he envisioned the Brotherhood of the Union as "a permanent, living, although unobtrusive, Order, pursuing its way, for the great Future, regardless of factions, parties, Presidential elections, or spasmodic Reform societies."[52]

The Brotherhood drew inspiration from other radical, mystical, and fraternal organizations, but it seems also to have modeled its underground ("permanent, living, unobtrusive") on those Lippard and others imagined in city mysteries. As Paul Erickson observes, although Lippard feared establishing chapters in large cities due to their "corrupting influence," B.G.C. stood for "Brotherhood of the Great City," meaning "this organization, which shunned urban members, was structured around a vision of utopic urbanism."[53] For such a prolific author of city mysteries, this "utopic urbanism" likely derived less from the street than the page. Certainly Lippard lifted much of the material for the Brotherhood's rites directly from *Adonai*. Its slogan, as I noted earlier, translated as "Light from the Grave," which the

Brotherhood represented visually in a seal that pictured a tomb with the letters "HF," for "Holy Flame," written on it. The primary officers held the title of "Washington," progressing from Chief Washington to Exalted Washington to Supreme Washington, Lippard's office. But the Brotherhood also completes the seizure of "THE SWORD OF WASHINGTON" by "THE LABORERS OF THE WHOLE WORLD" that Lippard first staged in *Adonai*. Its "Washingtons," of course, are regular members, and its underground, both literal and figurative, belongs to the multitude: in initiation rites, members vowed "to use my most earnest efforts to hasten the Day, when Humanity shall rise from its grave, and all nations and races, learn by heart, the Lost Word, Brotherhood."[54] Another initiation rite actually reenacts the scene in *Adonai* where the "Poor of the World" gather together but gives it a very different ending. In the novel, the poor crowd around a sepulchre set in the middle of rocks. Light shines out from within, but a group of rich men, kings, and priests blocks it—and when members of the multitude try to come forward, this group kills them, tears them to pieces, and eats them. In the Brotherhood's rites, however:

> The candidate is led to a curtain, behind which are seated, various Brothers, attired in the costumes of various nations and races. The space behind the curtain may be arranged to represent a cavern, with a single light, burning upon a rock, in the center.
> And in the center, stands a Brother, who is dressed in a garb of coarse grey, edged with scarlet. He leans his hand upon a cloaked Figure. He personates the U.W. or Unknown Worker.[55]

In *Adonai*, the ruling classes literally cannibalize the poor in their zeal to keep them from accessing the subterranean flame. In the Brotherhood of the Union's rites, by contrast, the subterranean flame becomes a point of entry into a mysterious anticapitalist secret society—that is, into a political underground.

The Politics of Unrecognizability

Read for the sense of revolutionary potentiality unleashed by their combination of the topographical and the political, the city mysteries' undergrounds join other nineteenth-century dreams like the "world not to come" that Raúl Coronado maps in Tejano print culture, the "ghosts of futures past" that Molly McGarry finds in spiritualist writing, or "the fantastic visions, excessive imaginings, and unforeclosed possibilities that *would not come to be*" that Peter Coviello sees flourishing in literature before the standardization of modern sexuality.[56] But crucially, as the underground's shadowiness and its corresponding figurative opacity attest, the contours of the worlds the city mysteries dream of are not perceptible—not only from our perspectives looking backward but also from the writers' perspectives looking forward. Rather, the city mysteries' undergrounds are sites of what Stefano Harney and Fred Moten call "prophetic organization."[57] The paradoxical quality of the phrase is key: *prophetic* at once characterizes *organization* and disorganizes it, questioning the necessity or desirability of advance knowledge. The underground is a site of prophetic organization precisely because, as Harney and Moten write of the undercommons, "it is too dark" to "see clearly" there, at least from the viewpoint of politics as we know it.[58] These undergrounds do not picture a better future so much as they situate us somewhere we cannot (yet) imagine; they offer not a program for action but a leap into the unknown.

Adonai, or the Pilgrim of Eternity expands subterranean potentiality into epic mysticism, but even in Lippard's more realistic city mysteries, radical disorientation flourishes underground. In *New York: Its Upper Ten and Lower Million*, it is the novel's very referentiality to the known world that renders its "subterranean world" (116) so disorienting. Lippard buries the Black Senate's chambers beneath a familiar location: a Five Points tavern in which various "persons, black, white and chocolate-colored, of all ages and both sexes, [are] drinking and dancing together" (116). Readers would likely have recognized this as a description of Pete Williams's dance hall, made famous by writers like Ned Buntline, Charles Dickens, and George Foster.[59] But for Lippard, this familiar scene marks the threshold of a deeper perplexity. Addressing us directly, he commands we undertake the dark, labyrinthine descent that began this chapter. If that descent leaves us "utterly bewildered" (116), the scene that greets us at the end only compounds this confusion, for there we find that the vigilance committees known to be scattered throughout the northeastern United States have coalesced into a national political body. More to the point, the Black Senate supplants the risible bickering of "some other senates" (117) with a revolutionary government, conducting a subterranean—and, to judge from the rest of the chapter, effective—war against slavery. Hidden below a well-known location, the Black Senate tantalizes the reader with the possibility of the city's unguessed underground activities. But Lippard's depiction is actually even stranger and more disorienting. As readers likely knew (it was key to the notoriety of the place), Pete Williams's dance hall was *itself* underground.⁶⁰ Its promise, then, is not only one of revelation, in which one might tunnel beneath this dance hall to discover the Black Senate fomenting revolution, but transfiguration as well, in which Pete Williams's dance hall might also *be* (or become, or already have been) the Black Senate.

That uncertainty is to the point. It is a motif that runs through Lippard's entire description of the Black Senate, from its physical location, which leaves one "utterly bewildered," to the "strange scene" the den contains (116). Indeed, obscurity is a feature of the city mysteries' undergrounds generally. Hidden beneath the surface and unknown to most residents, they exemplify the play between the "visible city" and the "invisible city" that Jeffrey Steele finds in much antebellum urban writing, which "is interested both in recording *the sights* of the city"—consider the ubiquitous references to landmarks, neighborhoods, and street names—"and also in measuring the *limits of urban vision.*"⁶¹ And even if one does penetrate the surface, one is still in the dark. Closed to sunlight, undergrounds by definition are spaces inimical to seeing. Moreover, their dimensions resist comprehension, as I noted earlier: they extend indefinitely, and although they are usually constructed, the novels rarely offer any account of how they came to be. Such resistance is not simply an act of negation, however. In place of knowing, the underground cultivates an attachment to the unknown. Thus if, as I stated at the beginning of the chapter, the city mysteries depict some of the earliest social formations recognizable as figurative undergrounds, in situating those formations physically underground, the novels actually elaborate the value of unrecognizability.

Returning to the Black Senate, we find that against mainstream nineteenth-century commitments to philosophical empiricism and what philosopher Charles Taylor calls the "politics of recognition," Lippard builds the episode around a transvaluation of the known and the unknown.⁶² The "speaker of the house," Royal Bill (whose name seems to be a defamiliarizing double of Royal Hill, the South Carolina plantation where he was formerly enslaved), tells the members that he has assembled them that night "by d'rection ob *somebody dat you don't know*" (118), and for good reason: kidnappers are in town, and the members need to arm themselves and leave immediately. When one of the kidnappers, Bloodhound, interrupts the meeting, the Senate closes in on him and Royal Bill asks, "Do you know de pris'ner?"

"He stole me fader!"

"He took me mother from Fildelfy and sold her down south."

"He kidnapped my little boy."

"Dam kidnapper! he stole my wife!"

"I knows him, I does—he does work for de man dat sells niggas in Baltimore."

"Don't you know how he tuk de yaller gal away from Fildelfy, making b'lieve dat her own fader was a-dyin', and sent for her?"

Such were a few of the responses to old Royal's question. It was evident that Bloodhound was *known*. And, although his hair had grown gray in the practice of all the virtues, it did not give him much pleasure to find that he was known. (121)

The "known" Bloodhound contrasts unfavorably with "*somebody dat you don't know*," the valiant tipster whose message to Royal Bill initiated the meeting. More broadly, his known quantity stands in opposition to the entire mysterious underground of the Black Senate—including the conditions under which we as readers have entered it, "descend[ing] into the subterranean world" without knowing where we are going. Directly and indirectly, the underground invites us to cast our lot with the unknown. (Recall here, too, the figure of the "Unknown Worker" in the cavern tableau who superintends the initiation of members of the Brotherhood of the Union.) The prefix *sub-* in *subterranean* resonates with this meaning, for in addition to "under," it also means "toward." The underground thus offers a kind of utopianism without a blueprint, which pitches itself toward another world without demanding that it already be recognizable.

In their recessiveness—in the way they draw the reader down into ever-deepening perplexities—the city mysteries' undergrounds present a mise en abyme of the genre itself. (The fact that the phrase *mise en abyme* itself contains an abyss—*abyme*—seems almost overdetermined at this point.) The term "city mystery," and even the novels' own idiom of exposure, may encourage us to go searching for answers in their undergrounds, but those undergrounds insist otherwise. For despite its promises of unmasking, lifting veils, and bringing secrets to light, one does not, after all, *solve* a city mystery. City mysteries recall an older, religious sense of the word "mysteries," exemplified in Egyptian, Greek, and Roman mystery cults and later Christian theology: forms of knowledge that defy reason. In the nineteenth century, fraternal organizations like Freemasonry reanimated this notion of "mysteries" and made it central to their rituals. As I noted in chapter 2, Black Freemasons gave particular emphasis to "mysteries," arguing that they showed Freemasonry's origins in ancient Egypt; recall Martin Delany's newspaper the *Mystery*, as well as the secret antislavery organizations the African-American Mysteries and the American Mysteries Secret U.G.R.R. Society, described in chapter 3. As "mysteries" in this respect, city mysteries do not reject revelation so much as recall a different understanding of it, one that predates its more familiar empiricist meaning. For long before it referred to the exposure of facts, revelation signified a supernatural communication of knowledge—the means, for medieval Christian theologians, by which we apprehend mysteries. To the extent that they resist totalizing knowledge, city mysteries point us back toward these earlier understandings of mystery and revelation. *New York: Its Upper Ten and Lower Million* stages this concept of mystery as a formal experiment in intertextuality. As Jeffrey Steele observes, the novel "covers basically the same narrative territory" as Lippard's earlier New York city mystery, *The Empire City; or, New York by Night and Day* (1850), returning to "the same cast of characters, the same thematic structures, and the same resolution." But rather than providing closure to the earlier novel, *New York* introduces what Steele describes as a Deleuzean "fold" that bends the story "infinitely inward," so that "there seems room for an unlimited number of complications."[63] It reopens the mysteries of *The Empire City* and makes still more "room" for mystery within them.

Two further examples of post-1848 city mysteries illuminate how their undergrounds' unbounded mysteries bring startling political possibilities into reach, if not into view. Both materialize Bataille's "immense and sinister caves" incubating "force and human liberty" by carving out a space of revolutionary potentiality—dubious or compromised as it may be—from underneath an accumulation of political disappointments. Through a convoluted series of events, the title character of the *Terrible and All Absorbing Narrative and Confession of Edwin Winters* finds himself in the headquarters of the Western Bandit and United Empire Association, an underground cave in Arkansas. Sumptuously furnished with velvet hangings, plush carpets, elegant furniture, rare books, and a magnificent art collection, the cave is populated by 250 bandits ruled by a sixteen-year-old queen, who rides around the cave in a gilded chariot pulled by fourteen servants. (Sometimes the floor underneath the chariot rises four feet, apparently just for effect.) He learns the goal of their confederation "is to establish in this country a monarchical government, by means of a revolution," that will "divide the republic of the United States into two Empires," east and west.⁶⁴ "An emperor is to reign over each of the two empires," and "titles of nobility are to be conferred on those who distinguish themselves in the struggle between the United States' government and the organization" (22). Winters is initiated into the organization, taking an oath of secrecy and vowing to "renounce all the laws of, and allegiance to, the United States' Government" (24), and he marries the queen. Given these events, the association's highly developed plans, its 72,000 members in high places, and its impressive assets of over $27 million, one might expect the novel to culminate with the realization of the scheme (21, 23). Instead, Winters departs before the Western Bandit and United Empire Association makes its move, and the novel leaves its fate in doubt, explaining portentously, "the time for the outbreak is not fixed upon" (22).

While the extravagantly reactionary underground of *Terrible and All Absorbing Narrative* seeks to install a monarchy in the United States, a rural city mystery from the same year, George W. L. Bickley's *Adalaska; or the Strange and Mysterious Family of the Cave of Genreva*, imagines the nation's underground spaces fulfilling the 1848 European revolutions. At the same time, it raises disquieting questions about the concept of unknowability that I have argued constitutes the underground's most utopian feature. In the early 1850s, Bickley actively participated in Lippard's Brotherhood of the Union; he founded a Cincinnati circle and, according to historian Mark Lause, likely several other Ohio circles as well.⁶⁵ By the end of the decade, however, he had founded a new organization that dramatically reimagined the Brotherhood of the Union's anticapitalist "circles": the secessionist Knights of the Golden Circle, a secret society that planned an empire for slavery that would encompass the US South, the Caribbean, Mexico, and Central America.⁶⁶ *Adalaska*'s spectacular tale of transnational revolution, utopian communities, economic leveling, and racial equality appears difficult to square with Bickley's later pro-slavery, imperialist fantasies. Perhaps his trajectory denotes the curdling of his revolutionary dreams, but I suggest that Bickley's two undergrounds are not as far apart as we might like to believe. This proposition is not only an accounting of *Adalaska*'s racial exclusions and stereotypes; it is also an argument that the novel's vision of the underground's radical unthinkability is itself animated by notions of unfathomable racial difference.

Adalaska revolves around the members of an aristocratic French family who flee to the United States after being accused of plotting against Napoleon Bonaparte. One branch of the family marries into the Shawnee, while the other takes up residence in a gaslit cave in Virginia more than three hundred feet underground. Separated from the rest of society, they attain the "perfection of human nature," according to the awestruck visiting narrator, a utopian state contingent upon their underground existence.[67] As one of the family explains, "If we intend to keep ourselves as pure and unsullied as we are now, we must be very cautious in our intercourse with those who are familiar with the upper world of society" (36). But their isolation is broken when the title character falls in love with the daughter of a rich white Kentuckian (conveniently named Major White), who gathers a party of men and pursues the couple back to the cave. The cave dwellers—led by Bolivar, an African "servant"—drive them back, and Adalaska and Eliza White finally marry.

The novel is far from over at this point, however. Adalaska's aunt Lenna, one of the original French refugees, periodically descends into deathlike trances in which she prophesies "things hidden deep in the womb of the future" (68). This peculiar description of a subterranean future, gestating but unknown, both images and models the "chaotic mess of metaphors" that Benjamin finds ricocheting amid the "allegorical depths" of the *Trauerspiel*.[68] Its metaphors multiply without adding up: Bickley analogizes the unknown both to the space of the cave itself and to Lenna's role as its visionary matriarch. The image confounds temporal and spatial registers, and its unknown "things" are themselves doubly recessive, not only "hidden deep" but "in the womb," undeveloped—another example of the feminization of the underground I discussed in relation to Mattie Griffith's *Madge Vertner* in chapter 3. In one trance, Lenna exclaims,

> The blood of my house, though royal itself, must flow in the veins of him who shall rise with the sword of the Lord in his hand, and lead the organized host to the field, not to battle against their brothers and sisters who do the labor of the world, but against the tyrant and his servants who sell their birthright for a mess of pottage. All Europe is trembling at the result, and well she may; for her masses shall rise as one man and destroy the oppressor. . . . From this home of ours—from this American country, the deliverer must go forth to accomplish what Christopher Columbus began but could not *then* finish. *Universal peace and universal love must prevail; but first the earth must be clothed in red.* (69)

Accordingly, Adalaska, his wife, and children leave the cave for Europe, where they spread the word that "the masses must rise as one man and swear, by heaven! to be free and to live like brothers" (102).

Here, just as the novel reaches its revolutionary crescendo, its politics abruptly moderate. Although Adalaska "brought about the revolution of 1848," he finds "insufficient organization of the people to effect their liberties" (106). Consequently, he resolves that "if we shall be unable to effect the work in Europe, we will plant the germ of future government" in the United States (102). The family returns to Virginia, where they build two thriving intentional communities—aboveground. Major White even comes to live in one and decides he is "no longer ashamed to acknowledge old Bolivar as his equal and Adalaska as his son-in-law" (102). Racial and class conflict dissolve in the sunlight. It is a happy ending, but its politics bear little resemblance to the full-tilt international uprising Lenna prophesied from within the cave. Still, that subterranean vision lingers. By the close, "Adalaska found the spirit of his aunt growing stronger in him" (106), an image of prophetic gestation that recalls Lenna's own spiritual encounters with "things hidden deep in the womb of the future." Adalaska may have left the cave behind, but like Abraham and Torok's cryptophoric subject on loop, he has incorporated it, with all of the presumed dead modes of existence it contains. In the final sentence of the novel, he "is now devoting himself, might and main, to bring about universal emancipation from the polluting tyranny of kings and priests" (107), an ongoing struggle that notably exceeds the narrative and political resolution the intentional communities provide. Although the revolutions of 1848 have been defeated, *Adalaska*'s vertiginous counterhistory of the present, like that of *Edwin Winters*, promises readers in 1853 that all manner of undergrounds are now agitating unguessed beneath their feet.

Adalaska exemplifies my earlier claim that the most radical aspects of the city mysteries' undergrounds lie in the way they question the known world and draw readers into an unknowable one. Even as the novel settles into a happy ending about terrestrial democracy and land reform, the revolution prophesied in the cave of Genreva still haunts it, all the more "strange and mysterious" for remaining unfulfilled. Although Adalaska has abandoned the cave, he has encrypted the prophetic gifts his aunt cultivated there, leaving readers with a "deep" vision of liberation at once portentous and significantly indeterminate. But especially in the unavoidable shadow of Bickley's career, *Adalaska* also enables us to return to this earlier claim about the radicalism of subterranean unrecognizability and discern the troubling racial politics that underpin it. As I have shown, city mysteries capitalize on images of Black undergrounds while being largely uninvested in Black liberation, a tradition Bickley joins by equipping the cave family with a heroic African "servant" named after a South American freedom fighter. And these fleeting images of Black undergrounds, rarely motivated by plot, together suggest a more expansive hypothesis: that even in the absence of any such references, the city mysteries' underground fantasies are fired by ideas of racial difference. In other words, these visions of the underground not only trade on images of Black undergrounds but fold an invisible "Africanist presence," to borrow Toni Morrison's famous formulation, into the nature of the underground itself, whose mystery materializes white notions of Black unintelligibility.[69] In this admittedly bleak reading, the most radical properties of the underground are unescapably an entailment of white supremacist thought; their vision of a world otherwise is inseparable from a history of racial othering.

The Mysteries of Demystification

Revolutionaries driven underground by Napoleon who reemerge in 1848, confront its failures, and promise to surface again: *Adalaska* reads a lot like a sensationalized version of Karl Marx's *The Eighteenth Brumaire of Louis Bonaparte*, which he wrote two years before for a New York publisher. Specifically, *Adalaska*'s underground narrative echoes the famous moment when Marx cites *Hamlet* to picture revolutionary consciousness as an "old mole" "grubb[ing]" in the earth.[70] Marx is borrowing from the scene when Hamlet tells his father's ghost, "Well sayd old Mole" (1.5.163), but his misquotation is telling. Hamlet calls the ghost a mole flippantly; the epithet is a mordant joke on the fact that he speaks from the grave (and that the actor voicing the ghost likely did so from below the stage). But Marx recuperates the mole in all its mole-ness by transforming the absurd image of a talking mole into one of a mole simply doing what moles do, digging in the earth: "Well grubbed, old mole!" Marx's effort to take the mole's work seriously becomes even clearer in light of Peter Stallybrass's reminder that he is also citing Hegel, who in *Lectures on the History of Philosophy* pictures the "Spirit" of humanity as the "mole that is within," which "forces its way on ... into the light of day."[71] As Stallybrass points out, Hegel's mole proceeds upward, a figure of progressive enlightenment, but "Marx's mole, unlike Hegel's, is not working toward the light; it is working in the earth."[72] Europe "will leap from its seat" once the mole's work is complete, but the mole itself remains underground. Marx, in other words, shifts the drama from above to below: while for Hegel, the mole burrows in "lifeless seclusion" before reaching the light, for Marx, the underground itself animates history.[73]

This would not be the last time Marx would turn Hegel upside down. In a well-known passage from the afterword to the second edition of *Capital*, volume 1, Marx explains, "My dialectic method is ... not only different from the Hegelian, but exactly opposite to it ... With him it is standing on its head. It must be inverted."[74] Here, too, Marx upends the trajectory of the dialectic: rather than proceeding through supersession or "lifting up" (*Aufhebung*), with all the faith in progress this ascent implies, he directs the dialectic downward. Famously, such descent becomes a motif for *Capital*, whose turning point comes when Marx leaves "this noisy sphere, where everything takes place on the surface and in view of all men" for "the hidden abode of production," in order to "force the secret of profit making."[75] As David McNally notes, Marx here "descends into a cellar of sorts—the underworld of work" and in doing so "reverses the whole trajectory of Western philosophy which, since Plato, has sought truth by means of an ascent from the cave."[76] Marx's invitation to induct us into the subterranean "secret" of capitalism's "hidden abode of production" resonates with his earlier reorientation of Hegel and, beyond that, with the plots of city mysteries. This might not be coincidence. Marx and Engels originated the image of a topsy-turvy Hegel thirty years earlier in *The Holy Family* (1844), in a splenetic discussion of none other than Sue's foundational city mystery, *Les Mystères de Paris*. There they excoriate the author and, more particularly, the Young Hegelian critics who embraced Sue's novel for ignoring the real mysteries of modern society and insisting instead that its mysteries lie in vaporous truths about human nature, which the intrepid writer can disclose. Marx and Engels observe that the critic is looking at the situation the wrong way up: "He stands the world *on its head* and can therefore *in his head* also dissolve all limitations."[77] Material conditions are not simply containers in which metaphysical questions take shape, Marx and Engels retort; mysteries lie in the material conditions themselves. Marx would famously turn this insistence on the mysteriousness of the material world into the critical method we know as demystification. Tracing demystification through *The Holy Family*'s anti-Hegelian reading of the city mysteries, however, gives this supposedly dour interpretative practice a surprisingly sensationalist cast. Even more surprisingly, this genealogy indicates that demystification, like city mysteries, addresses itself to mysteries that defy "absolute knowledge."[78] But to see mysteries in this way, we must take the view from below.

Demystification has come under attack from opponents of "deep reading" as an interpretive feat that whisks away the veils of ideology to expose the truth beneath. Yet such criticisms may too quickly assume we know what we do when we read deeply. Reading Marxist demystification through Marx's own reading of city mysteries allows us to reapproach demystification as something other than a totalizing critical project. City mysteries' topographies share the motifs of surface and depth familiar to us from those debates, and their desire to ferret out the intimate life of social inequality and political corruption can certainly look like a caricature of ideology critique, which Bruno Latour accuses of pulling "causal explanations . . . out of the deep dark below."[79] They may very well constitute part of the genealogy of these vertical frameworks for interpretation. But the city mysteries' digging hardly yields a sense of comprehension or mastery. They are "antihermeneutical," to borrow Scott Herring's description of the queer slumming literature that became one of the genre's twentieth-century successors.[80] And they are nowhere more so than in their undergrounds, where we most expect to discover hidden secrets.

Although the underground holds latent meaning beneath the city's manifest contents, the city mysteries do not equate the unseen with the truth. Hegel's mole, tunneling upward toward "the light of day," may aim for enlightenment, but the subterranean worlds of the city mysteries produce very different sensations of bewilderment and wonder. Recall that when Walter Howard of *The Secrets of the Twin Cities* exclaims at the Twin Cities from "the depths of his astonishment," his catachresis pictures astonishment as not only a response *to* the underground but also synonymous *with* it. Seeing Marxist demystification as akin to the disorienting sensations of the city mysteries highlights what Gayatri Chakravorty Spivak calls the "moments of productive bafflement" in Marx's work.[81] It attends, for instance, to the wildly unscientific passages of *Capital*—lurid, romantic, and shot through with the grotesque—and enables us to see them as indicating the dialectical tension between demystification and mystery, in which the former does not explain away the latter but extends it. For what person who has begun the work of demystification ever feels that they end it or ever feels that it makes the world feel less strange, rather than more so? Read by the gaslight of the city mysteries, demystification becomes, as Jordy Rosenberg has described Marx's related motif of dissection, a "theory of figuration" whose "propositions"—of a full reckoning of capitalism, of a space outside of it—are "unpositable."[82] Rather than solving mysteries, demystification incites an ever-unfolding process of astonishment. City mysteries' incessant surprises model a kind of reading that makes our knowledge less, not more, secure. Their unfathomable depths leave the known world in doubt, while inclining us toward worlds we do not yet know.

5 "To Drop beneath the Floors of the Outer World"

PASCHAL BEVERLY RANDOLPH'S
OCCULT UNDERGROUNDS

In the first four chapters, I described preemergent and emergent ideas of the underground in the early to mid-nineteenth-century United States. Through manifestos, songs, speeches, newspapers reports, poetry, travel narratives, and novels, I showed how a range of writers turned their attention to subterranean spaces and invested them with new possibilities. In these works, caves, tunnels, mines, volcanoes, and cellars became sites of agitation, collective refusal, freedom, or simply living otherwise. This vein of subterranean thinking, I argued, was deeply interwoven with contemporaneous racial thought. I traced the ways a range of thinkers racialized underground spaces as Black spaces to various different ends, and I suggested that the racialization of the underground both indicated its politicization and enabled it.

Those chapters highlighted how long the figurative meaning of the underground remained embedded in its literal meaning and studied how that literal meaning shaped the emergent figurative one. In this chapter and the next, I move into the mid- to late nineteenth century and explore what happened as the underground's figurative meaning became disembedded from its literal meaning and legible in its own right. Thus, where chapters 1 through 4 focused on writing *about* the underground, chapters 5 and 6 focus on writing that increasingly understands itself as coming *from* the underground. Examining two very different underground movements—occultism and anarchism—I read the work of writers dedicated to organizing secretive communities to challenge the authority of the world as they knew it. My hypothesis is that the crystallization, however uneven and heterogeneous, of the idea of the underground in the 1840s and 1850s made it feasible for these writers to identify themselves as belonging to undergrounds as their predecessors could not have done. It is tricky to mark this shift while also recognizing how different these undergrounds are from one another, as well as how different they are from how we tend to understand undergrounds today. But I think one can say, at least, that they shared a sense that they were building collectivities around specific beliefs or practices, which sat askew of the social order and held out a promise of life beyond it. The task will be to analyze how they conceived of this work as underground and to consider the roles that space and race continued to play in their efforts to theorize and enact these new underground movements.

This chapter centers on the extraordinary work of writer, orator, educator, and occult practitioner Paschal Beverly Randolph. Born in 1825 in Five Points, New York—site of George Lippard's Black Senate—to a Black mother and a white father who left soon after Randolph's birth, Randolph grew up in poverty that deepened after his mother died of cholera when he was six. After a difficult, itinerant childhood, he began lecturing on spiritualism and performing as a trance medium in the early 1850s. But in 1858 he publicly broke with the spiritualists, citing their racism, the hypocrisy of their radicalism, and their narrow view of the immaterial world. Although at times Randolph insisted that "not a drop of continental African, or pure negro blood runs through me," at this point he increasingly began to identify with the struggles of Black people.[1] When the Civil War began, he recruited Black troops for the Union army, and during Reconstruction he worked as a teacher and agent for Freedmen's Bureau schools in Louisiana, participated in important Black and Republican conventions, and served as a correspondent for the *Weekly Anglo-African*, the successor to the *Anglo-African Magazine* (which had serialized William J. Wilson's "Afric-American Picture Gallery" and Martin Delany's *Blake*). But from within these established institutions, Randolph was also developing a subterranean praxis that he called "angular and eccentric" and that L. H. Stallings describes as that of a "funky black freak."[2] He founded a series of secret societies organized around his idiosyncratic interpretation of Rosicrucianism, an esoteric European religious movement claiming to preserve the wisdom of a mysterious ancient order, and he dreamed of building still more. Randolph produced a huge body of writing, which he mostly self-published with his first wife, Mary Jane Randolph, and his second wife, Kate Corson Randolph, both gifted spiritual practitioners in their own right.[3] In handbooks, pamphlets, novels, newspaper articles, manifestos, historiography, a wildly embellished memoir, printed "private letters," handwritten manuscripts, and more, he taught the curious a kind of DIY occult practice that used their own bodies—through study, sex, and drugs—to make connections to the spirit world. But the gospel of a hallucinatory, cosmic sex magic was not an easy path for anyone in the late nineteenth century, much less a Black man. Randolph struggled against racism (which he deeply internalized), economic precarity, and an abiding sense of being an outsider his entire life. Even when it came to his own theories, he seems to have vacillated between belief and doubt. He shot himself in the head in his front yard in 1875, at age forty-nine.

Yet in a turn of events that fulfilled some of Randolph's grandest ambitions, after his death his work helped bring about an efflorescence of late nineteenth- and early twentieth-century transnational occultism. Better-remembered occult groups like the Theosophical Society, the Hermetic Brotherhood of Luxor, and the Hermetic Society of the Golden Dawn formed in the late 1870s and 1880s and drew heavily on Randolph's thought, as John Patrick Deveney shows in his invaluable biography.[4] The American Rosicrucian R. S. Clymer heralded Randolph as the founder of that order, although his accounts greatly simplified and regularized Randolph's beliefs.[5] Clymer's Philosophical Publishing Company, the California esoteric publisher Health Research, and other occult and new age publishing companies in the United States, South America, and Europe continued to reprint Randolph's writings through the twentieth century.

Randolph's legacy has made him a subject of renewed interest among scholars of religious esotericism, including Deveney, Joscelyn Godwin, Hugh Urban, Christine Ferguson, and Lana Finley, who have worked to restore Randolph's place in the history of occult thought.[6] More recently, L. H. Stallings and Benjamin Kahan have examined Randolph's experiments with sexual knowledge. In *Funk the Erotic: Transaesthetics and Black Sexual Culture*, Stallings argues that Randolph demonstrates how "another model of humanity" beyond conventional definitions of the human "could be made by individuals willing to articulate other means of embodiment and pleasure's significance to these alternatives."[7] Her work aptly demonstrates Randolph's own insistence that "the sexive principle, habitude, and instinct in the human ... means, implies, and leads to immeasurably more and deeper things than the average thinker ever dreams of."[8] Kahan includes a brief but illuminating discussion of Randolph in *The Book of Minor Perverts: Sexology, Etiology, and the Emergences of Sexuality*, arguing that he stands as "one of the earliest theorists and instantiators of sexual subjectivity."[9] Stallings and Kahan convincingly elevate Randolph from an eccentric footnote in the history of sexuality to one of its most inventive, important thinkers. Jayna Brown's brilliantly heady *Black Utopias: Speculative Life and the Music of Other Worlds* brings together the sexual and esoteric genealogies of Randolph's work by suggesting that for him, "sexual and spiritual ecstasy were porous." Brown places Randolph in a tradition of nineteenth-century Black mystics that includes Zilpha Elaw, Jarena Lee, Sojourner Truth, and Rebecca Cox Jackson, who understand touch as a means of accessing "alternatives senses of self."[10]

Randolph's relevance to this project may be less obvious. I will argue that he dedicated his life to building otherworldly undergrounds, in person and in print, as alternatives to the public spheres and counterpublics that so often excluded or insulted him. Yet I should say from the outset that his secret societies were sparsely populated and short-lived, and he struggled to keep his publishing business afloat. Although Randolph helped invent the late nineteenth-century occult underground, as a result of some combination of racism, personal eccentricity, and the circuitous paths of his influence, he did not enjoy the chance to participate in it. Thus it is hard to argue that Randolph wrote from an actually existing underground, or even that his idiosyncratic thought is representative of a broader underground imaginary. In his writings, Randolph most strongly identified as belonging nowhere at all—not to the abolitionist movement, not to the spiritualist movement, not to Black people, not to white people, not even to this earth. But if Randolph never fully got to inhabit the undergrounds he imagined, he seems to have fantasized all the more wildly for that. Here I try to thread through the sprawl of Randolph's work, while staying with its messiness, to explore how he used his position as an inveterate outsider to visualize ever more extraordinary undergrounds, which would not be social subgroups but worlds that vastly exceed this one.

Randolph's Occult Racial Theory

The spiritualist movement Randolph joined as a speaker and a trance medium in the 1850s was far removed from the esoteric theories and practices he would eventually espouse. Although detractors derided it as a fringe movement, spiritualism was widespread and visible. Its practitioners prided themselves on their rationality; they communicated with the spirits of the dead, but they insisted that they did so by scientific, not supernatural, means. Spiritualists tended to be active in progressive causes, including abolitionism, feminism, socialism, free love, temperance, land reform, and Native American rights. In their communications with the afterlife, they sought to use the wisdom of the next world to bring harmony to this one, and the spirits of the dead who appeared in spiritualist circles frequently spoke in support of social reform.

In 1858, however, Randolph renounced the spiritualist movement. In a series of lectures, he attacked the characters of leading spiritualists, ridiculed their trances as "jugglery" (or worse, demon possession), dismissed their "business of world-bettering" as hypocrisy, and railed against some of their central tenets, such as the belief popularized by Andrew Jackson Davis that only select souls are immortal and thus all spirits are good.[11] For all the spiritualists' professed antiracism, Randolph recalled that whenever he had questioned aspects of spiritualism or sought rest from his grueling work as a medium, they "openly taunted me with my natural, ethnological condition, and insulted my soul by denying me common intelligence."[12] He concludes, "My crime was *rete mucosmal*," or residing in the color of his skin.[13] He relates that after a harrowing suicide attempt (or, as he explained it elsewhere, a transformative experience with Egyptian hashish), he finally left spiritualism behind.[14] The spiritualists had "exhausted all logic trying to prove me a nobody,—themselves the only real thinkers," he recounts. "Still I survived; and—despite them all."[15]

Following Randolph's break with spiritualism, he began to develop his own theories about extraterrestrial spirit worlds. Moreover, he envisioned building a different kind of community around these beliefs: not a fringe movement but an underground. While midcentury spiritualism's reformist principles meant that it strove to be exoteric, Randolph's ideas were esoteric, cultivating secrecy as an essential component of knowledge. At the same time, this knowledge was more horizontal than that of spiritualism; whereas spiritualism's revelations were indirect, conveyed through a medium, Randolph instructed practitioners how to make direct contact with spirits themselves. The spirits, for their part, were freakier; while spiritualism communicated with the spirits of the (deserving) dead, occultists saw a universe full of spirits, some of whom had never taken human form and many of whom were decidedly nasty. Though spiritualists touted their practices as modern, rational, and scientific, Randolph traced his practices back to ancient traditions of magic. Finally, and perhaps most important, spiritualists adamantly denied that there was anything erotic about the supernatural connections that took place at séances and trances (even as many spiritualists were themselves sex radicals). But Randolph embraced sex as a key element of his occult practice.

To some extent, Randolph's ideas overlapped with contemporaneous European occultist movements, especially in England and France, and he often referred to himself as a Rosicrucian. But he cautioned that this was not the trifling version that passed for Rosicrucianism in Europe and the Americas. Rather, he explained, "the Rosicrucian system is, and never was other else than a door" to the "inner crypts" of his ancient, deeper, truer system.[16] Indeed, Randolph asserted that he had only ever used the label strategically, because it gave him passage over the color line:

> Very nearly *all* that I have given as Rosicrucianism originated in my soul; and scarce a single thought, only suggestions, have I borrowed from those who, in ages past, called themselves by that name—one which served me well as a vehicle wherein to take *my* mental treasures to a market, which gladly opened its doors to that name, but would, and did, slam its portals in the face of the tawny student of Esoterics.[17]

Ironically, even as Western occultists balked at a "tawny student of Esoterics" like Randolph, they often invested their knowledge with power by racializing it. Randolph similarly attributed his secrets to "Oriental," "Chaldaic," "Persian," "Egyptian," "Asiatic," or "Arab" sources. But his belief system may also have had other, less acknowledged influences. He spent almost two of his most productive writing years in Louisiana, and it is difficult to imagine that he did not study the area's rich African diasporic religious life. Although in one of his lectures he boasts of exposing "the whole tribe of VOUDEAUX in New Orleans," he also concedes "it was from one of the VOUDEAUX queens ... that I gained much of my knowledge," and elsewhere he cites hoodoo and obeah practices and flaunts the secrets he learned from "the quadroons of Louisiana."[18] Perhaps Randolph discovered, as the formerly enslaved magnetic physician Abraham Peters in Pauline Hopkins's novel *Contending Forces* put it, that "*Magnifyin'* [i.e., using magnetism] and *hoodooin'* is 'bout the same thing down thar."[19] (I'll say more about the relation between Hopkins and Randolph later.)

The connections Randolph makes between occultism and the knowledge of people of color, especially women, mean that, like various writers in previous chapters, he constructs an underground in part by racializing and feminizing it. But Randolph did not just traffic in manufactured exoticism; he also developed a more philosophically and politically complicated theory of the occult anchored in his own racialized identity. "I owe my successes,—mental,—to my conglomerate blood; my troubles and poverty to the same source," he asserted.[20] In nearly all of his published works, he refers to himself as "a *sang mêlée*," a term that derives from colonial intellectual Médéric Louis Élie Moreau de Saint-Méry's infamous taxonomy of racial mixture in Saint-Domingue, which describes those with the smallest fraction of African ancestry as *sang-mêlé*.[21] Two aspects of Randolph's use of the term bear noting here. One, he consistently identifies himself using the feminine version, *sang mêlée*, a self-description that may represent the logical extension of his arguments against any singular, permanent gender identity, which I discuss further below. Two, Randolph's spelling fuses Moreau de Saint-Méry's attempt to impose order on Saint-Domingue's multiracial society with a word for the event Moreau de Saint-Méry wished to prevent: a *mêlée*, or disorderly struggle. His use of the term invokes at once regimes of racialization and their defiance—a tension that runs through his life's work. Randolph asserted that his identity as a *sang mêlée* afforded him "peculiar mental power and almost marvelous versatility": because he already channeled multiple racial identities within his body, he reasoned, he was predisposed to channel other identities, not of this world. As Christine Ferguson observes, this theory accepts "the necessity of phenotypical difference" but turns it into the basis for a belief that would dissolve the bounded self in the "conscious, purposeful communion between mortals and higher cosmic intelligences."[22] Through this logic, Randolph transformed his racialization from a source of exclusion to a means of extraordinary connection.

Describing his powers as a *sang mêlée*, Randolph expounds a kind of strategic essentialism of the supernatural. But he also suggests that his occult abilities have been sharpened by the lived experience of anti-Blackness. He traces his abilities as a medium to an attunement to the power of others so acute that it verges on painful. Beginning from a young age, he recounts, "I could feel the influence and feelings of all with whom I was brought in contact; I became morbidly sensitive."[23] Randolph calls this condition "abnormal," but his unasked-for consciousness of others' "influence and feelings" evokes quotidian experiences of racism and the kinds of skills developed in hopes of surviving it.[24] In this origin story, Randolph reframes racialized hyperawareness and alienation as signs of supernatural capability. As he writes in *Dealings with the Dead*,

> There are seasons when men and women of a certain mould, without the least apparent cause, are plunged into the very midst of the blackest barathrum of misery and woe, and who ten times a year pass through the body of a death too fearful in its agonies to be even faintly imaged by those of a different make-up. They complain, and are met with the stereotyped: "Fancy! Hypochondrias! Delusion!" ... To the looker-on of surface, Yes; to the student of the soul and its mysteries, No![25]

Randolph insists that the suffering of "men and women of a certain mould"—a word that suggestively refers to both internal and external character—is not only real, despite others' dismissals, but it is the sign that their knowledge of the world exceeds that which others are willing to accept. (Note how Randolph describes both their suffering—"plunged into the very midst of the blackest barathrum"—and their knowledge, opposed to that of "the looker-on of surface," with analogous imagery and that this imagery is subterranean.) We might hear the echo of Randolph's connection between his racialization and his gifts as a medium nearly half a century later in the supernatural overtones of W. E. B. Du Bois's famous formulation of double consciousness in *The Souls of Black Folk*: the "peculiar sensation" of being "gifted with second sight in this American world."[26] As I will discuss further, I am almost certain that we hear much more than the echo of Randolph's thought in a novel by his onetime Boston neighbor Pauline Hopkins, *Of One Blood*, whose protagonist, Reuel Briggs, is—like Randolph—a melancholy, alienated, mixed-race medical doctor, born to a clairvoyant mother, who experiments with mesmerism and magic mirrors, writes magazine articles on "spiritualistic phenomena," and travels to Ethiopia.[27] Surely one could hardly find a better plot summary of *Of One Blood* than Randolph's description of his own turn to the occult underground: "Failing to find sympathy on earth," he searched for it "in the awful labyrinths that underlie the tomb."[28]

Cosmic Undergrounds

The details of Randolph's cosmology changed from work to work, but they might be summed up by Fred Moten's statement: "Fuck a home in this world, if you think you have one."[29] If we took a properly cosmic perspective, Randolph held, we could all recognize ourselves as adrift from the here and now. He generally believed that all beings begin as "monads," thoughts of

God that scatter over the universe like a kind of divine particulate. Some remain immaterial, and some reach worlds, including Earth, where they are embedded in rocks beneath its surface. Over a long period they materialize in a succession of geological, plant, and animal forms and finally become human souls—a trajectory leading from extraterrestrial worlds to the underground to human beings.[30] After death, human souls travel to a vast and heterogeneous system of spirit realms—some located on belts around the planets, some in a zone that encircles all the galaxies, and others still beyond them—and arrive at a location corresponding to their spiritual development. The souls may be stuck where they land, or they may continue the process of spiritual development and move through the "middle states" of the spirit world to reach an unimaginably radiant "soul world."

Randolph's criteria for these celestial divisions varied over the course of his career. At times he delineates them in starkly racist terms, asserting that souls of African, Native American, and some Asian people inhabit the lower realms and stand little chance of leaving them. At other times (sometimes within the same text), he contends, "Ties, blood, race, or family count for little or nothing over there."[31] And in his late work, he declares that the "choice abodes of spirit-land" primarily belong to people of color:

> There are people of all kinds there, even "N[—]" and *Sangs Melees*,— lots of them too, *vivat!*—and the dark-hued Southern and Oriental races and peoples outnumber the Northern and fair ones in the ratio of about twelve thousand to one hundred; besides excelling them in the same degree in mind, love, knowledge, force of character, and power of soul. . . . [D]ark-hued beings . . . constitute the population of the heavens proper.[32]

In his descriptions of the spirit realms, Randolph's racial thought oscillates excruciatingly between replicating the earthly categories that thwarted and hurt him and creating a world unto itself. In these latter instances, the spirit realms offer not only an exit from white supremacy but an eternity of redress, which gathers people of color from all over the earth to enjoy dominion beyond it.

Randolph pictures the spheres, divisions, zones, and sections of the spirit world in elaborate detail, including their distinctive environments, architecture, and cultural institutions. The magnitude and detail of Randolph's world-building recall Charles Fourier's intricate taxonomies of the forces of the universe, whose "ungovernable profusion," Jayna Brown argues, creates not order but a kind of sensuous accumulation of detail.[33] The appearance of each sphere, Randolph explains, corresponds to the spiritual development of its inhabitants, because they are a "projection" from the "souls who dwell together and create their own scenery and surrounding."[34] Randolph means this quite literally: in the spirit worlds, "each thought possesses an inherent vitality of its own, as also form, proportion, and coherence"; in short, spirit worlds are made of palpable ideas.[35] As such, they contain both familiar forms of animal life and "entirely different" ones that embody "some salient and positive love, principle, or affection."[36] Human souls look like earthly people but instead of blood, "only a pure, white, or colorless electric current" courses through them. They wear clothes and have no bad teeth or saliva.[37] They move through space using magnetism. They have musical sounds and note values, so the spheres in which they gather are literally harmonious and rhythmical.[38] They have buildings, cities, schools, art, and music, and more "fun" than we do.[39] They also have better sex, for "up there, and there only, can its deep mysteries be fully known, its keener joys be felt!"[40] Souls do get married, but these marriages do not depend on "justice, parson, or priest," and they "last just so long as the parties thereto are agreeably and mutually pleased with, and attracted, to each other, and no longer."[41]

Looking for language to describe the relation between our familiar world and the mysteries of the spirit realms, Randolph reached for the subterranean. "All the vast congeries of constellations yet revealed to the telescope, are but the archipelagos,—the island groups upon the bosom of the *abyss*," he explained.[42] Randolph's image of "the *abyss*" portrays the spirit world as unperceived by modes of empirical knowledge that only detect formations above the surface ("archipelagos"). Other occultists also invoked the image of the subterranean, most notably Randolph's contemporary Emma Hardinge Britten. But the differences between the meanings they attach to the underground are illuminating. Britten understood the subterranean as a location within a hierarchy of spiritual development. She envisioned a spirit world arrayed across realms of the "mundane," the "super-mundane" (consisting of those "who have attained to the highest conditions of Angelic exaltation"), and the "sub-mundane" (consisting of "those lower orders of being" who live "below, beneath the earth," in an "*anti-state* of mortal being").[43] Her novel *Ghost Land* (serialized in 1872, published as a book in 1876) elaborates this moral topography through the story of its narrator's conversion to occultism by the Brotherhood, an international secret society led by a powerful German adept, Professor Felix von Marx, who proves to be all too connected to the sub-mundane.⁴⁴ These connections manifest in a literal subterranean inclination: a "*mineral* quality in my organism" that Professor von Marx explains "attracts to me and easily subjects to my control the elementary spirits who rule in the mineral kingdoms," enabling him, among other gifts, to "tell the quality of mines, however distant."⁴⁵ As a consequence of his sub-mundane disposition, Professor von Marx's studies open "an abyss of mystery and unrest," and through them he has "sunk down to the sphere of elementary spirits," bringing the narrator with him; the second half of the novel recounts the feats required to "redeem them from the depths" of these "fathomless abysses."⁴⁶ But where Britten's subterranean imagery maps onto hierarchies of spiritual development, Randolph's subterranean imagery is unconnected to them. Rather, for him the underground becomes an expression of the most unimaginable possibilities of the occult.

Specifically, Randolph envisions the spirit world as this world's underground. Through occult study and practice, he promises, one could cultivate "the ability, by self-effort or otherwise, to drop beneath the floors of the outer world, and come up, as it were, upon the other side."⁴⁷ Randolph reused the phrase "to drop beneath the floors of the outer world" multiple times in his writings to describe practical occultism; its image of the spirit world's simultaneous proximity and exteriority to everyday life seems to have resonated with him.⁴⁸ But he also used the image of the underground to explain that the spirit world was interior, buried within a person's soul, because the "abysses, labyrinths, and most secret recesses of your being" themselves hold a microcosm of the universe.⁴⁹ To be clear, for Randolph, these subterranean regions of the soul are not a metaphor. They are an actual portal. Randolph charts their egress to unknown worlds in the first half of *Dealings with the Dead: The Human Soul, Its Migrations and Its Transmigrations*, which is narrated (through the medium of Randolph) by a disembodied soul named Cynthia Temple. After dying, Temple recounts how the "soul-principle" within her "rapidly sunk down into one of the profoundest labyrinths of its own vast caverns":

> Down, down, still lower and deeper into the awful abyss of itself it sank, until at last it stood solitary and alone in one of its own secret halls. The outer realm, with all its pains and joys, cares, sorrows and ambitions, hopes, likes, antipathies and aspirations; all its shadows and fitful gleams of light, were left behind, and naught of the great wide world remained.⁵⁰

Having descended into her own soul, Temple then finds herself in the "Soul-world," an inconceivably beautiful world of heightened sensory experience where she joins her fellow spirits, including an ancient Egyptian king and Rosicrucian with the enviable name Thotmor, who becomes her lover. This "boundless realm of mysteries," as Randolph described it elsewhere, reveals earthly existence to be simply "the outer realm" of unimaginably greater, unguessed worlds.[51] Imagine the city mysteries on a cosmic scale, in which the city becomes the planet and its mysterious tunnels and cellars extend across galaxies. Next I examine the secret societies Randolph founded to aid other "delvers into the mines of mystery" to plunge into "nature's deeper departments, and the subtler crypts of the unfathomable human soul," and access these spirit realms.[52]

"We Do Not Count Ourselves as Altogether of This World": Sex Magical Collectivities

We have seen how Randolph invoked images of underground spaces to describe occultism, picturing the subterranean as an access point to the unknown universe. But at the same time he was conceptualizing occultism in subterranean terms, Randolph was also working hard to build occultism into an underground movement. As he moved around the United States, propelled by hardship and restlessness, he founded a series of secret societies devoted to his interpretation of Rosicrucianism: the Supreme Grand Lodge of the Triple Order in San Francisco in 1861, the Rosicrucian Club in Boston in the late 1860s or early 1870s, the Brotherhood of Eulis in Nashville in 1874, and another incarnation of the Supreme Grand Lodge—now of the Triplicate Order—in San Francisco in late 1874. The precise relationships between these organizations remain unclear, but Randolph framed all of them as alternatives to the mainstream spiritualist circles that mistreated him. "Ostracized by those for, and with whom I had labored since 1848; met with ingratitude at every step, I gladly accept the ostracism of the many for the good companionship of the few," he declared, "yet not so few after all, for day by day . . . our Brotherhood of Thinkers has increased."[53]

Randolph's swelling "Brotherhood of Thinkers" was probably fantasy. None of the lodges seems to have lasted more than a few months, and John Patrick Deveney wonders to what extent they existed at all. Deveney points out, "The theoretical organization of Randolph's groups always outstripped the actual," so "how much of this structure was wishful thinking and how much reality is a matter of conjecture."[54] Yet it is Randolph's "wishful thinking" about undergrounds that particularly interests me. Evidence suggests he did a lot of it, and it is here that we can find his fullest accounting of the meaning and possibilities of subterranean life.[55] He inserted a manifesto for a Rosicrucian order in the 1863 novel *The Wonderful Story of Ravalette* and in 1871 issued another manifesto, "The Asiatic Mystery," which also appears in slightly different forms in Randolph's edition of the *Divine Pymander* of Hermes Trismegistus, *Soul!*, and *Eulis!* Randolph's last book, *The Book of the Triplicate Order*, was a handbook optimistically "Printed for the Use of the Brotherhood, Candidates for Membership, and all who Desire to Know Who and What We Are, and the Work we are Doing." An 1869 pamphlet commemorating the Rosicrucian Club's "grand day of Jubilee," *Rosicrucian: Out of the Shell*, suggests the pleasures to be had with "orgies" of "co-conspirators."[56] The celebration takes place on a boat, with "cans of Ice Cream" (6), a gymnastic performance, music by the poignantly named "Band of Hope" (3), and "that dinner!!!!!!!!!!!!" (5). It ends with a song in honor of the occasion, which begins,

> All hail! the Rosicrucian Club,
>   And let outsiders stare, Sir;
> They know us not—"aye there's the rub"—
>   Leave them to their despair, Sir. (8)

The song exults in the Rosicrucian Club's combination of idiosyncrasy ("let outsiders stare") and mystery ("they know us not—'aye there's the rub'"). Sung to the tune of "Yankee Doodle," it supersedes the familiar patriotic song with jubilant weirdness, much as the celebration of the Rosicrucian holiday on July 4 supersedes Independence Day and Randolph's dating of the year as "Anno Rosic. II" (presumably marking two years since the group's founding, as Deveney notes) supersedes the conventional calendar.[57] It is impossible to know if the Jubilee did occur as described. Given that the pamphlet references twelve people by name, some event probably did, although perhaps on a smaller scale than suggested by Randolph's reference to "the unnamed great" "who throng the Club" (11). But expansiveness was key to Randolph's underground imaginary. "Every Rosicrucian is known, and is the sworn brother of every other Rosicrucian the wide world over," he writes in "The Rosicrucians, Who and What They Are," and "after once becoming a true Rosicrucian, it is next to impossible that he can ever afterward come to want."[58] Read in light of Randolph's own hardships, this image of a secret mutual aid society on an international scale is moving, but the pamphlet *Guide to Clairvoyance* extends its mode of belonging even further. "I have associates," he declares there. "We do not count ourselves as altogether of this world."[59]

In addition to founding secret societies, Randolph sought to construct a virtual occult underground through a sub-rosa body of writing that his more widely available publications hinted at but could not themselves contain.[60] In interpolated statements, footnotes, and publishers' advertisements, Randolph promoted a shadow repertoire: pamphlets, "privately printed letters," handwritten manuscripts, formulas, and correspondence disclosing secrets that "cannot well be printed in [a] book."[61] Texts like "The Golden Letter," "The True Oriental Secret," "The Ansairetic Mystery," "The Mysteries of Eulis," and "The Golden Secret!" showed readers how they could use their sexuality—in combination with a good diet, drugs, devices like magnets and mirrors, mental concentration, and study—to exercise their paranormal capacities.[62] These practices constituted an extreme version of what Kyla Schuller calls "sensorial discipline," the regulation of bodily impressibility in order to secure membership in civilization that Schuller identifies as a primary technology of late nineteenth-century biopolitics.[63] But Randolph directed his sensorial discipline toward the amplification of feeling rather than its mitigation and toward membership in a sphere that lay outside civilization—or beneath it. In supplying "keys which open doors sealed from man, but which are ready to swing wide when the proper 'Open Sesame' is spoken by those worthy of admission," his precepts promised to transform strangers reading them into a subterranean society of adepts whose community extended far beyond earthly realms.[64]

Randolph may have run this clandestine mail-order business for profit, although the prices of most texts were so low (or in some cases, nonexistent) that this motive seems insufficient. It's also possible that Randolph created it in order to avoid scrutiny, particularly after New York passed a state law prohibiting the sale of obscene materials in 1868, which in turn prompted Anthony Comstock to lobby Congress successfully to outlaw the distribution of obscene materials through the US mail in 1873.[65] The fact that Randolph was a Black man writing about sex probably would have made him a particular target of state authorities; the fact that he was a Black man writing about how sex could "revolutionize the globe" could only have compounded his danger.[66] Randolph may also have concluded that such subterranean writing offered the best way to reach the "democratic underlayer of society," where he believed true sexual knowledge belonged, and to circumvent the media dominance of "the upper strata," whose "newspapers by myriads" spread "gross and culpable non-knowledge" about "all the vital points that cluster around the one word 'sex.'"[67] At the same time, Randolph's underground body of work recalls Foucault's argument that the power of an *ars erotica* derives from its secrecy: one needs to "hold it in the greatest reserve, since, according to tradition, it would lose its effectiveness and its virtue by being divulged."[68] (It's hard not to believe—at least, I want to believe—that Foucault intended his language here to echo the practice of intercourse without ejaculation that has been part of so many traditions of *ars erotica*, sometimes including Randolph's prescriptions.) Thus, in addition to being instrumental, the relation between the underground circulation of Randolph's writings to their sex magic content seems reciprocal: underground circulation heightens their occult capacity.

Randolph often explicitly addresses his writings about sex to the personal needs of heterosexual married couples, but this address is at odds with the powers he ascribes to sexual activity, as well as with the capaciousness of his ideas about gender and sexuality. "I believe in love, all the way through," he declared, "and while I live will help every man, woman, and the betweenities to win, obtain, intensify, deepen, purify, strengthen and keep it, and I will help all others to do the same. There! That's me! I mean it!"[69] He counted earthly gender identity as "provisional,—that is, limited to a given arc of the universal polygon of souls' duration," and God is both male and female in his account.[70]

Accordingly, while Randolph taught both "feminine" and "masculine" occult practices, these correspond not to the practitioner's gender identity but to the types of power they exercise.[71] The entire universe, he held, was organized around male and female forces, but he saw earthly notions of physiological sex difference as a ruse: "[I]t *don't* follow that all who wear the Penis are in soul true males, or that a vagina is the sign of womanness."[72] Randolph's conception of what Benjamin Kahan calls "misattuned bodies and souls" leads Kahan to identify him as "the first theorist of inversion," the late nineteenth-century sexological theory that explained same-sex desire as a matter of being externally one sex but internally another.[73] But I am less sure we can fold Randolph's ideas into the taxonomies of sexology. His ideas about sex exceed inversion's binary model, extending to the "betweenities," mutability, and the possibility of holding multiple sexual subjectivities simultaneously in a single body. Moreover, his sweeping rejection of physiological sex difference differs markedly from sexology's attempts to reify it, stigmatizing "perceived sexual ambiguity" through "a tendency to racialize it," as Siobhan Somerville observes.[74] Randolph seems not to be thinking in the emerging terms of modern sexuality so much as working out an erotic praxis that lies both in their shadow and on an entirely different plane.

Randolph's ideas about sex were uncontained not only by binary sex and gender identities but also by identity, period. Where Foucault writes that in "the nineteenth century sexuality . . . became the stamp of individuality," for Randolph, sex did not personalize; it made one porous to other, invisible presences, less like an individual and more like a force field.[75] In this respect, Randolph departs both from what Peter Coviello describes as the concurrent "turning of sex into another of the liberal self's secured properties" and from the most prominent sexual dissident movement of the day, free love, which by the late nineteenth century was dominated by individualist anarchists who saw sexual freedom as an expression of individual sovereignty.[76] Instead, Randolph called back to an earlier incarnation of free love, the Fourierist utopian communities of the 1850s, where "passional attraction" organized new forms of erotic and social life.[77] More specifically, Randolph's theory of sex amplified his theory of mediumship, which he believed did not involve yielding oneself to the direction of a spirit (as most spiritualists supposed) but was instead a "strange blending," by which the medium could hold "MIXED IDENTITIES" in a single body.[78] Both these theories, in turn, seem homologous to Randolph's belief that his position as what he called a "composite man" (i.e., racially mixed) specially qualified him for acts of supernatural communion.[79] Sex offered the most expansive possibilities for such communion because "soul-power and sex-power are co-efficients and co-dependents." By cultivating one's sexual capacities, practitioners could become connected to celestial forces and harness their "power, knowledge, energy, force." But this can happen "*only* at the moment, the very instant, of the holy, full, mutual and pure orgasm, or ejection of the three fluids and two auras—i.e., prostatic, seminal, and female lymph or lochia."[80] Mutual orgasm, in other words, opens a momentary pathway to the cosmos, enabling humans to connect with spirits. Thus, while Randolph may have addressed himself to couples, in his account the best sex always involves more than two participants. Moreover, the sexual fluids emitted at this moment of ecstatic extraterrestrial contact could enable even further connections: "Dolts and fools may laugh," but they could be used for "the charging of mirrors with the divine spiritual reflective powers which characterize them."[81] With a magic mirror, readers could practice clairvoyance, "leaping all the barriers of the outer senses and world" to become "*en rapport* with a thousand knowledges" on earth and beyond it.[82]

Randolph's sex magic promises an array of earthly benefits, including heightened pleasure, physical health, guaranteed love, the empowerment of women, and the production of superior children. But in his subterranean publications he reveals that its real value goes beyond this. "Churches and marriage exist as repressions,—our system in expansion," he asserts in "The Asiatic Mystery": "Love forever, *against* the world!"[83] In this declaration, Randolph's revelations about sex refuse the world as their proper sphere and even array themselves "*against*" it. Although the explosive potential Randolph claims for sex magic may be self-serving, it also recalls Audre Lorde's hypothesis in "The Uses of the Erotic" that the erotic is "so feared" because it "becomes a lens through which we scrutinize all aspects of our existence."[84] For Randolph, who believed that one could develop clairvoyance through sex, Lorde's description of the erotic as a "lens" for seeing the world anew is especially apt. Crucially, Randolph's notion of clairvoyance extends beyond the ability to see into the future; it also becomes an alternative means to move through the present. He advised in *Guide to Clairvoyance*, "Keep your design constantly before you, and your soul and inner senses will make grooves for themselves, and continue to move in them as cars on rails or wheels in ruts. Let your groove be clair-voyance!"[85] Rather than its conventional derivation from "to see" (like *voyeur*), Randolph's nonce etymology of *clairvoyance* derives the word from "way" (like *convoy*), picturing "clair-voyance" as a mode of transportation like a carriage or a railway, or the literalizations of the Underground Railroad in chapter 3. Once adepts cultivate their latent powers, he predicts they will "revolutionize the globe," "bidding farewell to many of [the] modes, moods, opinions, sentiments, thoughts, and procedures" of current civilization and ushering in "a new epoch of human history."[86]

We can never know how far Randolph's subterranean literature actually traveled, though it seems likely that, like his secret societies, the virtual underground he envisioned mostly failed to materialize. But if we think of these undergrounds as not only theoretical but also as *theorizing*, they assume a different cast: less half-baked, futile projects than sustained thinking and study about the nature, purpose, and possibilities of the underground. Randolph spins out an extraordinary account of its power in *P. B. Randolph, The "Learned Pundit," and "Man with Two Souls,"* a kind of patchwork memoir that combines a biography, a prison interview, letters, testimonials, and newspaper reports. These materials frame the story of how three men scheme to seize control of one of Randolph's sex magic manuscripts, "The Golden Secret," by informing the Boston police that Randolph is circulating obscene free love literature. The police raid his apartment, find his publications, arrest him, and jail him. Randolph is then arraigned in the last part of the book, "The Great Free Love Trial," a thirty-page judicial spectacular involving not two but three sides—Randolph, the government, and a representative of free love—and a jury "selected from all the religious sects in the State" and "African, Asiatic, German, English, American, Spanish" nationalities.[87] The trial is obviously fiction, and the story of the men's plot and Randolph's imprisonment seems likely to be so, too.[88] But their overheated account of the attempted repression of Randolph's sex magic underground indicates what he saw as its revolutionary potential.

At the trial, the prosecutor breathlessly describes the wide reach of Randolph's "alluring doctrines of freedom" (69). In his apartment, police found "vast numbers of letters to him" (72)—though Randolph "had taken the extraordinary precaution to number these letters, and then erase the mailing places, signatures and dates!" (72)—from people all over, "from crowded city to hillside cabin, men and women, married and single, rich and poor, of all lands, tongues, grades of life, custom, color and religion" (73). Indeed, the prosecutor himself has read Randolph's book on love and sex, *Casca Llana* (which attempts "to follow the Grand Passion into its very crypts"), and "only by the most herculean efforts of the will, was I able to resist its logic, or to avoid being utterly swept along its tide by the vast fascination centred in every page and in almost every line!" (71).[89] Even as he argues his case, he reports "something inside continually urging me to speak the words, 'Go, Randolph, you are free!'" (75). As a result, the prosecutor asks the court "to put an enduring injunction" on Randolph's works "and to totally suppress their future publication" (72).

What makes Randolph "*the* most *dangerous* man and author on the soil of America, if not of the entire globe" (70) is not so much his individual magnetism but the threat his ideas pose when taken up by an unknown, unidentifiable body of associates. "Is it safe to tolerate a body of men whose secrets are deeper than the grave?" the prosecutor demands (75). Although "none of us here know" these secrets, "and those who do are bound not to reveal it" (73), the prosecutor warns that they will inspire "the men, but especially the women," to "undermine" the "very foundations of a true and conservative social order" (77): "Fired by the enthusiasm of this weird magician, fascinated by the desire to test their new-found power, they grow restive and restless ... until at last, grown sharp, cunning, sure and fearless, they throw off all restraint, and we are plunged neck-deep in the resistless torrent of a social revolution and domestic cataclysm, wherein men must take back seats and universal woman come to the front!" (71). In the prosecutor's fears, Randolph voices his dreams of an occult underground that radicalizes its members by cultivating unsuspected powers in them, connecting their transformed consciousnesses to one another and to the cosmos, ultimately toppling hierarchies and "upheaving the world!" (77). The remainder of this chapter explores the recurrence of such visions of an occult underground in Randolph's writing and considers their relation to his political organizing during the Civil War and Reconstruction.

"This Is Possible Destiny!": Randolph's Black Revolutionary Prophecies

Randolph's occultism is both so totalizing and so *out there* that it can seem utterly disconnected from earthly events. Yet his most prolific writing years were also a period of intense political activism, when he was recruiting Black soldiers for the Union army, helping found the National Equal Rights League, teaching in and advocating for Freedmen's Bureau schools in Louisiana, participating in various Colored Conventions, and lecturing and writing in support of these endeavors. John Patrick Deveney describes this work as "almost entirely removed from Randolph's usual occult concerns," and other scholars have likewise tended to consider his occultism and his political activism as separate tracks in his life.[90] But references to anti-Black violence and scenes of Black liberation materialize in his occult writing like its own attendant spirits. These moments invite us to consider the politics of Randolph's occultism, particularly in light of the repeated frustration of his political activism, and to read his dreams of "upheaving the world" and joining other worlds alongside the unfulfilled promises of Emancipation. Given the irregularity of Randolph's stated politics, I am hesitant to overstate his political radicalism. Still, we might heed his avowal that "there are a great many more 'radical' and other passions in the human soul, than either [Welsh utopian socialist Robert] Owen, [French utopian socialist Charles] Fourier, [French socialist and anarchist forerunner Pierre-Joseph] Pro[u]dhon, [US spiritualist] Professor [Joseph Rodes] Buchanan, [German phrenologist Franz Joseph] Gall, [US phrenologist

Orson Squire] Fowler, or even [US occultist] William Fishbough ... ever thought or dreamed of."[91]

In particular, I want to suggest that the concurrence of Randolph's political activism and his efforts to build an occult underground place his extravagant thinking against the "double bind of emancipation" that Saidiya Hartman names "the burdened individuality of freedom."[92] Rather than breaking decisively from slavery, Hartman argues, legal emancipation introduced new modes of racial subjection, now centered in "liberal narratives of individuality" that "idealize mechanisms of domination and discipline."[93] She explains, "If the nascent mantle of sovereign individuality conferred rights and entitlements, it also served to obscure the coercion of 'free labor,' the transmutation of bonded labor, the invasive forms of discipline that fashioned individuality, and the regulatory production of blackness."[94] These new modes of racial subjection are not the unfortunate collateral damage of liberalism, nor do they mark a gradual incorporation into its privileges. "Rather, the excluded, marginalized, and devalued subjects that it engenders, variously contained, trapped, and imprisoned by nature's whimsical apportionments, in fact, enable the production of universality, for the denigrated and deprecated, those castigated and saddled by varied corporeal maledictions, are the fleshy substance that enable the universal to achieve its ethereal splendor."[95] But beyond this illusory universality, Randolph pictures an actual universe, whose far greater "ethereal splendor" outshines the earth and puts its arrangements to shame. To reach it, he rejects the bounds of the "sovereign individual" and instead envisions freedoms that would lie in extraordinary forms of collectivity—whether the preternaturally connected undergrounds he sought to build, what he called his "intromission" into other realms, or his understanding of one's own person as irreducibly plural, as never actually one's own.[96]

To get a sense of the connection between Randolph's occult undergrounds and his post-Emancipation politics, consider the migration of a phrase that recurs throughout his writing: "We may be happy yet!" In Randolph's occult works, this is an expression of esoteric knowledge: it appears in the mouths of all the spiritually gifted characters and as the "formula" (51) of the occult secret society the Mysterious Brotherhood in *The Wonderful Story of Ravalette*; he identifies it as his own "motto" (2) in another novel, *Tom Clark and His Wife*; and he uses it as the finale to the second part of *Eulis!*[97] But in between these works, Randolph reused the phrase in another context: the 1864 National Convention of Colored Men in Syracuse. The convention, which led to the founding of the National Equal Rights League, gathered a who's who of the leading Black political voices of the era, including Frederick Douglass, who was elected president, Henry Highland Garnet, William Howard Day, Frances Ellen Watkins Harper, J. W. C. Pennington, John Mercer Langston, William Wells Brown, Peter Clark, and Jermain Loguen. One wonders how the other delegates received Randolph. He had earned a reputation as a provocateur in antislavery meetings, often more concerned with proving his own "angular and eccentric" character than aiding the movement. Even as he wrote eloquently about his alienation from white people, he sometimes seemed actively to alienate himself from Black people.[98] At the same time, what room did the National Convention of Colored Men's resolution to "promote every thing that pertains to a well-ordered and dignified life" leave for a sex magician?[99]

Still, when Randolph had his turn to speak, he did not leave his occultism at the door. "Let the nations take warning!" he announced. When his "soul leaps onward a full century," he hears "the deep-toned melodies of an universal jubilee," which assures him that "we, the mourners, may and shall be happy yet."[100] In *The Wonderful Story of Ravalette* and his other writings, this indeterminately hopeful statement seems spoken out of the accumulation of personal grief that, according to Randolph, inevitably trails the spiritually gifted. But when Randolph uses it in his speech at the convention to speak of Black people collectively as "we, the mourners," he reframes this grief as something akin to Claudia Rankine's statement that "the condition of Black life is one of mourning."[101] His addition of "and shall" also uncovers new meanings in the motto: alone, "may be" indicates possibility, but paired with the confident prediction of "shall be," it appears as permission—a refusal of the interdiction of Black happiness that reminds us how radical his quest for erotic bliss in and out of this world was. Randolph's citation of his occult motto in the speech suggests political dimensions to his use of it elsewhere, while introducing into the convention configurations of power that were not necessarily on its agenda. Unlike his fellow delegates, Randolph pins his vision of Black freedom not on earnest progressivism but on a scene of clairvoyance, in which he sends his soul traveling into the future—a feat that Randolph very much believed in. Given this rhetoric and the history of the phrase "we may be happy yet," one might well wonder whether, when Randolph goes on to exhort his audience to cultivate their "latent powers," it may not be bootstrapping so much as a call to fire up their occult capacities.[102]

It was in his fiction—especially *The Wonderful Story of Ravalette*, first published in 1863—that Randolph delved most deeply, if bewilderingly, into occultism's racial politics. A wild tale of transmigration, clairvoyance, and shape-shifting, *The Wonderful Story of Ravalette* follows an "extremely enigmatical" young Rosicrucian, Beverly, whose physical appearance and biography closely resemble Randolph's.[103] A "*sang mêlée*" in whom "at least seven distinct strains of blood intermingled" (13), Beverly is "endowed with certain hyper-mental powers, among which was a strange intro-vision" (12). In Randolph's description, Beverly's powers take a shape that should by now sound familiar: "A volcano slumbered in that man's brain and heart, only it required a touch, a vent, in the right direction, to wake its fires and cause it to blaze forth vehemently" (10). No revolutions come to pass in *The Wonderful Story of Ravalette*. But Beverly's identification with the slumbering volcano forecasts how visions of Black liberation erupt without warning from the occult underground as the story unfolds. Throughout Beverly's life, he crosses paths with a series of mysterious men, some of whom seem trustworthy and some sinister, most of whose names are anagrams of Ravalette, and all of whom promise to initiate him into a recondite organization and its secrets. We finally learn that Ravalette is part of "a vast Association in the Spaces, known as the Power of the Shadow" (57) that seeks to "rule ... the world" by controlling its "crowned heads and officials" (222). Having heard of Beverly's reputation as a seer, the "Mysterious Brotherhood" wishes to recruit him to their numbers so that they can place him in the "sleep of Si-alam," a "magnetic slumber" (222) that Randolph describes elsewhere as a glimpse into a celestial underground, in which the seer could see "the wintry storm of falling worlds! lamps of God flickering in the Vault!—starry eyes glimpsing down into the Deeps!—pregnant earths waiting patiently to be delivered of the Humanity gestating in their bosoms."[104] Beverly resists the appeals of Ravalette (who is also Vatterale, Ettelavar, etc., as well as the transmigrated soul of a man Beverly's own transmigrated soul knew thousands of years before) to join the order. But out of gratitude for all Ravalette has taught him, he agrees to be put into the clairvoyant trance the Mysterious Brotherhood desires, in which he sees an astonishing series of earthly upheavals.

Racism drives the narrative in *The Wonderful Story of Ravalette*. It has "doomed [Beverly] from birth to strange and bitter experiences" (20), and Randolph connects Beverly's occult abilities to these experiences, much as he does his own. Aside from these brief expository remarks, Randolph rarely addresses racism directly. But apparitions of racial retribution repeatedly materialize, unexplained, in the novel's scenes of occult practice. At one séance, the disembodied hand of "a beautiful mulatto girl of fifteen or sixteen summers" appears from beneath the table and exposes one of the participants as her sexual abuser (180). It is the novel's centerpiece, though—an astonishing séance that Vatterale (Ravalette) leads in Paris—that most fully summons both anti-Black violence and the threat of its recoil. The séance begins when Vatterale places two rolls of paper in front of a visiting American, "Mr. Theodore Dwight" (199), whose name seems to refer to Theodore Dwight Jr., a member of the New York Colonization Society and one of the founders of the American Ethnological Society; the rolls of paper evoke the Arabic texts that Dwight collected from West Africa, sending Christian missionary materials in return.[105] (Randolph, who was also interested in Arabic texts, would likely have been familiar with Dwight's activities.) Suddenly, the papers vanish, and in their place appear "three horrible beings, somewhat resembling overgrown scorpions—only, that instead of claws, they had—hands and arms! for all the world like those of a newly-born negro child!" (200). The "detestable *things*" march in a circle before Dwight, "whirling and twirling" their limbs at him (200), "their eyes ... scintillating and flashing with the very essence of intense malignity" (203).

Randolph's comparison between the beings' limbs and those of a Black infant may constitute an especially grotesque example of his internalized racism. Yet the phantasmic nature of the beings, and their focus on Dwight in particular, suggests that they have more to do with the invented category called Blackness than with the people sorted into it. Vatterale explains to the participants in the séance that although the beings are not illusions, neither do they have an objective existence outside human thought: "The creatures you have beheld tonight are real, but ephemeral—they are Will-creations, and perish when the power ceases to act which called them into being" (206). Apparitional yet real, the human-scorpions of *The Wonderful Story of Ravalette*, which hold the onlookers in their "fearful spell" (201), graphically embody what Alexander Weheliye calls "racializing assemblages": "the political, economic, social, and cultural disciplining ... of the Homo sapiens species into assemblages of the human, not-quite-human, and nonhuman."[106] Notional as they are, these "Will-creations" are nonetheless "a genuine and horrid trinity of *facts*" (201) both because, as Weheliye explains, paraphrasing Marx, "race is a mysterious thing in that the social character of racial assemblages appears as an objective character stamped upon humans" and because this "objective character," despite being fictional, orders lived experience.[107] (Thus, while the human-scorpions ultimately disappear, they exhibit lasting material effects by leaving a trail of revolting green pus that makes a permanent mark on the carpet.) As they march implacably within the circle of the séance, waving their limbs and glaring, the "Will-creations" seem to be admonishing Dwight and the others for their own existence.

Yet the participants in the séance respond less to the shocking appearance of the beings than to some unnamed further danger they augur: "We were bound, chained, rooted, riveted to the spot, by a potentiality never to be questioned, never to be despised, for its might, when once it fastens upon its victim, is merciless, gripping, stern and unrelenting" (203). The participants' terror is directed toward "a potentiality," but it is "never to be questioned, never to be despised." They already envision how it will unfold: it will be "merciless, gripping, stern and unrelenting." If their response seems extraneous to their situation, their fear of this "potentiality never to be questioned," which would "bind" and "chain" those who consider themselves free, strongly evokes midcentury white Americans' fears about Black rebellion. Their fears seem confirmed when Vatterale removes the human-scorpion beings. After several minutes, vapor begins to rise from the floor and then "assumed a human semblance—but, Heavens! what a caricature!" It is "a hideous, half-naked, bow-legged, splay-footed monster," with "arms . . . longer than its entire body" and a "gigantic" head but no neck or face, just a "fearful-looking red gash" for a mouth (206). "From its horrible head there hung to the very ground the appearance of a tangled mass of wire-like worms" (206), which turn out to be chains. It drops these chains as, "stalking heavily across the floor right into the centre of the open space between us," it comes to stand in front of the audience, "slowly swaying to and fro, as if its heart was heavy" (206–7). Like the human-scorpions, this "caricature" manifests anti-Black visions of racialized Blackness, this time in sickeningly familiar form (a faceless, simian "monster"). Boasting of the chained being's subjection to his "will" (209), Vatterale commands that it give a musical performance. The header for this page of *The Wonderful Story of Ravalette* reads "How 'Spiritual' Music Is Made" (209), the quotation marks indicating a play on words that connects the "spiritual music" of the séance with the emergent term for Black religious music, especially that made by enslaved people.[108] The being's song bears out this connection: it sings "the most soul-stirring strains of music that ever fell on human hearing," in "tones that were so pathetic, so solemn, so supremely sorrow-freighted" that it "stirred depths" never before reached (209). (Compare Frederick Douglass's famous description of enslaved people's songs, whose "pathetic tone" "filled [him] with sadness" as they "pass through the chambers of his soul."[109]) But even as this being seems to embody anti-Blackness, it is also—like the minatory human-scorpions—unmistakably threatening, as if to warn the audience against the very ways of seeing that have given it form. Following the human-scorpions' conjuration of "a potentiality never to be questioned, never to be despised," when this being marches across the floor and drops its chains before the audience, it seems to bring the prospect of Black revolution even closer.

Such a revolution in fact materializes in the novel's occult climax. When Beverly, in his prophetic sleep, looks into the near future, he sees imminent uprisings of enslaved, colonized, and oppressed people—prefiguring Randolph's speech at the National Convention of Colored Men the following year, when he looked into the future and declared "Let the nations take warning!" These events include a second French Revolution; the independence of former Spanish colonies, which are reborn as "Black Republics" and soon surpass Spain in power; the end of the US Civil War; and the establishment by the "Black races" of the United States of "an empire which will extend from her southern borders to Brazil" (241–42). Randolph offers no further commentary on this final prophecy. But its unmistakable scenes of Black revolution amplify the more oblique references to slavery and subjugation that I have unpacked here. Together, they reframe the novel's twisty, unresolved story of Beverly and the Mysterious Brotherhood as an experiment in imagining how the world could be radically rearranged if Black people joined forces with strange powers.

The question of what futures occultism could open must have weighed on Randolph's mind particularly heavily around this time, because yet another prophecy of Black revolution flares up in the midst of a second novel he published the same year as *The Wonderful Story of Ravalette*. Narrated by a Rosicrucian named Paschal, *Tom Clark and His Wife* recounts how an unhappily married white couple come to appreciate each other through the interventions of dueling spirits and, somehow, Rosicrucian philosophy. The novel is a hodgepodge of comedy and melodrama, but halfway through Paschal interrupts the story to relate a vision in a very different register:

> See, yonder is a plain, miles in extent. In its centre there stands an obelisk. Go, Ministers of State, and plant on its top a banner, upon which

shall be emblazoned this magic sentence: "Freedom—Personal, Political, and Social, to the Black man—and protection of his Rights forever," and there will be more magnetic power in it than in ten thousand Ministers, with their little whims; . . . [C]ut the cords that now bind the Black man. Say to him: "Come as a man, not as a chattel! Come with me to Enfranchisement and Victory! Let us save the Nation!" and the swift-winged winds will bear the sound from pole to pole, from sea to sea, and from continent, island, and floating barks, from hills, valleys, and mountains, from hut, hovel, and dismal swamps, will come a vast and fearful host, in numbers like unto the leaves of a forest; and they will gather in that plain around that obelisk, rallying around that banner, and before their victorious march Rebellion will go down as brick walls before the storm of iron. . . . This is possible destiny![110]

Written at the same time Randolph was working to recruit Black troops for the Union army, this scene is to some extent a vision of military policy reform, in which "ministers of state" acknowledge the humanity of Black men, who respond with loyal service on the battlefield. Yet the grandeur and the mysticism of the scene exceed its call for policy change and even the frame of the Civil War. Randolph's picture of the international Black army—"pole to pole" and "sea to sea," enslaved, fugitive, and nominally free—suggests struggle on a larger scale. The reference to "dismal swamps," indelibly linked to Nat Turner, overlays the Civil War with the image of enslaved people's insurrection. Moreover, this army does not mobilize through ordinary channels but responds to the supernatural pull of an obelisk whose inscription gives it enormous "magnetic power"—a mechanism that closely echoes Randolph's methods for contacting the spirit world. The supernatural sweep of the scene makes it less than clear that the "Nation" to which the assembled forces stake a claim is the United States or even lies on Earth. Insofar as the scene extends the novel's Rosicrucian theme, Rosicrucianism here is no longer just an inheritance from the past but the key to a "possible destiny." Invoking an undetermined future that nevertheless already belongs to Black people by fate, the phrase's tension calls back to *The Wonderful Story of Ravalette*'s "potentiality never to be questioned." Both phrases vibrate between speculation and inevitability, taking as certainty what is not in sight.

Over the next six years, as the war ended, Reconstruction began, and Randolph moved south to take part in it, his vision of a revolutionary "possible destiny" for Black people took a different turn. *After Death; or, Disembodied Man* (1868), his fullest account of "the worlds of disbodied, unearthed peoples," builds to a prophecy of literally world-shattering upheaval.[111] The "disbodied, unearthed peoples" to whom Randolph refers are technically the spirits of the dead in the afterlife. But the adjectives' peculiar negative construction, which implies something done *to* peoples, and the word *peoples* itself, with its connotations of group rather than individual identity, also evoke the situations of Black people in "the afterlife of slavery," to borrow Saidiya Hartman's phrase—an association reinforced by references to racial violence that thread through the book. Randolph wrote *After Death* while working for the Freedmen's Bureau in Louisiana, where he first taught in New Orleans and then tried to build new schools in the countryside to the west, chronicling his experiences for the *Anglo-African Weekly* and the *Religio-Philosophical Journal*. The work was extremely dangerous. Randolph was in New Orleans on July 30, 1866, when a mob of armed white men, backed by the police, attacked a march of Black and white Radical Republicans and their supporters in what would be known as the New Orleans Massacre. "If hell is any worse than New Orleans, I pity the damned," he informed the *New York Tribune*, and in the countryside it was little better.[112] The writer Edmonia Goodelle Highgate, who was teaching just fifteen miles from Randolph, recounted that white supremacists shot at her and her students, and "the rebels here threatened to burn down the school and house in which I board before the first month was passed."[113]

While the politics of Randolph's other writing often remain below the surface, he explicitly frames *After Death*'s ideas in the context of his work for the Freedmen's Bureau and especially the experience of being terrorized by white supremacists. He explains that these circumstances shaped his conceptualization of the book:

> [F]or weeks together, I was obliged to sleep with pistols in my bed, because the assassins were abroad and red-handed Murder skulked and hovered round my door. Daily threats of summary strangling seasoned many of my meals, while writing out the first edition of this revelation, the offense being that, under the orders of my Country's officers, I taught some thousands of "negroes"—black and white too,— the sublime arts of reading and penmanship. And yet the work laid out was accomplished then,—finished now. (10)

Reminders of the book's conditions of production pepper the text, abruptly transporting the reader from the resplendent landscapes of the spirit worlds to the grim scenes of this one: "I am, at the writing of the first edition of this book, here in the carpenter shop of Auguste Landry, in St. Martinsville, St. Martin's Parish, Louisiana, May 12, 1866" (29); "I am in this barn in St. Martinsville, penning the lines now before the reader's eye" (133). These uncanny conduits between St. Martinsville and the soul realms suggest that Randolph's visions of life beyond the grave may be shaped by his anticipation of his own murder, his elaboration of extraterrestrial spirit realms an effort to create a line of flight out of this world.

In the second half of *After Death*, Randolph takes this fantasy a step further, picturing not only an exit from this world but the "upheaving" of it the prosecutor warns against in "The Great Free Love Trial." This time the world upheaval is literal and terrestrial as well as social. He notes that in his 1863 historical-theological-geological study *Pre-Adamite Man*, he had argued that thousands of years ago, the world was rocked by a cataclysm in which "the molten mass in the earth's bowels became disturbed, and it vomited forth . . . fire and flame from a hundred volcanic mouths." But since he wrote that book, he adds—which is also to say, in the five years since the Emancipation Proclamation—"I have become convinced that we are liable to such a catastrophe" occurring again "at any moment" (185). He predicts that soon "a family of asteroids" will strike the earth, which "will cause the northern pole to sink and the southern one to rise," tilting the planet dramatically on its axis. "Terrific storms, earthquakes, and volcanic eruptions" will follow; whole sections of the earth "will sink and again be thrown up," and "mountains and mountain-ranges will be leveled." In this tumult, "earth's bowels will be completely out-turned," and "gold, silver, precious stones, and metals will be thrown to the surface in quantities that will forever bar them as standards of value" (186), a prediction that upends David Walker's image of Black people held captive underground to "dig up gold and silver." Millenarian prophecies were not uncommon in the late nineteenth century, but *After Death*'s is distinctive for the way it frames apocalypse with Randolph's experiences of white supremacist violence. These incidents, along with the recent development of Randolph's conviction that "we are liable to" apocalypse, seem to tie the earth's imminent upheaval to the continuation of Black unfreedom after Emancipation. Notably, the forthcoming cataclysm, and the better world it ultimately inaugurates, coincides with the literal emergence of the underground. When Randolph concludes, "The earth is gestating new and better children: fearful will be her parturition; but joyous will the family be!" (188), he imagines the earth's gestation as the quickening of forces within it that will forge new communities above it.

We might read *After Death*'s vision of the earth turned inside-out as also imaging Randolph's conception of the occult underground: contiguous with the extraterrestrial, "*against* THE WORLD," in his words. Here I call back to Randolph's account of his racialized identity as the basis for his supernatural powers while reading it in light of Denise Ferreira da Silva's assertion that "Blackness knowing and studying announces the End of the World as we know it"—or more precisely, "the end of the World produced by the tools of reason."[114] Because this world, and the tools of reason that produce it, also produce and are produced by what Ferreira da Silva calls the "category of Blackness"—the sorting operations that create "a racial subject destined to obliteration"—it is evident why one would fantasize, as Randolph does, about its end.[115] But Ferreira da Silva also suggests that "the Category of Blackness already carries the necessary tools for dismantling the existing strategies for knowing, and opening the way for another figuring of existence," precisely because it constitutes a subject who violates the definition of the subject, by being "born into a World it cannot claim as its own."[116] (Recall Randolph's "disbodied, unearthed peoples.") Thus Ferreira da Silva urges that for "an unknowing and undoing of the World that reaches its core" and to "collectively design the framework for reconstruction" (here Randolph might want to capitalize the *r* in "reconstruction"), "we need ... to follow Blackness as it signals that knowing and doing can be released from a particular kind of thinking, which is necessary for opening up the possibility for a radical departure from a certain kind of World" and instead "opens the World as Plenum."[117] Ferreira da Silva's analysis allows us to understand Randolph's prophecy of earthly destruction as the logical endpoint of his occultism itself, whose "knowing and doing ... released from a particular kind of thinking" might bring about the end of this meager world and discover an unimaginably more bountiful one.

Yet by the time Randolph issued a revised edition of *After Death* five years later, this vision of extraterrestrially induced, seismic cataclysm had vanished. He rewrites the prophecy to predict instead a future of "modified republicanism" in the United States, anchored in racial segregation. He asserts that "Indians" and "the unfortunate mixed race" are destined for "extinction"; white Americans will "dictate laws to the habitable globe" (but benignly), and "the nation will give the negro a vast territory freely."[118] Then, before the end of 1875, there will come "a literal and unprecedented outpouring of the Spirit (world)," "especially in the Southern States among the blacks, who will, with almost a frenzied zeal, march off to their Zion in the south-west." "If I am in the body on that day, I will be their Peter the Hermit, and cast my lot with theirs," Randolph vowed.

> The new empire and the new civilization yet to come out of that poor yet rich and mighty people is destined to be as great in peace and spiritual goodness, as their masters have been in intellect and war. In that new Zion, Science will erect her halls and Art shall build her schools; and in them African genius, untainted for the cuticular hue, God's doings, not theirs, shall pursue the triumphs of investigation. Ay! And by its warmth and fervor open new doors to the mysterious realms above and around us, that the colder white can never penetrate; and thus the black shall add his quota to the common stock of human knowledge, and the word Justice will have a meaning in this world.[119]

The apocalyptic fervor and subterranean upheaval of the 1867 edition have dropped out, replaced by the prospect of a spiritually developed Black colony.[120] We might see Randolph's faith in Reconstruction in this vision. But it is hard not to hear despair in his prediction of white global rule, however peaceful; the eradication of Indigenous and mixed-race people; and the relegation of Black people to the desert to commune with "the mysterious realms above and around us," especially in the shadow of his suicide two years later. This vision of a Black occult eminence is beguiling in its way but fundamentally different from the occult undergrounds ringing in the end of the world as we know it that Randolph had pictured in the 1860s. Instead, concluding that "the races can never live side by side on equal terms," Randolph looks toward a colonization project, directed by the US government, that strongly resembles the efforts of the white-led American Colonization Society to send free African Americans to West Africa in the early nineteenth century.[121] As the frontier replaces the underground, Randolph no longer contemplates destroying the world to remake it; he just wants to be left in peace. In this attenuated future, "justice will have a meaning in this world" not when it is upturned but once Black people "open new doors" into other ones.

Randolph in Telassar

Thirty years later, Pauline Hopkins would place the relation between occultism and racialized Blackness—as well as the tension the two editions of *After Death* capture, between fierce hope in the underground and its exhaustion—at the center of her novel *Of One Blood*. As I observed earlier,

Hopkins's protagonist, medical student Reuel Briggs, closely resembles Randolph in temperament (melancholy), background (mixed-race child of a clairvoyant mother, ambivalent about his Blackness), profession (medicine, writing about the occult), and interests (trance states, prophecy, magic mirrors). As with Randolph, who capitalizes on the occult knowledge of his wives Mary Jane Randolph and Kate Corson Randolph, the "VOUDEAUX QUEENS" of New Orleans, and anonymous lovers like "a dusky maiden of Arabic blood . . . in far-off Jerusalem or Bethlehem, I really forget which," Reuel's spiritual gifts tend to eclipse those of the women around him: his sister/lover Dianthe, his mother Mira, and his grandmother Hannah, "the most noted 'voodoo' doctor or witch in the country."[122] The religion of Telassar, centered on an "ever-living faculty or soul Ego" (562) distributed to all living things that constantly strives to return to its divine origins, strongly recalls Randolph's beliefs. Lana Finley, who has also hypothesized that Hopkins based Reuel on Randolph, notes that Hopkins was growing up in the Beacon Hill neighborhood of Boston in the late 1860s when Randolph moved there to practice medicine and clairvoyance.[123] In Boston Randolph became "something of a celebrity," according to John Patrick Deveney; is it any wonder his work or reputation would have captured the attention of a budding Black writer interested in the occult?[124]

In *Of One Blood*, Reuel quite literally fulfills Randolph's injunction "to drop beneath the floors of the outer world, and come up, as it were, upon the other side." Having joined an exploring party to Ethiopia, he leaves the camp late one night to seek out a nearby pyramid and, once inside, descends into a chasm in the center. He then loses consciousness. When he comes to, he has been transported through subterranean passages to the hidden city of Telassar, where the ancient civilization of Meroë survives. With its stunning physical beauty, its extraordinary arts and sciences, and its prophetic traditions, Telassar is a living rejoinder to the arrogance of the white members of the exploring party, who see in Ethiopia "no future . . . [n]othing but the monotony of past centuries dead and forgotten" (526). Their archaeological episteme, with its assumption that what is buried belongs to the past, gravely misreads both Ethiopia and the underground. Where they dismiss Africa as "a played-out hole in the ground" (590), Telassar returns their slur to them transfigured, as an immortal Black underground. It is also a distinctly occult underground, complete with a magic mirror housed in an "underground room" (575), in which Reuel sees the past, present, and future.

In chapter 3, I suggested that in Telassar, Hopkins extends a line of thinking about the underground that she had developed in *Peculiar Sam* and *Winona*. In these texts, Hopkins revives a set of antislavery discourses that picture the underground as a place out of keeping with the space and time of the world above it and for that reason a site of otherwise unimaginable freedom for African Americans. For Hopkins, reopening these earlier freedom dreams offers some way out of, and beyond, the terribly partial and compromised version of freedom that had arrived with legal emancipation. But reading *Of One Blood* through Hopkins's engagement with Randolph's thought allows us to see how her fascination with the underground's escape from earthly space and time becomes dimmed, in her final novel, by increasing pessimism about ever realizing that freedom above ground. Written after the overthrow of Reconstruction and during the emergence of Jim Crow, the story of Telassar founders on the fear discernible in Randolph's revisions to *After Death*: that the underground might be a dead end.

Although the residents of Telassar assure Reuel that his destiny is "the upbuilding of humanity and the restoration of the race of our fathers" (573), the novel gives us little material with which to imagine Telassar's future. The final paragraphs militate against those earlier prophesies of resurgence:

> [Reuel's] days glide peacefully by in good works; but the shadows of great sins darken his life, and the memory of past joys is ever with him. He views, too, with serious apprehension, the advance of mighty nations penetrating the dark, mysterious forests of his native land.
>
> "Where will it stop?" he sadly questions. "What will the end be?" (621)

Prophesied to "restore the former glory of his race," Reuel settles for pursuing "good works." While his "days glide peacefully by" him, the forces of European colonialism march across Africa, encroaching on Telassar. If the underground was once a resource for enacting Black freedom in the world, this function now becomes difficult for Hopkins to imagine. Rather, as Claudia Tate writes, "*Of One Blood*'s ending in the fantastic underground city of Telassar adds to the reader's uneasiness by making the acquisition of equal justice an even more remote possibility."[125] Telassar's underground turns out to be what Lauren Berlant describes as an "impasse," a "space of time" that registers a historical present of "ongoing crisis" with no apparent way out.[126] Where at first Randolph's vision of the possibilities the occult underground holds for Black liberation seem to animate *Of One Blood*, the doubts he expresses in the second edition of *After Death* come to overtake Hopkins's novel by its end. The occult underground may offer a "hidden city of refuge" (529) from the world for Black diasporic peoples, but Hopkins is less clear that it could offer any ingress back into that world.

6 Subterranean Fire

ANARCHIST VISIONS OF THE
UNDERGROUND

In 1886, the underground became infamous in the United States. The story has been told many times: on May 4, Chicago anarchists and socialists held a meeting in Haymarket Square to protest an attack by police on striking workers the day before, when police had shot into the crowd, killing two people. As the meeting was drawing to a close, police marched in and commanded the crowd to disperse. The last speaker, teamster and organizer Samuel Fielden, explained that he was just finishing his speech, but when the police captain insisted, he stepped down from the speaker's wagon. At that moment a bomb flew through the air, landing in the ranks of police. Once again, the police began shooting wildly into the crowd—and, inadvertently, at their fellow officers. Eight police officers and unknown numbers of civilians died as a result of the chaos.

Within a month, as newspapers across the country screamed for revenge, a grand jury indicted ten Chicago anarchists on charges of conspiracy to murder. Eight were convicted and seven sentenced to death a year and a half later in a trial marked by flagrant bias, a stacked jury, dubious evidence, and the most tenuous of legal arguments.[1] After the sentencing, the defendants had the chance to address the court. They turned the courtroom into a platform, and the speeches they made would be printed, reprinted, and translated many times over, in newspapers, pamphlets, and books, for years to come. August Spies, upholsterer and editor of the labor newspaper the *Arbeiter-Zeitung*, went first. After explicating anarchism for an audience bent on misrepresenting it and excoriating the court's travesty of justice, he delivered a ringing prophecy:

> If you think that by hanging us, you can stamp out the labor movement—the movement from which the downtrodden millions, the millions who toil and live in want and misery—the wage slaves—expect salvation—if this is your opinion, then hang us! Here you will tread upon a spark, but there, and there, and behind you and in front of you, and everywhere, flames will blaze up. It is a subterranean fire. You cannot put it out.[2]

Spies's image of the movement as a "subterranean fire" promises that anarchism's apparent defeat at the hands of the court is only superficial. Against the crushing forces of law and order, which would "stamp out" the struggles of the already "downtrodden millions," the phrase envisions a movement whose power derives from its subjacency, or what Spies described as its "unfathomable depths."[3] "Subterranean fire" pictures anarchism as a force that cannot be contained by the state because it exceeds the vision of the state; as Spies told the servants of capital assembled in the courtroom, "You can't understand it."

Taking its cue from Spies's "subterranean fire," this chapter explores the underground imaginary of the International Working People's Association (IWPA), the loose organization held responsible for the deaths in Haymarket Square. Although the IWPA had highly visible elements, I argue that it theorized and built a movement closer than any other in this book to what we would now recognize as an underground, one defined by what their founding manifesto called "the work of revolutionary conspiracy." I trace the IWPA's construction of an anarchist underground through an intensive reading of the *Alarm*, their English-language weekly, which ran from 1884 to 1886, when it was suppressed following the Haymarket affair, before being revived from 1887 to 1889. The *Alarm* reported on the IWPA's activities, those of other anarchist and socialist organizations, and the latest outrages of the capitalists, and it published poetry and short fiction that remain little studied by literary critics. That said, Chicago's IWPA-affiliated German newspapers were more numerous and claimed a larger readership than the *Alarm*, and the city was also home to Czech and Danish IWPA-affiliated newspapers. While the papers often reprinted content from each other, as well as from other anarchist papers in the United States and beyond, this chapter's focus on literature in English makes its account of the IWPA's underground imaginary necessarily incomplete. Still, it may prove illuminating even without aspiring to comprehensiveness. My goal is not to use the *Alarm* to reconstruct a full picture of the IWPA's activities (many of which remain elusively underground, even considering the materials in German, Czech, and Danish) so much as to explore the interlocking strands of underground imagery that ran through it. Attending to the literary contents of the *Alarm* highlights writing that might not otherwise appear politically important; it also tries to move away from a tendency to treat the *Alarm* solely as background to the Haymarket bombings. Moreover, a method that accepts and preserves some element of incomprehension may actually be particularly well suited to studying the anarchist underground. It avoids the will to knowledge exemplified by the fatal actions of the Chicago police and the legal system and instead draws on the thinking of the anarchists themselves, who doggedly worked toward a revolution whose outcome they did not believe they could script in advance.

Some of the richest examples of the anarchists' subterranean thinking appear in the *Alarm*'s poetry column and in the short fiction regularly contributed by assistant editor Lizzie Swank, a feminist writer and labor organizer who had grown up on a free love commune in Ohio. In particular, I examine three recurring motifs through which Swank and other writers in the *Alarm* elaborate the anarchist underground: the figure of the tramp, the itinerant non-worker that the *Alarm* writers often depicted as consigned to death; the image of dynamite, with its misleading dormancy; and the paper's elegiac yet frustrated invocations of the abolitionist movement. I am especially interested in the morbid and macabre quality of these works, which suggest an underground saturated—and, ironically, animated—by the buried dead. Thus, where the previous chapter underscored the political aspects of Paschal Beverly Randolph's occultism, this chapter underscores the occult aspects of the IWPA's politics, hypothesizing that this language has as much to tell us about anarchist visions of the underground as their more declarative statements do. Taking seriously the anarchists' figurative language helps us heed the words of Samuel Fielden, whose call in Haymarket Square to "throttle the law" was fatally interpreted as justifying a massive police intervention; as Fielden noted incredulously at the trial, "It is a word widely used as meaning to abolish; if you take the metaphors from the English language, you have no language at all."[4] Doing so also picks up on my earlier discussion of the relationship between demystification and mystery in Marx's writing and extends this inquiry into the role of mystery in nineteenth-century radical thought. The conclusion follows Spies's invocation of a "subterranean fire" as it makes a surprising reappearance in Herman Melville's *Billy Budd*. Written mostly during and just after the Haymarket trial, Melville's novella about a sailor hanged, under pressure of the state, for the accidental killing of the ship's "chief of police" bears the imprint of the Haymarket affair. Yet I am most interested in how Melville relocates the roiling anarchist underground inside the individual self, a transformation indexed by his use of the phrase "subterranean fire" to describe the inner turmoil of John Claggart, the slain officer. In the introduction, I suggested that nineteenth-century ideas of the underground become displaced by the twentieth-century concept of subculture; here I suggest that one place they go is into emerging psychological models of the unconscious.

"Commune il faut": Building an Anarchist Underground

The International Working People's Association, or the Black International, was founded in London in 1881, but state crackdowns on anarchists hampered its growth in Europe. One target of these crackdowns was the German firebrand Johann Most, writer, orator, and editor of the newspaper *Freiheit*. In 1882, fresh out of prison in London, Most emigrated to New York. The following fall, he organized a convention of anarchists and revolutionary socialists in Pittsburgh that launched a US branch of the IWPA, announcing itself in a manifesto that became known as the Pittsburgh Proclamation.[5] Many IWPA members had previously been active in socialist organizations and trade unions, and many continued to maintain ties. But the depressions of the 1870s, along with the increasingly brutal suppression of labor, especially during the 1877 railroad strike, convinced them that nothing less than the overthrow of the state could end capitalism. As an IWPA member in Milwaukee put it, "Reform doodles are out of the times and the people are ready for radical ideas as well as radical means."[6]

Historians argue about what exactly those radical ideas and radical means entailed—whether the IWPA inclined more toward revolutionary unionism or revolutionary agitation—but our eagerness to classify the movement can obscure the movement's own willingness to remain unclassifiable. The *Alarm* advertised itself as "the only Communist-Anarchist newspaper published in the English language in the United States" but carried the subtitle "A Socialistic Weekly."[7] Some urged the IWPA-affiliated groups to agree on a unified political position, but editor Albert Parsons and others seemed to relish being impossible to pin down. Even "anarchist," as they often pointed out, was simply a term they had appropriated from their enemies. Parsons gleefully ventriloquized the ruling class's exasperation at the idiosyncrasy of the "strange fellows" who gather under "the red flag": "Revolutionary Socialists, Anarchists, Internationalists, or whatever you may call the 'ignorant foreigners' . . . 'Cranks,' *commune il faut* these Socialists—'ain't they?'"[8] Parsons's punning *commune il faut* rejects the propriety of *comme il faut* ("as it should be") while transforming its French from bourgeois affectation into invocation of the Paris Commune ("the commune it should be"). Bemused and dismissive as Parsons's imaginary capitalist grouch may be, his slip of the tongue suggests that he, too, is unwittingly drawn in to the IWPA's orbit.

For a group calling for the violent overthrow of capitalism and the state, the IWPA was extraordinarily visible. They organized regular open-air meetings, parades, demonstrations, picnics, dances, and concerts, often in combination.[9] On July 26, 1885, for example, several thousand workers marched through downtown Chicago, accompanied by four brass bands and the uniformed and armed Lehr und Wehr Verein (Education and Defense Association), pulling floats with tableaus ridiculing the police and the government, and carrying banners inscribed "Down with the throne, altar and money-bag," "Private capital is robbery," "Our civilization: the bullet and policeman's club," "Freedom without equality is a lie," and "The fountain of right is might. Workingmen, arm!" According to the *Alarm*, "spectators lined the sidewalks" for three miles to watch. At the end of the route, "fully ten thousand people" gathered to eat, dance, and listen as a series of speakers in English and German exhorted them to "prepare mentally and physically for the inevitable conflict of force between capitalists and their laborers."[10] Each year the IWPA organized an especially enthusiastic celebration for the anniversary of the Paris Commune, and beginning in 1884, they held an annual counter-Thanksgiving march for "everyone who feels the sting of mockery" in the state's official observation of Thanksgiving. (Signs among the crowd included "Shall we thank our lords for our misery, destitution and poverty?" and "Our capitalist robbers may well thank *their* Lord, we their victims have not yet strangled them."[11]) The IWPA's Chicago members also regularly sent representatives around the country on "agitation trips" to organize new groups and energize existing ones. The Bureau of Information extended the organization's reach even further by circulating numerous free pamphlets and circulars, including Lucy

Parsons's broadside "Address to Tramps," Johann Most's instructions on the manufacture of dynamite, the Pittsburgh Proclamation, and the *Communist Manifesto*; they also offered for sale heftier books by Marx, Mikhail Bakunin, and anarchist geographer Élisée Reclus, as well as Russian revolutionary Sergey Stepnyak-Kravchinsky's *Underground Russia*, whose title illustrates the legibility of the underground by the 1880s.[12]

Yet the Pittsburgh Proclamation acknowledged that a confrontational public presence was not enough to build a movement: "The work of peaceful education and revolutionary conspiracy well can and ought to run in parallel lines."[13] The proclamation's image of "parallel lines" pictures "peaceful education" taking place in full view of the world while "revolutionary conspiracy" runs below it. At an organizational level, the IWPA built the movement's underground dimensions by cultivating a "rapidly extending" cellular structure, as an article in the *Alarm* explained:

> The organization is composed of "groups," which are in agreement upon fundamental principles, as set forth in the Pittsburg manifesto of October, 1883. But in all other matters each "group" is autonomous, or independent of all the others in matters of propaganda, etc. There are over one hundred groups in the United States, located principally in the centers of industry, with a membership for each group from 20 to 300 persons. In Chicago alone there are over 2,000 active members, with a sympathetic membership of at least 10,000 more.... The organization is also to be found in Mexico and British Columbia, and parts of South America, while all of Europe, England included, is honeycombed with "groups" of the International.[14]

Some members sought to take the IWPA even further underground: several months later, an item in the Letter Box column replying to "many correspondents" advised, "If you wish to organize secret groups you can do that and make such regulations as will best suit you."[15] But the earlier article suggests that the IWPA's organizing did not need to be explicitly secret to be subterranean. It functioned as an underground in part by being so radically horizontal: its decentralized structure made full knowledge of the organization impossible, even for its own members. The article likely exaggerates the IWPA's numbers: despite its name, it had little presence outside the United States, and dispatches in the *Alarm* from struggling groups around the country suggest that many did not grow much beyond the required nine members. But its inflated accounting also indicates the speculative character of 1880s anarchism, which measured its reach in terms of possibilistic "sympathetic membership" as much as card-carrying members, and which understood internationalism less as an accomplished goal than as a spatialized embodiment of potentiality. Anarchists "honeycombed" the world, carving out holes and passages from underneath whose sweetness lay in their secrets. They were "to be found" all over, a thrillingly portentous construction that promises that the full forces of anarchism lie undiscovered.

The *Alarm*'s regular reports about organizing document the arduous, dangerous process of building an anarchist underground that was at once less and more than it appeared. The paper explicitly encouraged readers to create their own hand-to-hand distribution networks, inserting regular reminders to "circulate the *Alarm* among your friends and neighbors." Letters from readers suggest they took the charge seriously. Those from towns where the movement had little support or was especially heavily policed write of trying to identify trustworthy associates to whom they could pass along copies of the *Alarm* or repeat its contents.[16] An agitator traveling through Colorado explains that when his plans to organize new groups of the IWPA hit a wall, he "quietly slipped copies of THE ALARM and of [Denver socialist newspaper] *The Labor Enquirer* into the hands of persons to whom their contents was a revelation. And I have reason to believe that some of these seed have fallen upon ground not altogether barren."[17] Reader Lewis York reported his attempts to spread anarchist ideas in his hometown of Logansport, Indiana: "The shop bosses have drove me out twice" and the editors of two local newspapers "have stopped me from giving *Alarm* to their hands in their offices," he writes, "but they cannot stop me from street working on the principles of anarchy."[18] Other readers took the principle of "street working" more literally, like the correspondent in Joplin, Missouri, who posted "several of Mrs. P[arsons]'s little notices to tramps upon the most public corners" in town, then hung around to savor his handiwork. "I have to laugh as I stand on the corner and see first one and then another step up and read it," he wrote jubilantly, adding, "There is the rumble of an earthquake 'round and about."[19] In Indianapolis, another correspondent posted handbills "all over the city last week" featuring a series of anarchist mottoes—"WORKINGMEN, TO ARMS! WAR TO THE PALACE, PEACE TO THE COTTAGE, AND DEATH TO LUXURIOUS IDLENESS! . . . One pound of DYNAMITE is better than a bushel of BALLOTS!"[20] "Police pulled them down wherever they found them," but a Portland, Oregon, correspondent maintained that even when "the most benighted, hard-hearted and relentless class of sharks and vampires that ever soiled

God's green earth" seemed to have the advantage, "they are unaware of the mine they are standing upon."[21] In at least one instance, the state actually had a mole in its ranks. An anonymous US Army officer stationed at Alcatraz decided to "show the 'lower strata' their power" by revealing "the weak points in our prescribed tactics for suppressing riots." In a letter to the *Alarm*, he carefully detailed the military's preferred maneuvers and diagrammed a plan for anarchist street fighters to resist them, which the newspaper reproduced using dashes, O's, and periods.[22]

While the IWPA adopted subterranean tactics for its own organizing purposes, the "hirelings of capital" aggressively drove the anarchists further underground. Mainstream newspapers threatened to rotten-egg, mob, and lynch speakers; landlords refused to rent space to them; police and Pinkertons followed, attacked, and tried to infiltrate them. Chicago business owners assembled an armed guard of 150 men to confront "the armed organizations of the Communists," and when the Chicago groups held their second counter-Thanksgiving demonstration in 1885, Illinois sent out the military for a menacing street riot drill.[23] Anarchists denounced the repressive measures that forced their work into subterranean channels, but some, like the secretary of the IWPA's American Group (and husband of Lizzie Swank), William Holmes, also suggested that "repression but makes us stronger."[24] An item in the capitalist press supports his theory: upon seeing a copy of the Pittsburgh Proclamation, the popular religious weekly the *Christian Union* fretted, "How many of this tract have been printed, and what its circulation, we do not know."[25] In the *Alarm*, an article on the history of the Lehr und Wehr Verein, the largest of Chicago's labor militias, explained how going underground created unforeseen possibilities for the movement. Chicago workers formed the Lehr und Wehr Verein after the brutal suppression of the 1877 railroad strike showed the need for an "armed proletarian corps."[26] In response, the state legislature outlawed any militia not authorized by the governor, a law the Lehr und Wehr Verein and the other anarchist militias like the Jaeger Verein, the Bohemian Sharpshooters, and the armed section of the American Group resisted by drilling secretly in saloons, nearby woods, or just over state lines.[27] But "that militia law has also had its beneficial effects," the article noted. It ends,

> Where there once was a military body of men publicly organized, whose strength could easily be ascertained, there exists an organization now whose strength cannot even be estimated, a network of

destructive agencies of a *modern* military character that will defy any and all attempts of suppression. We don't grumble! Make more "laws" if you like.[28]

Driven underground, anarchism's "strength cannot even be estimated"; it becomes immeasurable and potentially boundless. The final line reads like a missive from another world, where laws have become mere "laws," their spell broken. The *Alarm* writer's glee, like the *Christian Union* writer's dismay, confirms August Spies's triumphant assertion about "subterranean fire": it is precisely because "you can't understand it" that "you cannot put it out."

To Breathe Together: The Disinspirited and the Risen Dead

Refusing to heed Spies's warning, Chicago police captain Michael J. Schaack made it his mission to apprehend the anarchist underground, in both senses of the word *apprehend*. Charged with investigating the Haymarket bombing, Schaack relentlessly hounded the city's anarchists; after the trial, he published a tour de force of fearmongering and self-promotion, *Anarchy and Anarchists*, whose nearly seven hundred pages flail at comprehensiveness. Schaack's attempt to grasp the anarchist underground returned repeatedly to the idea that anarchists were literally lurking beneath the public's feet. In the months following the Haymarket bombing, he fed newspapers stories that "secret 'anarchist arsenals' were still being discovered, in basements, and under sidewalks"; in *Anarchy and Anarchists*, he regaled readers with accounts of "underground conspirators" meeting in candlelit basements and dropping through secret cellar doors for "underground rifle practice" with the Lehr und Wehr Verein (figure 6.1).[29] When *New York World* reporter Charles Edward Russell observed of Schaack, "He saw more anarchists than vast hell could hold," he perfectly captured both the police officer's murderous zeal and its subterranean cast.[30]

Popular fiction took up Schaack's feverish efforts to unearth anarchist plots. The 1888 dime novel *Deadwood Dick Jr. in Chicago; or, the Anarchist's Daughter*, for example, sends its titular detective to a city where "although the bomb-throwers of the fearful Haymarket massacre were even now mouldering in their tombs, anarchy was still rife" and "growing stronger each and every day." Deadwood Dick discovers as much for himself when anarchists take him captive in the sub-cellar of a saloon that is "a sort of

6.1 "Underground Conspirators," from Michael J. Schaack, *Anarchy and Anarchists* (1889). Courtesy of the Chicago Public Library, Special Collections Division.

hang-out for the laboring people who are in favor of revolution." ("There is another cellar still, under you," his guard reveals.)[31] In chapter 4, I argued that the literal undergrounds that mine mid-nineteenth-century city mysteries indicate the unknowability of their figurative undergrounds, but thirty years or so later, once the idea of a political underground had more fully emerged, this literalization reads differently—as an epistemological strategy that tries to fix the underground in place.[32] We can see a similar desire for containment play out in the 1885 dystopian novel *The Fall of the Great Republic (1886–88)* by the pseudonymous Sir Henry Standish Coverdale, which recounts an anarchist revolution that begins in Chicago. There, "below the thin and treacherous surface, the volcanic fires of a socialistic agitation were blazing up with daily increasing fierceness," and eventually they topple the US government.[33] (Ultimately invading British troops and US Southerners team up to put down the revolution, an alliance that brings to mind responses to earlier slumbering volcanoes.)

But Coverdale ultimately reveals the "fungus-like growth" of an international revolutionary groundswell to be the contrivance of "a mysterious centre known among outsiders and to most of the socialists themselves as 'The Council of Seven,' but whom the few fully initiated knew to be a single individual" who directs the activities of revolutionaries all over the United States and Europe.[34] In other words, there is no anarchist fungus among us, merely one fanatic who can easily be eliminated. Similarly, in *Deadwood Dick Jr. in Chicago*, the anarchists turn out to be a "lodge" of forty people, which cloaks a "secret lodge" of just six.[35] These novels frighten readers with the threat of anarchist underground but then dispel the threat twice over, first by crushing the movement and then by exposing it as merely a cover for authoritarian machinations.

Despite the fantasies of Schaack, *Deadwood Dick*, and Coverdale, the Chicago anarchists' "bomb-talking" far outstripped their "bomb-throwing," as Floyd Dell observed a century ago.[36] However, this does not mean we should dismiss their "bomb-talking" as primarily a "bluff," as Dell does. The IWPA's interest in propaganda of the deed was real, and they regularly taught the manufacture of dynamite at meetings and in print.[37] But they were also captivated by dynamite "in the synecdochal sense of that term," as Eau Claire, Wisconsin–based anarchist C. L. James put it.[38] In the "synecdochal" sense, dynamite is not only an instrument of revolutionary conspiracy; it also stands for the revolutionary conspiracy in which it plays a part. Besides being cheap, what made dynamite such "a genuine boon for the disinherited," Gerhard Lizius explained in the *Alarm*, was its easy concealment: "The dear stuff can be carried around in the pocket," and "the more you prohibit it, the more will it be done." With dynamite in the anarchists' pockets, they became a new incarnation of a familiar subterranean trope: "Our law makers might as well try to sit down on the crater of a volcano," Lizius warned.[39] Dynamite figures an anarchist underground, not least because it was invented as a mining technology and so, as its proponents often instructed, it worked best when placed underground. (The *Alarm* was ecstatic when striking coal miners in Ohio's Hocking Valley repurposed dynamite to blow up their own mines and tunnels.[40])

"Election Day," a dystopian anti-ballot parable by Lizzie Swank, imagines how dynamite's literally subterranean properties might become figuratively subterranean ones. In a "colony in a strange new country," several men have been imprisoned in a cave for "some fancied misdemeanors." They are forced to work constantly and given little to eat, but their rulers insist that "they did not wish to be cruel or unjust," so they congratulate themselves on giving the prisoners the right to vote. Finally, however, one of the prisoners assails the "great privilege to allow us a voice in your affairs" when "these rough damp walls, this darkness, this close air is all we can receive." He is reported a "dangerous character" and a "crank," but in the meantime the prisoners "brooded and studied over a discovery they had made, which promised the only gleam of hope they had known in years."[41] Swank never names the discovery. But readers of the *Alarm* would likely have recognized it as dynamite, "the latest discovery of science by which power is placed in the hands of the weak and defenseless to protect them against the domination of others," as Albert Parsons had exulted in a speech to strikers at the McCormick Reaper Works several months earlier.[42] The story ends on this portentous note, with the prisoners "brooding and studying" in their cave, transformed by their discovery from being underground to being *an* underground.

Attending to the "synecdochal sense" of dynamite helps us avoid the temptation to see "the work of revolutionary conspiracy" retrospectively, as prefiguring the Haymarket affair, and thus to conflate the IWPA's understanding of conspiracy with the conspiracy charges brought against the Haymarket defendants by the state. This is the mode of historian Timothy Messer-Kruse's study *The Haymarket Conspiracy*, for example, which attempts to reconstruct the bombing as an intricate terrorist plot. Messer-Kruse offers a useful caution against narratives of innocence that obscure the anarchists' militancy, and his hypothesis invites readers to take seriously the movement's commitment to revolutionary violence. But his interpretation of the bombing relies not only on police captain Michael Schaack's account and other evidence from the defendants' grossly unfair trial but also on a narrow, teleological, legalistic definition of "the work of revolutionary conspiracy," which depicts the bombing as the culmination of a tightly choreographed plan and that plan as the cause of the IWPA.[43] Such an instrumentalized reading of "the work of revolutionary conspiracy" obscures much of what makes the anarchist underground (1) anarchist and (2) an underground. Following the "synecdochal sense" of dynamite allows us to understand "revolutionary conspiracy," instead, as referring to the construction of an underground movement that might include terrorist plots but cannot be reduced to them. This interpretation does not follow the legal meaning of the word *conspiracy* so much as its Latin etymology, from the wonderfully nebulous "to breathe together." It was this etymology that August Spies threw back at his accusers when he exclaimed at his trial, "You want to 'stamp out the conspirators'?"

Ah, stamp out every factory lord who has grown wealthy upon the unpaid labor of his employees. Stamp out every landlord who has amassed fortunes from the rent of overburdened workingmen and farmers. Stamp out every machine that is revolutionizing industry and agriculture, that intensifies the production, ruins the producer, that increases the national wealth, while the creator of all these things stands amidst them, tantalized with hunger! Stamp out the railroads, the telegraph, the telephone, steam and yourselves—for *everything breathes the revolutionary spirit*.[44]

Spies's dialectical riposte takes the conspiracy charge and inverts it: conspiracy here is not the action of the eight defendants against the capitalist state but the joint action of all the elements of the capitalist state (against) itself. Landlords, factories, the technologies of speed-up that increase profit—"everything breathes the revolutionary spirit." The work of the anarchists, then, is to inhale "the revolutionary spirit" already exhaled all around them, to "aid and direct its forces," as Spies's codefendant Albert Parsons put it.[45]

The power of breathing together through revolutionary conspiracy becomes clearer when we place it alongside the anarchists' contention that workers were hardly breathing at all. The *Alarm* regularly depicts the capitalist state as oppressive to the point of being murderous, willing to press workers to their limits even at the risk of destroying their labor power. So the worker always lives in the shadow of death. More than that, the worker lives in an even stranger half-light of being without a place in the world at all—for even as capitalism regularly shatters and ejects its proletarian subjects, it also teaches that work is not only an "economic necessity and a social duty" but also "an individual moral practice and collective ethical obligation," Kathi Weeks explains, the grounds for human belonging.[46] Another short story by Lizzie Swank lays out the process by which capitalism makes anyone not working—which, as the *Alarm* consistently emphasized, could be anyone at any moment—an outcast. It recounts the brief life of a boy who, after being replaced by machinery at his factory, hears a preacher at church promise that "somewhere in the wide world there is a place for everyone." With the preacher's words "re-echo[ing] in his thoughts," he goes out to look for a new job, and "constantly he reproved himself for not having the steadiness, ability, and determination to find [his place] out." But his efforts are fruitless, and when he finally freezes to death, his fate belies the preacher's words: "[T]he world and that place in it which was for him, never missed him."⁴⁷ This framing of the proletariat as exiled from the world recurs frequently in the literary contents of the *Alarm*. As the Chartist Ernest Jones asks in the refrain of "Song of the Wage Slave," which the paper reprinted twice, "The rich have got the earth, / But what remains for me?"⁴⁸ Another uncredited poem has a ready answer: "All things have a home save one: / Thou, O proletaire, hast none."⁴⁹ When Albert Parsons bitterly observed at the Haymarket trial, "A wage-worker is no part of society," he invoked a familiar subterranean metaphor to describe this position of being so far below society as to be outside of it: "They are part of the society as the mud-sills who do the work, but have no part of the benefits."⁵⁰

For the IWPA, proletarian dispossession was embodied by the tramp, the itinerant worker, implicitly white, who is chewed up and spit out by capitalism, then pathologized and criminalized for not working.⁵¹ Lucy Parsons's call to arms "A Word to Tramps," published in the first issue of the *Alarm* and later as the broadside that accosted readers on street corners in Joplin, Missouri, addresses those "for whom life has become a burden and existence a mockery." "Have you not worked hard all your life, since you were old enough for your labor to be of use in the production of wealth?" Parsons demands. Yet when the worker's "employer saw fit to create an artificial famine by limiting production," they were turned out on to the street and told it was their own fault. "You were only a tramp now, to be execrated and denounced as a 'worthless tramp and vagrant' by that very class who had been engaged all those years in robbing you and yours," who "will say to you that you drank up all your wages last summer when you had work, and that is the reason why you have nothing now, and the workhouse or the woodyard is too good for you, and you ought to be shot."⁵² (Parsons does not exaggerate: newspapers railed against the dangers of tramps so vehemently that a writer for the *Chicago Tribune* could advise readers, seemingly only half-jokingly, "to put a little arsenic in the meat and other supplies furnished the tramp" as a "warning to other tramps to keep out of the neighborhood" and "save . . . one's chickens and other portable property from constant destruction."⁵³) For Parsons, the tramp crystallizes the growing biopolitical imperative of capitalism, which squeezes the life out of workers while insisting that only those who work deserved to live. Circulated to working readers, as well as the tramps it addresses, "A Word to Tramps" intimates that all workers are potentially tramps, or as the *Alarm* repeatedly put it, "every workingman is a tramp in embryo."⁵⁴ For these reasons, "this is a movement of tramps," as IWPA stalwart W. J. Gorsuch declared at one mass meeting.⁵⁵

In a report from one of his agitation tours, Albert Parsons recounts distributing copies of "A Word to Tramps" to coal miners in the Monongahela valley.[56] He gives the broadside's subtitle as "the Unemployed, the Destitute, and Disinspirited," and while it was actually "the Unemployed, the Disinherited, and Miserable," his term *disinspirited*, with its suggestion of stolen breath, underscores how much the tramp stands in need of "conspiracy." It also highlights the oddly spiritual undertones of much IWPA propaganda. If the proletariat has no place in the world, as Swank, the Parsonses, and others contend, then there could be something otherworldly about them; if capitalism relentlessly wrings the life out of the proletariat, then in these moments the IWPA imagines itself as the risen dead, an organization of ghosts. In fact, as rousing a manifesto as "A Word to Tramps" is, it is also morbid. Lucy Parsons doesn't argue with the tramp's desire for suicide but with his method: rather than drown himself, she urges him to "stroll down the avenues of the rich and look through the magnificent plate-glass windows into their voluptuous homes." Then, with the aid of dynamite, "let your tragedy be enacted *here*."[57] We could read Parsons's endorsement of the tramp's suicide as nihilist (a word maligners of anarchism used as synonymous with *anarchist*) or as a predilection for martyrdom, but I'm more curious about how Parsons looks outside the realm of life for a vision of militant action. "A Word to Tramps" insists that the anarchist response to capitalism cannot lie in the reclamation of life, as long as life remains synonymous with survival under capitalism. Instead, for Parsons, it is the dead who initiate revolution.

"A Word to Tramps" inaugurates a strikingly macabre strain of writing in the *Alarm*. "They think us dull, they think us dead, / But we shall rise again," warns Jones in "Song of the Wage Slave," and note that the second line does not contradict the presumed death of the workers in the first so much as it owns the threat of an insurrection of the resurrected:

> A trumpet through the lands will ring;
> A heaving through the mass;
> A trampling through the palaces,
> Until they break like glass.[58]

Jones borrows the imagery of millenarianism to picture revolution, but here the end of the world is driven by "a heaving through the mass" rather than divine agency. The IWPA's Pittsburgh Proclamation ends on a similar note: "Tremble! Oppressors of the world: Not far beyond your purblind sight there dawns the scarlet and sable lights of the JUDGMENT DAY!"[59] Stripped of its Christian associations, judgment day arrives in the colors of "scarlet and sable," the red and black of anarchist iconography. Such visions of the dead as buried but not stilled, I argue, quicken the IWPA's anarchist underground. It is these ghostly bodies that might breathe together in "the work of revolutionary conspiracy."

For the *Alarm*, the defeated Paris Commune offered a particularly compelling model of an underground in which death and burial promise resurgence in transfigured form. (That the last Communards occupied Père Lachaise Cemetery before the army shot them against a wall and threw them into a trench only adds to the Commune's resonance.) S. Robert Wilson's poem "Revolution," written for the fourteenth anniversary celebration of the Commune held by the San Francisco branch of the IWPA, begins, "They say she is dead, the Commune is dead," and pictures the personified Commune accordingly, shot and bleeding. But after several stanzas, we hear the Commune's "earthquake tread," and she appears and seizes control of the poem:

> But know ye this, I am not dead,
> The spirit of revolt can never die,
> Upon ten thousand battle fields I've bled
> And with my martyr'd slain did lie.
>
> But every soul your bloody steel set free,
> My spirit absorbed into its own;
> So now I'm the sum, the majesty,
> Of every rebel the world hath known.

In a remarkable twist, the fallen Commune reveals that she has used death to effect a kind of subterranean communion, by which she "absorbed" the spirits of "every rebel the world hath known." Interment and decomposition instigate a dissolution of boundaries that galvanizes unprecedented collective power. (This fantasy shows the distance between the IWPA's communist anarchism and the individualist anarchism of contemporaries and intermittent comrades like Benjamin Tucker and Ezra Heywood, whose principles, much closer to what we would now call libertarianism, centered on personal sovereignty.) Physically underground, the Commune adopts a new strategy of going politically underground, "no more an open war to wage; / Or braggart like to scour the field, / And overt cast the battle gage." In the final stanza, the Commune triumphantly returns from the dead:

I am not dead, I am not dead,
I live a life intense, divine;
Yours were the days forever fled,
But all the morrows shall be mine.[60]

Wilson's poem enjoyed an afterlife of its own in both the late nineteenth-century anarchist and, interestingly, the spiritualist press; we might also see its influence, or at least a shared aesthetic of revivification, in the Popular Front anthem "I Dreamed I Saw Joe Hill Last Night." It became a particular touchstone for feminist anarchist Voltairine de Cleyre, who quoted the final stanza in one of her annual Commune anniversary speeches, "The Commune Is Risen," as well as in an 1895 speech memorializing the Haymarket defendants who had joined the subterranean army of the dead.[61] (The commemorative celebration, which was a regular feature of late nineteenth-century radical politics, offers still another example of the revolutionary macabre.) J. Michelle Coghlan describes de Cleyre's 1912 Commune address as "a vital index of the way the Commune's memory continued to animate radical feeling and speak to contemporary revolutionary struggles some four decades after its sensational demise."[62] What strikes me most about "The Commune Is Risen" is how it uses the Commune to "animate radical feeling" in the present by picturing its demise as the catalyst for its quite material reanimation. "We do not stand today as mourners at the bier of a Dead Cause, but with the joy of those who behold it living in the Resurrection," de Cleyre begins. Much as the Pittsburgh Proclamation imagines judgment day wrought by anarchism instead of by God, she seems less interested in resurrection as a Christian affair than as a subterranean one. "A portentous sound has risen from the depths; in the roots of human life, in coal-caverns, Revolt speaks," she continues. "Underground the earthquake rumbles wide," and across the earth "the mines growl." Returning to Wilson's poem, she concludes, "We hear the Commune's 'earthquake tread,' and know that out of the graves at Père-la-Chaise, out of the trenches of Satory, out of the fever-plains of Guiana, out of the barren rural sands of Caledonia, the Great Ghost has risen, crying across the world, *Vive la Commune!*"[63] De Cleyre's riff on Wilson spins out the eeriness of his poem, as she envisions the fallen Communards charging the underground and sowing an unearthly internationalism.

The IWPA's interest in the occult possibilities of the physical underground returns us once more to Marx's "old mole" and allows us to build out its literary genealogy further. For Marx was not the first radical to adapt the mole that Hegel had adapted from Shakespeare into a figure for revolution; his future antagonist Mikhail Bakunin did so six years earlier. Bakunin, whose anarchist ideas would split the First International in 1872 (in part because of his embrace of the revolutionary power of secret associations), was a key influence on the Chicago anarchists, and the *Alarm* sold translations of his works alongside those of Marx. The revolutionary mole appears in Bakunin's early essay "The Reaction in Germany" (1842), an argument for the primacy of negation in the dialectical process best remembered for its famous final lines: "The passion for destruction is a creative passion, too." But a few pages earlier he writes,

> The Spirit of revolution is not subdued, it has only sunk itself in order soon to reveal itself again as an affirmative, creative principle, and right now it is burrowing—if I may avail myself of this expression of Hegel's—like a mole under the earth.... Nevertheless, visible manifestations are stirring around us, hinting that the Spirit, this old mole, has brought its underground work to completion and that it will soon come again to pass judgment.[64]

Even more than Marx's mole, Bakunin's mole melds the earthly with the unearthly. It descends "under the earth" and then, like the risen Christ, returns to "pass judgment." Bakunin retains from Hegel the image of the mole as a "Spirit," but he specifies that it is "the Spirit of revolution" rather than Hegel's broader sense of *Geist* as human consciousness. At the same time, Bakunin amplifies the ghostliness of *Geist* (a cognate of "ghost"), which Hegel had muted with his emphasis on the historical agency of reason. Borrowing a spiritualist idiom for worldly signs of otherworldly activity, his revolutionary mole-spirit is attended by "visible manifestations... stirring around us" that signal the completion of its "underground work." In Bakunin's old mole, we can find—as perhaps the Chicago anarchists did—an image of the underground as a site where revolution becomes endowed with supernatural power.

"Underground Railways"

The month after the *Alarm* published S. Robert Wilson's ode to the Paris Commune's risen dead, it published an anonymous poem called "On a Cartridge of 'Hercules' Dynamite," which pictured the Commune in the company of another revolutionary "a-mouldering in the grave," even as "his soul is marching on." The poem reads in full:

> Infant destroyer of dragons! There are labors for you to do,
> Woe to the crown'd king of serpents if he sets his proud hoofs upon you!
> Louise Michel is mad, they say again;
> Well, for the knaves, she has too long been sane.
> They who have hanged John Brown, hung him so high
> That, like Orion, he bestrides the sky.[65]

The speaker urges on the work of dynamite, icon of the anarchist underground, by placing it alongside Louise Michel, the imprisoned Communard, and John Brown, executed twenty-six years earlier. In fact, "On a Cartridge of 'Hercules' Dynamite" was one of several poems about Brown to appear in the *Alarm*.[66] These poems evince the anarchists' attachment to another movement besides the Paris Commune that seemed over: radical abolitionism. Yet the poem also raises a question about the nature of this attachment. The terse structure of three rhyming couplets and the nebulous theme of repression recoiling suggest some relation between the Paris Commune, Harpers Ferry, and the present. But with no framing, the relation between the juxtaposed times and places remains ambiguous. When anarchists called on the memory of antislavery—which, as I will show, they did often—what did they understand it to mean to anarchism?

Unlike the Paris Commune, abolitionism had not suffered a spectacular defeat. Instead, many white Americans, eager to forget the terrible destruction of the Civil War, had papered over the struggle against slavery with narratives of mutual sacrifice and reconciliation.[67] Abolitionists themselves were dismissed as fanatics or "annoying relic[s]," in Holly Jackson's words, their fight relegated to a distant past with no bearing on the present.[68] (Jackson recounts that in 1870 the celebrated abolitionist Wendell Phillips "was booed in Faneuil Hall," the site of so many antislavery meetings, "by someone who yelled that his message was 'played out.'"[69]) At the same time, the Union's victory had allowed the state to take on the mantle of the antislavery cause—even as the betrayal of Reconstruction proved how little it deserved to do so. Yet while many were working to forget or supersede antebellum abolitionism, the *Alarm* frequently called on its memory, and the IWPA explicitly identified itself as an abolitionist movement. Its goal, of course, was not the abolition of slavery but the abolition of the entire economic system that slavery had played such a crucial role in creating: "ABOLISH CAPITAL," as a headline in the second issue of the *Alarm* proclaimed.[70]

Since the end of slavery, labor activists and socialists, including many former abolitionists, had identified the workers' movement as abolitionism's logical next cause. But whereas these activists advocated for a more equitable distribution of wealth, the IWPA insisted the entire system of private property must be destroyed. Most of its members had not participated in the antislavery movement. Many were recent immigrants; many were too young. Nonetheless, Black freedom struggles were politically formative for a number of the Chicago anarchists. Perhaps most significantly, Lucy Parsons was born enslaved in Virginia and then brought to Texas; although she identified herself as "Spanish-Indian" after she and Albert Parsons left Texas together for Chicago in 1873, the anti-Black epithets that police and the mainstream press regularly hurled at her prevented her from making a complete break with the past.[71] After fighting in the Confederate army as a teenager, Albert Parsons began his political career as a Radical Republican organizing with Black Texans; Samuel Fielden was radicalized when a series of Black antislavery lecturers visited his hometown in England; Dyer Lum descended from the well-known abolitionist family the Tappans; Josef Dietzgen, who became editor of the *Arbeiter-Zeitung* after August Spies's imprisonment, emigrated from Germany to Montgomery, Alabama, in the 1850s, where he lived until the lynching of some antislavery friends prompted his return to Germany. However, these personal and political genealogies were never straightforward.

Subtending the IWPA's abolitionist framework was an analogy between waged labor and enslaved labor familiar from antebellum white men's labor activism, which the *Alarm* took up and developed. The article in the *Alarm* before "Abolish Capital," titled "Enslaved Labor," explained, "Slavery is where one person is compelled to render service for the benefit of another. And this is precisely what the capitalistic system, based upon private property in the implements of labor, compels the wage laborer to do."[72] Furthermore, another article in the same issue observed that enslavers' claims about the benevolence of the ruling class and the elevating effects of labor were "precisely the argument used to defend capitalism—the wage-slavery system—to-day."[73] In a similar vein, C. L. James compared state socialists, philanthropists, and others who would reform capitalism rather than destroy it to pro-slavery colonizationists who made "the error of assuming that the existing, crying, fundamental abuse, must be preserved, whatever else happens."[74] The history of slavery showed the folly of trying to ameliorate a ruthless system when it needed to be entirely uprooted, James argued. But it also showed the folly of believing its end to be impossible.

The parallels the anarchists drew between the defense of capitalism and the defense of slavery could be illuminating. But the parallels they drew between slavery and capitalism themselves, of course, fundamentally misrecognized slavery as defined by coerced labor alone. More than that, as David Roediger and others have shown, the description of white workers as "wage slaves" historically did not create solidarity between enslaved and waged workers so much as it served as a means of distinction, which jarred white audiences with its image of the "wrong" people enslaved.[75] The metaphor's resurgence among anarchists indicates a limit of their critique of capitalism: their inability to understand its racial character, even as the "wage slave" analogy symptomatically exhibited it. Despite the Pittsburgh Proclamation's call for "equal rights for all without distinction to sex or race," the IWPA kept its focus on white male workers.[76] It did so even as the xenophobic mainstream press consistently racialized the anarchists themselves as non-white, depicting them with dark complexions, unruly hair and beards, and unplaceable accents. (A sketch in the humor magazine *Puck*, for example, represents "the Supreme Anarchist" as a Polish immigrant who is also "the shapeless fungus of a human Dismal Swamp," an image whose muddle does not obscure its reference to Black fugitives from slavery.)[77] The *Alarm*'s embrace of tramps as the heart of the movement never considered the relation between Northern vagrancy laws and Southern Black Codes. Nowhere in the contributors' critiques of waged labor or property did they consider whiteness either as a wage or as property, in W. E. B. Du Bois's and Cheryl Harris's respective formulations.[78] The *Alarm* paid almost no attention to the struggles of Black workers in any sector, and the IWPA rarely attempted to organize with them. There are glimpses of other possibilities in the movement: For example, in February 1885, new organizer Harry A. Blakesley wrote in to report that his Topeka, Kansas, group (one of the few consisting of students) was planning to organize "a large group among our colored friends," having "engaged a skating rink for the purpose."[79] And a month before the Haymarket affair, Lucy Parsons responded to the massacre of Black residents of Carrolton, Mississippi, by their white neighbors with an article urging Black Southerners to abandon the ballot and the church and to take up "the torch of the incendiary" against "these loafers" whose "land you tilled as a chattel slave [and] still till as a wage-slave."[80] But these instances remained exceptions. The circle around the *Alarm* embraced the idea that "anarchism is a kind of abolitionism," as Marquis Bey writes.[81] Yet they did not "reckon full force with Blackness," as Bey argues anarchists must do to see how "Blackness serves as the distinct angle of vision for encountering the effects of State-sanctioned enslavement and oppression."[82] They neither recognized the historical role Blackness played in the constitution of capitalism and the state nor reckoned with the possibilities of anarchism expressed through Blackness.

We cannot disavow how an anti-Black worldview at once enabled and limited the IWPA's invocations of abolitionism. Yet it does not fully explain the question "On a Cartridge of 'Hercules' Dynamite" poses about what abolitionism meant to them. To some extent, we can understand the anarchists who called back to abolitionism as celebrating their movement's continuity with earlier radical movements. In regular reports on anniversary celebrations of the attack on Harpers Ferry, for example, the *Alarm* explicitly held Brown up as "a model for men to copy," in the words of one member of the John Brown Association of Jersey City.[83] But I am struck by the sense of melancholy that pervades the *Alarm*'s invocations of abolitionism, especially its undergrounds. Writers for the paper did not celebrate the accomplishments of abolitionist undergrounds so much as they "brooded and studied over them," to return to the subterranean prisoners pondering dynamite in Swank's "Election Day." I hypothesize that the anarchists felt themselves to be working in the shadow of a movement over but not yet *done*. At times this was a source of inspiration for them and at times a source of frustration. When the Boston Unitarian journal the *Index* lambasted the anarchists' embrace of violence, for instance, the *Alarm* countered with a comparison to Brown, whose memory the *Index* venerated. "For was not he too one of the 'worst enemies of democratic institutions,' as they existed in his day?" the writer demanded. "A 'riot' in any large city under a crimson flag of labor" would "fall upon the country like the report from Harpers Ferry did in 1859," the article continued hopefully, "and might even convince our good friend the *Index* that freedom did not wholly lie in the direction his pointer is set to indicate."[84] The final proposition suggests that the anarchists not only saw in Brown's actions a revolutionary precedent; they also understood him to have discerned a definition of freedom—beyond the state and its laws—out of sight of liberal outlets like the *Index*. Doing so figures Brown's death as a defeat, like the Commune, rather than as the first shot of a victory later achieved, as the writer for the *Index* and other good Republicans wished to think. Like their summoning of the Paris Commune's presumed dead, then, the anarchists' melancholic dwelling on abolitionist undergrounds shaped a subterranean imaginary that was wondrously coincident with the past.

Consider still another story by Lizzie Swank, "Two Stories in One," which appeared in the same issue of the *Alarm* in which Lucy Parsons urged Black workers to take up "the torch of the incendiary." A diptych that sets Black fugitives on the Underground Railroad alongside contemporary white workers, its form echoes the juxtapositions of "On a Cartridge of 'Hercules' Dynamite." The first part, "Slavery in 1850," recounts the escape from slavery of Rose, Jerry, and Jeptha in a story notable for its emphasis on Black militancy during a period when many writers were renovating the Underground Railroad into a stage for white heroism. The three reach Sandusky, Ohio—which readers may remember from chapter 3 as the location of the American Mysteries Secret U.G.R.R. Society, an armed Black organization with links to the African-American Mysteries and to John Brown—and then proceed on "over the 'underground.'"[85] Before they reach Canada, however, four marshals catch up with them, and Rose and Jerry hide in the bushes while Jeptha confronts the marshals. When he refuses to give away his companions' hiding place, the head marshal lunges for him with a horse whip, and Jeptha quickly stabs him. Then, before the deputy marshals can kill him, Jeptha turns the knife on himself. Rose and Jerry, we learn, successfully reach Canada disguised as young boys.

The second part, "Slavery in 1886," begins as a pay cut threatens the family of John, a factory worker, his wife, Nellie, and their children. John's unsavory foreman, Gray, proposes that if their young son Willie will leave school and take a job at the factory, he can make up the lost wages. He then offers John a better-paying job that would require him to leave home, paralleling Jerry's enslaver's attempt in the first story to compel him to marry another woman. When John declines, Gray attempts to assault Nellie, recalling Rose's sale "to a bad man who frightened me so that I prayed over and over again to die," but John arrives in time to throw him out of the house. Soon after, the workers go on strike, and when Gray receives a blow in the fray, he blames John. Gray brings the police to search the house and they notice Nellie sitting on a trapdoor. Gray brutally attacks her and the children until he can access the door, and the police discover John in the cellar, a subterranean hiding place that both literalizes the Underground Railroad of the first story and recuperates one of its archetypal sanctuaries. The story closes as Nellie prematurely delivers a stillborn child and dies herself a few hours later, Willie enters factory life, John becomes a tramp, and Gray prospers. Swank ends by demanding,

"Have we no Jepthas among us? Is not the freedom of the white slave—the revolution—near at hand?"[86]

Although Swank adopts the facile analogy of the "white slave," the emphasis of her story ultimately falls less on an actual parallel with slavery than on a wishful parallel with antislavery resistance, calling for a present-day underground that would model itself on the historical example of Black fugitives. An unidentified speaker at the 1884 counter-Thanksgiving march had similar thoughts, admonishing the crowd, "When the slaves wanted liberty they did not stop for anything. We got our guns, and that is the way to do."[87] The problem, as the speaker and Swank saw it, was that white workers lacked the clarity of enslaved people's political analysis. Freedom could not be "near at hand" so long as they believed themselves already to be free, so long as "with a copy of the Declaration in one hand and the ballot in the other, the wage worker is deluded into the belief that he is a free man and a sovereign!"[88] In an article titled "Slavery—White and Black," Swank contrasted this delusion with enslaved people's understanding:

> In the old slavery days every slave owner had three votes for every five slaves he owned. To-day every great manufacturer has a vote for each slave and his political influence amounts to a several hundred vote power. The only difference is that black slaves never dreamed the power their ownership gave their master could help *their* cause; while white wage-slaves are ingeniously hood-winked into thinking *they* are wielding a power, and asserting their freedom.[89]

Enslaved people, whose lack of a vote gave their enslavers even greater voting power, recognized that electoral politics was rigged for the benefit of the ruling class, so they never mistook it for a means of liberation. White workers, who believed the power of the ballot evinced their freedom, needed to learn that same lesson in order to understand that the "freedom" they claimed was only "the shadow of freedom," as Swank put it, and even that was "fast dematerializing." Parsons's and Swank's frustration is palpable. Without a racial analysis of capitalism, neither one could understand why white workers would be so invested in believing themselves to be free.

The frustration Swank expresses in "Two Stories in One" helps us discern something wishful in the way "On a Cartridge of 'Hercules' Dynamite" moves from the anarchist underground to John Brown. The poem's juxtapositional structure enacts a descent from the present into the past: from the dynamite the speaker addresses, to Louise Michel and the Paris Commune, to John Brown. At the same time, when the poet declares that "[t]hey who have hanged John Brown, hung him so high / That, like Orion, he bestrides the sky," they question whether John Brown belongs to the past at all. The lines' odd syntax transforms the past tense of Brown's death ("hanged") into the present perfect ("have hanged"), an aspect that pulls this event toward the speaker's moment. "On a Cartridge of 'Hercules' Dynamite" tries to make the past contiguous, if not continuous, with the present. Its morbid preoccupations, too, turn out to be a ruse: Brown's hanging becomes his celestial apotheosis, while Michel's ostensible madness becomes her regeneration. Both promise a revolutionary movement that traverses time, in which history's apparent failures invest the anarchist underground with unreckoned power. This was also the hope Albert Parsons expressed in what would be the final issue of the *Alarm* to appear before police shut down the paper after the Haymarket affair. In the conclusion to his report about a "Law and Order League" that property holders in Ottawa, Kansas, had formed against the supposedly "dangerous, lawless element taking root there," Parsons quoted the refrain of "John Brown's Body," reminding readers, "John Brown's body lies moulding [sic] in the grave, / But his soul goes marching on." His exhortatory final lines connect Ottawa, Kansas, with Osawatomie, just to the northwest, where Brown famously battled proslavery forces, and Brown's underground—literal and figurative—with forces "taking root" that would "emancipate the laborers of the world from wage-slavery and capitalistic domination."[90] Brown offered the anarchists not just a usable past, which would reclaim abolitionism as a doctrine against the state, but also the image of an infinite revolutionary present, in which the question of freedom, seemingly closed after the end of slavery, could be reopened.

In late 1887, after the Haymarket bombing, the trial, the executions, and the *Alarm*'s shutdown by the police and subsequent resurrection, new editor Dyer D. Lum "brooded and studied" over the crushing of his own movement and fantasized about how things might have turned out differently. In an article titled "Underground Railways," Lum wrote,

> When black slavery was legal—when law and gospel smiled approvingly on that "peculiar institution," and statesmen proclaimed the constitutional "covenant with hell" to be above human rights and an effectual bar against justice—the sturdy common sense of the people showed itself in contempt for the prevailing law and order by "conspiring" to establish secure routes for runaway slaves on their way to Canada. The fact that men would band together to "throttle law," to connive

at depriving planters of their legal property, and to make themselves liable by furnishing food and shelter to these poor outlaws, demonstrated that the law had been tried in the balance and found wanting.... A spirit was born that damns the law and refuses obedience to injustice.

Who doubts today that had any one of our heroic comrades, recently put out of the way by an arrogant state, succeeded in effecting an escape, he could in like manner have passed from city to city, cared for by loving hands, from the Atlantic to the Pacific?[91]

Lum's fantasy asks readers not to recall the Underground Railroad but to picture "Underground Railways"—plural—and to envision a world in which such subterranean activity thwarted the legal system and kept August Spies, Albert Parsons, George Engel, and Adolph Fischer alive. His redescription of the Underground Railroad as "the people...'conspiring'" draws a direct line between its underground and that of the IWPA's Pittsburgh Proclamation, with its injunction to do "the work of revolutionary conspiracy." Attributing Samuel Fielden's call at Haymarket Square to "throttle [the] law" to the Underground Railroad's participants, he merges them in a transhistorical subterranean movement. When the article ends with a call for "the new abolitionist" to "raise ... his warning voice," it makes this genealogy explicit. But its counterfactual mode also reminds us that this genealogy has yet to be realized; the inheritor of radical antislavery's underground is not anarchism as it exists but anarchism as it could be.

The Underground Inside

Several years after August Spies warned a Chicago courtroom of a "subterranean fire" that the state could neither understand nor extinguish, it flashed up again in an unexpected place. In his unfinished novella *Billy Budd*, Herman Melville describes the "natural depravity" that burns inside master-at-arms John Claggart as follows: "As to Claggart, the monomania in the man—if that indeed it were—as involuntarily disclosed by starts in the manifestations detailed, yet in general covered over by his self-contained and rational demeanor; this, like a subterranean fire, was eating its way deeper and deeper in him. Something decisive must come of it."[92] Spies had not coined the expression "subterranean fire," which appears periodically in nineteenth-century writing. Usually the fire to which the phrase refers is literal, but occasionally authors use it figuratively, as

Spies and Melville do. In an excursus on geothermal heat in the 1843 essay "A Winter Walk," for example, Henry David Thoreau hypothesizes that this "subterranean fire in nature which never goes out" has its analogue in the human heart.[93] Still, it is hard not to wonder at the phrase's appearance in a novella, primarily written between the Haymarket bombing and the execution, about an accidental killing, an unjust trial meant to quell an uprising against the state, and the hanging of an innocent man that results.

In fact, almost fifty years ago, Melville scholar Robert K. Wallace published a note in *American Literature* positing that *Billy Budd*, "whatever else it might be, reflects the author's imaginative response to the Haymarket affair."[94] This assertion departs from the customary understanding that Melville based *Billy Budd* on the 1842 *Somers* mutiny case, to which the novella directly refers. But Wallace points out that it was Haymarket that had "revived" *Somers* in the press while Melville was writing, as an outgrowth of the inescapable newspaper coverage of the bombing, trial, and executions.[95] Moreover, Melville's revision of the text "parallels major Haymarket developments." While Billy Budd was "simply a mutineer" in the first version of the story, the second version, which Melville wrote between the bombing and the executions of the anarchists, "emphasized Claggart's death and the punishment of Billy, just as in real life emphasis fell on the deaths of the Chicago policemen and the punishment of anarchists." Finally, the third version of the story, written a year after the executions, "shifts the focus from Billy and Claggart to Vere just as the national concern over the Haymarket affair shifted from the individual anarchists and the Chicago police to the way the legal system had dealt with the case."[96]

Wallace confines his analysis to plot and themes, but a closer reading discovers further parallels, beginning with Melville's use of the phrase "subterranean fire." Melville repeatedly describes Claggart as "a sort of chief of police" (64) for the ship, evoking the police officers whose deaths led to the Haymarket defendants' murder convictions. Captain Vere refers to Billy, for his part, as "the striker" (107) because Claggart dies after Billy hits him, but the term inescapably recalls the workers striking for an eight-hour day whose attack by police prompted the protest at Haymarket Square. The Haymarket connection may also explain Vere's puzzling exclamation after Billy kills Claggart: "It is the divine judgment on Ananias!" (100). One of a group of early Christians who had abolished private property, believing that none "of the things which he possessed was his own, but they had all things in common" (Acts 4:32), Ananias was struck down after he sold a parcel of land and kept the money for himself. The allusion thus shadows the conflict between Billy and Claggart with the conflict between anarchism and capitalism. Billy's trial, too, proceeds along lines familiar from the Haymarket trial: the way Vere intervenes in the drumhead court, reframing the officers' qualms as a struggle between private feelings and public responsibilities, echoes Haymarket trial judge Joseph Gary's prejudicial instructions to the jury. If we follow Barbara Johnson's bleak reading of the politics of Billy Budd's trial, they certainly seem to chime with those of Haymarket as well: "The legal order," Johnson concludes, "can only eliminate violence by transforming violence into the final authority."[97] Like the Haymarket executions, Billy's execution generates conflicting media responses. Afterward, a newspaper account surmises that he "was no Englishman, but one of those aliens adopting English cognomens" (130), much as the mainstream press depicted the anarchists as foreigners, whether or not they were born in the United States. Meanwhile, a sailor writes and circulates a ballad memorializing Billy Budd, like the elegies for the Haymarket defendants that Kristin Boudreau shows proliferated after their executions, and other sailors cherish chips of the beam from which Billy was hung, just as supporters of the Haymarket defendants wore brass pins in the shape of gallows (a trinket displaying the morbid aspects of anarchism this chapter has described).[98]

Yet if Haymarket haunts *Billy Budd*, what is interesting about Melville's use of the phrase "subterranean fire" is how removed it is from this subtext. It does not refer to the threat of mutiny that grips Vere, leading him to sacrifice Billy to martial law. Instead, it refers to Claggart's individual "pent frenzy," as Melville put it in one revision of the passage (360): the particular conjunction of desire for Billy Budd and aversion to that desire that Eve Sedgwick terms "homosexual-homophobic knowing."[99] Sedgwick argues that these two are related: "Not an alternative to the plot of male-male desire and prohibition, the mutiny plot is the form it takes at the (inseparable) level of the collective."[100] In other words, the crew's subterranean fire—its potential for mutiny—is homologous to Claggart's own mutinous desire. I would add that the work the homology does is to displace the former with the latter. The crew's subterranean fire proves phantasmal: although Vere's suspicion of incipient mutiny makes him determined to hang Billy, Melville offers no evidence that any such plot exists; he hints that even the afterguardsman's midnight invitation to join "a gang of us" (82) was only Claggart's contrivance to entrap Billy. As the crew's subterranean fire flickers and fades from the story, however, it rematerializes as Claggart's homosexuality, which comes to drive the plot.

The work of this transposition comes into focus if we compare *Billy Budd* to Pauline Hopkins's *Of One Blood*, where Reuel's interiority, "the hidden self" of the subtitle, parallels the hidden city of Telassar. There, however, each site builds out the other, while the underground inside Claggart supplants the ship's underground. Like Telassar and so many of the other undergrounds I trace in this book, Claggart's "subterranean fire" entails a "mystery," but as Vere attests, "it is a 'mystery of iniquity,' a matter for psychologic theologians to discuss" (108), not a social or political phenomenon. It is born, not made. The "mystery" of Claggart's desires, private yet defining, makes him an avatar of emerging models of homosexual identity, as Sedgwick and subsequent queer theory scholars have shown. It is also, I argue, the enclosure of anarchism's subterranean fire.

Moreover, by examining *Billy Budd*'s transformation of the underground from mutiny to interiority, we can perceive what Fredric Jameson calls its "vanishing mediator": the notion of homosexuality's own potentially anarchic spirit.[101] That is, what shuttles from Haymarket to Claggart but gets privatized there is homosexuality as a subterranean fire: the notion, brought into focus by the famously homoerotic space of the ship, that queers could be everywhere, that you don't know what they are doing, but that they're in it together—and whatever *it* is could explode the ground at your feet. It is this version of homosexuality that enables the transit from the crew's mutiny to Claggart's mutinous desires. But in the transition, subterranean fire moves from outside to inside, from collective to individual, from discomposing the world to discomposing John Claggart.

To point out how *Billy Budd* converts the dangers of an anarchist underground into an emerging model of homosexual identity (via a less particularized, more politicized version of homosexuality it supplants) is to add to other critics' observations of the novella's tendency to transform one thing into another, from Cesare Casarino's analysis of the ship as a place where "old and obsolescent modes of production are superimposed onto new and dynamic ones," engendering "the crisis of modernity," to Hiram Pérez's argument that Billy Budd's supersession of the African "Handsome Sailor" who opens the story stages "the figure of the primitive as an invisible component of the modern gay."[102] I propose that in transposing anarchism's subterranean fire to Claggart's tumultuous subjectivity, Melville indexes the beginning of the underground's transformation into "an inside narrative," in the words of *Billy Budd*'s subtitle—a figure for interiority that would reach its fullest expression in emerging theories of the unconscious. This is not to say that the expression of the unconscious as subterraneanity was new at the end of the nineteenth century; almost half a century before writing *Billy Budd*, in *Moby-Dick*, Melville himself had analogized the workings of "unconscious understandings" to the untraceable shafts dug by "the subterranean miner that works in us all."[103] But the expression of the unconscious as subterraneity expands, intensifies, and becomes institutionalized in these decades. As William James observed in 1901, looking back at recent achievements in the study of psychology,

> In the wonderful explorations by Binet, Janet, Breuer, Freud, Mason, Prince, and others, of the subliminal consciousness of patients with hysteria, we have revealed to us whole systems of underground life, in the shape of memories of a painful sort which lead a parasitic existence, buried outside the primary fields of consciousness, and making irruptions thereunto with hallucinations, pains, convulsions, paralyses of feeling and of motion, and the whole procession of symptoms of hysteric disease of body and mind.[104]

Pierre Janet named these "whole systems of underground life" the "subconscious" and compared them to stacked subterranean streams that periodically break the surface of consciousness.[105] Freud described the idea that certain thoughts "exist and are operative beneath the threshold of consciousness," as he and Josef Breuer put it in *Studies in Hysteria* (1893–95), as the "topographical model" of the psyche, or "depth-psychology."[106] The method of analyzing it was "one of clearing away the pathogenic material layer by layer, and we liked to compare it with the technique of excavating a buried city."[107] The unconscious, in short, was the self's underground.

By tracking *Billy Budd*'s relocation of the anarchist underground to Claggart's psyche, we can discern the waning of certain concepts of the underground whose development I have traced over the course of this book. As the underground becomes a figure for interiority, it helps create what Sedgwick calls the novella's "privacy effect: the illusion that a reader of *Billy Budd* has witnessed a struggle between private and public realms that are distinguished from one another with quite unusual starkness." Sedgwick identifies Vere as "the character who seems most identified with and responsible for the austerity of this definitional segregation," to the extent that he labors to present his decision to condemn Billy Budd as an agonized "choice between public and private."[108] But Claggart's "subterranean fire," "in general covered over by his self-contained and rational demeanor" and only "involuntarily disclosed by starts," likewise partakes of this logic, and Claggart reproduces it in his caution that Billy is "a deep one" whose "fair cheek," "under the ruddy-tipped daisies," may hide "a mantrap" (94). It still isn't clear to me whether the novella believes in "the privacy effect" or seeks to expose the illusion; to make this call requires deciding whether or not it is on Vere's side. But restoring the impressions the Haymarket affair made on *Billy Budd* allows us to reconstruct how the privacy effect is manufactured through the evocation and suppression of a countervailing idea of a smoldering underground.

Reading *Billy Budd* alongside the Haymarket affair indicates that as earlier ideas of the underground recede at the end of the nineteenth century, they become incorporated into the developing discourse of psychoanalysis. But they hint, too, that the underground eludes full capture, just as its advocates intended. Consider what happens following Billy's execution, when the silence of the watching crew "was gradually disturbed by a sound not easily to be verbally rendered," an "ominous low sound": "The seeming remoteness of its source was because of its murmurous indistinctness, since it came from close by, even from the men massed on the ship's open deck. Being inarticulate, it was dubious in significance further than it seemed to indicate some capricious revulsion of thought or feeling such as mobs ashore are liable to" (126). If Haymarket gets internalized and individualized in *Billy Budd*, it spills back out with the sound that "mobs ashore are liable to." The story this book has told enables us to recognize this "ominous low sound" as the sound of the underground. "Not easily to be verbally rendered," of "murmurous indistinctness," and "dubious in significance," it confounds knowledge. It does not articulate direct resistance but "seemed to indicate some capricious revulsion of thought or feeling." It has no single origin or place. It appears far away but is dangerously close. Vere responds by ordering the crew to "pipe down" (126). Nonetheless, the "mobs ashore" eventually get Vere, who, believing he has quelled a mutiny aboard the *Bellipotent*, is ultimately felled by a French Revolutionary battleship.

But this finale, as readers of *Billy Budd* well know, turns out not to be the end—and that inconclusiveness, too, evinces the persistence of the underground. The narrator's account of Vere's death is followed by two accounts by other hands: first a report in a naval newspaper vilifying Billy and eulogizing Claggart, then a sailor's ballad written from Billy's perspective and circulated among the navy's crews. Having begun as an "inside narrative" promising authoritative knowledge, *Billy Budd* disperses into a jumble of incommensurate texts, each of which casts the others into doubt. As Barbara Johnson quips, the story "begins to repeat itself—retelling itself first in reverse, and then in verse." The ending thus "problematizes the very *idea* of authority," Johnson continues, because "to repeat is to be ungovernably open to revision, displacement, and reversal."[109] Surely Spies and the other members of IWPA would find something congenial in being so ungovernable—something like solidarity, however unintentional. We, too, can recognize something familiar in the ungovernability that finally mires *Billy Budd*'s story of governance. The solid ground of the narrative opens up, branches out, and folds back on itself, like the passages of Mammoth Cave, the tunnels and sewers of the city mysteries, or Paschal Beverly Randolph's soul world. These repetitions and displacements double and discompose the story we have been told, like David Walker's rewriting of the US Constitution, Bernice's underground studio in William J. Wilson's "Afric-American Picture Gallery," or the subterranean Twin City of Charles Averill's *The Secrets of the Twin Cities*. Like each of these undergrounds and all of the others in this book, the ending of *Billy Budd* scuttles what we think we know and leaves us in the dark, which is also a place of multiplying possibilities. If *Billy Budd* indexes the waning of nineteenth-century ideas of the underground, it also testifies that, as August Spies said of the anarchists' subterranean fire, "you cannot put it out."

Epilogue

STAYING UNDERGROUND

This book has traced the emergence of the underground as an idea over the nineteenth century, before its eventual subsumption in the concept of subculture and psychological discourses of the unconscious. The media coverage of the Underground Railroad in the 1840s occupies a key place in this story as a catalyst for new meanings of the underground. Its marvelously literal images of a mysterious subterranean train themselves went underground in the late nineteenth century, I suggest, overtaken by narratives about a heroic network of abolitionists deftly ferrying fugitives to Canada, as well as by the invention of actual subways. But one thing that the previous chapters, for all their linear chronology, underscore is that the underground's temporalities are rarely linear; the underground doubles back, loops, and suspends time. And during the time I was writing this book, the weirdness of the Underground Railroad made an unexpected return.

In 2016, Colson Whitehead published *The Underground Railroad*, a harrowing picaresque that topped the *New York Times* best seller list; it went on to win both the 2016 National Book Award for fiction and the 2017 Pulitzer Prize for fiction, and Barry Jenkins adapted it into a television series for Amazon in 2021. Besides *The Underground Railroad*, 2016 saw the publication of Ben H. Winters's *Underground Airlines*, a counterfactual detective novel set in a version of the present where slavery is still legal in four states, as well as the WGN debut of Misha Green and Joe Pokaski's historical drama *Underground*, which ran for two seasons. The following year, photographer Dawoud Bey made the series *Night Coming Tenderly, Black*, whose images of nineteenth-century buildings and the Ohio countryside inhabit the perspective of fugitives on the Underground Railroad; it was installed in a Cleveland church known as an Underground Railroad site in 2018 and then exhibited at the Art Institute of Chicago in 2019. All of these works tap deep into nineteenth-century history, but they are uncontained either by the boundaries of realism or by the Underground Railroad's familiar legends. Nor do they comport with efforts to incorporate the Underground Railroad into an affirmational national history, exemplified most recently by the misbegotten plan to put Harriet Tubman's face on the twenty-dollar bill. In these respects, not only do they take the Underground Railroad as their subject; they also call back to nineteenth-century ideas of the underground. They revel in anachronism, fantasy, and mystery. In *Underground Airlines*, it's hard to say which is more disconcerting: the picture of slavery's continued existence or the fact that this alternate reality doesn't look so different from our own. *Underground*, at once pulpy and demanding, punctuates a devotion to period accuracy—one episode consists entirely of Harriet Tubman (played by Aisha Hinds) lecturing to abolitionists—with flashes of the present, as when Tubman turns to face the camera and condemns those who would "kill everything good and right in the world and call it 'making it great again.'" Even as *Night Coming Tenderly, Black* depicts sites of the Underground Railroad, the soft darkness of Bey's photographs refuses to elucidate its subjects. In taking up the Underground Railroad, these works confront a world that every day gives new evidence that it has not left slavery in the past, while reaching toward concepts of the underground that world has lost.

Whitehead's *The Underground Railroad* calls back to these earlier undergrounds especially distinctly. The novel's premise is the same idea that I trace in chapter 3 in newspaper reports, poetry, and antislavery songs in the mid-nineteenth century: that of the underground railroad as an actual subterranean train, built by unknown Black people who "toiled in the belly of the earth for the deliverance of slaves."[1] (In discussing the novel, I follow Whitehead in not capitalizing *underground railroad*.) Cora, the novel's shattered but determined protagonist, and her fellow fugitive Caesar first get there through a trapdoor in a barn that leads down steep stairs to a platform:

> The black mouths of the gigantic tunnel opened at either end. It must have been twenty feet tall, walls lined with dark and light colored stones in an alternating pattern. The sheer industry that had made such a project possible. Cora and Caesar noticed the rails. Two steel rails ran the visible length of the tunnel, pinned into the dirt by wooden crossties. The steel ran south and north presumably, springing from some inconceivable source and shooting toward a miraculous terminus. Someone had been thoughtful enough to arrange a small bench on the platform. Cora felt dizzy and sat down. (67)[2]

But Cora and Caesar learn that there is no "miraculous terminus." Instead, Cora observes, "[t]he heading of the underground railroad was laid in the direction of the bizarre" (90). One train pulls a bare platform, the next a sumptuous passenger car. Rather than taking a certain path to Canada, the underground railroad rambles and dead-ends. The destination of any given train cannot be determined in advance. No one knows the railroad's full extent. Its timetable is unpredictable, and its historical temporalities are discontinuous, too; it carries its passengers through an antebellum South where skyscrapers crop up without explanation. What's miraculous about the underground railroad is not its terminus but its kaleidoscopic (yet unseen) deviations, its bounded boundlessness.

The underground railroad has this in common with Cora, who, even in bondage, is "a stray in every sense" (145). That is to say that the underground railroad of Whitehead's novel, like its nineteenth-century antecedents, has a tendency to proliferate. It tunnels through the novel as it does through the nation, and it reappears in disparate places, including in Cora. Like many of Whitehead's protagonists, Cora is somewhat elusive. Maybe she is hollowed out by a lifetime of violence and loss; maybe she simply keeps her distance from the reader. But over the course of the novel, Whitehead delicately builds an analogy between his novel's protagonist and its central conceit. Whitehead first makes the parallel explicit when Cora attacks the kidnapper Ridgeway, and her scream "came from deep inside her, a train whistle echoing in a tunnel" (226). A few pages later, Whitehead shifts to Caesar's point of view as he recalls when he first asked Cora to run with him "for good luck—her mother was the only to ever make it out." But this time he acknowledges this was "probably a mistake": "She wasn't a rabbit's foot to carry with you on the voyage but the locomotive itself" (234). Caesar's realization prefigures the climax of the novel, when Ridgeway forces Cora to take him to the underground railroad station in Indiana—"the sorriest, saddest station yet" (256), unconnected to the rest of the line, with only a handcar because the tunnel is too small for a locomotive—and she pushes him down the stairs as they descend. Throwing herself into the handcar,

> She pumped and pumped and rolled out of the light. Into the tunnel that no one had made, that led nowhere.
>
> She discovered a rhythm, pumping her arms, throwing all of herself into movement. Into northness. Was she traveling through the tunnel or digging it? (303)

In this final journey, the apparatus of the underground railroad disappears. Cora is both a passenger on the train and, as Caesar recognized, "the locomotive itself," powering her way through the tunnel, making it as she goes.

Nor is Cora's embodiment of the underground railroad the only instance in the novel when the underground railroad unexpectedly recurs somewhere else. In a brief chapter right before Cora's final journey on the underground railroad, we at last learn the fate of Cora's mother, Mabel, whom Cora believes abandoned her when she was a child. We see Mabel flee the plantation for a swamp, where for a few moments she lies on her back, eats some young turnips she has grown, watches the sky, and listens to the animals around her.

> On the bed of damp earth, her breathing slowed and that which separated herself from the swamp disappeared. She was free.
>
> This moment.
>
> She had to go back. The girl was waiting on her. This would have to do for now. (294)

But on Mabel's way back, a cottonmouth bites her leg. She struggles on, until "she stumbled onto a bed of soft moss and it felt right. She said, Here, and the swamp swallowed her up" (295). Cora never learns that Mabel died trying to return to her. But if we recall the underground's nineteenth-century refractions, we might notice how Cora's contiguity with the underground railroad in the next chapter echoes the experience of Mabel, who finds a momentary freedom in blurring into the swamp (while relishing a root vegetable!) and finally sinks down into its depths. And when, underground, Cora comes to understand "the secret triumph you keep in your heart" (304) that the builders of the underground railroad must have cherished, her description evokes Mabel's determination, in the swamp, to "keep this moment close, her own treasure" (294). Cora's climactic journey on and as the underground railroad allows her, finally, some closeness to Mabel and her taste of freedom, even though Mabel herself never got to find "the words to share it with Cora" (294). Attending to the recurrences of the underground railroad—in Cora and in the swamp into which Mabel melts—in Whitehead's novel allows us to see it in the nineteenth-century ways that this book has sought to recuperate: not as a singular formation but as part of a burgeoning idea of the subterranean that takes shape through the proliferation and convergence of disparate versions of itself.

The Underground Railroad ends, though, with Cora leaving the underground behind. Once her arms are exhausted from pumping the handcar, she gets out and walks, running her hand along the side of the tunnel as she goes. "Her fingers danced over valleys, rivers, the peaks of mountains, the contours of a new nation hidden beneath the old" (304), perceptible only by touch. When a pinpoint of light appears ahead, she climbs out of the darkness of the tunnel she has at once traveled and made and finds herself in the mouth of a cave. She walks north until she meets a wagon train and joins the wagons as they head west. This conclusion, with its familiar overland route to a better life in America, reads as hopeful, if not exactly happy. Having gone underground, Cora reemerges transformed, just as she imagines those who first built the underground railroad must have done: "On one end there was who you were before you went underground, and on the other end a new person steps out into the light. The up-top world must be so ordinary compared to the miracle beneath, the miracle you made with your sweat and blood" (304). The underground railroad turns out to be a vehicle of self-knowledge that opens the way toward the novel's cautiously optimistic ending. Still, when Cora joined the convoy west, I questioned whether this expansionist fantasy could compare to that of the "new nation hidden beneath the old." I couldn't help but remember Paschal Beverly Randolph, in his revision of *After Death*, trading a future of subterranean upheaval for a Black colonization project in "their Zion in the south-west."[3] I thought uneasily, too, about what historians such as Shirley Ann Wilson Moore have taught us about the brutal exploitation of Black women on the wagon trains and in the West.[4] It was hard to forget Whitehead's own demonstrations of white Americans' tireless commitments to exploiting and destroying Black people's lives. Is there any reason to believe that Cora, heading west, would not continue to find cause to go underground? I wondered about the different life Cora might live if "the tunnel pulled at her" (68) even once she left it. What if she found a way, like Mabel, to say "Here," but one that wasn't fatal? If the underground did not forge a path to a better future but remained a necessary part of her daily existence? If it offered not self-discovery but the experience of thinking and acting collectively? In keeping with Whitehead's close study of history, I pictured Cora joining the United Order of Tents, the secret society of Black women founded in the mid-nineteenth century and continuing into the present, which has guarded its rituals, songs, and handshakes even as it has also engaged in the visible offices of caring for the needy and the sick and of burying the dead. The United Order of Tents' determination to remain, as an 1888 article in the New York *Sun* put it, "so mysterious," despite "the many efforts that have been made to invade it," suggests something of what Cora has discovered—but the novel finally forgets—about the singular refusal, respite, and possibility of going underground.[5]

This book tries to remember those things. By excavating the nineteenth-century undergrounds that precede and exceed *The Underground Railroad*, it asks how we could go elsewhere without "step[ping] out into the light," into clarity, or into the future. In search of some alternative to the institutions, systems, and beliefs that make up what Frederick Douglass, in "Slavery, the Slumbering Volcano," called "the ground" of our existence, the thinkers I study looked under it. Many took the underground as an analytical viewpoint that offered new purchase on life aboveground. Others saw in the underground a different way of living that might be closer than we guess. From the guides of Mammoth Cave to the authors of city mysteries, they rearranged society underground and summoned even stranger worlds. They envisioned exiting linear time to dwell in what Pauline Hopkins called "the eternal now" of subterranean time. They fantasized about what it would mean to live in "profound mystery," as William J. Wilson put it, out of sight of institutions and other forms of authority, and in ways one could not understand in advance. Some saw going underground as a means to foment revolution, but one need not always prepare to meet the forces above. Going underground could also be a means of escaping, creating, thinking, or simply breathing together, to cite the etymology of *conspiracy* I explored in chapter 6. These formations of the underground have themselves since been submerged. But this book has tried to recollect and reopen them for us now. When the future has never been more of a trap, the subterranean visions of the nineteenth century promise that there could be depths in the present, and they call us to imagine all these depths could hold.

Notes

Introduction. A Basement Shut Off and Forgotten during the Nineteenth Century

A version of the introduction appeared as "Going Underground: Race, Space, and the Subterranean," *American Literary History* 33 (Fall 2021): 510–26, in a special issue on second book projects.

1. Ellison, *Invisible Man*, 568, 571, 6, 581.

2. Melville, *Moby-Dick*, xvii.

3. Sociologist Milton M. Gordon first defined the term *subculture* in "The Concept of the Sub-Culture and Its Application," although the *Oxford English Dictionary* records earlier nonce uses of the word.

4. For a helpful sampling and overview of this work, see Gelder, *Subcultures Reader*.

5. Hebdige, *Subculture*, 18.

6. Stallybrass, "'Well Grubbed, Old Mole,'" 13; Marx, *Eighteenth Brumaire of Louis Bonaparte*, 121.

7. See Valencius, *Lost History of the New Madrid Earthquakes*.

8. On the scientific and infrastructural significance of the underground, see Williams, *Notes on the Underground*, chaps. 2 and 3.

9. Luciano, "Sacred Theories of Earth," 716. John McPhee coins the phrase "deep time" in *Basin and Range*, 142.

10. Yusoff, *Billion Black Anthropocenes or None*, 5. I read Yusoff's book as I was finishing this one, and I wish I could have had it from the beginning. Denise Ferreira

da Silva points out that to the extent that "blackness refers to matter"—and that *matter* was once defined as "that without form"—"it functions as a nullification of the whole signifying order that sustains value in both its economic and ethical scenes" ("1 (life) ÷ 0 (blackness)= ∞ − ∞ or ∞/∞").

11. Yusoff, *Billion Black Anthropocenes or None*, 67, 6.

12. Yusoff, *Billion Black Anthropocenes or None*, 107, 108.

13. Estes, *Our History Is the Future*, 19; "Short Bull's Speech, October 31, 1890," 313; "Kicking Bear's Speech, October 9, 1890," 310.

14. Knox, *Underground, or Life Below the Surface*, 5.

15. "New Publications," *Cincinnati Daily Gazette*, June 6, 1873, 5.

16. Marx, "Contribution to the Critique of Hegel's *Philosophy of Right*," 64.

17. Wynter elaborates this idea through much of her writing, but see especially "Unsettling the Coloniality of Being/Power/Truth/Freedom."

18. Hammond, "Speech on the Admission of Kansas, under the Lecompton Constitution," 318. My thinking about the mudsill and the slumbering volcano has benefited from conversations with Geo Maher, who also writes about both in his book *Anticolonial Eruptions: Racial Hubris and the Cunning of Resistance*.

19. Robinson, *Black Marxism*, 19.

20. Robinson, *Black Marxism*, 26.

21. Robinson, *Black Marxism*, 9.

22. Mirabeau quoted in James, *Black Jacobins*, 55; Smith, *Lecture on the Haytien Revolutions*, 15; Martineau, *Hour and the Man*, 1:18.

23. Enoch Lewis, "Proposals for Publishing a New Periodical Work, to Be Entitled *The African Observer*," *Berks and Schuylkill Journal*, April 7, 1827, 1.

24. "African Colonization," *Freedom's Journal*, December 21, 1827, 2.

25. Daut, *Tropics of Haiti*, 5.

26. Du Bois, "Comet," 253, 254; Wright, "Man Who Lived Underground," 54; Mayfield, "Underground"; Shockley, "ode to my blackness," 30. The underground promise of Puryear's "Old Mole" stands in contrast to his "Ladder for Booker T. Washington" (1996), a long wooden ladder that narrows so dramatically toward the top that it appears to recede indefinitely, a wry joke on the unattainability of Washingtonian uplift.

27. Gumbs, *M Archive*, 139. *M Archive* expands on Gumbs's 2015 short story "Evidence."

28. On the circulation of Walker's *Appeal*, see Hinks, *To Awaken My Afflicted Brethren*, 116–72.

29. Foucault, *Archaeology of Knowledge*, 144–45.

30. Williams, *Marxism and Literature*, 123.

31. Williams, *Marxism and Literature*, 112.

32. Williams, *Marxism and Literature*, 126.

33. Walker, *Appeal to the Coloured Citizens of the World*, 68.

34. Peterson, "Subject to Speculation," 111; Hartman, "Venus in Two Acts," 11. Hartman further develops critical fabulation as a method in *Wayward Lives, Beautiful Experiments*, xiii–xv.

35. Johnson, "'He Was a Lion, and He Would Destroy Much,'" 196, 197, 202, 207. Johnson's essay is part of a discussion of Ada Ferrer's *Freedom's Mirror: Cuba and Haiti in the Age of Revolution*.

36. Herring, *Queering the Underworld*, 21, 209.

37. Eburne, *Outsider Theory*, 352. Eburne uses this term to describe the writings and music of Sun Ra, who drew on the writings of Helena Blavatsky, who in turn seems to have been strongly influenced by Randolph (see Deveney, *Paschal Beverly Randolph*, chaps. 12–13).

38. Brown, *Black Utopias*, 17, 18, 17.

39. Quashie, *Sovereignty of Quiet*; Simpson, *Mohawk Interruptus*; Campt, *Listening to Images*, chap. 2; Crawley, *Black Pentecostal Breath*; Gordon, *Hawthorn Archive*. The work on fugitivity grows every day, but for influential statements see Best, *Fugitive's Properties*; Harney and Moten, *Undercommons*; Hartman, *Lose Your Mother*, chap. 12, and *Wayward Lives, Beautiful Experiments*; Mackey, "Other" and "Cante Moro"; Moten, *In the Break*; and Roberts, *Freedom as Marronage*. Rinaldo Walcott, however, cautions that *fugitivity* is a "limited frame . . . for thinking Black freedom" because it "only makes sense in the space of unfreedom and thus cannot be constituted as freedom." Rather, fugitivity "mark[s] the interstices of Black desires for freedom" (*Long Emancipation*, 106).

40. Ellison, *Invisible Man*, 9.

Chapter 1. The "Blackness of Darkness" in Mammoth Cave

A version of chapter 1 appeared as "The Blackness of Darkness: Mammoth Cave and the Racialization of the Underground," *History of the Present* 11 (Spring 2021): 2–22.

1. Bird, *Peter Pilgrim*, 2, 65. "Monarch of caves" became something of a stock phrase in Mammoth Cave literature.

2. Earlier in the 1830s, before the cave became a full-scale tourist attraction, two white guides had led small numbers of visitors through parts of it, and later in the century, new Black and white guides joined the descendants of the antebellum

guides. But as far as I can tell, the guides were all enslaved men from 1838 until after the Civil War.

3. Crary, "Blackness of Darkness."

4. West, "Trying the Dark."

5. Fanon, *Black Skin, White Masks*, 176; Musser, *Sensational Flesh*, 47–48. Fanon explains this masochistic tendency as deriving from the "guilt complex" that anti-Blackness induces in a "democratic culture" (177).

6. On the ugly exploring costumes, see Willis, *Health Trip to the Tropics*, 153, 160.

7. McKittrick, *Demonic Grounds*, x.

8. McKittrick, *Demonic Grounds*, xii, xiii.

9. McKittrick, *Demonic Grounds*, 7.

10. Finch, *Englishwoman's Experience in America*, 351.

11. Lydia Maria Child, "Mammoth Cave," *Anglo American*, October 28, 1843, 9.

12. Rusert, *Fugitive Science*, 4, 5.

13. This anecdote appears regularly in accounts of Mammoth Cave—for example, "The Mammoth Cave, Edmondson County, Kentucky," *Friend*, August 28, 1847, 389; Barnwell, "Mammoth Cave," 304.

14. Barnwell, "Mammoth Cave," 304; Silliman, "On the Mammoth Cave of Kentucky," 334.

15. Peterson, "Two Days in the Mammoth Cave," 157.

16. McKittrick, *Demonic Grounds*, 7.

17. Martin, *Pictorial Guide to the Mammoth Cave*, 10.

18. Rogers, *Incidents of Travel in the Southern States and Cuba*, 302–3.

19. Surtees, "Emancipation," 282; Finch, *Englishwoman's Experience in America*, 351.

20. Surtees, "Emancipation," 282. Surtees expanded this piece in "Recollections of North America."

21. Rusling, *Trip to the Mammoth Cave, K.Y.*, 6.

22. Stadler, *Troubling Minds*, especially chaps. 1–3.

23. Rogers, *Incidents of Travel in the Southern States and Cuba*, 280.

24. See, for example, Barnwell, "Mammoth Cave," 304; Rosenberg, *Jenny Lind in America*, 194; Willis, *Health Trip to the Tropics*, 151.

25. Child, "Mammoth Cave," 7. Thank you to David Anderson for encouraging me to think about Mammoth Cave and the sublime.

26. Willis, *Health Trip to the Tropics*, 204.

27. Peterson, "Two Days in the Mammoth Cave," 157.

28. Peterson, "Two Days in the Mammoth Cave," 155.

29. Barnwell, "Mammoth Cave," 309.

30. Thank you to R. J. Boutelle for help working through this passage.

31. Barnwell, "Mammoth Cave," 304.

32. Zabriskie, "Visit to the Mammoth Cave of Kentucky," 152.

33. Emerson, "Illusions," 244.

34. Barnwell, "Mammoth Cave," 309.

35. Willis, *Health Trip to the Tropics*, 172; Barnwell, "Mammoth Cave," 303.

36. Willis, *Health Trip to the Tropics*, 172. Peter West observes that when Lydia Maria Child visited the cave in 1843, she reported that this branch was called "the Jordan," but by the time Alexander Clark Bullitt's *Rambles in Mammoth Cave* appeared in 1845, it had been renamed Echo River. West hypothesizes that "we might read the 'Jordan' River as a site where Bishop and his fellow guides attempted to bring the vocabulary of slavery into a place that its proprietor sought to depoliticize" but that his enslaver John Croghan, who had a significant hand in *Rambles*, shut this down ("Trying the Dark").

37. "My Gropings Nine Miles Underground," 60.

38. "Tour in the Mammoth Cave." Joseph C. Douglas's essay "Music in the Mammoth Cave" gives a very helpful overview of music-making in the cave; I am indebted to it for this reference. Sometimes the guides seem to have varied their repertoire to include popular "white" songs, but the visitors identify most as "Negro songs" or sometimes "one of the wild songs of [Bishop's] Indian fathers" (Barnwell, "Mammoth Cave," 303).

39. Finch, *Englishwoman's Experience in America*, 35. We might gauge the traction of the analogy between Mammoth Cave and racialized blackness by way of an 1861 travelogue through the US South in which the author describes how an elderly enslaved man's face, breaking into a laugh, "opened till it looked like the entrance to the Mammoth Cave" ("Through the Cotton States," 315). Since the author is referring to the inside of the man's body, rather than the outside, his racialization might appear beside the point. But while presumably anyone's mouth *might* look like Mammoth Cave when opened widely to laugh, in what Cedric Robinson, in another context, calls a "confident declaration from the bleached bowels of mid-nineteenth-century American intelligentsia" (*Black Marxism*, 75), it is this enslaved Black man's mouth that *does*. We glimpse here how the racialization of Mammoth Cave intersected with the popularization of theories of comparative anatomy, whose focus on internal structures attempted to find a basis for racial categories below the surface of the skin. Thank you to Britt Rusert for suggesting the connection between the racialization of Mammoth Cave and comparative anatomy's search for a deeper science of racial difference.

40. Griffith, *Madge Vertner*, October 29, 1859, 4. On *Madge Vertner*, see Lockard, "'Light Broke Out Over My Mind.'"

41. Griffith, *Madge Vertner*, October 29, 1859, 4.

42. Griffith, *Madge Vertner*, October 8, 1859, 4.

43. Griffith, *Madge Vertner*, December 24, 1859, 4.

44. Spillers, "Mama's Baby, Papa's Maybe," 207.

45. Hammonds, "Black (W)holes and the Geometry of Black Female Sexuality," 139. Although Hammonds's account of the silences in Black feminist theory helps me conceptualize the absent presence of Black female sexuality in Mammoth Cave, it's important to note the differences between these scenes: unlike the silences Hammonds seeks to redress, Mammoth Cave's Black (w)holes were not produced by Black women and thus cannot yield the reclamation of "pleasure, exploration, and agency" that Hammonds seeks (134).

46. Child, "Mammoth Cave," 7.

47. Bullitt, *Rambles in the Mammoth Cave*, 99; Rogers, *Incidents of Travel in the Southern States and Cuba*, 278.

48. Taylor, *At Home and Abroad*, 214–15.

49. Willis, *Health Trip to the Tropics*, 153.

50. Diouf, *Slavery's Exiles*, 278–84.

51. Allewaert, *Ariel's Ecology*, 35–50. See also Sayers, *Desolate Place for a Defiant People*.

52. Willis, *Health Trip to the Tropics*, 185.

53. The popular writer J. T. Trowbridge's antislavery novel *Cudjo's Cave* may also belong in the category of literature speculating on Mammoth Cave as an autonomous Black community. The novel centers on a cave occupied by two fugitives from slavery, Cudjo and Pomp, who take in a group of unionists trying to escape from their secessionist neighbors. In the cave, Cudjo sings a song urging on Judgment Day ("appearing to take delight in hearing the echoes resound through the cavern"), while Pomp declares that the Civil War is just the beginning of the fight that awaits. "This continent is going to shake with such a convulsion as was never before. It is going to shake till the last chain of the slave is shaken off, and the sin is punished, and God says, 'It is enough!'" (117). Although Trowbridge sets *Cudjo's Cave* in Tennessee, he hints that the cave comes at least partly from elsewhere. "In order to give form and unity to the narrative," he explains, "[t]wo separate and distinct caves have been connected, in the story, by expanding both into one, which is for the most part imaginary" (146).

54. Letcher, *Wonderful Discovery!*, 16, 17.

55. Parker, "New Wonders of the Mammoth Cave," 153, 165.

56. Parker, "New Wonders of the Mammoth Cave," 168.

57. Parker, "New Wonders of the Mammoth Cave," 168.

58. Moreton-Robinson, *White Possessive*, 51. Two years into Reconstruction, a tale by Nathan Ryno Smith demonstrated that one could also switch these positions and use a submerged Native American tribe to elevate whiteness and undermine Black life. In a multiply framed narrative, Smith's narrator learns the story of "a venerable Indian," who recounts how white settlers drove his "once powerful tribe" to Mammoth Cave and surrounded them on all sides. Faced with annihilation, the members of the tribe "plunge into" the cave. Years later, the narrator discovers a new cavern in the cave, where an unidentified Native chief suddenly appears and informs him of the "great and terrible events" that "our Seers" foresee: first, the North will triumph over the South in the Civil War—and then, after many years, "shall the Southern panther rise from his lair, and avenge his wrongs" (*Legends of the South*, 46, 48, 61). Through what Jodi A. Byrd calls the "transit" of "paradigmatic Indianness," which serves as the "ontological ground" for so many other types of violence in the United States, the prophecy evacuates the underground of its familiar associations with racialized Blackness and remakes it as a guarantor of white resurgence and the return of slavery (*Transit of Empire*, xxi, xix).

59. Parker, "New Wonders of the Mammoth Cave," 158.

60. Parker, "New Wonders of the Mammoth Cave," 160.

61. Chiles, *Transformable Race*. Compare Parker's account with the more conventional connection W. E. Surtees makes between Mammoth Cave's fish and climatological theories of race: "Would their descendants, if removed into the light, obtain their sight? Ay! And would the foot, the skin, the hair, the skull, and the intellect of the negro, if his race were for countless ages engrafted on Europe, develop the European peculiarities?" ("Recollections of North America," 22). The eyeless fish prompted a Canadian travel writer named John Francis Campbell to even crueler fantasies of Black evolution: "If . . . a healthy tribe of n[—] were to breed there, and feed upon each other—as do the fish, crawfish, crickets, lizards, bats, and rats, a new human species of 'Underjordiske' [underground peoples of Norwegian folklore] might people Kentucky down-stairs" (*Short American Tramp in the Fall of 1864*, 350).

62. Agassiz, "Observations on the Blind Fish of Mammoth Cave," 127.

63. Grier, "Why (and How) August Wilson Marginalized White Antagonism."

64. Willis, *Health Trip to the Tropics*, 152.

65. Carpenter, *Observations on American Slavery*, 46, 47.

66. Lyons, *Making Their Mark*, 21.

67. Kazanjian, *Brink of Freedom*, 32.

68. Kazanjian, *Brink of Freedom*, 31, 111–12. Kazanjian quotes the phrase "action toward" from Moten, "Knowledge of Freedom," 303.

69. Hartman, "On Working with Archives."

70. Symmes, "Light Gives Light, to Light Discover."

71. On Symmes and the anonymous *Symzonia: A Voyage of Discovery*, one of the earliest hollow earth fictions inspired by Symmes's ideas, see Blum, "John Cleves Symmes and the Planetary Reach of Polar Exploration."

72. Symmes Pit and Symmes Pit Branch appear on Edmund Lee's 1835 map of Mammoth Cave.

73. Ellison, *Invisible Man*, 9.

74. Moten, *In the Break*, 68.

Chapter 2. Early Black Radical Undergrounds

1. Robinson, *Black Marxism*, xxx.

2. Hartman, "Belly of the World," 167.

3. Robinson, *Black Marxism*, 170.

4. Fanon, *Black Skin, White Masks*, 8, 109.

5. Maldonado-Torres, *Against War*, 18.

6. Fanon, *Black Skin, White Masks*, 8. On Fanon's images of hell and damnation, see Gordon, "Through the Hellish Zone of Nonbeing."

7. In *What Fanon Said: A Philosophical Introduction to His Life and Thought*, Lewis R. Gordon argues that Fanon's quotation of "L'Internationale" was mediated by the Haitian communist poet Jacques Roumain's citation of it in "Sales nègres" (112–13). George Ciccariello-Maher connects it to another poem by Roumain, "Nouveau sermon nègre," from the same book, *Bois d'Ebène* (1945). "Nouveau sermon nègre" is a "decolonial adaptation" of "L'Internationale," Ciccariello-Maher writes, which recognizes that "the truly condemned cannot simply 'arise,' as the 'Internationale' exhorts them to do, imprisoned as they are to a subontological hell that itself lies *beneath* the foundation (*base*) to be changed" (*Decolonizing Dialectics*, 75, 76).

8. Glissant, *Poetics of Relation*, 6, 7.

9. Glissant, *Poetics of Relation*, 8.

10. Glissant, *Poetics of Relation*, 7.

11. Glissant, *Poetics of Relation*, 8.

12. Wynter, "Sambos and Minstrels," 149, 156, 149. Wynter's fullest discussion of "underlife" appears in the long unpublished book manuscript "Black Metamorphosis: New Natives in a New World." I glean my understanding of her use of it there from quotations and analysis in the special section devoted to "Black

Metamorphosis" in the March 2016 issue of *Small Axe*, especially Cunningham, "Resistance of the Lost Body."

13. Cunningham, "Resistance of the Lost Body," 117.

14. Hartman, *Lose Your Mother*, 6; Sharpe, *In the Wake*.

15. Gikandi, *Slavery and the Culture of Taste*, x. Gikandi's concept of slavery's crypt draws on Nicolas Abraham and Maria Torok's psychoanalytic theorization of the crypt in "Mourning or Melancholia."

16. Hartman, "Venus in Two Acts," 2. For an excellent overview of the debates about slavery and archival recovery, see Helton, Leroy, Mishler, Seeley, and Sweeney, introduction to "Question of Recovery: Slavery, Freedom, and the Archive."

17. Hartman, "Venus in Two Acts," 11, 13.

18. Wilderson, *Red, White, and Black*, xi.

19. Sharpe, *In the Wake*, 71, 100.

20. Moten, "Blackness and Nothingness," 743. These lines reappear in Harney and Moten, *Undercommons*, 94.

21. Moten, "Blackness and Nothingness," 739, and "Black Op," 1746; Harney and Moten, *Undercommons*, 26.

22. Walker, *Appeal to the Coloured Citizens of the World*, 75; Sharpe, *In the Wake*, 17. All further citations from Walker will appear parenthetically in the text.

23. See Hinks, *To Awaken My Afflicted Brethren*, 116–72.

24. Lenin, *Collapse of the Second International*, 16–20.

25. Yusoff, *Billion Black Anthropocenes or None*, 68.

26. Marx, *Capital*, 715, 760.

27. Thank you to Chioma Anomnachi and Faith Booker for helping me think through Walker's image of the mist in the abyss.

28. Dinius, "'Look!! Look!!! At This!!!,'" 55.

29. For a related reading of the relation between footnote and main text, see Rusert's "Plantation Ecologies," which reads the copious footnotes of James Grainger's poem *The Sugar-Cane* as "a kind of wild overgrowth that territorializes, or counter colonizes, the cultivated space of the colonial plantation" (353).

30. Dinius, "'Look!! Look!!! At This!!!,'" 56.

31. I am indebted to Maya Deutsch for pointing out the particular radicalism of Walker's footnotes, as well as for conversation about how to read them aloud.

32. Jefferson, *Notes on the State of Virginia*, 272.

33. Jefferson to William Stephens Smith, November 13, 1787, 356.

34. Apess, "Indian's Looking-Glass for the White Man," 55. For example, compare Apess's declaration that Native Americans on New England reservations are "the most mean, abject, miserable race of beings in the world" (53) to Walker's statement "We, (colored people of these United States) are the most degraded, wretched, and abject set of beings that ever lived since the world began" (3).

35. Glaude, *Exodus!*, 115.

36. Apess, "Indian's Looking-Glass for the White Man," 55. Here Apess seems to echo Walker's thunderstruck calculation that in Jamaica 15,000 white people are "ruling and tyrannizing over 335,000" "coloured people" (66).

37. Douglass, "Slavery, the Slumbering Volcano," 149, 150. All further citations to this source will appear parenthetically in the text.

38. Ciccariello-Maher, "Dialectics of Standing One's Ground." Ciccariello-Maher expands this analysis of Fanon's decolonization of Hegel's master-slave dialectic in *Decolonizing Dialectics*, 54–58.

39. Douglass, *Life and Times of Frederick Douglass*, 198–99.

40. Six years after Douglass described the revolt plotted below the *Creole*'s decks in "Slavery, the Slumbering Volcano," Herman Melville reached for the same expression in *Benito Cereno* to characterize the *San Dominick*, the ship seized by its enslaved cargo whose name hints at the enduring threat of the Haitian Revolution. "Might not the San Dominick, like a slumbering volcano, suddenly let loose energies now hid?" wonders the visiting Captain Delano, oblivious to the fact that it already has (68).

41. McGann, "Editor's Note," in Delany, *Blake; or, the Huts of America; a Corrected Edition*, xxxiv. Floyd J. Miller, editor of the earlier Beacon Press edition, estimates that "perhaps six chapters" remain (ix).

42. Quoted in Ernest, *Resistance and Reformation in Nineteenth-Century African-American Literature*, 112.

43. Ernest, *Resistance and Reformation in Nineteenth-Century African-American Literature*, 128.

44. Delany, *Origin and Objects of Ancient Freemasonry*, 67, 64.

45. Delany, *Blake; or, the Huts of America*, 39. All further citations to *Blake* will come from the Miller edition and appear parenthetically in the text.

46. Quoted in Ernest, *Resistance and Reformation in Nineteenth-Century African-American Literature*, 111.

47. Harney and Moten, *Undercommons*, 132.

48. In emphasizing the collective organization that precedes and enables Blake's scheme, I differ from Jerome McGann, who asserts, "It is a scheme 'adapted to all times and circumstances' because it involves a personal choice that anyone anywhere can make. That is its 'secret'" (introduction to Delany, *Blake; or, the Huts of*

America; a Corrected Edition, xiv). McGann makes the provocative argument that Delany planned in the final chapters to abandon the plan for insurrection in favor of one for "Black emigration from America" (xxv).

49. Marlene Daut argues that although Placido dismisses the idea that Haiti could assist the Army of Emancipation, Haiti is nonetheless "omnipresent" for Delany—in the form of the novel, which Daut compares to other historical fiction by Black Atlantic authors on the Haitian Revolution; in the pages of the *Anglo-African Magazine*, where *Blake* ran alongside regular coverage of Haiti; and in the presences of Delany's sons Toussaint L'Ouverture Delany and Faustin Souloque Delany ("Martin Delany's *Blake* in Black Revolutionary Context," 83).

50. Historians have long questioned whether such a conspiracy actually existed. But Aisha K. Finch's groundbreaking study, *Rethinking Slave Rebellion in Cuba*, persuasively shows how enslaved people on rural plantations did mobilize a powerful insurgency in the early 1840s.

51. Madera, *Black Atlas*, 133.

52. On Plácido's reputation in the United States, see Nwankwo, *Black Cosmopolitanism*, chaps. 1 and 2; and Boutelle, "'Greater Still in Death.'" I use "Plácido" to refer to the historical figure but follow Delany in using "Placido" to refer to his character.

53. Sundquist, *To Wake the Nations*, 210.

54. Leary, *Cultural History of Underdevelopment*, 41.

55. The *Anglo-African Magazine* published chapters 28–30 of *Blake* as a stand-alone feature in the January 1859 issue before starting it from the beginning in the February 1859 issue, when it also began serializing "Afric-American Picture Gallery."

56. While the use of pseudonyms was a convention of periodical writing, Carla Peterson points out that the particular pseudonyms of Wilson and his fellow columnists for *Frederick Douglass' Paper*, Communipaw (James McCune Smith) and Cosmopolite (Phillip A. Bell), signaled a "serious debate about the place of blacks in the city, the nation, and the cosmos" (*Black Gotham*, 217). I would add that Wilson also expanded the horizontal dimensions of this debate to contemplate the prospects of Black life below the surface of the earth as well as above and beyond it.

57. Wilson, "From Our Brooklyn Correspondent," *Frederick Douglass' Paper*, July 30, 1852, quoted in Clytus, "Visualizing in Black Print," 29.

58. Clytus, "Visualizing in Black Print," 31, 47, 30.

59. Clytus, "Visualizing in Black Print," 52, 51, 52.

60. Wilson, "Ethiop Before the Convention—No. I," *Frederick Douglass' Paper*, August 24, 1855, 1, quoted in Clytus, "Visualizing in Black Print," 53.

61. Wilson, "Afric-American Picture Gallery," no. 2 (February): 52, 53. I cite the original installments in order to address their print context in the *Anglo-African Magazine*, but Leif Eckstrom and Britt Rusert have produced an excellent digital edition of "Afric-American Picture Gallery" for the Just Teach One: Early African American Print project: http://jtoaa.common-place.org/welcome-to-just-teach-one-african-american/introduction-afric-american-picture-gallery/.

62. Wilson, "Afric-American Picture Gallery," no. 8 (August): 245.

63. Wilson, *Specters of Democracy*, 156.

64. Wilson, *Specters of Democracy*, 160.

65. Wilson, *Specters of Democracy*, 154.

66. Wilson, "Afric-American Picture Gallery," no. 3 (March): 89; Sharpe, *In the Wake*, chap. 4.

67. Wilson, "Afric-American Picture Gallery," no. 3 (March): 89.

68. Wilson, "Afric-American Picture Gallery," no. 3 (March): 90.

69. Wilson, "Afric-American Picture Gallery," no. 4 (April): 101.

70. Leif Eckstrom and Britt Rusert, "Introduction," Just Teach One: Early African American Print, http://jtoaa.common-place.org/welcome-to-just-teach-one-african-american/introduction-afric-american-picture-gallery/.

71. Wilson, "Afric-American Picture Gallery," no. 6 (June): 174.

72. Wilson, "Afric-American Picture Gallery," no. 6 (June): 174.

73. Wilson, "Afric-American Picture Gallery," no. 4 (April): 101.

74. Spires, *Practice of Citizenship*, 190–91.

75. Wilson, "Afric-American Picture Gallery," no. 4 (April): 103; no. 7 (July): 216. In fact, while the story's other installments consist of numbered "sketches," the installment that describes Bernice's cave defies this order by containing no numbered sketches; moreover, as Derrick Spires points out, while the sketch that precedes this installment is numbered 14, once Ethiop returns, "his next sketch is numbered 19, suggesting that either something should be there, but Ethiop has not or cannot write it down, or that the scenes in Bernice's hut were supposed to be numbered, but they exceeded Ethiop's ability to organize them" (*Practice of Citizenship*, 196).

76. Wilson, "Afric-American Picture Gallery," no. 7 (July): 216.

77. Wilson, "Afric-American Picture Gallery," no. 6 (June): 173.

78. Wilson, "Afric-American Picture Gallery," no. 4 (April): 102, 103.

79. Wilson, "Afric-American Picture Gallery," no. 6 (June): 174, 175, 176. Half a year later, Wilson, again writing as Ethiop, would return to white people's self-inflicted doom in an essay titled "What Shall We Do with the White People?" In

language that recalls the tablet, Ethiop declares, "And verily they have triumphed; and in that triumph and what else we have instanced, who does not see that this people are on the direct road to barbarism" (44). The essay is hilarious, but as Mia Bay notes, it is "at least half serious" (*White Image in the Black Mind*, 76). Wilson arrives at no solution for white people's implacable destructiveness, besides concluding that "[w]e have arrived at a period where they could easily be spared" (45).

80. Wilson, "Afric-American Picture Gallery," no. 6 (June): 174.

81. Wilson, "Afric-American Picture Gallery," no. 3 (March): 89.

82. Wilson, "Afric-American Picture Gallery," no. 6 (June): 177.

83. Blyden, "Chapter in the History of the African Slave Trade," 184. Interestingly, the next article, J. Theodore Holly's "Thoughts on Hayti," ends on a prayer that Black people everywhere will honor Haiti's example.

84. Wilson, "Afric-American Picture Gallery," no. 6 (June): 177.

85. Rusert, "From Wilson's Cave Gallery to Jemisin's The Stone Sky." My thinking about "Afric-American Picture Gallery" is greatly indebted to conversations with Rusert and our collaboration on this panel.

86. Wilson, "Afric-American Picture Gallery," no. 7 (July): 218.

87. Wilson, "Afric-American Picture Gallery," no. 10 (October): 321.

88. Wilson, "Afric-American Picture Gallery," no. 10 (October): 324.

89. Fraser, "Rethinking the Public Sphere," 67.

90. Fraser, "Rethinking the Public Sphere," 67.

91. Wilson, "Afric-American Picture Gallery," no. 4 (April): 102.

Chapter 3. The Underground Railroad's Undergrounds

1. Wilson, "Afric-American Picture Gallery," *Anglo-African Magazine* 1, no. 2 (February 1859): 54.

2. Wilson, "Afric-American Picture Gallery," *Anglo-African Magazine* 1, no. 2 (February 1859): 54.

3. My analysis of these pictures follows Ivy Wilson's observation that the paintings in the Afric-American Picture Gallery "experiment with compositional zones" (*Specters of Democracy*, 159).

4. Gara, *Liberty Line*, 2.

5. Examples of postbellum histories of the Underground Railroad include *Reminiscences of Levi Coffin, the Reputed President of the Underground Railroad* (1876); Alexander Milton Ross, *Recollections and Experiences of an Abolitionist* (1876); Eber M. Petitt, *Sketches in the History of the Underground Railroad* (1879); Laura S.

Haviland, *A Woman's Life-Work* (1882); *Autobiography of the Rev. Luther Lee, D.D.* (1882); Robert C. Smedley, *History of the Underground Railroad in Chester and the Neighboring Counties of Pennsylvania* (1883); Homer Uri Johnson, *From Dixie to Canada: Romance and Realities of the Underground Railroad* (1894); and Wilbur H. Siebert, *The Underground Railroad from Slavery to Freedom* (1898).

6. Among others, see Blackett, *Making Freedom*; Foner, *Gateway to Freedom*; Griffler, *Front Line of Freedom*; Jackson, *Force and Freedom*; LaRoche, *Free Black Communities and the Underground Railroad*; and Weik, *Archaeology of Anti-Slavery Resistance*.

7. Charles T. Torrey, letter to Milton M. Fisher, Esq., November 16, 1844, Hixon Family Papers, Massachusetts Historical Society, Ms. N-1409, 2.

8. See *New York Observer*, September 28, 1842; *Vermont Telegraph*, October 5, 1842, 11; *Liberator*, October 14, 1842, 163. I have not found any surviving copies of the issue of the *Tocsin of Liberty* that contains the original item.

9. McGill, *American Literature and the Culture of Reprinting*; and Cordell, "Reprinting, Circulation, and the Network Author in Antebellum Newspapers."

10. Ruggles, *First Annual Report of the New York Committee of Vigilance*, 13. On vigilance committees, see Boromé, "Vigilant Committee of Philadelphia"; Quarles, *Black Abolitionists*, 150–56; Horton and Horton, *Black Bostonians*, chaps. 5, 8, and 9; Collison, "Boston Vigilance Committee"; Hodges, *David Ruggles*, chaps. 3 and 4; Finkenbine, "Community Militant and Organized"; and Sinha, *Slave's Cause*, 383–93.

11. Douglass, *Narrative of the Life of Frederick Douglass*, 101.

12. "Rev. John Cross, of Illinois," *Liberator*, August 23, 1844, 1.

13. Reprinted in "The Brazilian Slaves," *New York Evangelist*, August 26, 1847, 135. Mahommah Gardo Baquaqua, who was one of the enslaved passengers, recounts the escape in *Biography of Mahommah G. Baquaqua*, 54–56.

14. An 1849 article in *Scientific American* on a proposal to build an actual underground railroad in New York, for instance, called the idea "original, but any thing except feasible" ("Under-ground Railroad in Broadway," 53).

15. A. S. Myrick, "The Underground Railroad," *Liberator*, June 10, 1853, 92.

16. I thank Jocelyn Proietti, in her response to the Fugitive Recordings panel at the Black Sound in the Archives symposium, February 7–8, 2019, Yale University, for encouraging me to think about what death looks like from below in this material.

17. On Simpson, see Eaklor, "Songs of *The Emancipation Car*"; Sherman, *Invisible Poets*, 35–41; and Wilson, *Specters of Democracy*, 74–76, where Wilson reads Simpson's settings of his songs to popular music as an example of "double voicing."

18. "The Son's Reflections," "The Slaveholder's Rest," "Away to Canada," and "They Are Still Traveling North" appear unattributed in *Blake*; see, respectively,

100–101, 105–6, 141–42, and 143. At the time of *Blake*'s publication(s), only "Away to Canada" seems to have appeared in print, which suggests that Delany may have had been in correspondence with Simpson. Delany may have also arranged the publication of two of Simpson's poems in the *North Star* when he was coeditor: "A Voice from Jamaica on the First of August" (July 28, 1848, 4) (a longer version than the one that appears in *Original Anti-Slavery Songs* and *The Emancipation Car*) and (again) "The Slaveholder's Rest" (December 7, 1849, 4).

19. On the Colored Conventions movement, see Foreman, Casey, and Patterson, *Colored Conventions Movement*. Cheryl Janifer LaRoche's essay for the volume, "Secrets Well Kept," argues that antebellum Colored Conventions nurtured Underground Railroad activism by creating "overt socially sanctioned, politically tolerated meeting spaces where public activists brought hidden agendas" (247).

20. *Minutes of the State Convention of the Colored Citizens of Ohio*, 4–5; *Minutes of the Second U.G.R.R. Convention*, 3. The Colored Conventions Project has digitized the Minutes for the State Convention of the Colored Citizens of Ohio at http://coloredconventions.org/items/show/249.

21. Moten, "Black Op," 1743.

22. Moten, "Black Op," 1745.

23. Moten, "Black Op," 1743, 1745.

24. Simpson, *Emancipation Car*, iii–iv. The 1874 edition is a reprint of the 1854 edition, printed by E. C. Church.

25. Simpson, *Original Anti-Slavery Songs*, n.p.; *Emancipation Car*, v.

26. Simpson, *Emancipation Car*, 17.

27. Simpson, *Emancipation Car*, 59.

28. Simpson, *Emancipation Car*, 13.

29. Simpson, *Emancipation Car*, 27–29.

30. Simpson, *Emancipation Car*, 49, 50–51.

31. Simpson, *Emancipation Car*, 147, 148.

32. Simpson, *Emancipation Car*, 119.

33. Simpson, *Emancipation Car*, 7–9. The term "emancipation car" derives from the song "Get off the Track!" by the popular singing group the Hutchinson Family Singers, which became something of an abolitionist anthem in the 1840s. "Get off the Track!" does not itself mention the Underground Railroad; there, the "car, Emancipation" is a metaphor for liberty, which rolls unstoppably "through our nation," gathering supporters and scattering naysayers as it goes. But antislavery writers matched train with train to analogize the "car, Emancipation" to the popular image of a literal Underground Railroad.

34. Simpson, *Emancipation Car*, 85–86.

35. McKittrick, "'Freedom Is a Secret,'" 102. This is not to say that Simpson rejected the idea of Canada as a site of freedom; in fact, one of his songs is called "Away to Canada." But most of the song is sung by the fugitive in mid-flight, when Canada is more idea than reality. When the fugitive does finally arrive in Canada, the song ends on a note of disappointment and sorrow, as he thinks of his wife still enslaved in Tennessee.

36. Hartman, *Scenes of Subjection*, 68; McKittrick, "Freedom Is a Secret," 101.

37. Even "The Fugitive in Montreal" and "The Fugitive at Home," which take place in Canada, still refer to the speaker as "the fugitive"—a name that may bespeak Simpson's expansive take on fugitivity, his skepticism about legal freedom, or both.

38. Simpson, *Emancipation Car*, iv.

39. Williams, *History of the Negro Race in America*, 2:59.

40. Siebert, *Underground Railroad from Slavery to Freedom*, 340; Du Bois, *John Brown*, 94, and *Black Reconstruction in America*, 13.

41. *Minutes of the Second U.G.R.R. Convention*, 3.

42. *Minutes of the Second U.G.R.R. Convention*, 9.

43. Pittsburgh *Morning Post*, March 8, 1855, quoted in Blackett, "'Freemen to the Rescue!,'" 137.

44. The narrator notes that although she cannot reveal the full story of the Slaves Masonic League, "If the whites in the south knew everything that is going on, and has been going on for years, around them, they would not sleep soundly in their beds for any two consecutive hours" (*Six Months in Secessia*, 29). Barclay's politics seem to have been fairly opportunistic; four years earlier he published *Disclosures and Confessions of Frank A. Wilmot, the Slave Thief and Negro Runner, with an Accurate Account of the Underground Railroad! What It Is, and Where Located*, which depicts the Underground Railroad as a secret society whose real purpose is to siphon money from abolitionists. The novel not only refuses to imagine enslaved people's acts of self-emancipation; it refuses even to concede their desires to be free or to credit the existence of any antislavery belief.

45. Dickson, *Manual of the International Order of Twelve of Knights and Daughters of Tabor*, 15, 9, 17. After the Civil War, the "original warlike order" transformed into a more orthodox Black fraternal organization.

46. "Freedom's Railway," quoted in Lumpkin, "'General Plan Was Freedom,'" 71.

47. "Freedom's Railway," quoted in Lumpkin, "'General Plan Was Freedom,'" 71, 72, 76.

48. Quarles, *Allies for Freedom*, 60–61.

49. *Calendar of Virginia State Papers and Other Manuscripts*, 319.

50. Lumpkin, "'General Plan Was Freedom,'" 74.

51. In *John Brown and His Men*, Richard Josiah Hinton identifies Reynolds as "a leading member of the 'League of Liberty'" (180), a group of "armed and drilled men along the United States border, whose duty it was to help the slaves escape to Canada" (174). It's not clear to me if the League of Liberty was another name for the American Mysteries Secret U.G.R.R. Society or a different organization.

52. Richard Realf, letter to Dear Uncle [John Brown], May 31, 1858, John Brown Collection, Kansas State Historical Society, http://www.kansasmemory.org/item/4846.

53. "Meeting in Detroit," *Weekly Anglo-African*, December 17, 1859.

54. Higginson, *Cheerful Yesterdays*, 139.

55. Higginson, *Cheerful Yesterdays*, 148.

56. Henry Ingersoll Bowditch, "Thirty Years War of Anti-Slavery," unpublished manuscript quoted in Bowditch, *Life and Correspondence of Henry Ingersoll Bowditch*, 1:276. Thank you to Susanna Ashton, who first told me about the Anti-Man-Hunting League.

57. Bowditch, *Life and Correspondence*, 1:279.

58. "Declaration of Sentiments of the Colored Citizens of Boston on the Fugitive Slave Bill," *Liberator*, October 11, 1850, 162.

59. Bearse, *Reminiscences of Fugitive-Slave Law Days in Boston*, 36.

60. Sidney Kaplan ascribes the tribute to Melville's friend Richard Henry Dana Jr., a member of the Boston Vigilance Committee ("Moby Dick in the Service of the Underground Railroad," 175). However, Sandra Harbert Petrulionis points out that Dana, one of the committee's more squeamish members, would be unlikely to involve himself in Bearse's scheme. Instead, she hypothesizes that another committee member, Theodore Parker, devised the name to twit Melville's father-in-law, Lemuel Shaw, whose decisions as chief justice of the Massachusetts Supreme Judicial Court upheld the Fugitive Slave Law ("Fugitive Slave-Running on the *Moby Dick*," 74). Both Kaplan and Petrulionis confine their inquiries into the boat's name to Melville's personal connections, and Petrulionis cautions against looking further, doubting that Bearse would have read the novel as closely as literary critics have done. But it's worth considering the opposite possibility: that Bearse and his associates' antislavery commitments would have made them *especially* attuned to *Moby-Dick*'s reflections on race and slavery. At any rate, the history of the *Moby Dick* broadens our picture of African Americans' engagements with Melville. John Stauffer identifies James McCune Smith as "the only known African American in the nineteenth century to have read Melville's *Moby-Dick*," which Smith references in his 1856 essay "Horoscope" (*The Works of James McCune Smith*, 143). But the history of the *Moby Dick* indicates that several years earlier, a number of African Americans—Joshua Bowen Smith and Lewis Hayden, who collaborated with Bearse on the runs; the unnamed "four or five

colored men" who accompanied Bearse; the longshoremen who alerted him; and the enslaved people he rescued in the boat—at the very least interacted with the novel's namesake and may have chosen or helped to choose that name.

61. Melville, *Moby-Dick*, 568.

62. Melville, *Moby-Dick*, 456.

63. Countless critics have analyzed Melville's preoccupation with questions about race, slavery, and freedom in *Moby-Dick*. But provocative as Melville's remarks are, they never seem to add up to a clear political position, often following Ishmael's tendency to slide into metaphor instead ("Who ain't a slave?"). The novel gestures toward critiques from which it withdraws, less interested, as C. L. R. James observes, in specific arguments than in acts of argumentation (*Mariners, Renegades and Castaways*, 17).

64. Brown, "Words of Advice; Branch of the United States League of Gileadites, Adopted January 15, 1851," quoted in Sanborn, *Life and Letters of John Brown*, 125.

65. Brown to Thomas Wentworth Higginson, February 12, 1858, quoted in Higginson, *Cheerful Yesterdays*, 218.

66. Douglass, *Life and Times of Frederick Douglass*, 390. Earlier, Brown had suggested to Douglass that liberating enslaved people was less the ends of Subterranean Pass Way than the means: "The true object to be sought is first of all to destroy the money value of slavery property; and that can only be done by rendering such property insecure" (*Life and Times of Frederick Douglass*, 340–41). But over the next twelve years, the purpose of the Subterranean Pass Way seems to have shifted from undermining the economic basis of slavery to waging a guerrilla war against it.

67. Du Bois, *John Brown*, 274.

68. Rollin, *Life and Public Services of Martin R. Delany*, 84. Delany also told Rollin that Brown had appointed him president of the "permanent organization" of the Subterranean Pass Way and that he had first suggested the name (89), although Richard Josiah Hinton's assertion that the flag Brown holds in a ca. 1847 daguerreotype is marked "S.P.W." for Subterranean Pass Way contradicts this claim (*John Brown and His Men*, 716).

69. Hinton, *John Brown and His Men*, 674.

70. Douglass, "John Brown," 499, 497.

71. Brown to Rev. McFarland, November 23, 1859, in Sanborn, *Life and Letters of John Brown*, 598; Brown to E. N., November 1, 1859, in Sanborn, *Life and Letters of John Brown*, 582.

72. Brown to his family, November 30, 1859, in Sanborn, *Life and Letters of John Brown*, 613. On the construction of Brown's martyrdom, see Finkelman, "Manufacturing Martyrdom."

73. Martineau, "John Brown," 387.

74. Anderson, *A Voice from Harper's Ferry*, 4.

75. *Report of the Select Committee of the Senate Appointed to Inquire into the Late Invasion and Seizure of the Public Property at Harper's Ferry*, 97.

76. Jackson, *American Radicals*, 210. Jackson's description subtly rewrites Martin Delany's interpretation of the Provisional United States as existing "*within* and *under* the government of the United States"; in Jackson's formulation, "under" no longer quite indicates submission to state authority.

77. Both Simpson and Day were delegates to the 1851 State Convention of the Colored Citizens of Ohio, where Simpson opened and closed each session with an "anti-slavery song," and Day announced his plans to start a newspaper he then planned to call *Voice of the Disenfranchised* (*Minutes of the State Convention of the Colored Citizens of Ohio*, 5, 13). His newspaper finally appeared two years later under the title the *Aliened American*. Along with Charles Henry Langston, Simpson and Day also coauthored a call for a National Convention of Colored Freemen to take place in Buffalo in September 1851. See Martin Delany's polite rebuttal in the *North Star*, April 3, 1851.

78. Quarles, *Allies for Freedom*, 47–51.

79. "John" to "Friend Henrie," September 8, 1859, in *Report of the Select Committee of the Senate Appointed to Inquire into the Late Invasion and Seizure of the Public Property at Harper's Ferry*, 66, 65.

80. Sanborn, *Memoirs of John Brown*, 77.

81. Brown to Miss Sterns, November 27, 1859, in Sanborn, *Life and Letters of John Brown*, 607.

82. Du Bois, *John Brown*, 121.

83. Wood, *Horrible Gift of Freedom*, 2. Wood borrows the term *emancipation moment* from David Brion Davis, *The "Emancipation Moment,"* 22nd Annual Robert Fortenbaugh Memorial Lecture (Gettysburg, PA: Gettysburg College Press, 1983).

84. Logan, *Negro in American Life and Thought*.

85. Still, "Preface to the Revised Edition," in *Underground Rail Road*.

86. On the formal strategies of *The Underground Rail Road*, see Black, "'New Enterprise in Our History.'"

87. Brown, *Pauline Elizabeth Hopkins*, 110. Jessica Metzler gives a meticulous account of the play's performance history in "'Course I Knows Dem Feet!" See also Shockley, "Pauline Elizabeth Hopkins," 23.

88. Hopkins, *Peculiar Sam*, 105.

89. Hopkins, *Peculiar Sam*, 109.

90. Brooks, *Bodies in Dissent*, 287.

91. Brown, *Pauline Elizabeth Hopkins*, 120; Brooks, *Bodies in Dissent*, 12–13.

92. Daphne Brooks's stunning reading of Juno suggests that she, too, voices the play's expansive sense of the subterranean, her alto register acting as a foil to the sopranos of Virginia and Mammy to sound the "the lower ('underground') frequencies of musical as well as thematic performance" (*Bodies in Dissent*, 288).

93. Brown, *Pauline Elizabeth Hopkins*, 367.

94. Hopkins, *Winona*, 336. Further citations will appear parenthetically in the text.

95. Carby, *Reconstructing Womanhood*, 155.

96. Aunt Vinnie's predictions echo those of Judah, "a true prophet," who sees visions of a "storm . . . gathering force" that will "end in the breaking of every chain that binds human beings to servitude in this country" (*Winona*, 351–52).

97. Beam, *Style, Gender, and Fantasy in Nineteenth-Century American Women's Writing*, 185. As JoAnn Pavletich and Daniel Hack have noted, Hopkins borrows this passage, along with others in the novel, from *The White Islander*, a popular 1893 novel by Mary Hartwell Catherwood. See Pavletich, "'. . . We Are Going to Take That Right,'" 118–21; and Hack, *Reaping Something New*, 137.

98. Hopkins, *Of One Blood*, 582. Further citations will appear parenthetically in the text.

99. Peterson, "Commemorative Ceremonies and Invented Traditions," 39; Rohy, *Anachronism and Its Others*, 86.

100. Albanese, "Unraveling the Blood Line," 230. Albanese finds "an alternative geography beneath the Africa-oriented *Of One Blood*": "Haitian valences" in "the spiritual practices of the matrilineage of Hannah-Mira-Dianthe" (228) and "the uncolonized kingdom Telassar" (229). In light of Albanese's essay, we might see Telassar connecting the Subterranean Pass Way, as Brown himself did, with the hemispheric "underground" of Haiti explored in the introduction and the previous chapter.

101. I thank Barbie Halaby for pointing out the parallel between the locations of Telassar and Harpers Ferry.

102. Quoted in Redpath, *Public Life of Captain John Brown*, 144.

Chapter 4. The Depths of Astonishment

A version of chapter 4 appeared as "The Depths of Astonishment: City Mysteries and the Antebellum Underground," *American Literary History* 29 (Spring 2017): 1–25.

1. Lippard, *New York*, 116. Further citations will appear parenthetically in the text.

2. Old Royal's backstory appears in the companion book to *New York*, *The Empire City; or, New York by Night and Day*, 105. Brown was a celebrity at the time,

performing widely on the lecture circuit, publishing *The Narrative of Henry Box Brown* in 1849, and exhibiting his panorama, "The Mirror of Slavery," in 1850.

3. The most complete study of city mysteries remains Erickson, "Welcome to Sodom"; see also his "New Books, New Men." Arguably, as violent and sexually explicit material often written under pseudonyms and printed by fly-by-night publishers, city mysteries themselves constituted a print underground.

4. Tyler Roeger persuasively argues that outside of eastern cities, "city-mysteries became a counterintuitive and sensationalized form of boosterism, a means to demonstrate imagined urban legitimacy" ("Sensationalizing the Urban West," 562).

5. Lippard, *Quaker City*, 46. Further citations will appear parenthetically in the text.

6. Ingraham, *Dancing Feather*, 28.

7. Testut, *Les Mysteres de la Nouvelle-Orleans*, 6, 24. Translation mine.

8. "A Street View," *Weekly Rake*, July 9, 1842, reprinted in Cohen et al., *Flash Press*, 12.

9. "Personal Sketches; Recollections and Memoranda of Prominent Public Men Recently Deceased," *New York Times*, January 11, 1860, 2.

10. "Sudden Death of Mike Walsh," *New York Herald*, March 18, 1859, 1.

11. Foster, *New York by Gas-Light*, 69, 123.

12. Vose, *Seven Nights in Gotham*, 86, 82. Although "journalistic" accounts like those by Foster and Vose share the city mysteries' fascination with undergrounds, it should be said that they portray them quite differently, arguably working to stabilize the novels' more fantastical visions.

13. Whitman, "Two Vaults," quoted in Levin and Whitley, introduction to *Whitman among the Bohemians*, xi.

14. On the Free Love League, see Lause, *Antebellum Crisis and America's First Bohemians*, 31–33; and Jackson, *American Radicals*, 136–37; on Menken at Pfaff's, see Sentilles, *Performing Menken*, chap. 5.

15. Whitman, *Leaves of Grass*, 373; Blalock, "'Tell What I Meant by *Calamus*.'"

16. "Ballard's What Is It," *New Yorker Clipper*, February 20, 1864, reprinted in Slout, *Broadway below the Sidewalk*, 29.

17. Brian P. Luskey cites the comic journal *Vanity Fair*'s descriptions of clerks as "a third sex" and a separate species (*Homo counter-jumperii*) in *On the Make*, 102; and Ruth L. Bohan further explores *Vanity Fair*'s depictions of clerks' effeminacy in "*Vanity Fair*, Whitman, and the Counter Jumper." Thank you to Edward Whitley and Paul Erickson for these references.

18. See Streeby, *American Sensations*; Helwig, "Denying the Wages of Whiteness"; Otter, *Philadelphia Stories*; Stewart, *Reading and Disorder in Antebellum America*; Cohen and Wong, introduction to Lippard, *Killers*, 1–41; and Altschuler, "'Picture It All, Darley.'"

19. Although the authors of city mysteries were white, Black authors adapted the genre's conventions to other genres. Jennifer Rae Greeson argues that Harriet Jacobs incorporates the generic conventions of city mysteries into *Incidents in the Life of a Slave Girl*; see "'Mysteries and Miseries' of North Carolina." Carl Ostrowski proposes a wider intertextual relationship between the slave narrative and the city mystery in "Slavery, Labor Reform, and Intertextuality in Antebellum Print Culture." City mysteries were also a point of reference for the incarcerated Black writer Austin Reed, who gave his ca. 1858–59 manuscript prison memoir *The Life and Adventures of a Haunted Convict* the subtitle *Or the Inmate of a Gloomy Prison, with the Mysteries and Miseries of the New York House of Refuge and Auburn Prison Unmasked*.

20. Clytus, "Visualizing in Black Print," 31.

21. Denning, *Mechanic Accents*, 87. The genre's Americanization itself amounts to a sharp critique of existing democracy in the mid-nineteenth century. It was one thing to spin a tale of conniving aristocrats and the urban underclass they exploited in Europe; it was quite another thing to restage this narrative in the putatively egalitarian United States. Asserting that the same plots could be recycled in cities across the United States belied flattering distinctions between new-world opportunity and old-world inequality. Interestingly, Eugène Sue introduced *Les Mystères de Paris* as an urban, European version of James Fenimore Cooper's romances of US settler colonialism: "We are about to place before our readers some episodes of the lives of other barbarians, as far removed from civilization as the savage people so well described by Cooper; only the barbarians of whom we speak live among us, and around us" (3).

22. Looby, "George Thompson's 'Romance of the Real,'" 666–67.

23. The tension between description and narrative is fundamental to Fredric Jameson's classic essay "Of Islands and Trenches." However, where Jameson finds utopian fiction's "more garrulous explanatory passages" (95) to be much less radical than the "blank or gap" that results from their tension with the story, which marks "the absence of a theoretical discourse yet to be developed" (97), I contend that the city mysteries' undergrounds offer precisely the "incapacity to produce [Utopia] as a vision" that is, in Jameson's apt words, "Utopia's deepest subject" (101).

24. "Barnum's Gallery of Wonders No. 26" (New York: Currier and Ives, ca. 1860).

25. Vose, *Seven Nights in Gotham*, 86–87.

26. David L. Pike surveys these undergrounds and the imaginary worlds they inspired in *Subterranean Cities* and *Metropolis on the Styx*.

27. An 1851 newspaper article titled "Underground Life" reported that there were 3,742 cellars in New York holding 18,456 people, "so that one person out of every twenty, in this metropolis, eats, drinks, and sleeps under ground. When we

consider this startling fact, we no longer wonder at the vice of our great cities" (*New-York Organ*, March 31, 1851, 414).

28. Sedgwick, *Touching Feeling*, 8.

29. Averill, *Secrets of the Twin Cities*, 111. Further citations will appear parenthetically in the text.

30. Carl Ostrowski calls *The Quaker City* an "anti-exposé," and while he is specifically referring to its critique of popular anti-Catholic and anti-Mormon exposés, one might extend his term to the novel's formal structure. See "Inside the Temple of Ravoni."

31. Foucault, "Of Other Spaces," 25.

32. Bataille, "'Old Mole' and the Prefix *Sur*," 35.

33. Noys, "George Bataille's Base Materialism," 501.

34. Thompson, *City Crimes*, 134.

35. Thompson, *City Crimes*, 250.

36. Bataille, "'Old Mole' and the Prefix *Sur*," 35.

37. Bataille, "Base Materialism and Gnosticism," 51.

38. Otter, *Philadelphia Stories*, 168–69.

39. Bataille, "'Old Mole' and the Prefix *Sur*," 43.

40. Benjamin contrasts the "genuine," "theological" meaning of allegory with its "modern" meaning, which assumes "a conventional relationship between an illustrative image and its abstract meaning" (*Origin of German Tragic Drama*, 162). Further citations will appear parenthetically in the text. Although Michael Denning does not specifically engage Benjamin's definition of allegory in his analysis of city mysteries, he argues that nineteenth-century popular fiction was especially responsive to allegorical modes of reading (*Mechanic Accents*, 72–74).

41. For comparison, note the climactic role of Devil-Bug's dream in *The Quaker City* (and the presence of dreams and visions in many city mysteries); the timing of the narrative, which begins at midnight and mostly unfolds at night; the novel's tendency to absorb its critique of capitalism into what Denning calls a "seduction-rape plot" (*Mechanic Accents*, 93); and its determination to make place the key to history, by "describ[ing] all the phases of a corrupt social system, as manifested in the city of Philadelphia" (Lippard, *Quaker City*, 2).

42. Emerson, *Nature*, 49.

43. Buck-Morss, *Dialectics of Seeing*, 168.

44. Jay, "Against Consolation," 228, 238.

45. Abraham and Torok, "Mourning *or* Melancholia," 130–31, and *Wolf Man's Magic Word*, chap. 8. In *The Psychic Life of Power*, Judith Butler introduces another wrinkle into this spatial understanding of melancholia, arguing, "The internal topography

by which melancholia is partially explained is itself the effect of that melancholia" (174), which "produces a set of spatializing tropes for psychic life" (171). I will return to the relation between the underground and psychological discourse in chap. 6.

46. Rogin, *Subversive Genealogy*, 102–54.

47. Thompson, *City Crimes*, 234.

48. Lippard, *Adonai, the Pilgrim of Eternity*, 16. Further citations will appear parenthetically in the text.

49. "Key to figure [216] of the B.G.C.," Brotherhood of the Union Collection, the Library Company of Philadelphia, box 1, folder 1; Flatley, *Affective Mapping*, 65.

50. "Key to figure [216] of the B.G.C."

51. Quoted in Lause, *Secret Society History of the Civil War*, 28.

52. George Lippard, letter to William McFarlane, Brotherhood of the Union Collection, the Library Company of Philadelphia, box 1, folder 3.

53. Erickson, "Welcome to Sodom," 108n90.

54. "Key to figure [216] of the B.G.C."

55. "Key to figure [231] of the B.G.C.," Brotherhood of the Union Collection, the Library Company of Philadelphia, box 1, folder 2.

56. Coronado, *World Not to Come*; McGarry, *Ghosts of Futures Past*; Coviello, *Tomorrow's Parties*, 19.

57. Harney and Moten, *Undercommons*, 27.

58. Harney and Moten, *Undercommons*, 79.

59. On Pete Williams, see Cook, "Dancing across the Color Line."

60. As Cook notes, the dance hall, which was originally called Almack's and then later renamed Dickens's Place in honors of its celebrated visitor, actually relocated between 1848 and 1850, but both locations seem to have been underground.

61. Steele, "Visible and Invisible City," 185.

62. Taylor, "Politics of Recognition."

63. Steele, "Visible and Invisible City," 188–89.

64. *Terrible and All Absorbing Narrative and Confession of Edwin Winters*, 22. Further citations will appear parenthetically in the text.

65. Lause, *Secret Society History of the Civil War*, 55.

66. In *Knights of the Golden Circle*, David C. Keehn argues that the KGC conducted extensive operations before and during the Civil War, although Mark Lause believes they existed largely on paper. Nonetheless, Lause emphasizes that the fascination they held for the press gave them outsized power—and he notes that when the Ku Klux Klan formed after the Civil War, they drew on the example

of the KGC, including for their name, from the Greek for "circle," *Kuklos* (*Secret Society History of the Civil War*, 92–103, 153). Naturally, the KGC was the subject of a sensationalist novel, in which the protagonist plunges through a trapdoor "down continually to a depth that seemed unfathomable, down to the very bowels of the earth, dark and cheerless as the realms of despair!" and into a cave where his initiation takes place (*Narrative of Edmund Wright*, 43). All the KGC chapters in the novel also meet in subterranean caverns.

67. Bickley, *Adalaska*, 31. Further citations will appear parenthetically in the text.

68. Benjamin, *Origin of German Tragic Drama*, 173, 166.

69. Morrison, *Playing in the Dark*, 6.

70. Marx, *Eighteenth Brumaire of Louis Bonaparte*, 121.

71. Hegel, *Lectures on the History of Philosophy*, 3:553.

72. Stallybrass, "'Well Grubbed, Old Mole,'" 13. See also de Grazia, "Teleology, Delay, and the 'Old Mole.'"

73. Hegel, *Lectures on the History of Philosophy*, 3:553.

74. Marx, *Capital*, 102–3.

75. Marx, *Capital*, 269.

76. McNally, *Monsters of the Market*, 133. McNally's description of the "hidden abode of production" as a "cellar" riffs on Marx's citation of the "Auerbach's Cellar" chapter of Goethe's *Faust* in the *Grundrisse*.

77. Marx and Engels, *Holy Family*, 226. On *The Holy Family* and *Les Mystères de Paris*, see Prawer, *Karl Marx and World Literature*, 86–102.

78. Marx and Engels, *Holy Family*, 225.

79. Latour, "Why Has Critique Run Out of Steam?," 229.

80. Herring, *Queering the Underworld*, 21.

81. Spivak, "Can the Subaltern Speak?," 286. See also Denning, "Mysteries of *Capital*," which argues that *Capital* should be read as "one of the major imaginative works of the socialist tradition." Note that Denning's title is not "The Mysteries of Capital," which might suggest that the book solves the mysteries of capital, but "The Mysteries of *Capital*," the book itself.

82. Rosenberg, "Monstrously Unpositable," 201, 203.

Chapter 5. "To Drop beneath the Floors of the Outer World"

1. Randolph, *P. B. Randolph, The "Learned Pundit," and "Man with Two Souls,"* 4. For examples of Randolph identifying as Black, see "The Fremont Legion—Negro Convention," *Daily National Intelligencer*, July 27, 1863, 2; *National Convention of*

Colored Men, 11; "The Loyal Convention Adoption of the Report Advising Negro Suffrage," *Boston Journal*, September 8, 1866, 2. Given Randolph's own words, the racism found in even progressive corners of the nineteenth-century United States, and what we know of other public figures' strategic disidentifications in the face of anti-Blackness, I follow other scholars of Randolph, including Jayna Brown, John Patrick Deveney, Lana Finley, and L. H. Stallings, in referring to him as Black.

2. Randolph, *P. B. Randolph, The "Learned Pundit," and "Man with Two Souls*," 18; Stallings, *Funk the Erotic*, 35.

3. Mary Jane Randolph wrote spiritual pamphlets of her own, contributed material to Randolph's work, and sold "medicinal formulas." Kate Corson Randolph was a medium who collaborated with Randolph to receive the secrets in *The New Mola!* (1873) and may have also contributed to his other work. More research on both women is necessary, especially in relation to nineteenth-century Black self-publishing.

4. Deveney, *Paschal Beverly Randolph*, chaps. 11–13. Deveney's study remains the most comprehensive account of Randolph's work, and I am indebted to it throughout this chapter. However, Deveney is primarily interested in Randolph as a forerunner of later esoteric religious groups, and his account accordingly emphasizes the elements of his thought that would prove most influential. I am at least as interested in the elements of his thought that *did not* endure—that proved less durable or transportable.

5. Clymer published copiously from the early to mid-twentieth century, but see, for example, *Rose Cross Order*. Later, Clymer elaborated a longer genealogy that reached back to William Lloyd Garrison, John Brown, and George Lippard. See *Book of Rosicruciae*, 2:134–73. Clymer also republished several books by Randolph, although his editions are significantly abridged and altered.

6. In addition to Deveney, see Ferguson, *Determined Spirits*, chap. 4; Finley, "Paschal Beverly Randolph in the African American Community"; Godwin, *Theosophical Enlightenment*; and Urban, *Magia Sexualis*.

7. Stallings, *Funk the Erotic*, 41.

8. Randolph, *Eulis!*, 27.

9. Kahan, *Book of Minor Perverts*, 79.

10. Brown, *Black Utopias*, 25.

11. Randolph, *Wonderful Story of Ravalette*, iii; Randolph, *Eulis!*, 112.

12. "The Converted Medium," *New-York Daily Tribune*, November 25, 1858, 3.

13. Randolph, *Eulis!*, 122.

14. Randolph gives the suicide narrative in the lecture transcribed in "Converted Medium" and the hashish narrative in *Unveiling*, 58.

15. Randolph, *Eulis!*, 123.

16. Randolph, *Eulis!*, 48.

17. Randolph, *Eulis!*, 47.

18. Randolph, *Guide to Clairvoyance*, 27; Randolph, *Seership!*, 17–21, 82.

19. Hopkins, *Contending Forces*, 132.

20. Randolph, *P. B. Randolph, The "Learned Pundit," and "Man with Two Souls,"* 3.

21. Moreau de Saint-Méry, *Description Topographique, Physique, Civile, Politique et Historique*, 1:71.

22. Ferguson, *Determined Spirits*, 128.

23. Quoted in A. B. Child, "P. B. Randolph at Washington Hall, Charlestown, Sunday Afternoon, November 27, 1859," *Banner of Light*, December 3, 1859, 5.

24. Randolph often discusses the racist insults he received, and white supremacist violence nearly claimed the life of his twelve-year-old son Lorenzo, a printer's apprentice, during the 1863 New York City draft riots. A white mob broke into his bedroom, forcing him to jump out the window "in the midst of a fierce shower of brickbats hurled by the rampant fiends." He wandered the streets for the rest of the night, while the rioters looted the house where he boarded and took everything he owned ("The Late Riot," *New York Tribune*, July 20, 1863, 3).

25. Randolph, *Dealings with the Dead*, 91.

26. Du Bois, *Souls of Black Folk*, 3. As Susan Gilman and others have noted, Du Bois borrows the metaphor of the veil from the spiritualists' idiom; see *Blood Talk*, 8. Reading his description of "two souls, two thoughts, two unreconciled strivings; two warring ideals in one dark body, whose dogged strength alone keeps it from being torn asunder," one wonders if he could have been thinking of Randolph, who referred to himself as "the man with two souls."

27. Hopkins, *Of One Blood*, 444. Randolph at least claimed to have traveled to Ethiopia.

28. Randolph, *Dealings with the Dead*, 84.

29. Harney and Moten, *Undercommons*, 140.

30. Randolph recounts the life of a monad from the monad's point of view in "Story of a Monad," embedded in *Dealings with the Dead*, 44–48. John Patrick Deveney provides a helpful summary of Randolph's cosmology in *Paschal Beverly Randolph*, 103–12.

31. Randolph, *After Death; or, Disembodied Man*, 100–101, 110. Even within *After Death*, his most comprehensive account of the spirit worlds, Randolph takes contradictory positions on the meaning of race there. At one point he states, "A thousand eternities will not be long enough to enable Cuffee to catch Carlyle, or low Pompey to overtake Theodore Parker. *It can never be!* There is no democracy

in the spheres!" (101). Yet just over twenty pages later he writes, "There is a vast difference between Cuffee and Carlyle; yet the former will bridge it in time, just as the latter will leap the chasm between himself and the myriad Cuffees of ages lang syne" (122). Randolph's perspective on Black spirits seems to relate to his teaching in the Freedmen's Schools, and perhaps it shifted with his day-to-day experiences there. He reports, "Schools of the primary order are established among them," and "already they begin to appreciate their teachers, and to comprehend their lessons," though the teachers in the spirit world come not from the North but from "higher sections and grand divisions of the zone" (123).

32. Randolph, *Eulis!*, 185.

33. Brown, *Black Utopias*, 151. Brown draws here on Roland Barthes in *Sade, Fourier, Loyola*.

34. Randolph, *Dealings with the Dead*, 132.

35. Randolph, *Dealings with the Dead*, 135.

36. Randolph, *After Death; or, Disembodied Man*, 153, 154.

37. Randolph, *After Death; or, Disembodied Man*, 51–53.

38. Randolph, *Dealings with the Dead*, 103–5.

39. Randolph, *After Death; or, Disembodied Man*, 51–54.

40. Randolph, *After Death; or, Disembodied Man*, 138.

41. Randolph, *After Death; or, Disembodied Man*, 156, 157. Randolph's description of soul marriages closely resembles the ideas promulgated by proponents of free love, despite his vociferous opposition to that movement.

42. Randolph, *After Death; or, Disembodied Man*, 151.

43. [Britten], *Art Magic*, 112, 106; [Britten], *Ghost Land*, 213. Britten describes herself as the translator and editor of both these works, which she explains she received from the clairvoyant narrator, Louis.

44. One has to ask: Were Professor von Marx and his Brotherhood inspired by Karl Marx? Do Professor Marx's sub-mundane tendencies bear any relation to Marx's old mole? Could Britten, working as a clairvoyant and actress in London in the 1840s, have heard through the demimonde of the secret societies Marx joined, the League of the Just or its successor, the Communist League? Could she have read the English translation of *The Communist Manifesto* in *Woodhull and Claflin's Weekly* when she was living in the United States in 1871? Certainly by 1878, when Britten delivered a lecture on "The Chinese Labour Question; or the Problem of Capital versus Labour," she had an analysis of anti-immigrant sentiment as a symptom of the degradation of labor created by driving down wages.

45. Britten, *Ghost Land*, 36.

46. Britten, *Ghost Land*, 181, 283, 284.

47. Randolph, *Love and Its Hidden History; A Book for Man, Woman, Wives, Husbands, and for the Loving and the Unloved*, 166.

48. Randolph reuses the line about "drop[ping] beneath the floors of the outer world" in *P. B. Randolph, The "Learned Pundit," and "Man with Two Souls"* (29) and *Seership!* (28). He varies the language in *Seership!*, where he writes that magic mirrors allow one "to penetrate the floors of the waking world, and come up, all brilliant and keen, upon the other side" (37).

49. Randolph, *Dealings with the Dead*, 8.

50. Randolph, *Dealings with the Dead*, 33.

51. Randolph, *Unveiling*, 7. Randolph uses the word *mysteries* habitually and with the same sense of unknowability that I argue in chapter 4 it carries in midcentury city mysteries.

52. Randolph, *Wonderful Story of Ravalette*, 50; Randolph, *Book of the Triplicate Order*, quoted in Deveney, *Paschal Beverly Randolph*, 232.

53. Randolph, *Eulis!*, 121.

54. Deveney, *Paschal Beverly Randolph*, 145.

55. Randolph's own writing questions whether the distinction between thought and being even holds. In *Dealings with the Dead*, he realizes, "THOUGHTS WERE LIVING THINGS, ENDOWED WITH A BEING IN THEMSELVES!" (199). While we are living, they "loom up in the deep, distant depths of the mind"; "after death, these become the realities of our then existence, are the spontaneous out-births or out-creations of our souls" (254). Thus, while I have been drawing a distinction between the undergrounds of fantasy and reality, he might respond that every underground he dreams up in his writing, precisely by being dreamed up, takes on an obscure but no less real life of its own. In this analysis, fantasy constitutes our reality's underground, dismissed and discredited on earth yet sure of fulfillment some time, somewhere.

56. Randolph, *Rosicrucian*, 1. Further citations will appear parenthetically in the text.

57. Deveney, *Paschal Beverly Randolph*, 175. Deveney identifies the group as the Boston Rosicrucian Club, but the locations Randolph mentions them visiting on the previous year's outing are all around the Raritan Bay, suggesting that he may have started a New York group as well.

58. Randolph, *Wonderful Story of Ravalette*, 81.

59. Randolph, *Guide to Clairvoyance*, 42.

60. Most of Randolph's writing was published by himself, Mary Jane Randolph, Kate Corson Randolph, or some combination of these. However, some of his works appeared through other publishers specializing in reform or fringe movements, and cheap print impresario Sinclair Tousey, founder of the megadistributor American News Company, published *The Wonderful Story of Ravalette*

and the historical-theological-geological study *Pre-Adamite Man*. Tousey also acted as agent for some of Randolph's other works. See the advertisement for Randolph's publications in the *New York Tribune*, September 26, 1863; and "Appendix C: Bibliography of the Works of Paschal Beverly Randolph" in Deveney, *Paschal Beverly Randolph*, 343–68.

61. Randolph, *Love and Its Hidden History; also, the Master Passion*, 69.

62. Only a few copies of most of these texts survive. For some understanding of those I could not access, I have relied on the detailed synopses of other works Randolph includes at the end of *Eulis!* and on John Patrick Deveney's invaluable bibliography of Randolph's works. Deveney also reprints "The Ansairetic Mystery" ("A Private Letter, Printed, But Not Published") and the manuscript "The Mysteries of Eulis" as appendices to *Paschal Beverly Randolph*.

63. Schuller, *Biopolitics of Feeling*, 18.

64. Randolph, *Eulis!*, 219.

65. Comstock undertook his crusade in response to the feminist/sex radical/spiritualist/socialist *Woodhull & Claflin's Weekly*, coedited by Victoria Woodhull, whom Randolph openly supported. Molly McGarry posits that the spiritualist component of *Woodhull & Claflin's Weekly* may have shaped obscenity laws as much as its embrace of free love did. While the spiritualist movement of the 1850s had contacted disembodied spirits, a second wave of spiritualists in the 1870s contacted embodied, often sexualized ones; the entrance of these embodied spirits into the home, McGarry argues, became displaced onto fears about the dangerous flow of sexualized bodies through the US mail. See *Ghosts of Futures Past*, chap. 3.

66. Randolph, *Seership!*, 1.

67. Randolph, *Eulis!*, 4.

68. Foucault, *History of Sexuality*, 1:57.

69. Randolph, *Love! At Last!*, 45.

70. Randolph, *Casca Llanna*, 18; Randolph, "Mysteries of Eulis," 340.

71. Randolph, "Mysteries of Eulis," 334.

72. Randolph, "Mysteries of Eulis," 340.

73. Kahan, *Book of Minor Perverts*, 82–83.

74. Somerville, *Queering the Color Line*, 27.

75. Foucault, *History of Sexuality*, 1:146.

76. Coviello, *Tomorrow's Parties*, 22.

77. On Fourier and Fourierist communities, see Beecher, *Charles Fourier*; Guarneri, *Utopian Alternative*; Jackson, *American Radicals*, chaps. 6–7; and Brown, *Black Utopias*, chap. 5.

78. Randolph, *Dealings with the Dead*, 11; Randolph, *New Mola!*, 14, quoted in Deveney, *Paschal Beverly Randolph*, 116. Randolph explains that both he and Cynthia Temple are the authors of *Dealings with the Dead* due to the process he called "THE BLENDING": "I did not seem to be myself, but ... instead of who and what I am ... I was myself and Cynthia ... at first very imperfectly, but gradually approaching an absolute and complete mergement of Soul" (10).

79. Randolph, *P. B. Randolph, the "Learned Pundit," and "Man with Two Souls,"* 18.

80. Randolph, "Ansairetic Mystery," 316.

81. Randolph, *Eulis!*, 206.

82. Randolph, *Guide to Clairvoyance*, 14.

83. Randolph, "Asiatic Mystery," 120, 113.

84. Lorde, "Uses of the Erotic," 57. Even leaving aside its transformative effects, the scrupulous intentionalism of Randolph's sex magic contravenes the "dominant mythology" of Black sex that Hortense Spillers describes, which sees it as "a state, of vicious, routinized entanglement ... untrammeled by consciousness" ("Interstices," 164).

85. Randolph, *Guide to Clairvoyance*, 5. Randolph repeats the passage in *Seership!*, 3.

86. Randolph, *Seership!*, 2.

87. Randolph, *P. B. Randolph, The "Learned Pundit," and "Man with Two Souls,"* 70. Further citations will appear parenthetically in the text.

88. I differ here from Deveney, who considers the trial fiction but accepts the scheme to seize Randolph's work as fact. I see no evidence for this.

89. Randolph, *Casca Llanna*, 10.

90. Deveney, *Paschal Beverly Randolph*, 154.

91. Randolph, *After Death; or, Disembodied Man*, 76.

92. Hartman, *Scenes of Subjection*, 115.

93. Hartman, *Scenes of Subjection*, 116.

94. Hartman, *Scenes of Subjection*, 120.

95. Hartman, *Scenes of Subjection*, 122.

96. Randolph, *After Death; or, Disembodied Man*, 10.

97. In *The Wonderful Story of Ravalette*, the protagonist Beverly hears the phrase from his dead mother's spirit (30), from his beloved Evlambéa (51), and from the mysterious Ravalette in one of his guises (123), and he finally reads it on a scroll in a prophetic trance (245).

98. For example, in 1858 a writer to the *Liberator* accused Randolph of trolling William Wells Brown at one of his lectures and stealing money from a hat containing contributions ("John Randolph," *Liberator*, November 5, 1858, 177).

99. *National Convention of Colored Men*, 36.

100. *National Convention of Colored Men*, 21.

101. Claudia Rankine, "The Condition of Black Life Is One of Mourning," *New York Times Magazine*, June 22, 2015. https://www.nytimes.com/2015/06/22/magazine/the-condition-of-black-life-is-one-of-mourning.html.

102. *National Convention of Colored Men*, 22.

103. Randolph, *Wonderful Story of Ravalette*, 14. Further citations will appear parenthetically in the text.

104. Randolph, *Eulis!*, 184.

105. On Theodore Dwight's interest in Arabic writing from Africa, see Ala Alryyes's introduction to *A Muslim American Slave*, 3–46.

106. Weheliye, *Habeas Viscus*, 43.

107. Weheliye, *Habeas Viscus*, 51.

108. The *Oxford English Dictionary* gives the earliest usage of this sense of "spiritual" from 1858, five years before the publication of *The Wonderful Story of Ravalette*.

109. Douglass, *Narrative of the Life of Frederick Douglass*, 13, 14.

110. Randolph, *Tom Clark and His Wife*, 39–40.

111. Randolph, *After Death; or, Disembodied Man*, 10. Further citations will appear parenthetically in the text.

112. Quoted in an untitled paragraph, *Portsmouth Journal of Literature and Politics*, August 11, 1866, 2.

113. Highgate to Strieby, December 17, 1866, in Sterling, *We Are Your Sisters*, 299. On Highgate's own remarkable writing, see Gardner, "'Each Atomic Part'"; and Gardner, *Black Print Unbound*, chap. 6. Highgate almost certainly knew Randolph; in a letter she wrote to the *Colored Tennessean* about the Freedmen's Schools in New Orleans, she mentions him as "that gifted, eccentric genius" and praises a performance his students gave at the New Orleans Theatre. "The superb scenes, tableaux, declamations, and songs were many of them written by the doctor for that occasion," she reported; one can only imagine what he devised for them ("New Orleans Correspondence," *Colored Tennessean*, March 24, 1866).

114. Ferreira da Silva, "Toward a Black Feminist Poethics," 84.

115. Ferreira da Silva, "1 (life) + 0 (blackness)= $\infty - \infty$ or ∞/∞."

116. Ferreira da Silva, "Toward a Black Feminist Poethics," 82, 89.

117. Ferreira da Silva, "Toward a Black Feminist Poethics," 85–86, 91.

118. Randolph, *After Death: The Disembodiment of Man*, 259–60.

119. Randolph, *After Death: The Disembodiment of Man*, 260.

120. Randolph does add that "a baptism of fire and blood upon the heads of all civilized peoples,—the battle of Armageddon" (260) will also occur, but he says nothing further about it.

121. Randolph, *After Death: The Disembodiment of Man*, 260.

122. Randolph, *Eulis!*, 48; Hopkins, *Of One Blood*, 603. Further citations to *Of One Blood* will appear parenthetically in the text.

123. Finley, "Paschal Beverly Randolph in the African American Community," 47–49; Deveney, *Paschal Beverly Randolph*, 176.

124. Hopkins seems to have been well versed in spiritual literature: in Daniel Hack's analysis of the richly intertextual *Of One Blood*, he finds that the text it borrows from most extensively is Emma Hardinge Britten's novella *L'Improvvisatore*. See Hack, *Reaping Something New*, 169.

125. Tate, *Domestic Allegories of Political Desire*, 207. In both its invocation of antislavery undergrounds and its ultimate difficulty in imagining the underground leading anywhere, *Of One Blood* resembles Sutton Griggs's *Imperium in Imperio* (1899), published three years earlier. The story of two friends who join a secret Black "compact government exercising all the functions of a nation" (132), in many ways *Imperium in Imperio* exemplifies nineteenth-century undergrounds in all their multiplicity. The Imperium is headquartered underneath a college (Jefferson College, of course); it has united all the Black secret societies created before the Civil War; it circulates a "secret newspaper" that "spread[s] fire-brands everywhere in the ranks" (137), and through its work, "beneath the South a mine had been dug and filled with dynamite" (176). Yet the novel ends before it can "strike a blow for freedom" (149) and seize Texas, with the Imperium in disarray and its plans betrayed by a self-declared "traitor" (176).

126. Berlant, *Cruel Optimism*, 199, 201.

Chapter 6. Subterranean Fire

1. George Engel, Samuel Fielden, Adolph Fischer, Louis Lingg, Albert Parsons, Michael Schwab, and August Spies were sentenced to death, Oscar Neebe to a fifteen-year prison term. Fielden's and Schwab's sentences were later commuted; Lingg killed himself in prison by putting a cartridge of dynamite in his mouth and lighting the fuse.

2. *Accused the Accusers*, 10. The Cuban writer and revolutionary José Martí, living in New York at the time of the trial, seems to have been especially struck by Spies's image of anarchism as an embodiment of subterranean fire. He observed of the defendants:

Así como la vida del hombre se concentra en la medulla espinal, y la de la tierra en las masas volcánicas, surgen de entre esas muchedumbres, erguidos y vomitando fuego, seres en quienes parece haberse amasado todo su horror, sus desperaciones y sus lágrimas.

Del infierno vienen: ¿qué lengua han de hablar sino la del infierno?

[As human life concentrates itself in the spinal cord and that of the earth in the volcanic masses, there surge from amid these multitudes, erect and spewing fire, beings in whom all of their horror, desperation, and tears seem to have gathered.

From hell they come: what language would they speak but that of hell?] (Martí, "Un drama terrible," 338; my translation).

3. *Accused the Accusers*, 11.

4. *Accused the Accusers*, 69.

5. On Johann Most and the Pittsburgh Congress, see Goyens, *Beer and Revolution*, chap. 3.

6. J. S., "The Bullet or the Ballot!," *Alarm*, April 18, 1885, 4.

7. Untitled item, *Alarm*, February 28, 1885, 2.

8. "Eight Hour Movement," *Alarm*, January 23, 1886, 2.

9. Nelson, *Beyond the Martyrs*, chap. 6.

10. "Revolutionary! A Great Demonstration by the Working People of Chicago under the Auspices of the International," *Alarm*, August 8, 1885, 1.

11. "The Black Flag!," *Alarm*, November 29, 1884, 1.

12. The November 28, 1885, issue of the *Alarm* reported that "387,527 books, pamphlets and circulars had been distributed and sold by the International" in the preceding six months ("Semi-Annual Report," 1).

13. "To the Workingmen of America," *Alarm*, October 4, 1884, 2 (originally issued October 16, 1883).

14. "The International," *Alarm*, April 18, 1885, 4.

15. "Letter Box," *Alarm*, November 14, 1885, 3.

16. For example, see untitled item, *Alarm*, December 18, 1884, 1; "A Voice from North Carolina," *Alarm*, July 25, 1885, 2; "The Revolutionary Movement in the United States," *Alarm*, February 6, 1886, 1.

17. J. Allen Evans, "Greeley, Colorado," *Alarm*, April 4, 1885, 3.

18. Lewis York, "Capitalists Afraid," *Alarm*, March 20, 1886, 2.

19. "Friends Everywhere," *Alarm*, February 28, 1885, 2.

20. "Workingmen to Arms!," *Alarm*, April 24, 1886, 1.

21. "Workingmen to Arms!," 1; "The Far West," *Alarm*, April 24, 1886, 2.

22. "Street Fighting," *Alarm*, July 25, 1885, 3.

23. Quotation from "capitalist papers all over the country" in "Arming," *Alarm*, February 21, 1885, 3; "Thanksgiving! Response of the Working People to the Command to Give Thanks," *Alarm*, December 12, 1885, 1.

24. W[illiam]. H[olmes]., "The London Excitement," *Alarm*, February 20, 1886, 2.

25. "The Communist Programme," *Christian Union*, April 30, 1885, 3.

26. "The Right to Bear Arms," *Alarm*, January 9, 1886, 2.

27. Avrich, *Haymarket Tragedy*, 46.

28. "Right to Bear Arms," 2.

29. Nelson, *Beyond the Martyrs*, 193; Schaack, *Anarchy and Anarchists*, 220, 289.

30. Quoted in Clymer, *America's Culture of Terrorism*, 49.

31. Wheeler, *Deadwood Dick Jr. in Chicago*, 2, 4, 5.

32. Edward Bellamy's 1888 utopian novel *Looking Backward* offers an interesting variation on the attenuating wildness of literal undergrounds: wealthy Julian West seals himself in a subterranean sleeping chamber to protect himself from anarchists and other "labor agitators," only to wake up in the year 2000, where he learns the error of his ways. In Bellamy's bourgeois socialist view, the underground is educative, a place for the moral regeneration of bad capitalists.

33. Coverdale, *Fall of the Great Republic*, 27. The image of "a volcano smoldering underfoot" also appears on p. 9. Will Hansen, assistant curator of collections at Duke University's David M. Rubenstein Rare Book and Manuscript Library, has identified Coverdale as journalist Abner Hitchcock; see Amy McDonald, "An Anonymous Author Unveiled, 125 Years Later," The Devil's Tale, March 4, 2011, https://blogs.library.duke.edu/rubenstein/2011/03/04/hitchcock/.

34. Coverdale, *Fall of the Great Republic*, 32, 52.

35. Wheeler, *Deadwood Dick Jr. in Chicago*, 8.

36. Dell, "Socialism and Anarchism in Chicago," 391.

37. See, for example, "The Meeting Attended by Two Thousand Working Men on the Lake Front," *Alarm*, November 15, 1884, 1; "Dynamite: Professor Mezzeroff Talks About It," *Alarm*, January 13, 1885, 4; "Explosives: A Practical Lesson in Popular Chemistry," *Alarm*, April 4, 1885, 1.

38. Dell, "Socialism and Anarchism in Chicago," 391; C. L. James, "Anarchy's Apostles, IV: Bakounine—The Organizer," *Twentieth Century*, January 7, 1892, 7.

39. T. Lizius, "Dynamite," *Alarm*, February 21, 1885, 3. The article is signed from Indianapolis, so my guess is that the *T* is a mistake and the writer is regular *Alarm*

contributor Gerhard Lizius, who lived in Indianapolis at the time and would shortly become an editor at the *Arbeiter-Zeitung*.

40. "All Honor to Them," *Alarm*, January 13, 1885, 2; and "The Hocking Valley," *Alarm*, January 13, 1885, 3.

41. Lizzie M. Swank, "Election Day," *Alarm*, November 14, 1885, 2.

42. "Victory," *Alarm*, April 18, 1885, 1.

43. For a useful critique of Messer-Kruse's *Haymarket Conspiracy*, see Kenyon Zimmer's review in *Labor* 11 (2014): 125–27.

44. *Accused the Accusers*, 11.

45. Quoted in Avrich, *Haymarket Tragedy*, 163.

46. Weeks, *Problem with Work*, 11.

47. L[izzie]. M. S[wank]., "A Short Story for Moral Teachers," *Alarm*, January 23, 1886, 3.

48. Ernest Jones, "Song of the Wage-Slave," *Alarm*, December 6, 1884, 4.

49. Untitled poem, *Alarm*, October 18, 1884, 4.

50. *Accused the Accusers*, 162.

51. The expendability of the tramp is emphatically different from Black social death, beginning with the fact that it is not ontological. However, the perception that tramps approach a condition racialized as Black may be part of what makes them so intolerable. Note that many of the vagrancy laws that criminalized tramps in the North in the 1880s were modeled on post–Civil War vagrancy laws passed to control Black people's mobility in the South. See Stanley, *From Bondage to Contract*, chap. 3. On tramps in Chicago and the contradictions of free labor, see Black, "Crime to Live without Work."

52. Lucy Parsons, "A Word to Tramps," *Alarm*, October 4, 1884, 1.

53. Quoted in Cresswell, *Tramp in America*, 9.

54. Untitled item, *Alarm*, October 11, 1884, 3; untitled item, *Alarm*, October 18, 1884, 3.

55. "The Proletariat," *Alarm*, January 13, 1885, 1.

56. "Monongahela Valley," *Alarm*, January 23, 1886, 1.

57. Parsons, "Word to Tramps," 1.

58. Jones, "Song of the Wage-Slave," 4.

59. "To the Workingmen of America," 2.

60. S. Robert Wilson, "Revolution," *Alarm*, April 4, 1885, 4.

61. De Cleyre, "Fruit of the Sacrifice," 5.

62. Coghlan, *Sensational Internationalism*, 100–101.

63. De Cleyre, "Commune Is Risen," 10, 13, 15.

64. Bakunin, "Reaction in Germany," 56, 57.

65. "On a Cartridge of 'Hercules' Dynamite," *Alarm*, May 30, 1885, 3.

66. See also "Old John Brown," *Alarm*, November 8, 1884, 1; and Dyer D. Lum, "John Brown," *Alarm*, April 3, 1886, 3.

67. Travis Foster gives a stunning account of the role that postwar elegies played in such attempts to console and forget in *Genre and White Supremacy in the Postemancipation United States*, chap. 3, where he shows how even the dissenting elegiac strains he identifies as "antiwar" and "melancholic" worked to reinforce patently nationalist ones.

68. Jackson, *American Radicals*, 294.

69. Jackson, *American Radicals*, 294.

70. "Abolish Capital," *Alarm*, October 11, 1884, 2.

71. Jones, *Goddess of Anarchy*, 11–12.

72. "Enslaved Labor," *Alarm*, October 11, 1884, 2.

73. Untitled item, *Alarm*, October 11, 1884, 1.

74. C. L. James, "An Open Letter," *Alarm*, March 20, 1886, 3.

75. See Roediger, *Wages of Whiteness*, especially chap. 4.

76. "To the Workingmen of America," 2.

77. Fish, "Water Cure for Anarchists," 186.

78. See Du Bois, *Black Reconstruction in America*, 700; and Harris, "Whiteness as Property."

79. "Agitation in Topeka, Kansas: The Students Organized into a Group of the International, Are Now Organizing the Colored People into Groups Also," *Alarm*, February 28, 1885, 2.

80. Lucy E. Parsons, "The Negro," *Alarm*, April 3, 1886, 2. Even as she acknowledges Black workers to be subject to "deep-seated, blind, relentless prejudice," however, Parsons denies the significance of racism, demanding, "Are there any so stupid as to believe these outrages have been, are being and will be heaped upon the Negro because he is black? Not at all. It is because he is poor."

81. Bey, *Anarcho-Blackness*, 94. By "abolitionism," Bey refers not only to antislavery but to "the political strategy of eradicating rather than reforming systems, discourses, and institutions that structure life and livability" (91). In terms of nineteenth-century abolitionism, perhaps more surprising than Bey's claim that anarchism is abolitionist is their corresponding claim that "abolition is fundamentally anarchic" (27). However, Holly Jackson's *American Radicals* describes

Garrisonianism as anarchist in nature, emphasizing its absolute rejection of government; see chap. 4.

82. Bey, *Anarcho-Blackness*, 15.

83. "Old John Brown," 1; "New York City: Comrade Lum, John Brown, and Cyrus W. Field," *Alarm*, December 12, 1885, 2.

84. "A Stationary Index," *Alarm*, September 19, 1885, 2.

85. Lizzie M. Swank, "Two Stories in One," *Alarm*, April 3, 1886, 3.

86. Swank, "Two Stories in One," 3.

87. "The Black Flag!," *Alarm*, November 29, 1884, 1.

88. [Albert] P[arsons]., "The Dynamite Terror," *Alarm*, February 21, 1885, 2.

89. L[izzie]. M. S[wank]., "Slavery—White and Black," *Alarm*, March 20, 1886, 2.

90. [Albert] P[arsons]., "Law and Order League," *Alarm*, April 24, 1886, 1.

91. Dyer D. Lum, "Underground Railways," *Alarm*, December 3, 1887, 2.

92. Melville, *Billy Budd*, 360. Further citations will appear parenthetically in the text.

93. Thoreau, "Winter Walk," 215.

94. Wallace, "*Billy Budd* and the Haymarket Hangings," 108.

95. Wallace, "*Billy Budd* and the Haymarket Hangings," 111.

96. Wallace, "*Billy Budd* and the Haymarket Hangings," 109–10.

97. Johnson, "Melville's Fist," 599.

98. Boudreau, "Elegies for the Haymarket Anarchists."

99. Sedgwick, *Epistemology of the Closet*, 97.

100. Sedgwick, *Epistemology of the Closet*, 101.

101. Jameson, "Vanishing Mediator."

102. Casarino, "Gomorrahs of the Deep," 11, 12; Pérez, *Taste for Brown Bodies*, 26.

103. Melville, *Moby-Dick*, 187.

104. James, *Varieties of Religious Experience*, 234.

105. Janet, *L'automatisme psychologique*, 335.

106. Breuer and Freud, *Studies on Hysteria*, 222–23; Freud, "Unconscious," 173.

107. Breuer and Freud, *Studies on Hysteria*, 139. For a useful survey of the development of the topographical model in Freud's thought, see Gill, *Topography and Systems in Psychoanalytic Theory*. On Breuer and Freud's archaeological metaphors, see Hake, "Saxa loquuntur"; Khanna, *Dark Continents*, chap. 1; and O'Donoghue, "Negotiations of Surface."

108. Sedgwick, *Epistemology of the Closet*, 115.

109. Johnson, "Melville's Fist," 569.

Epilogue. Staying Underground

1. Whitehead, *Underground Railroad*, 303. Further citations will appear parenthetically in the text. I don't know if antebellum accounts of the Underground Railroad number among Whitehead's extensive historical references (Harriet Jacobs, David Walker, Martin Delany, J. Marion Sims, etc.). In interviews he has described his inspiration as the "childhood notion" of the Underground Railroad as an "actual subway" (Whitehead, "Colson Whitehead's 'The Underground Railroad' Is a Literal Train to Freedom"). The Underground Airlines of Winters's novel is metaphorical and even somewhat misleading. There is "[n]o such thing as the Underground Airlines, not really, not in any grand, organized sense," explains the narrator, a fugitive from slavery who becomes an agent tracking fugitives for the government (Winters, *Underground Airlines*, 9). But its literalization also becomes a motif, as the underground materializes in places like the tunnel where a fugitive hides—"He'd gone underground," the narrator notes wryly (166)—as well as the basement kitchen that is the headquarters of an Underground Airlines cell and the subterranean room where the narrator is imprisoned after he becomes a double agent.

2. Whitehead's underground railroad in some ways seems like an inverted version of the elevators in his first novel, *The Intuitionist*, whose operations are likewise shrouded in mystery.

3. Randolph, *After Death: The Disembodiment of Man*, 260.

4. See Moore, *Sweet Freedom's Plains*. Thank you to Paula Austin for connecting Whitehead's final scene to Moore's book and for talking through the trajectory of *The Underground Railroad* with me.

5. "Women Who Can Keep a Secret: All That Can Be Learned about the Grand United Order of Tents," *Sun*, May 6, 1888, 5. I first learned of the United Order of Tents through the work of sculptor and installation artist Simone Leigh, who draws on it in her works *Free People's Medical Clinic* (2014) and *The Waiting Room* (2016). In an interview with Rizvana Bradley, Leigh comments, "Perhaps it is time to do as the Tents do, go back underground" ("Going Underground"). See also Richter, "Reflections on Black Sisterhood and the United Order of Tents."

Bibliography

Abraham, Nicolas, and Maria Torok. "Mourning *or* Melancholia: Introjection *versus* Incorporation." In *The Shell and the Kernel: Renewals of Psychoanalysis*, vol. 1, edited and translated by Nicholas Rand, 125–38. Chicago: University of Chicago Press, 1994.

Abraham, Nicolas, and Maria Torok. *The Wolf Man's Magic Word: A Cryptonomy*. Translated by Nicholas Rand. Minneapolis: University of Minnesota Press, 1986.

The Accused the Accusers: The Famous Speeches of the Eight Chicago Anarchists in Court. Chicago: Socialistic Publishing Society, 1886.

Agassiz, Louis. "Observations on the Blind Fish of Mammoth Cave." *American Journal of Science and the Arts* 11 (January 1851): 127–28.

Albanese, Mary Grace. "Unraveling the Blood Line: Pauline Hopkins's Haitian Genealogies." *J19* 7 (Fall 2019): 227–48.

Allewaert, Monique. *Ariel's Ecology: Plantations, Personhood, and Colonialism in the American Tropics*. Minneapolis: University of Minnesota Press, 2013.

Alryyes, Ala, ed. and trans. *A Muslim American Slave: The Life of Omar Ibn Said*. Madison: University of Wisconsin Press, 2011.

Altschuler, Sari. "'Picture It All, Darley': Race Politics and the Media History of George Lippard's *The Quaker City*." *Nineteenth-Century Literature* 70 (June 2015): 65–101.

Anderson, Osborne P. *A Voice from Harper's Ferry: A Narrative of the Events at Harper's Ferry*. Boston, 1861.

Apess, William. "An Indian's Looking-Glass for the White Man." In *The Experiences of Five Christian Indians of the Pequod Tribe*, 53–60. Boston: James B. Dow, 1833.

Averill, Charles E. *The Secrets of the Twin Cities; or, the Great Metropolis Unmasked*. Boston: George H. Williams, 1849.

Avrich, Paul. *The Haymarket Tragedy*. Princeton, NJ: Princeton University Press, 1984.
Bakunin, Michael [Mikhail]. "The Reaction in Germany." In *Selected Writings*, edited by Arthur Lehning, 37–58. London: Jonathan Cape, 1973.
Baquaqua, Mahommah Gardo. *Biography of Mahommah G. Baquaqua, a Native of Zoogoo, in the Interior of Africa . . . Written and Revised from His Own Words, by Samuel Moore, Esq.* Detroit: Geo. E. Pomeroy, 1854.
Barnwell. "The Mammoth Cave." *Knickerbocker* 33 (April 1849): 301–12.
Bataille, George. "Base Materialism and Gnosticism." In *Visions of Excess: Selected Writings, 1927–1939*, edited by Allan Stoekl, translated by Allan Stoekl, Carl R. Lovitt, and Donald M. Leslie Jr., 45–52. Minneapolis: University of Minnesota Press, 1985.
Bataille, George. "'The Old Mole' and the Prefix *Sur*." In *Visions of Excess: Selected Writings, 1927–1939*, edited by Allan Stoekl, translated by Allan Stoekl, Carl R. Lovitt, and Donald M. Leslie Jr., 32–44. Minneapolis: University of Minnesota Press, 1985.
Bay, Mia. *The White Image in the Black Mind: African-American Ideas about White People, 1830–1925*. Oxford: Oxford University Press, 2000.
Beam, Dorri. *Style, Gender, and Fantasy in Nineteenth-Century American Women's Writing*. Cambridge: Cambridge University Press, 2010.
Bearse, Austin. *Reminiscences of Fugitive-Slave Law Days in Boston*. Boston: Printed by Warren Richardson, 1880.
Beecher, Jonathan. *Charles Fourier: The Visionary and His World*. Berkeley: University of California Press, 1983.
Benjamin, Walter. *The Origin of German Tragic Drama*. Translated by John Osborne. London: NLB, 1977.
Berlant, Lauren. *Cruel Optimism*. Durham, NC: Duke University Press, 2011.
Best, Stephen. *The Fugitive's Properties: Law and the Poetics of Possession*. Chicago: University of Chicago Press, 2004.
Bey, Marquis. *Anarcho-Blackness*. Chico, CA: AK Press, 2020.
Bickley, George W. L. *Adalaska; or the Strange and Mysterious Family of the Cave of Genreva*. Cincinnati, OH: H.M. Rulison, 1854.
Bird, Robert Montgomery. *Peter Pilgrim; or, a Rambler's Recollections*. 2 vols. Philadelphia: Lea and Blanchard, 1838.
Black, Alex W. "'A New Enterprise in Our History': William Still, Conductor of *The Underground Rail Road* (1872)." *American Literary History* 32 (2020): 668–90.
Black, Joel E. "A Crime to Live without Work: Free Labor and Marginal Workers in Industrial Chicago, 1870–1920." *Michigan Historical Review* 36 (Fall 2010): 63–93.
Blackett, R. J. M. "'Freemen to the Rescue!' Resistance to the Fugitive Slave Law of 1850." In *Passages to Freedom: The Underground Railroad in History and Memory*, edited by David W. Blight, 133–48. Washington, DC: Smithsonian Books, 2004.
Blackett, R. J. M. *Making Freedom: The Underground Railroad and the Politics of Slavery*. Chapel Hill: University of North Carolina Press, 2013.

Blalock, Stephanie M. "'Tell What I Meant by *Calamus*': Walt Whitman's Vision of Comradeship from Fred Vaughn to the Fred Gray Association." In *Whitman among the Bohemians*, edited by Joanna Levin and Edward Whitley, 172–91. Iowa City: University of Iowa Press, 2014.

Blum, Hester. "John Cleves Symmes and the Planetary Reach of Polar Exploration." *American Literature* 84 (June 2012): 243–71.

Blyden, Edward W. "A Chapter in the History of the African Slave Trade." *Anglo-African Magazine* 1, no. 6 (June 1859): 178–84.

Bohan, Ruth L. "*Vanity Fair*, Whitman, and the Counter Jumper." *Word and Image* 33 (2017): 57–69.

Boromé, Joseph A. "The Vigilant Committee of Philadelphia." *Pennsylvania Magazine of History and Biography* 92 (July 1968): 320–51.

Boudreau, Kristin. "Elegies for the Haymarket Anarchists." *American Literature* 77 (June 2005): 319–47.

Boutelle, R. J. "'Greater Still in Death': Race, Martyrology, and the Reanimation of Juan Placido." *American Literature* 90 (September 2018): 461–93.

Bowditch, Vincent Y. *Life and Correspondence of Henry Ingersoll Bowditch*. 2 vols. Boston: Houghton, Mifflin, 1902.

Bradley, Rizvana. "Going Underground: An Interview with Simone Leigh." *Art in America*, August 20, 2015. https://www.artnews.com/art-in-america/interviews/going-underground-an-interview-with-simone-leigh-56438/.

Breuer, Josef, and Sigmund Freud. *Studies on Hysteria*. Vol. 2 of *The Standard Edition of the Complete Psychological Works of Sigmund Freud*, translated and edited by James Strachey. London: Hogarth Press, 1955.

Britten, Emma Hardinge. *Art Magic; or, Mundane, Sub-Mundane and Super-Mundane Spiritism*. New York, 1876.

Britten, Emma Hardinge. *Ghost Land; or Researches into the Mysteries of Occultism*. Boston, 1876.

Brooks, Daphne A. *Bodies in Dissent: Spectacular Performances of Race and Freedom, 1850–1910*. Durham, NC: Duke University Press, 2006.

Brown, Jayna. *Black Utopias: Speculative Life and the Music of Other Worlds*. Durham, NC: Duke University Press, 2021.

Brown, Lois. *Pauline Elizabeth Hopkins: Black Daughter of the Revolution*. Chapel Hill: University of North Carolina Press, 2008.

Buck-Morss, Susan. *The Dialectics of Seeing: Walter Benjamin and the Arcades Project*. Cambridge, MA: MIT Press, 1989.

Bullitt, Alexander Clark. *Rambles in the Mammoth Cave, during the Year 1844*. Louisville, KY: Morton and Griswold, 1845.

Butler, Judith. *The Psychic Life of Power: Theories in Subjection*. Stanford, CA: Stanford University Press, 1997.

Byrd, Jodi A. *The Transit of Empire: Indigenous Critiques of Colonialism*. Minneapolis: University of Minnesota Press, 2011.

Calendar of Virginia State Papers and Other Manuscripts, vol. 11. Richmond, 1893.

Campbell, John Francis. *A Short American Tramp in the Fall of 1864*. Edinburgh: Edmonston and Douglas, 1865.

Campt, Tina M. *Listening to Images*. Durham, NC: Duke University Press, 2017.

Carby, Hazel V. *Reconstructing Womanhood: The Emergence of the Afro-American Woman Novelist*. New York: Oxford University Press, 1987.

Carpenter, Russell Lant. *Observations on American Slavery: After a Year's Tour in the United States*. London: Edward T. Whitfield, 1852.

Casarino, Cesare. "Gomorrahs of the Deep; or, Melville, Foucault, and the Question of Heterotopia." *Arizona Quarterly* 51 (Winter 1995): 1–25.

Chiles, Katy L. *Transformable Race: Surprising Metamorphoses in the Literature of Early America*. Oxford: Oxford University Press, 2014.

Ciccariello-Maher, George. *Decolonizing Dialectics*. Durham, NC: Duke University Press, 2017.

Ciccariello-Maher, George. "The Dialectics of Standing One's Ground." *Theory and Event* 15, no. 3 (2012).

Clymer, Jeffory A. *America's Culture of Terrorism: Violence, Capitalism, and the Written Word*. Chapel Hill: University of North Carolina Press, 2003.

Clymer, R. Swinburne. *The Book of Rosicruciae: A Condensed History of the Fraternitas Rosae Crucis or Rosy Cross*. 3 vols. Quakertown, PA: Philosophical Publishing, 1946–49.

Clymer, R. Swinburne. *The Rose Cross Order: A Short Sketch of the History of the Rose Cross Order in America, Together with a Sketch of Dr. P. B. Randolph, the Founder of the Order*. Allentown, PA: Philosophical Publishing, 1916.

Clytus, Radiclani. "Visualizing in Black Print: The Brooklyn Correspondence of William J. Wilson, aka 'Ethiop.'" *J19* 6 (Spring 2018): 29–66.

Coghlan, J. Michelle. *Sensational Internationalism: The Paris Commune and the Remapping of American Memory in the Long Nineteenth Century*. Edinburgh: Edinburgh University Press, 2016.

Cohen, Patricia Cline, Timothy J. Gilfoyle, Helen Lefkowitz Horowitz, and the American Antiquarian Society. *The Flash Press: Sporting Male Weeklies in 1840s New York*. Chicago: University of Chicago Press, 2008.

Collison, Gary L. "The Boston Vigilance Committee: A Reconsideration." *Historical Journal of Massachusetts* 12 (1984): 104–15.

Cook, James W. "Dancing across the Color Line." *Common-place* 4, no. 1 (October 2003). http://commonplace.online/article/dancing-across-the-color-line/.

Cordell, Ryan. "Reprinting, Circulation, and the Network Author in Antebellum Newspapers." *American Literary History* 27 (August 2015): 417–45.

Coronado, Raúl. *A World Not to Come: A History of Latino Writing and Print Culture*. Cambridge, MA: Harvard University Press, 2013.

Coverdale, Sir Henry Standish [pseud.]. *The Fall of the Great Republic (1886–88)*. New York: Roberts Brothers, 1885.

Coviello, Peter. *Tomorrow's Parties: Sex and the Untimely in Nineteenth-Century America*. New York: NYU Press, 2013.

Crary, B. F. "The Blackness of Darkness." *Ladies' Repository* (February 1853): 70–72.
Crawley, Ashon T. *Black Pentecostal Breath: The Aesthetics of Possibility*. New York: Fordham University Press, 2017.
Cresswell, Tim. *The Tramp in America*. London: Reaktion Books, 2001.
Cunningham, Nijah. "The Resistance of the Lost Body." *Small Axe* 20 (March 2016): 113–28.
Curtis, Newton M. *The Matricide's Daughter. A Tale of Life in the Great Metropolis*. New York: W. F. Burgess, 1850.
Daut, Marlene L. "Martin Delany's *Blake* in Black Revolutionary Context." *American Periodicals* 28, no. 1 (2018): 82–84.
Daut, Marlene L. *Tropics of Haiti: Race and the Literary History of the Haitian Revolution in the Atlantic World, 1789–1865*. Liverpool: Liverpool University Press, 2015.
de Cleyre, Voltairine. "The Commune Is Risen." *Mother Earth* 7 (March 1912): 10–15.
de Cleyre, Voltairine. "The Fruit of the Sacrifice." In *The First Mayday: The Haymarket Speeches, 1895–1910*, edited by Paul Avrich, 1–5. Sanday, Orkney: Cienfuegos Press, 1980.
de Grazia, Margreta. "Teleology, Delay, and the 'Old Mole.'" *Shakespeare Quarterly* 50 (Autumn 1999): 251–67.
Delany, Martin R. *Blake; or, the Huts of America*. Edited by Floyd J. Miller. Boston: Beacon Press, 1970.
Delany, Martin R. *Blake; or, the Huts of America; a Corrected Edition*. Edited by Jerome McGann. Cambridge, MA: Harvard University Press, 2017.
Delany, Martin R. *The Origin and Objects of Ancient Freemasonry: Its Introduction into the United States and Legitimacy among Colored Men*. In *Martin R. Delany: A Documentary Reader*, edited by Robert M. Levine, 49–67. Chapel Hill: University of North Carolina Press, 2003.
Dell, Floyd. "Socialism and Anarchism in Chicago." In *Chicago: Its History and Its Builders*, vol. 2, edited by J. Seymour Currey, 361–405. Chicago: S. J. Clarke, 1912.
Denning, Michael. *Mechanic Accents: Dime Novels and Working-Class Culture in America*. London: Verso, 1998.
Denning, Michael. "The Mysteries of Capital." *Amerikastudien/American Studies* 62, no. 4 (2017): 531–38.
Deveney, John Patrick. *Paschal Beverly Randolph: A Nineteenth-Century Black American Spiritualist, Rosicrucian, and Sex Magician*. Albany: State University of New York Press, 1997.
Dickson, Rev. Moses. *Manual of the International Order of Twelve of Knights and Daughters of Tabor*. St. Louis, MO: A. R. Fleming, 1891.
Dinius, Marcy J. "'Look!! Look!!! At This!!!': The Radical Typography of David Walker's *Appeal*." PMLA 126 (January 2011): 55–72.

Diouf, Sylviane A. *Slavery's Exiles: The Story of the American Maroons*. New York: NYU Press, 2014.

Douglas, Joseph C. "Music in the Mammoth Cave: An Important Aspect of Nineteenth-Century Cave Tourism." *Journal of Spelean History* 32 (July–September 1998): 47–59.

Douglass, Frederick. "John Brown: An Address by Frederick Douglass at the Fourteenth Anniversary of Storer College, Harpers Ferry, West Virginia, May 30, 1881." In *The Tribunal: Responses to John Brown and the Harpers Ferry Raid*, edited by John Stauffer and Zoe Trodd, 492–99. Cambridge, MA: Belknap Press, 2012.

Douglass, Frederick. *The Life and Times of Frederick Douglass*. Hartford, CT: Park Publishing, 1881.

Douglass, Frederick. *Narrative of the Life of Frederick Douglass, an American Slave*. Boston: American Anti-Slavery Office, 1845.

Douglass, Frederick. "Slavery, the Slumbering Volcano." In *The Frederick Douglass Papers*, series 1, vol. 2, edited by John W. Blassingame, 148–58. New Haven, CT: Yale University Press, 1982.

Du Bois, W. E. B. *Black Reconstruction in America*. New York: Free Press, 1998.

Du Bois, W. E. B. "The Comet." In *Darkwater: Voices from Within the Veil*, 253–73. New York: Harcourt, Brace, and Howe, 1920.

Du Bois, W. E. B. *John Brown*. Philadelphia: George W. Jacobs, 1909.

Du Bois, W. E. B. *The Souls of Black Folk*. Chicago: A. C. McClurg, 1903.

Eaklor, Vicki L. "The Songs of *The Emancipation Car*: Variations on an Abolitionist Theme." *Gateway Heritage: Quarterly Journal of the Missouri Historical Society* 36 (1980): 92–102.

Eburne, Jonathan P. *Outsider Theory: Intellectual Histories of Unorthodox Ideas*. Minneapolis: University of Minnesota Press, 2018.

Ellison, Ralph. *Invisible Man*. New York: Vintage, 1952.

Emerson, Ralph Waldo. "Illusions." In *The Conduct of Life*, 241–56. Boston: Ticknor and Fields, 1860.

Emerson, Ralph Waldo. *Nature: Addresses and Lectures*. Boston: James Munroe, 1849.

Erickson, Paul. "New Books, New Men: City-Mysteries Fiction, Authorship, and the Literary Market." *Early American Studies* 1, no. 1 (Spring 2003): 273–312.

Erickson, Paul. "Welcome to Sodom: The Cultural Work of City-Mysteries Fiction in Antebellum America." PhD diss., University of Texas at Austin, 2005.

Ernest, John. *Resistance and Reformation in Nineteenth-Century African-American Literature: Brown, Wilson, Jacobs, Delany, Douglass, and Harper*. Jackson: University Press of Mississippi, 1995.

Estes, Nick. *Our History Is the Future: Standing Rock versus the Dakota Access Pipeline, and the Long Tradition of Indigenous Resistance*. London: Verso, 2019.

Fanon, Frantz. *Black Skin, White Masks*. Translated by Charles Lam Markmann. New York: Grove Press, 1967.

Ferguson, Christine. *Determined Spirits: Eugenics, Heredity and Racial Regeneration in Anglo-American Spiritualist Writing, 1848–1930*. Edinburgh: Edinburgh University Press, 2012.

Ferreira da Silva, Denise. "1 (life) ÷ 0 (blackness)= ∞ − ∞ or ∞/∞: On Matter Beyond the Equation of Value." *e-flux* 79 (February 2017). https://www.e-flux.com/journal/79/94686/1-life-0-blackness-or-on-matter-beyond-the-equation-of-value/.

Ferreira da Silva, Denise. "Toward a Black Feminist Poethics: The Quest(ion) of Blackness toward the End of the World." *Black Scholar* 44, no. 2 (2014): 81–97.

Finch, Aisha K. *Rethinking Slave Rebellion in Cuba: La Escalera and the Insurgencies of 1841–1844*. Chapel Hill: University of North Carolina Press, 2015.

Finch, Marianne. *An Englishwoman's Experience in America*. London: Richard Bentley, 1853.

Finkelman, Paul. "Manufacturing Martyrdom: The Anti-Slavery Response to John Brown's Raid." In *His Soul Goes Marching On: Responses to John Brown and the Harpers Ferry Raid*, edited by Paul Finkelman, 41–66. Charlottesville: University Press of Virginia, 1995.

Finkenbine, Roy. "A Community Militant and Organized: The Colored Vigilant Committee of Detroit." In *A Fluid Frontier: Slavery, Resistance, and the Underground Railroad in the Detroit River Borderland*, edited by Karolyn Smardz Frost and Veta Smith Tucker, 154–64. Detroit, MI: Wayne State University Press, 2016.

Finley, Lana. "Paschal Beverly Randolph in the African American Community." In *Esotericism in African American Religious Experience: "There Is a Mystery . . . ,"* edited by Stephen C. Finley, Margarita Simon Guillory, and Hugh R. Page Jr., 37–51. Leiden, Netherlands: Brill, 2015.

Fish, Williston. "The Water Cure for Anarchists." *Puck*, May 18, 1886.

Flatley, Jonathan. *Affective Mapping: Melancholia and the Politics of Modernism*. Cambridge, MA: Harvard University Press, 2008.

Foner, Eric. *Gateway to Freedom: The Hidden History of the Underground Railroad*. New York: W. W. Norton, 2015.

Foreman, P. Gabrielle, Jim Casey, and Sarah Lynn Patterson, eds. *The Colored Conventions Movement: Black Organizing in the Nineteenth Century*. Chapel Hill: University of North Carolina Press, 2021.

Foster, George G. *New York by Gas-Light*. Berkeley: University of California Press, 1990.

Foster, Travis. *Genre and White Supremacy in the Postemancipation United States*. Oxford: Oxford University Press, 2019.

Foucault, Michel. *The Archaeology of Knowledge and the Discourse on Language*. Translated by A. M. Sheridan Smith. New York: Pantheon Books, 1972.

Foucault, Michel. *The History of Sexuality*. Vol. 1, *An Introduction*, translated by Robert Hurley. New York: Vintage Books, 1990.

Foucault, Michel. "Of Other Spaces." Translated by Jay Miskowiec. *diacritics* 16, no. 1 (1986): 22–27.
Fraser, Nancy. "Rethinking the Public Sphere: A Contribution to the Critique of Actually Existing Democracy." *Social Text* 25/26 (1990): 56–80.
Freud, Sigmund. "The Unconscious." In *The Standard Edition of the Complete Psychological Works of Sigmund Freud*, vol. 14, translated and edited by James Strachey, 166–204. London: Hogarth Press, 1957.
Gara, Larry. *The Liberty Line: The Legend of the Underground Railroad*. Lexington: University of Kentucky Press, 1961.
Gardner, Eric. *Black Print Unbound: The Christian Recorder, African American Literature, and Periodical Culture*. New York: Oxford University Press, 2015.
Gardner, Eric. "'Each Atomic Part': Edmonia Goodelle Highgate's African-American Transcendentalism." In *Toward a Female Genealogy of Transcendentalism*, edited by Jana L. Argersinger and Phyllis Cole, 228–46. Athens: University of Georgia Press, 2014.
Gelder, Ken, ed. *The Subcultures Reader*. 2nd ed. London: Routledge, 2005.
"Get Off the Track! A Song for Emancipation, Sung by the Hutchinsons." Boston, 1844.
Gikandi, Simon. *Slavery and the Culture of Taste*. Princeton, NJ: Princeton University Press, 2011.
Gill, Merton M. *Topography and Systems in Psychoanalytic Theory*. Psychological Issues vol. 3, no. 2, monograph 10. New York: International Universities Press, 1963.
Gilman, Susan. *Blood Talk: American Race Melodrama and the Culture of the Occult*. Chicago: University of Chicago Press, 2003.
Glaude, Eddie S., Jr. *Exodus! Religion, Race, and Nation in Early Nineteenth-Century Black America*. Chicago: University of Chicago Press, 2000.
Glissant, Édouard. *Poetics of Relation*. Translated by Betsy Wing. Ann Arbor: University of Michigan Press, 1997.
Godwin, Joscelyn. *The Theosophical Enlightenment*. Albany: State University of New York Press, 1994.
Gordon, Avery F. *The Hawthorn Archive: Letters from Utopian Margins*. New York: Fordham University Press, 2018.
Gordon, Lewis R. "Through the Hellish Zone of Nonbeing: Thinking through Fanon, Disaster, and the Damned of the Earth." *Human Architecture* 5 (Summer 2007): 5–12.
Gordon, Lewis R. *What Fanon Said: A Philosophical Introduction to His Life and Thought*. New York: Fordham University Press, 2015.
Gordon, Milton M. "The Concept of the Sub-Culture and Its Application." *Social Forces* 26 (October 1947): 40–42.
Goyens, Tom. *Beer and Revolution: The German Anarchist Movement in New York City, 1880–1914*. Urbana: University of Illinois Press, 2007.

Greeson, Jennifer Rae. "The 'Mysteries and Miseries' of North Carolina: New York City, Urban Gothic Fiction, and *Incidents in the Life of a Slave Girl.*" *American Literature* 73 (June 2001): 277–309.

Grier, Miles P. "Why (and How) August Wilson Marginalized White Antagonism: A Note for Hollywood Producers." *Los Angeles Review of Books*, April 12, 2021. https://lareviewofbooks.org/article/why-and-how-august-wilson-marginalized-white-antagonism-a-note-for-hollywood-producers/.

Griffith, Mattie. *Madge Vertner. National Anti-Slavery Standard*, July 30–December 24, 1859.

Griffler, Keith P. *Front Line of Freedom: African Americans and the Forging of the Underground Railroad in the Ohio Valley*. Lexington: University Press of Kentucky, 2015.

Griggs, Sutton E. *Imperium in Imperio*. New York: Modern Library Classics, 2004.

Guarneri, Carl J. *The Utopian Alternative: Fourierism in Nineteenth-Century America*. Ithaca, NY: Cornell University Press, 1991.

Gumbs, Alexis Pauline. "Evidence." In *Octavia's Brood: Science Fiction Stories from Social Justice Movements*, edited by adrienne maree brown and Walidah Imarisha, 33–41. Oakland, CA: AK Press, 2015.

Gumbs, Alexis Pauline. *M Archive: After the End of the World*. Durham, NC: Duke University Press, 2018.

Hack, Daniel. *Reaping Something New: African American Transformations of Victorian Literature*. Princeton, NJ: Princeton University Press, 2017.

Hake, Sabine. "Saxa Ioquuntur: Freud's Archaeology of the Text." *boundary 2* 20 (Spring 1993): 146–73.

Hammond, James Henry. "Speech on the Admission of Kansas, under the Lecompton Constitution, Delivered in the Senate of the United States, March 4, 1858." In *Selections from the Letters and Speeches of the Hon. James H. Hammond*, 301–22. New York: John F. Trow, 1866.

Hammonds, Evelynn. "Black (W)holes and the Geometry of Black Female Sexuality." *Differences: A Journal of Feminist Cultural Studies* 6 (Summer–Fall 1994): 127–45.

Harney, Stefano, and Fred Moten. *The Undercommons: Fugitive Planning and Black Study*. Wivenhoe, UK: Minor Compositions, 2013.

Harris, Cheryl I. "Whiteness as Property." *Harvard Law Review* 108, no. 6 (June 1993): 1707–91.

Hartman, Saidiya V. "The Belly of the World: A Note on Black Women's Labors." *Souls* 18, no. 1 (2016): 166–73.

Hartman, Saidiya V. *Lose Your Mother: A Journey along the Atlantic Slave Route*. New York: Farrar, Straus, and Giroux, 2008.

Hartman, Saidiya V. "On Working with Archives." Interview with Thora Siemsen, Creative Independent, April 18, 2018. https://thecreativeindependent.com/people/saidiya-hartman-on-working-with-archives.

Hartman, Saidiya V. *Scenes of Subjection: Terror, Slavery, and Self-Making in Nineteenth-Century America*. New York: Oxford University Press, 1997.

Hartman, Saidiya V. "Venus in Two Acts." *Small Axe* 26 (June 2008): 1–14.

Hartman, Saidiya V. *Wayward Lives, Beautiful Experiments*. New York: Norton, 2019.

Hebdige, Dick. *Subculture: The Meaning of Style*. London: Methuen, 1979.

Hegel, Georg Wilhelm Friedrich. *Lectures on the History of Philosophy*. 3 vols. Translated by Elizabeth S. Haldane and Frances H. Simson. London: Kegan Paul, Trench, Trübner, 1896.

Helton, Laura, Justin Leroy, Max A. Mishler, Samantha Seeley, and Shauna Sweeney. Introduction to "The Question of Recovery: Slavery, Freedom, and the Archive." Special issue, *Social Text* 33 (December 2015): 1–18.

Helwig, Timothy. "Denying the Wages of Whiteness: The Racial Politics of George Lippard's Working-Class Protest." *American Studies* 47 (Fall/Winter 2006): 87–111.

Herring, Scott. *Queering the Underworld: Slumming, Literature, and the Undoing of Lesbian and Gay History*. Chicago: University of Chicago Press, 2007.

Higginson, Thomas Wentworth. *Cheerful Yesterdays*. Boston: Houghton, Mifflin, 1898.

Highgate, Edmonia Goodelle. Letter to M. E. Strieby, December 17, 1866. In *We Are Your Sisters: Black Women in the Nineteenth Century*, edited by Dorothy Sterling, 298–300. New York: Norton, 1984.

Hinks, Peter. *To Awaken My Afflicted Brethren: David Walker and the Problem of Antebellum Slave Resistance*. University Park: Pennsylvania State University Press, 1997.

Hinton, Richard Josiah. *John Brown and His Men*. New York: Funk and Wagnalls, 1894.

Hodges, Graham Russell Gao. *David Ruggles: A Radical Black Abolitionist and the Underground Railroad*. Chapel Hill: University of North Carolina Press, 2010.

Hopkins, Pauline Elizabeth. *Contending Forces: A Romance Illustrative of Negro Life North and South*. New York: Oxford University Press, 1988.

Hopkins, Pauline Elizabeth. *Of One Blood; or, the Hidden Self*. In *The Magazine Novels of Pauline Hopkins*, 439–621. Oxford: Oxford University Press, 1988.

Hopkins, Pauline Elizabeth. *Peculiar Sam; or, the Underground Railroad*. In *The Roots of African American Drama: An Anthology of Early Plays, 1858–1938*, edited by Leo Hamalian and James V. Hatch, 100–123. Detroit, MI: Wayne State University Press, 1991.

Hopkins, Pauline Elizabeth. *Winona: A Tale of Negro Life in the South and Southwest*. In *The Magazine Novels of Pauline Hopkins*, 285–437. Oxford: Oxford University Press, 1988.

Horton, James Oliver, and Lois E. Horton. *Black Bostonians: Family Life and Community Struggle in the Antebellum North*. New York: Holmes and Meier, 1979.

Ingraham, J. H. *The Dancing Feather, or The Amateur Freebooters*. Boston: George Roberts, 1842.

Jackson, Holly. *American Radicals: How Nineteenth-Century Protest Shaped the Nation*. New York: Crown Books, 2019.
Jackson, Kellie Carter. *Force and Freedom: Black Abolitionists and the Politics of Violence*. Philadelphia: University of Pennsylvania Press, 2019.
James, C. L. R. *The Black Jacobins: Toussaint L'Ouverture and the San Domingo Revolution*. 1938; repr., New York: Vintage, 1963.
James, C. L. R. *Mariners, Renegades and Castaways: The Story of Herman Melville and the World We Live In*. 1953; repr., Hanover, NH: University Press of New England, 2001.
James, William. *The Varieties of Religious Experience: A Study in Human Nature*. New York: Longmans, Green, 1902.
Jameson, Fredric. "Of Islands and Trenches: Neutralization and the Production of Utopian Discourse." In *The Ideologies of Theory: Essays, 1971–1986*, vol. 2, 75–102. Minneapolis: University of Minnesota Press, 1988.
Jameson, Fredric. "The Vanishing Mediator; or, Max Weber as Storyteller." In *The Ideologies of Theory: Essays, 1971–1986*, vol. 2, 3–34. Minneapolis: University of Minnesota Press, 1988.
Janet, Pierre. *L'automatisme psychologique: Essai de psychologie expérimentale sur les formes inférieures de l'activité humaine*. Paris: Félix Alcan, 1889.
Jay, Martin. "Against Consolation: Walter Benjamin and the Refusal to Mourn." In *War and Remembrance in the Twentieth Century*, edited by Jay Winter and Emmanuel Sivan, 221–39. Cambridge: Cambridge University Press, 1999.
Jefferson, Thomas. Letter to William Stephens Smith, November 13, 1787. In *The Papers of Thomas Jefferson*, vol. 12, edited by Julian P. Boyd, 355–57. Princeton, NJ: Princeton University Press, 1955.
Jefferson, Thomas. *Notes on the State of Virginia*. London: John Stockdale, 1787.
Johnson, Barbara. "Melville's Fist: The Execution of Billy Budd." *Studies in Romanticism* 18 (Winter 1979): 567–99.
Johnson, Sara E. "'He Was a Lion, and He Would Destroy Much': A Speculative School of Revolutionary Politics." *Small Axe* 58 (March 2019): 195–207.
Jones, Jacqueline. *Goddess of Anarchy: The Life and Times of Lucy Parsons, American Radical*. New York: Basic Books, 2017.
Kahan, Benjamin. *The Book of Minor Perverts: Sexology, Etiology, and the Emergences of Sexuality*. Chicago: University of Chicago Press, 2019.
Kaplan, Sidney. "The Moby Dick in the Service of the Underground Railroad." *Phylon* 12, no. 2 (1951): 173–76.
Kazanjian, David. *The Brink of Freedom: Improvising Life in the Nineteenth-Century Atlantic World*. Durham, NC: Duke University Press, 2016.
Keehn, David C. *Knights of the Golden Circle: Secret Empire, Southern Secession, Civil War*. Baton Rouge: Louisiana State University Press, 2013.
Khanna, Ranjana. *Dark Continents: Psychoanalysis and Colonialism*. Durham, NC: Duke University Press, 2003.

"Kicking Bear's Speech, October 9, 1890." In *The Lakota Ghost Dance of 1890*, by Rani-Henrik Andersson, 309–11. Lincoln: University of Nebraska Press, 2008.

Knox, Thomas Wallace. *Underground, or Life Below the Surface: Incidents and Accidents Beyond the Light of Day; Startling Adventures in All Parts of the World; Mines and the Mode of Working Them; Under-Currents of Society; Gambling and Its Horrors; Caverns and Their Mysteries; The Dark Ways of Wickedness; Prisons and Their Secrets; Down in the Depths of the Sea; Strange Stories of the Detection of Crime*. Hartford, CT: J. B. Burr, 1873.

LaRoche, Cheryl Janifer. *Free Black Communities and the Underground Railroad: The Geography of Resistance*. Urbana: University of Illinois Press, 2014.

LaRoche, Cheryl Janifer. "Secrets Well Kept: Colored Conventioneers and Underground Railroad Activism." In *The Colored Conventions Movement: Black Organizing in the Nineteenth Century*, edited by P. Gabrielle Foreman, Jim Casey, and Sarah Lynn Patterson, 246–60. Chapel Hill: University of North Carolina Press, 2021.

Latour, Bruno. "Why Has Critique Run Out of Steam? From Matters of Fact to Matters of Concern." *Critical Inquiry* 30 (Winter 2004): 225–48.

Lause, Mark. *The Antebellum Crisis and America's First Bohemians*. Kent, OH: Kent State University Press, 2013.

Lause, Mark. *A Secret Society History of the Civil War*. Urbana: University of Illinois Press, 2011.

Leary, John Patrick. *A Cultural History of Underdevelopment: Latin America in the U.S. Imagination*. Charlottesville: University of Virginia Press, 2016.

Lenin, Vladimir. *The Collapse of the Second International*. Translated by A. Sirnis. Glasgow: Socialist Labour Press, 1920.

Letcher, Montgomery E. *Wonderful Discovery! Being an Account of a Recent Exploration of the Celebrated Mammoth Cave*. New York: R. H. Elton, 1839.

Levin, Joanna, and Edward Whitley. Introduction to *Whitman among the Bohemians*, edited by Joanna Levin and Edward Whitley, xi–xxiv. Iowa City: University of Iowa Press, 2014.

Lippard, George. *Adonai, the Pilgrim of Eternity*. Philadelphia, 1851.

Lippard, George. *The Empire City; or, New York by Night and Day*. New York: Stringer and Townsend, 1850.

Lippard, George. *The Killers*. Edited by Matt Cohen and Edlie L. Wong. Philadelphia: University of Pennsylvania Press, 2014.

Lippard, George. *New York: Its Upper Ten and Lower Million*. Cincinnati, OH: H. M. Rulison, 1853.

Lippard, George. *The Quaker City; or, The Monks of Monk Hall*. Amherst: University of Massachusetts Press, 1995.

Lockard, Joe. "'A Light Broke Out Over My Mind': Mattie Griffith, *Madge Vertner*, and Kentucky Abolitionism." *Filson History Quarterly* 76 (2002): 245–85.

Logan, Rayford. *The Negro in American Life and Thought: The Nadir, 1877–1901*. New York: Dial Press, 1954.

Looby, Christopher. "George Thompson's 'Romance of the Real': Transgression and Taboo in American Sensation Fiction." *American Literature* 65 (December 1993): 651–72.

Lorde, Audre. "The Uses of the Erotic: The Erotic as Power." In *Sister Outsider: Essays and Speeches*, 53–59. Freedom, CA: Crossing Press, 1984.

Luciano, Dana. "Sacred Theories of Earth: Matters of Spirit in *The Soul of Things*." *American Literature* 86 (December 2014): 713–36.

Lumpkin, Katherine DuPre. "'The General Plan Was Freedom': A Negro Secret Order on the Underground Railroad." *Phylon* 28, no. 1 (1967): 63–77.

Luskey, Brian P. *On the Make: Clerks and the Quest for Capital in Nineteenth-Century America*. New York: NYU Press, 2010.

Lyons, Joy Medley. *Making Their Mark: The Signature of Slavery at Mammoth Cave*. Fort Washington, PA: Eastern National, 2006.

Mackey, Nathaniel. "Cante Moro." In *Paracritical Hinge: Essays, Talks, Notes, Interviews*, 181–98. Madison: University of Wisconsin Press, 2005.

Mackey, Nathaniel. "Other: From Noun to Verb." In *Discrepant Engagement: Dissonance, Cross-Culturality, and Experimental Writing*, 265–85. Cambridge: Cambridge University Press, 1993.

Madera, Judith. *Black Atlas: Geography and Flow in Nineteenth-Century African American Literature*. Durham, NC: Duke University Press, 2015.

Maher, Geo. *Anticolonial Eruptions: Racial Hubris and the Cunning of Resistance*. Oakland: University of California Press, 2022.

Maldonado-Torres, Nelson. *Against War: Views from the Underside of Modernity*. Durham, NC: Duke University Press, 2008.

Martí, José. "Un drama terrible." In *Obras Completas*, vol. 11, 331–56. Havana: Editorial Nacional de Cuba, 1963.

Martin, Horace. *Pictorial Guide to the Mammoth Cave, Kentucky*. New York: Stringer and Townsend, 1851.

Martineau, Harriet. *The Hour and the Man*. 2 vols. New York: Harper and Brothers, 1841.

Martineau, Harriet. "John Brown: South's Political Posturing." In *The Tribunal: Responses to John Brown and the Harper's Ferry Raid*, edited by John Stauffer and Zoe Trodd, 386–88. Cambridge, MA: Belknap Press, 2012.

Marx, Karl. *Capital*, vol. 1. Translated by Ben Fowkes. New York: Penguin, 1976.

Marx, Karl. "A Contribution to the Critique of Hegel's *Philosophy of Right*: Introduction." In *Early Political Writings*, edited by Joseph J. O'Malley, 57–70. Cambridge: Cambridge University Press, 1994.

Marx, Karl. *The Eighteenth Brumaire of Louis Bonaparte*. New York: International Publishers, 1963.

Marx, Karl, and Friedrich Engels. *The Holy Family, or Critique of Critical Criticism*. Moscow: Progress Publishers, 1956.

Mayfield, Curtis. "Underground." On *Roots*, Curtom Records, 1971.

McGarry, Molly. *Ghosts of Futures Past: Spiritualism and the Cultural Politics of Nineteenth-Century America*. Berkeley: University of California Press, 2008.

McGill, Meredith L. *American Literature and the Culture of Reprinting, 1834–1853*. Philadelphia: University of Pennsylvania Press, 2003.

McKittrick, Katherine. *Demonic Grounds: Black Women and the Cartographies of Struggle*. Minneapolis: University of Minnesota Press, 2006.

McKittrick, Katherine. "'Freedom Is a Secret': The Future Usability of the Underground." In *Black Geographies and the Politics of Place*, edited by Katherine McKittrick and Clyde Woods, 97–114. Toronto: Between the Lines, 2007.

McNally, David. *Monsters of the Market: Zombies, Vampires and Global Capitalism*. Leiden, Netherlands: Brill, 2011.

McPhee, John. *Basin and Range*. New York: Farrar, Straus, and Giroux, 1981.

Melville, Herman. *Benito Cereno*. In *The Piazza Tales, and Other Prose Pieces, 1839–1860*, 47–117. Evanston, IL: Northwestern University Press, 1987.

Melville, Herman. *Moby-Dick; or, the Whale*. Evanston, IL: Northwestern University Press, 1988.

Messer-Kruse, Timothy. *The Haymarket Conspiracy: Transatlantic Anarchist Networks*. Urbana: University of Illinois Press, 2012.

Metzler, Jessica. "'Course I Knows Dem Feet!': Minstrelsy and Subversion in Pauline E. Hopkins's *Slaves' Escape; or, the Underground Railroad*." In *Loopholes and Retreats: African American Writers and the Nineteenth Century*, edited by John Cullen Gruesser and Hanna Wallinger, 101–23. Berlin: Lit Verlag, 2009.

Minutes of the Second U.G.R.R. Convention, For the State of Ohio, Held in the City of Zanesville, On the 6th, 7th, and 8th of January, 1858. N.p., [1858].

Minutes of the State Convention of the Colored Citizens of Ohio, Convened at Columbus, Jan. 15th, 16th, 17th, and 18th, 1851. Cincinnati, OH: E. Glover, 1851.

Moore, Shirley Ann Wilson. *Sweet Freedom's Plains: African Americans on the Overland Trails, 1841–1869*. Norman: University of Oklahoma Press, 2016.

Moreau de Saint-Méry, M. L. E. *Description Topographique, Physique, Civile, Politique et Historique de la Partie Française de l'Isle Saint-Domingue*. 2 vols. Philadelphia: Chez l'auteur, 1797.

Moreton-Robinson, Aileen. *The White Possessive: Property, Power, and Indigenous Sovereignty*. Minneapolis: University of Minnesota Press, 2015.

Morrison, Toni. *Playing in the Dark: Whiteness and the Literary Imagination*. New York: Vintage, 1993.

Moten, Fred. "Black Op." PMLA 123, no. 5 (October 2008): 1743–47.

Moten, Fred. "Blackness and Nothingness (Mysticism in the Flesh)." *South Atlantic Quarterly* 112 (Fall 2013): 737–80.

Moten, Fred. *In the Break: The Aesthetics of the Black Radical Tradition*. Minneapolis: University of Minnesota Press, 2003.

Moten, Fred. "Knowledge of Freedom." *New Centennial Review* 4, no. 2 (2004): 269–310.

Musser, Amber Jamilla. *Sensational Flesh: Race, Power, and Masochism.* New York: NYU Press, 2014.

"My Gropings Nine Miles Underground." *National Magazine* 7 (1855): 58–63.

Narrative of Edmund Wright; His Adventures with and Escape from the Knights of the Golden Circle. Cincinnati, OH: J. R. Hawley, 1864.

National Convention of Colored Men, Held in the City of Syracuse, October 4, 5, 6, and 7, 1864; with the Bill of Wrongs and Rights. Boston: J. S. Rock and Geo. L. Ruffin, 1864.

Nelson, Bruce C. *Beyond the Martyrs: A Social History of Chicago's Anarchists, 1870–1900.* New Brunswick, NJ: Rutgers University Press, 1988.

Noys, Benjamin. "George Bataille's Base Materialism." *Cultural Values* 2 (October 1998): 499–517.

Nwankwo, Ifeoma Kiddoe. *Black Cosmopolitanism: Racial Consciousness and Transnational Identity in the Nineteenth-Century Americas.* Philadelphia: University of Pennsylvania Press, 2005.

O'Donoghue, Diane. "Negotiations of Surface: Archaeology within the Early Strata of Psychoanalysis." *Journal of the American Psychoanalytic Association* 52 (Summer 2004): 653–71.

Ostrowski, Carl. "Inside the Temple of Ravoni: George Lippard's Anti-Exposé." *ESQ* 55 (2009): 1–26.

Ostrowski, Carl. "Slavery, Labor Reform, and Intertextuality in Antebellum Print Culture: The Slave Narrative and the City-Mysteries Novel." *African American Review* 40 (Fall 2006): 493–506.

Otter, Samuel. *Philadelphia Stories: America's Literature of Race and Freedom.* Oxford: Oxford University Press, 2010.

Parker, Henry Webster. "New Wonders of the Mammoth Cave." In *Poems*, 153–68. Auburn: J. M. Alden, 1850.

Pavletich, JoAnn. "'. . . We Are Going to Take That Right': Power and Plagiarism in Pauline Hopkins's *Winona*." *CLA Journal* 59 (December 2015): 115–30.

Pérez, Hiram. *A Taste for Brown Bodies: Gay Modernity and Cosmopolitan Desire.* New York: NYU Press, 2015.

Peterson, Carla L. *Black Gotham: A Family History of African Americans in Nineteenth-Century New York City.* New Haven, CT: Yale University Press, 2011.

Peterson, Carla L. "Commemorative Ceremonies and Invented Traditions: History, Memory, and Modernity in the 'New Negro' Novel of the Nadir." In *Post-Bellum, Pre-Harlem: African American Literature and Culture, 1877–1919*, edited by Barbara McCaskill and Caroline Gebhard, 34–56. New York: NYU Press, 2006.

Peterson, Carla L. "Subject to Speculation: Assessing the Lives of African-American Women in the Nineteenth Century." In *Women's Studies in Transition: The Pursuit of Interdisciplinarity*, edited by Kate Conway-Turner, Suzanne Cherrin, Jessica Schiffman, and Kathleen Doherty Turkel, 109–17. Newark: University of Delaware Press, 1998.

Peterson, Charles J. "Two Days in the Mammoth Cave." *Peterson's Magazine* 22 (October 1852): 155–61.

Petrulionis, Sandra Harbert. "Fugitive Slave-Running on the *Moby Dick*: Captain Austin Bearse and the Abolitionist Crusade." *Resources for American Literary History* 28 (2002): 53–81.

Pike, David L. *Metropolis on the Styx: The Underworlds of Modern Urban Culture, 1800–2001*. Ithaca, NY: Cornell University Press, 2007.

Pike, David L. *Subterranean Cities: The World beneath Paris and London, 1800–1945*. Ithaca, NY: Cornell University Press, 2005.

Prawer, S. S. *Karl Marx and World Literature*. Oxford: Oxford University Press, 1976.

Quarles, Benjamin. *Allies for Freedom: Blacks and John Brown*. New York: Oxford University Press, 1974.

Quarles, Benjamin. *Black Abolitionists*. New York: Oxford University Press, 1969.

Quashie, Kevin. *The Sovereignty of Quiet: Beyond Resistance in Black Culture*. New Brunswick, NJ: Rutgers University Press, 2012.

Randolph, Paschal Beverly. *After Death; or, Disembodied Man*. Boston, 1868.

Randolph, Paschal Beverly. *After Death: The Disembodiment of Man*. Boston: Colby and Rich, 1873.

Randolph, Paschal Beverly. "The Ansairetic Mystery; A New Revelation Concerning Sex! A Private Letter, Printed, But Not Published; It Being Sacred and Confidential." In John Patrick Deveney, *Paschal Beverly Randolph: A Nineteenth-Century Black American Spiritualist, Rosicrucian, and Sex Magician*, 311–26. Albany: State University of New York Press, 1997.

Randolph, Paschal Beverly. "The Asiatic Mystery; The Fire Faith! The Religion of Flame! The Force of Love! The Energos of Will! The Magic of Polar Mentality! First Rosicrucian Manifesto to the World Outside the Order!" *The Initiates and the People* 3 (May/June 1930–May/June 1931): 107–23.

Randolph, Paschal Beverly. *The Book of the Triplicate Order, Rosicrucia, Eulis, Pythianae*. San Francisco: Women's Publishing, Printed for the Brotherhood, Candidates, and Truth-Seekers, 1875.

Randolph, Paschal Beverly. *Casca Llanna (Good News): Love, Woman, Marriage: The Grand Secret! A Book for the Heartful*. Boston: Randolph Publishing, 1872.

Randolph, Paschal Beverly ["The Rosicrucian"]. *Dealings with the Dead; The Human Soul, Its Migrations and Its Transmigrations*. Utica, NY: M. J. Randolph, 1861–62.

Randolph, Paschal Beverly. *Eulis! The History of Love*. Toledo, OH: Randolph Publishing, 1874.

Randolph, Paschal Beverly. *Guide to Clairvoyance, and Clairvoyant's Guide: A Practical Manual for Those Who Aim at Perfect Clear Seeing and Psychometry*. Boston: Rockwell and Rollins, 1867.

Randolph, Paschal Beverly, ed. *Hermes Mercurius Trismegistus; His Divine Pymander*. Boston: Rosicrucian Publishing, 1871.

Randolph, Paschal Beverly ["Count de St. Leon"]. *Love and Its Hidden History; A Book for Man, Woman, Wives, Husbands, and for the Loving and the Unloved: The Heart-Reft, Pining Ones*. Boston: William White, 1869.

Randolph, Paschal Beverly. *Love and Its Hidden History; also, the Master Passion, or the Curtain Raised on Woman, Love, and Marriage*. Boston: Randolph, 1870.

Randolph, Paschal Beverly. *Love! At Last! The Seven Magnetic Laws of Love*. Boston: Randolph, 1870.

Randolph, Paschal Beverly. "The Mysteries of Eulis." In *Paschal Beverly Randolph: A Nineteenth-Century Black American Spiritualist, Rosicrucian, and Sex Magician*, by John Patrick Deveney, 327–41. Albany: State University of New York Press, 1997.

Randolph, Paschal Beverly. *P. B. Randolph, The "Learned Pundit," and "Man with Two Souls": His Curious Life, Works, and Career; The Great Free-Love Trial*. Boston: Randolph Publishing House, 1872.

Randolph, Paschal Beverly ["Historicus"]. *Rosicrucian: Out of the Shell*. N.p., 1869.

Randolph, Paschal Beverly. *Seership! The Magnetic Mirror; A Practical Guide to Those Who Aspire to Clairvoyance-Absolute; Original and Selected from Various European and Asiatic Adepts*. Boston: Randolph, 1870.

Randolph, Paschal Beverly ["The Rosicrucian"]. *Soul! The Soul World: The Homes of the Dead*. Boston: Randolph Publishing, 1872.

Randolph, Paschal Beverly. *Tom Clark and His Wife*. New York: Sinclair Tousey, 1863.

Randolph, Paschal Beverly. *The Unveiling: or, What I Think of Spiritualism*. Newburyport, MA: William H. Huse, 1860.

Randolph, Paschal Beverly. *The Wonderful Story of Ravalette*. New York: Sinclair Tousey, 1863.

Redpath, James. *The Public Life of Captain John Brown*. Boston: Thayer and Eldridge, 1860.

Reed, Austin. *The Life and Adventures of a Haunted Convict*. Edited by Caleb Smith. New York: Random House, 2016.

Report of the Select Committee of the Senate Appointed to Inquire into the Late Invasion and Seizure of the Public Property at Harper's Ferry. Senate, 36th Cong., 1st sess., 1860, report 278.

Richter, Annette Lane Harrison. "Reflections on Black Sisterhood and the United Order of Tents." *e-flux* 105 (December 2019). https://www.e-flux.com/journal/105/305114/reflections-on-black-sisterhood-and-the-united-order-of-tents/.

Roberts, Neil. *Freedom as Marronage*. Chicago: University of Chicago Press, 2015.

Robinson, Cedric J. *Black Marxism: The Making of the Black Radical Tradition*. 1983; repr., Chapel Hill: University of North Carolina Press, 2000.

Roediger, David. *The Wages of Whiteness: Race and the Making of the American Working Class*. London: Verso, 1991.

Roeger, Tyler. "Sensationalizing the Urban West: City-Mysteries and Urban Boosterism." *ESQ* 63 (2017): 561–95.

Rogers, Carlton Holmes. *Incidents of Travel in the Southern States and Cuba, with a Description of the Mammoth Cave.* New York: R. Craighead, 1862.

Rogin, Michael Paul. *Subversive Genealogy: The Politics and Art of Herman Melville.* New York: Knopf, 1983.

Rohy, Valerie. *Anachronism and Its Others: Sexuality, Race, Temporality.* Albany: State University of New York Press, 2009.

Rollin, Frank [Frances] A. *Life and Public Services of Martin R. Delany.* Boston: Lee and Shepard, 1883.

Rosenberg, C. G. *Jenny Lind in America.* New York: Stringer and Townsend, 1851.

Rosenberg, Jordan/a. "Monstrously Unpositable: Primitive Accumulation and the Aesthetic Arc of Capital." *J19* 3 (Spring 2015): 197–204.

Ruggles, David. *First Annual Report of the New York Committee of Vigilance, for the Year 1837.* New York: Piercy and Reed, 1837.

"Rural, Ralph." *The Mountain Village: or, Mysteries of the Coal Region.* Pottsville, PA: G. L. Vliet's Cheap Job Printing Office, 1849.

Rusert, Britt. "From Wilson's Cave Gallery to Jemisin's *The Stone Sky*." Paper presented at the biennial conference of C19: The Society of Nineteenth-Century Americanists, Albuquerque, New Mexico, March 2018.

Rusert, Britt. *Fugitive Science: Empiricism and Freedom in Early African American Culture.* New York: NYU Press, 2017.

Rusert, Britt. "Plantation Ecologies: The Experimental Plantation in and against James Grainger's *The Sugar-Cane*." *Early American Studies* 13 (Spring 2015): 341–73.

Rusling, J. F. *A Trip to the Mammoth Cave, K.Y.* Nashville, TN, 1864.

Sanborn, F. B. *The Life and Letters of John Brown: Liberator of Kansas, and Martyr of Virginia.* Boston: Roberts Brothers, 1885.

Sanborn, F. B. *Memoirs of John Brown.* Concord, MA, 1878.

Sayers, Daniel O. *A Desolate Place for a Defiant People: The Archeology of Maroons, Indigenous Americans, and Enslaved Laborers in the Great Dismal Swamp.* Gainesville: University Press of Florida, 2014.

Schaack, Michael J. *Anarchy and Anarchists: A History of the Red Terror and the Social Revolution in America and Europe.* Chicago: F. J. Schulte, 1889.

Schuller, Kyla. *The Biopolitics of Feeling: Race, Sex, and Science in the Nineteenth Century.* Durham, NC: Duke University Press, 2018.

Sedgwick, Eve Kosofsky. *Epistemology of the Closet.* Berkeley: University of California Press, 1990.

Sedgwick, Eve Kosofsky. *Touching Feeling: Affect, Pedagogy, Performativity.* Durham, NC: Duke University Press, 2003.

Sentilles, Renée M. *Performing Menken: Adah Isaacs Menken and the Birth of American Celebrity.* New York: Cambridge University Press, 2003.

Sharpe, Christina. *In the Wake: On Blackness and Being*. Durham, NC: Duke University Press, 2016.

Sherman, Joan R. *Invisible Poets: Afro-Americans of the Nineteenth Century*. Urbana: University of Illinois Press, 1974.

Shockley, Ann Allen. "Pauline Elizabeth Hopkins: A Biographical Excursion into Obscurity." *Phylon* 33 (1972): 22–26.

Shockley, Evie. "ode to my blackness." In *the new black*, 30. Middletown, CT: Wesleyan University Press, 2012.

"Short Bull's Speech, October 31, 1890." In *The Lakota Ghost Dance of 1890*, by Rani-Henrik Andersson, 312–13. Lincoln: University of Nebraska Press, 2008.

Siebert, Wilbur H. *The Underground Railroad from Slavery to Freedom*. New York: Macmillan, 1899.

Silliman, B., Jr. "On the Mammoth Cave of Kentucky." *American Journal of Science and the Arts* 11 (May 1851): 332–39.

Simpson, Audra. *Mohawk Interruptus: Political Life across the Borders of Settler States*. Durham, NC: Duke University Press, 2014.

Simpson, Joshua McCarter. *The Emancipation Car, Being an Original Composition of Anti-Slavery Ballads, Composed Exclusively for the Under Ground Rail Road*. N.p.: J. Mc. C. Simpson, 1874.

Simpson, Joshua McCarter. *Original Anti-Slavery Songs*. Zanesville, OH, 1852.

Sinha, Manisha. *The Slave's Cause: A History of Abolition*. New Haven, CT: Yale University Press, 2016.

Six Months in Secessia. Philadelphia: Barclay, 1864.

Slout, William L., ed. *Broadway below the Sidewalk: Concert Salons of Old New York*. San Bernardino, CA: Borgo Press, 1994.

Smith, James A. McCune. *A Lecture on the Haytien Revolutions*. New York: Printed by Daniel Fanshaw, 1841.

Smith, James A. McCune. *The Works of James McCune Smith: Black Intellectual and Abolitionist*. Edited by John Stauffer. Oxford: Oxford University Press, 2006.

Smith, Nathan Ryno [Viator]. *Legends of the South, by Somebody Who Desires to Be Considered Nobody*. Baltimore: Steam Press of William K. Boyle, 1869.

Somerville, Siobhan B. *Queering the Color Line: Race and the Invention of Homosexuality in America*. Durham, NC: Duke University Press, 2000.

Spires, Derrick R. *The Practice of Citizenship: Black Politics and Print Culture in the Early United States*. Philadelphia: University of Pennsylvania Press, 2019.

Spillers, Hortense. "Interstices: A Small Drama of Words." In *Black, White, and in Color: Essays on American Literature and Culture*, 152–75. Chicago: University of Chicago Press, 2003.

Spillers, Hortense. "Mama's Baby, Papa's Maybe: An American Grammar Book." In *Black, White, and in Color: Essays on American Literature and Culture*, 203–29. Chicago: University of Chicago Press, 2003.

Spivak, Gayatri Chakravorty. "Can the Subaltern Speak?" In *Marxism and the Interpretation of Culture*, edited by Cary Nelson and Lawrence Grossberg, 271–313. Urbana: University of Illinois Press, 1988.

Stadler, Gustavus. *Troubling Minds: The Politics of Genius in the United States, 1840–1890*. Minneapolis: University of Minnesota Press, 2006.

Stallings, L. H. *Funk the Erotic: Transaesthetics and Black Sexual Cultures*. Champaign: University of Illinois Press, 2015.

Stallybrass, Peter. "'Well Grubbed, Old Mole': Marx, *Hamlet*, and the (Un)fixing of Representation." *Cultural Studies* 12, no. 1 (1998): 3–14.

Stanley, Amy Dru. *From Bondage to Contract: Wage Labor, Marriage, and the Market in the Age of Slave Emancipation*. Cambridge: Cambridge University Press, 1998.

Steele, Jeffrey. "The Visible and Invisible City: Antebellum Writers and Urban Space." In *The Oxford Handbook of Nineteenth-Century American Literature*, edited by Russ Castronovo, 179–96. Oxford: Oxford University Press, 2012.

Stewart, David M. *Reading and Disorder in Antebellum America*. Columbus: Ohio State University Press, 2011.

Still, William. *The Underground Rail Road; a Record of Facts, Authentic Letters, &c., Narrating the Hardships, Hair-breadth Escapes and Death Struggles of the Slaves in Their Efforts for Freedom*. Rev. ed. Philadelphia: People's Publishing, 1879.

Streeby, Shelley. *American Sensations: Class, Empire, and the Production of Popular Culture*. Berkeley: University of California Press, 2002.

Sue, Eugène. *The Mysteries of Paris*. Translated by Charles H. Town. New York: Harper and Brothers, 1843.

Sundquist, Eric J. *To Wake the Nations: Race in the Making of American Literature*. Cambridge, MA: Harvard University Press, 1993.

Surtees, W. E. "Emancipation: From the *National Intelligencer*." *African Repository*, September 1851, 282.

Surtees, W. E. "Recollections of North America, in 1849–50–51." *New Monthly Magazine* 94 (1852): 1–22.

Symmes, John Cleves. "Light Gives Light, to Light Discover—'Ad Infinitum.'" St. Louis, MO, 1818.

Tate, Claudia. *Domestic Allegories of Political Desire: The Black Heroine's Text at the Turn of the Century*. Oxford: Oxford University Press, 1992.

Taylor, Bayard. *At Home and Abroad*. New York: G. P. Putnam, 1860.

Taylor, Charles. "The Politics of Recognition." In *Multiculturalism: Examining the Politics of Recognition*, edited by Amy Gutman, 25–73. Princeton, NJ: Princeton University Press, 1994.

Terrible and All Absorbing Narrative and Confession of Edwin Winters; With an Authentic Statement of the Horrible Assassination of Miss Eugenia Blakeman, on Board a Western Steamer. New York: Randall, 1854.

Testut, Charles. *Les Mysteres de la Nouvelle-Orleans*. New Orleans: Imprimerie de A. Gaux et de L. Dutuit, 1852.

Thompson, George. *City Crimes*. In *Venus in Boston and Other Tales of Nineteenth-Century City Life*, edited by David S. Reynolds and Kimberly R. Gladman, 105–310. Amherst: University of Massachusetts Press, 2002.
Thoreau, Henry David. "A Winter Walk." *The Dial* 4 (October 1843): 211–26.
"Through the Cotton States." *Knickerbocker* 58 (October 1861): 314–23.
"A Tour in the Mammoth Cave." *All the Year Round* 4 (1861): 343–47.
Trowbridge, J. T. *Cudjo's Cave*. Boston: J. E. Tilton, 1864.
"An Under-ground Railroad in Broadway." *Scientific American*, November 3, 1849.
Urban, Hugh. *Magia Sexualis: Sex, Magic, and Liberation in Modern Western Esotericism*. Berkeley: University of California Press, 2006.
Valencius, Conevery Bolton. *The Lost History of the New Madrid Earthquakes*. Chicago: University of Chicago Press, 2013.
Vose, John D. *Seven Nights in Gotham*. New York: Bunnell and Price, 1852.
Walcott, Rinaldo. *The Long Emancipation: Moving toward Black Freedom*. Durham, NC: Duke University Press, 2021.
Walker, David. *Appeal to the Coloured Citizens of the World*. Edited by Peter Hinks. University Park: Pennsylvania State University Press, 2000.
Wallace, Robert K. "*Billy Budd* and the Haymarket Hangings." *American Literature* 47 (March 1975): 108–13.
Wally, R. T. *The Cesspool of Crime, or, Important Discoveries and Disclosures in Demolishing the Old Brewery at the Five Points, N. Y*. Albany: McGoun and Kewin, 1852.
Weeks, Kathi. *The Problem with Work: Feminism, Marxism, Antiwork Politics, and Postwork Imaginaries*. Durham, NC: Duke University Press, 2011.
Weheliye, Alexander G. *Habeas Viscus: Racializing Assemblages, Biopolitics, and Black Feminist Theories of the Human*. Durham, NC: Duke University Press, 2014.
Weik, Terrance M. *The Archaeology of Anti-Slavery Resistance*. Gainesville: University Press of Florida, 2012.
West, Peter. "Trying the Dark: Mammoth Cave and the Racial Imagination, 1839–1869." *Southern Spaces*, February 9, 2010. https://southernspaces.org/2010/trying-dark-mammoth-cave-and-racial-imagination-1839-1869.
Wheeler, E. L. *Deadwood Dick Jr. in Chicago; or, the Anarchist's Daughter*. New York: Beadle and Adams, 1888.
Whitehead, Colson. "Colson Whitehead's 'The Underground Railroad' Is a Literal Train to Freedom." Interview with Terry Gross. *Fresh Air*, NPR, August 8, 2016.
Whitehead, Colson. *The Underground Railroad*. New York: Doubleday, 2016.
Whitman, Walt. *Leaves of Grass*. Boston: Thayer and Eldridge, 1860.
Wilderson, Frank B., III. *Red, White, and Black: Cinema and the Structure of U.S. Antagonisms*. Durham, NC: Duke University Press, 2010.
Williams, George W. *History of the Negro Race in America, from 1619 to 1880*. 2 vols. New York: G. P. Putnam's Sons, 1882.

Williams, Raymond. *Marxism and Literature*. Oxford: Oxford University Press, 1977.

Williams, Rosalind. *Notes on the Underground: An Essay on Technology, Society, and the Imagination*. Boston: MIT Press, 1990.

Willis, N. P. *Health Trip to the Tropics*. New York: Charles Scribner, 1853.

Wilson, Ivy G. *Specters of Democracy: Blackness and the Aesthetics of Politics in the Antebellum U.S.* Oxford: Oxford University Press, 2011.

Wilson, William J. [Ethiop]. "Afric-American Picture Gallery." *Anglo-African Magazine* 1, nos. 2–10 (February–October 1859).

Wilson, William J. [Ethiop]. "What Shall We Do with the White People?" *Anglo-African Magazine* 2, no. 2 (February 1860): 41–45.

Winters, Ben H. *Underground Airlines*. New York: Mulholland Books, 2016.

Wood, Marcus. *The Horrible Gift of Freedom: Atlantic Slavery and the Representation of Emancipation*. Athens: University of Georgia Press, 2010.

Wright, Richard. "The Man Who Lived Underground." In *Eight Men*, 19–84. New York: HarperCollins, 1989.

Wynter, Sylvia. "Sambos and Minstrels." *Social Text* 1 (Winter 1979): 149–56.

Wynter, Sylvia. "Unsettling the Coloniality of Being/Power/Truth/Freedom: Towards the Human, after Man, Its Overrepresentation—An Argument." CR: *The New Centennial Review* 3 (Fall 2003): 257–337.

Yusoff, Kathryn. *A Billion Black Anthropocenes or None*. Minneapolis: University of Minnesota Press, 2018.

Zabriskie, James C. "A Visit to the Mammoth Cave of Kentucky." *Rutgers Literary Miscellany* (October 1842): 148–54.

Index

Abeokuta, 66
Abraham, Nicolas, 116, 128
abyss, 124; and Glissant, 18, 48–49; and Paschal Beverly Randolph's works, 142, 143; and *Appeal to the Coloured Citizens of the World* (Walker), 52
Africa, 30, 96; and *Adalaska* (Bickley), 127; and Barnum's Museum, 109; and *Billy Budd* (Melville), 194; and "New Wonders of the Mammoth Cave" (Parker), 41–42; in *Of One Blood* (Hopkins), 102, 163; in Paschal Beverly Randolph's works, 134, 138, 139, 141, 150, 155, 162; and slavery, 51, 71
African Observer (magazine), 10
African-American Mysteries, 4, 13, 17, 19, 88–89, 125, 188; and John Brown, 89, 93; formation of, 88; and militancy, 90
the *Alarm* (newspaper), 167–91; and abolitionism, 184–87; and anti-work politics, 178; close reading of, 167–68; complex politics of, 169, 170; and dynamite, 176, 177; and the macabre, 168, 180–83; poetry in, 168, 179–183, 189–90; reports on organizing in, 172–73; short fiction in, 176–79, 188–89. *See also* Blakesley, Harry A.; Holmes, William; James, C. L.; Jones, Ernest; Lizius, Gerhard; Lum, Dyer D.; Parsons, Albert; Parsons, Lucy; Swank, Lizzie; Wilson, S. Robert
Albanese, Mary Grace, 102
Alcott, Louisa May, 94
Aliened American (newspaper), 95
allegory, Benjamin's analysis of, 114–17, 119
Allewaert, Monique, 40
All the Year Round, 35
Altschuler, Sari, 108
American Colonization Society (ACS), 57, 162
American Mysteries Secret U.G.R.R. Society, 87, 89, 90, 93, 125, 188
anarchism, 2, 3, 21, 107, 134; and the *Alarm*, 167, 172, 173; and Mikhail Bakunin, 183; and *Billy Budd* (Melville), 169, 191–97; and John Brown, 189, 190; and Chicago, 166, 168; and dynamite, 176, 177, 184, 189; and the International Working People's Association, 170; and the Paris Commune, 181, 182; and the Pittsburgh Proclamation, 171; and Paschal Beverly Randolph, 148, 151; and *Anarchy and Anarchists* (Schaack), 174, 175; and "Two Stories in One" (Swank), 188; and whiteness, 186, 187; and "A Word to Tramps" (Parsons), 180

Anderson, Jeremiah, 95
Anderson, Osborne P., 95
Andrews, Stephen Pearl, 107
Anglo-African Magazine, 60, 61, 64–66, 70, 71, 134, 159
Anti-Man-Hunting League, 19, 90, 91
Apess, William, 56, 57
Arbeiter-Zeitung (newspaper), 167, 185
archaeology, 5, 6, 14
Armstrong, Louis, 44
Autobiography of a Female Slave (Griffith), 36
Averill, Charles E., 111, 112, 197

Bakunin, Mikhail, 171, 183
Barclay, E. E., 87
Barnum, P. T., 109, 110
Bataille, Georges, 112–14, 125
Beam, Dorri, 101
Bearse, Austin, 91, 92
Benjamin, Walter, 114–17, 119, 127
Bey, Dawoud, 199
Bey, Marquis, 187
Bickley, George W. L., 106, 117, 126, 128, 129
Billy Budd (Melville), 21, 169, 191–97; compared to *Of One Blood* (Hopkins), 194; ending of, 196–97; and the Haymarket affair, 21, 169, 192–194, 196; and homosexuality, 193, 194; revisions of, 192; and "subterranean fire," 21, 193, 195; the underground as a figure for interiority in, 194–96
biopolitics, 146
Bishop, Stephen, 12, 25, 26, 28–35, 36, 39, 42–44, 45
blackface minstrelsy, 34–36, 82, 98
Black geographies (McKittrick), 28, 30, 42
Black Marxism: The Making of the Black Radical Tradition (Robinson), 46
"The Blackness of Darkness" (Crary), 26, 32, 45
Blakesley, Harry A., 186
Blue Ridge Mountains, 103
Blyden, Edward Wilmot, 71

Boston, MA, 41, 50; Anti-Man-Hunting League, 19, 91; and the boat *Moby Dick*, 92; Boston Vigilance Committee, 90, 91; and city mysteries, 106; and Paschal Beverly Randolph, 140, 144, 150, 163
bourgeois public sphere, 72
Bowditch, Henry Ingersoll, 90
Brand, Dionne, 49
Bransford, Materson, 25–28, 30, 3–32, 35, 36, 45
Bransford, Nicholas, 25–28, 30, 45
Brazil, 77, 157
breath, 174, 177–81, 203
Breuer, Josef, 195
Britten, Emma Hardinge, 142, 143
Brooks, Daphne, 99
Brotherhood of Eulis, 144
Brotherhood of the Union, 118–21, 124, 126
Brown, Henry "Box," 105, 109, 117
Brown, Jayna, 22, 23, 136, 141
Brown, John, 19, 88–90, 92–97, 184; and Black radical secret societies, 88–90; John Brown Association of Jersey City, 187; Du Bois's biography of, 97; influence on Haymarket anarchists, 184, 187–90; in Pauline Hopkins's writings, 100–103; and raid on Harpers Ferry, 94, 95; and the Subterranean Pass Way, 100, 101, 103; use of mining language as code, 95–96
Brown, John, Jr., 96
Brown, Lois, 98, 99
Brown, William Wells, 153
Buck-Morss, Susan, 115
Bullitt, Alexander Clark, 28, 29, 36, 38, 39
Buntline, Ned, 122
Burns, Anthony, 90
burrowing, 2, 15–16, 107, 130, 183

Camp of Israel, 87
Campt, Tina, 16, 23
Canada, 74, 188, 190, 198, 200; and Austin Bearse, 91; and *Peculiar Sam* (Hopkins), 98; and mythology of the Underground Railroad, 75, 198; and Joshua McCarter

Simpson, 85. *See also* Chatham Convention
capitalism, 178, 180; and *Adonai* (Lippard), 119; and "American 1848," 116; and anarchism, 187, 189, 193; city mysteries, 19, 108, 132; and International Working People's Association, 169, 170, 179, 180; and Marx, 130; and racial capitalism, 10; and "wage slavery," 185, 186
Carby, Hazel, 100
Carpenter, Russell Lant, 43
Casarino, Cesare, 194
caves, 6, 22, 88, 112, 113, 114, 130, 133; and *Adalaska* (Bickley), 106, 126–29; and "Afric-American Picture Gallery" (Wilson), 3, 8, 18, 47, 67–72; and "Election Day" (Swank); 176–77; and *Invisible Man* (Ellison), 44; and *Terrible and All Absorbing Narrative and Confession of Edwin Winters*, 106, 125; and *The Underground Railroad* (Whitehead), 202; and *Winona* (Hopkins), 101–2. *See also* Mammoth Cave
Centre for Contemporary Cultural Studies (University of Birmingham), 2
Channing, William E., 94
Chatham Convention, 89, 95
Chicago, 199; and anarchism, 3, 21, 22, 167, 168; and *Billy Budd* (Melville), 191, 192; Chicago school of sociology, 2; Chicago *Western Citizen*, 77, 78; *Deadwood Dick Jr. in Chicago*, 174–75, 176; and Haymarket affair, 166; in *The Fall of the Great Republic (1886–88)* (Coverdale), 175–76; and influence of Bakunin on Chicago anarchists, 183; and International Working People's Association, 170, 171; and Lucy Parsons, 185; and police repression in the 1880s, 173–74; and tramps, 179
Child, Lydia Maria, 28–29, 31, 32, 38
Chiles, Katy, 41
Christian Union (newspaper), 173, 174
Ciccariello-Maher, George, 58, 212n7

city mysteries: and demystification, 110, 130–32; politics of, 108–9, 116–17, 122, 124–29; and popular nonfiction, 106–7; and racialization of the underground as Black, 109, 117, 126; rural city mysteries, 106, 126; settings of, 105–6, 109; and underground taverns, 107–8. *See also* mystery
clairvoyance, 149, 153, 154, 163
Clapp, Henry, 107
Clarkson, Thomas, 57
Clymer, R. S., 135
Clytus, Radiclani, 65, 66, 108
Coghlan, J. Michelle, 182
Cohen, Matt, 108
Colored American Magazine, 99
Colored Conventions, 66, 80, 151, 219n19
Compromise of 1850, 116
Comstock, Anthony, 146, 234n65
Conspiración de la Escalera, 64
conspiracy: and *Billy Budd* (Melville), 21; and Cuba, 63–64; and dynamite, 176–78; etymology of, 177–78, 203; "revolutionary conspiracy," 167, 171, 176, 177–78, 180, 191; and Haymarket trial, 166, 177, 178
Cordell, Ryan, 76
Cornish, Samuel, 66
Coronado, Raúl, 121
counterpublic: as a fantasy, 72; versus underground, 72, 136
Coviello, Peter, 122, 148
Crary, Reverend B. F., 26, 31, 45
Crawley, Ashon, 23
Crazy Horse, 6
Creole (ship), 59, 60
Croghan, John, 25, 27, 31, 43, 209n36
Cross, John, 77, 78
Cuba, 16, 18, 39, 60, 62–65, 69, 106
Cunningham, Nijah, 48
Curtis, Newton M., 106

Daut, Marlene, 11, 215n49
Davis, Andrew Jackson, 137
Davis, David Brion, 97
Day, William Howard, 95, 153

Deadwood Dick Jr. in Chicago; or, the Anarchist's Daughter, 174–76
DeBaptiste, George, 88, 89
Declaration of Independence, 55
de Cleyre, Voltairine, 182
Delany, Martin R., 66, 93, 125; *Blake; or, the Huts of America*, 11, 18, 47, 50, 60–64, 80, 105, 134; and Freemasonry, 61; on John Brown, 93–94; and Joshua McCarter Simpson, 80; the *Mystery* (newspaper), 17, 61, 125
Dell, Floyd, 176
Denning, Michael, 108
Detroit, MI, 4, 13, 19, 79, 88–90
Deveney, John Patrick, 135, 144, 145, 151, 163
Dickens, Charles, 122
Dickson, Moses, 88
Dietzgen, Josef, 185
Dinius, Marcy, 53
Diouf, Sylviane, 39
doubling, 55, 56, 69, 72, 111, 123, 197
Douglass, Frederick, 43, 50, 77, 153, 157; and John Brown, 93, 94; *Frederick Douglass' Paper*, 65; *The Life and Times of Frederick Douglass*, 58; *Narrative of the Life of Frederick Douglass*, 83; *North Star*, 34; "Slavery, the Slumbering Volcano," 11, 12, 18, 47, 57–60, 63, 64, 203; and subterranean wordplay, 57–58
dreams, 86, 99, 101–2; and allegory, 114; freedom dreams, 36, 100, 164. *See also* trances; visions
Dred Scott case, 70
Du Bois, W. E. B., 46, 86; *John Brown*, 93, 96, 97, 100; "The Comet," 12; *The Souls of Black Folk*, 140; and whiteness as a wage, 186
Dwight, Theodore, Jr., 155, 156
dynamite: and the *Alarm*, 21, 168, 177; and anarchist propaganda, 172, 176; Johann Most's pamphlet on the manufacture of, 171; "On a Cartridge of 'Hercules' Dynamite," 183, 184, 187–90; "in the synecdochal sense," 176–77; and "A Word to Tramps" (Parsons), 180

Eburne, Jonathan, 20
Eckstrom, Leif, 67
1886, 21, 88, 166, 167
1848, 106, 116, 117, 120, 125–29, 144
The Eighteenth Brumaire of Louis Bonaparte (Marx), 5, 12, 20, 113, 129
Elaw, Zilpha, 136
Ellison, Ralph, 1, 4, 12, 23, 26, 44, 45, 67
"emancipation car," 84, 219n33
The Emancipation Car (Simpson), 80, 82, 85, 86
Emerson, Ralph Waldo, 34, 114
Engel, George, 191
Engels, Friedrich, 20, 110, 130
Erickson, Paul, 120
Ernest, John, 61
Estes, Nick, 6
estrangement, and the underground, 39, 69, 103, 112, 123
Ethiopia, 12, 21, 102, 103, 140, 163

The Fall of the Great Republic (1886–88) (Coverdale), 175
Faneuil Hall, 184
Fanon, Frantz: critique of Hegel's masterslave dialectic, 58; and racial masochism, 27; and "zone of nonbeing," 18, 48, 49, 50
Ferguson, Christine, 135, 139
Ferreira da Silva, Denise, 161
Ferrer, Ada, 16
Fielden, Samuel, 185, 191
Finch, Marianne, 28
Finley, Lana, 135, 163
First International, 183
Fischer, Adolph, 191
Fisk Jubilee Singers, 102
Five Points (New York City neighborhood), 104, 106, 107, 110, 122, 134
flash press, 107
Flatley, Jonathan, 119
footnotes: in *Appeal to the Coloured Citizens of the World* (Walker), 15, 18, 47, 53–55, 64, 69; in Paschal Beverly Randolph's work, 146
Foster, George G., 107, 122

Foster, Stephen, 83
Foucault, Michel, 14, 112, 147, 148
Fourier, Charles, 141, 148, 151
Fraser, Nancy, 72
Fred Gray Association, 107
Free Love League, 107
free love movement, 137, 148, 150, 168
Freedom's Journal (newspaper), 11
Freiheit (newspaper), 169
Freud, Sigmund, 195
Fuentes, Marisa, 16
fugitives and fugitivity, 23, 75, 90, 91, 99, 100, 207n39, 220n37; and "Afric-American Picture Gallery," 3, 70, 71, 72, 74; and African-American Mysteries, 88; and anarchism, 186, 188–89; and John Brown, 93, 103; contemporary scholarship on fugitivity, 23; and Delany on origins of Freemasonry, 61, 80; *Fugitive Science* (Rusert), 16, 29; Fugitive Slave Law, 91, 92, 93; and maroon communities, 39; and *New York: Its Upper Ten and Lower Million* (Lippard), 104–5; and *Night Coming Tenderly, Black* (Bey), 199; and the North Star, 34; and *Of One Blood* (Hopkins), 103; and *Peculiar Sam* (Hopkins), 98–99; and Joshua McCarter Simpson, 80, 84–86; and "Slavery, the Slumbering Volcano" (Douglass), 59; and Underground Railroad, 76, 78; and *The Underground Railroad* (Whitehead), 199–202; and vigilance committees, 77; and *Winona* (Hopkins), 99–101
Fugitive Slave Law, 29, 67, 91, 92

Gara, Larry, 75
Garnet, Henry Highland, 64, 153
geography, 11, 40, 63
geology, 5, 6, 29
Get Out (Peele), 13, 52
Gikandi, Simon, 49
Gill, George R., 89
Glaude, Eddie S., Jr., 56
Glissant, Édouard, 18, 48, 49
Godwin, Joscelyn, 135

Gordon, Avery, 23
Gorin, Franklin, 25, 27
Great Dismal Swamp, 39–40, 103, 158, 186
Green, Misha, 199
Griffith, Mattie, 36, 37, 38, 127
the grotesque, 131, 155; and the grotesque-sublime, 113–14
Gumbs, Alexis Pauline, 13
gypsum, 25, 34

Haiti, 11, 18, 39, 63
Haitian Revolution, 10, 11, 59, 63, 94
Hamilton, Thomas, 66
Hamlet, 5, 12, 129
Hammond, James Henry, 9, 10. *See also* "mudsill theory"
Hammonds, Evelynn, 38
Harney, Stefano, 18, 50, 122
Harpers Ferry, 19, 93–95, 100, 103, 184, 187, 224
Hartman, Saidiya, 16, 43, 46, 49, 85, 152, 159
Haymarket affair, 166–69, 174, 177, 179, 190–91; and *Billy Budd* (Melville), 21, 169, 192–94, 196
Hebdige, Dick, 3
Hegel, G. W. F., 58, 129–31, 183
Helwig, Timothy, 108
Hermetic Brotherhood of Luxor, 135
Hermetic Society of the Golden Dawn, 135
Herring, Scott, 16, 131
Heywood, Ezra, 181
hieroglyphics, 40–41
Higginson, Thomas Wentworth, 90, 93
Hinton, Richard Josiah, 94
hollow earth theories, 22, 44
Holmes, William, 173
Hopkins, Pauline, 76, 97, 203; and John Brown, 100–103; *Contending Forces*, 138; *Of One Blood*, 12, 21, 97, 102–3, 140, 162–65, 194; and Paschal Beverly Randolph, 12, 21, 140, 162–65; *Peculiar Sam*, 19, 98–99, 102, 103, 164; *Winona*, 19, 97, 99–102, 103, 164

"I Dreamed I Saw Joe Hill Last Night," 182
Ingraham, J. H., 106

International Working People's Association (IWPA), 21, 167–73, 176, 177, 179–82, 184–87, 191, 197; American Group, 173; founding of, 169; and July 26, 1885, march through Chicago, 170; and "revolutionary conspiracy," 167, 171, 176, 177–78, 180, 191. *See also* the *Alarm*; Lehr und Wehr Verein

Invisible Man (Ellison), 1, 4, 12, 26, 44, 45, 67

"I Wish I Was a Mole in the Ground," 1

Jackson, Andrew, 56, 137
Jackson, Holly, 95, 184,
Jackson, Rebecca Cox, 136
Jackson, Shona, 9
James, C. L., 176, 185, 186
James, C. L. R., 46
James, William, 195
Jameson, Fredric, 194, 226n23
Janet, Pierre, 195
Jay, Martin, 116
Jefferson, Thomas, 55, 56, 59, 70
Jim Crow, 164
Johnson, Barbara, 193, 196, 197
Johnson, Sara E., 16
Jones, Ernest, 179, 180
jubilee, 101, 145, 153

Kagi, John Henry, 94, 95
Kahan, Benjamin, 135, 136, 147
Kansas-Nebraska Act of 1854, 39
Kazanjian, David, 16
"Kentucky Mummy," 6
King, Tiffany Lethabo, 9
Knickerbocker, 30, 33, 41
Knights of the Golden Circle, 125
Knox, Thomas Wallace, 6–8

Labor Enquirer (newspaper), 172
Lambert, William, 88–90
land reform, 128, 137
Latour, Bruno, 131
Laymon, Kiese, 13
Leary, John Patrick, 64

Lee, Jarena, 136
Lehr und Wehr Verein, 170, 173, 174
Lenin, V. I., 51
Letcher, Montgomery E., 40
Lewis, Enoch, 10, 11
Liberator (newspaper), 77, 79, 91
Liberia, 30, 31, 39, 43, 44, 71, 82
Liberty Line, 77
Lippard, George: *Adonai, the Pilgrim of Eternity*, 117, 119–21; and Brotherhood of the Union, 117–21, 124, 126; *The Empire City*, 125; *New York: Its Upper Ten and Lower Million*, 104–5, 108, 109, 122–24; *The Quaker City*, 106, 112, 113, 114
Lizius, Gerhard, 176
Logan, Rayford, 97
Looby, Christopher, 109
López, Narciso, 106
Lorde, Audre, 149
Louisiana, 20, 39, 70, 134, 138, 151, 159, 160
L'Ouverture, Toussaint, 66, 96, 215
"lower frequencies" (Ellison), 1
Luciano, Dana, 5
Lum, Dyer D., 190
Lumpkin, Katherine DuPre, 86

Madge Vertner (Griffith), 36–38, 127
Maldonado-Torres, Nelson, 48, 58
Mammoth Cave (Kentucky), 8, 25–45, 67, 105, 110, 197, 203; and archaeology, 6; and Stephen Bishop, 12, 25, 26, 28–35, 36, 39, 42–44, 45; and Black geographies (McKittrick), 28; and the "Blackness of Blackness," 45; and Materson Bransford, 25–28, 30, 31–32, 35, 36, 45; and Nicholas Bransford, 25–28, 30, 45; contemporaneous literature regarding, 26; Echo River, 35; eyeless fish in, 28, 39, 41, 42; feminization of, 37–38; and Haiti, 39; historical background of, 17, 25; and Indigenous history of, 32, 41; and *Madge Vertner* (Griffith), 36–38; and "Mammoth Cave" (Barnwell), 33–35; and "New Wonders of the Mammoth Cave" (Parker), 40–42; and *Pictorial Guide to the Mammoth*

Cave (Martin), 30; as racialized space, 4, 9, 18, 47; Star Chamber, 34, 35; Symmes Pit Branch, 44; and "Two Days in Mammoth Cave" (Peterson), 30, 33; and visions of a sovereign Black underground, 39, 40, 42. *See also* Black geographies (McKittrick); Bullitt, Alexander Clark; Carpenter, Russell Lant; Child, Lydia Maria; Finch, Marianne; Letcher, Montgomery E.; Peterson, Charles J.; Rogers, Carlton Holmes; Rusling, J. F.; Silliman, Benjamin, Jr.; Surtees, W. E.; Taylor, Bayard; Willis, N. P.; Zabriskie, James C.

maroon communities, 39, 50, 70, 93, 95, 103

Martin, Trayvon, 58

Martineau, Harriet, 10, 95

martyrdom, 94, 180, 181

Marx, Karl, 8, 52, 129–32, 155, 171, 183; and *Black Marxism* (Robinson), 10; *Capital*, 130, 131; and demystification, 131–32, 168; *The Eighteenth Brumaire*, 5, 12, 20, 113, 129–30; and Emma Hardinge Britten, 232n44; *The Holy Family*, 20, 110, 130–31; and the "old mole," 20, 113, 129–30, 182, 183

Mayfield, Curtis, 12

McCormick Reaper Works, 177

McGann, Jerome, 60

McGarry, Molly, 121

McGill, Meredith, 76

McKittrick, Katherine, 28, 30, 85

McNally, David, 130

melancholy, 116, 119, 140, 163, 187

Melville, Herman: *Billy Budd*, 21, 169, 191–97; *Moby-Dick*, 2, 91–92, 195

Menken, Adah Isaacs, 107

Messer-Kruse, Timothy, 177

Michel, Louise, 184, 189, 190

Miles, Tiya, 9

mines and mining, 5, 8, 9, 18, 47, 51, 69, 95, 96, 105, 133, 143, 144, 176, 182

Minkins, Shadrach, 90

minstrelsy, 35, 82, 98

Moby Dick (boat), 91–92

Moby-Dick (Melville), 2, 91–92, 195

moles, 1, 5, 6, 12, 20, 22, 113, 129–30, 131, 182–83

Moore, Shirley Ann Wilson, 202

Moreau de Saint-Méry, Médéric Louis Élie, 139

Moreton-Robinson, Aileen, 41

Morrison, Toni, 12, 129

Most, Johann, 169, 171

Moten, Fred, 45, 49, 62, 82, 122

"mudsill theory," 9, 10. *See also* Hammond, James Henry

Muñoz, José Esteban, 22, 23

music, and Pauline Hopkins, 98, 102; and *Invisible Man*, 44; and Mammoth Cave, 27, 35–36, 209n38; and Paschal Beverly Randolph, 142, 145, 156; and Joshua McCarter Simpson, 80, 82–85; and subculture, 2

Musser, Amber, 27

Myrick, A. S., 79, 80

mystery, 110, 124, 129, 194, 199, 203; and city mysteries, 19, 114, 115, 117, 124, 130; in Martin Delany's fiction, 63, 67, 68; and Marx, 20, 131, 168, 169; the *Mystery* (Martin Delany's newspaper), 17, 61, 125; and *Of One Blood* (Hopkins), 102, 103; and Paschal Beverly Randolph, 143–46, 149; versus secrecy, 3, 68, 79; and the underground, 3; and Underground Railroad, 74, 79

Nashville, TN, 31, 144

Native Americans, 6, 32, 41, 51, 56, 141, 161, 162, 211n58

New Madrid earthquakes (1811–12), 5

New York Colonization Society, 155

nonviolence, critiques of, 51, 55, 90

North Star (newspaper), 34, 75

Noys, Benjamin, 112

"On a Cartridge of 'Hercules' Dynamite," 183, 188–90

Order of Twelve, 88, 90

Otter, Samuel, 108, 113

Owen, Robert, 151

paranoia, 87
Paris Commune, 181, 184, 187, 189
Parker, Henry Webster, 40–42, 43
Parks, Suzan-Lori, 12
Parsons, Albert, 170, 177, 178, 179, 180, 185, 190, 191
Parsons, Lucy, 171, 172, 179, 180, 185, 186, 188
Peele, Jordan, 13, 52
Pérez, Hiram, 194
Peterson, Carla, 16, 102
Peterson, Charles J., 30, 33
Peterson's Magazine, 30
Pfaff's beer cellar, 107
Phillips, Wendell, 184
pirates, 91, 106
Pittsburgh, PA, 169
Pittsburgh Proclamation, 171, 173, 180, 181, 186. *See also* International Working People's Association (IWPA)
Pokaski, Joe, 199
the popular, 2, 3, 57, 59, 173; and popular culture, 75, 111; and popular fiction, 19, 108, 174; popular music, 82, 83; and popular nonfiction literature, 106; and popular opinion, 80
Prince Hall Freemasonry, 61, 125
Puryear, Martin, 12

Quashie, Kevin, 23

racial capitalism, 10
Randolph, Paschal Beverly, 3, 12, 20, 21, 133, 168, 197; and abolitionism, 136, 153, 235n98; and African diasporic religions, 138, 163; *After Death; or, Disembodied Man*, 159–62, 202; biography of, 134, 135; *The Book of the Triplicate Order*, 145; *Casca Llana*, 150; cosmological theories of, 140–42; *Dealings with the Dead*, 143; and Freedmen's Bureau, 3, 20, 134, 151, 159–60; and gender identities, 139, 147, 148; *Guide to Clairvoyance*, 146, 149; and Pauline Hopkins, 140, 162–65; and the occult underground, 136, 138, 151; *P. B. Randolph, The "Learned Pundit,"* 149–51;

racial self-identification as *sang-mêlée*, 139, 140; renunciation of spiritualism, 137; *Rosicrucian: Out of the Shell*, 145; and Rosicrucianism, 134, 138, 144, 158; and sex, 142, 146–49, 150; and the "soul world," 197; *Tom Clark and his Wife*, 157; *The Wonderful Story of Ravalette*, 152–55, 158. *See also* clairvoyance; sex magic
Rankine, Claudia, 153
Realf, Richard, 89, 95
Reclus, Élisée, 171
Reconstruction, 21, 134, 151, 158–62, 184
Redpath, James, 102
revolution, 203; and *Adalaska* (Bickley), 126, 128–29; and the African-American Mysteries, 88–90; and *Appeal to the Coloured Citizens of the World* (Walker), 15, 47, 51, 53, 56, 57; and *Blake* (Delany), 18, 47, 60–61, 63–64, 80; and Chicago anarchists, 167, 168, 171, 175–78, 180–83, 189–91; and 1848, 106, 125, 126, 128–29; and Frantz Fanon, 48, 49; French Revolution, 83, 118, 196; Haitian Revolution, 10, 11, 59, 63, 94; and the International Working People's Association, 169–71; and George Lippard, 119, 120, 122–23; and Marx, 5, 129; and Paschal Beverly Randolph, 149–51, 154, 157, 158; and sex, 146; and Joshua McCarter Simpson, 83; and "Slavery, the Slumbering Volcano" (Douglass), 58–59; and the "slumbering volcano," 11, 59; and *Terrible and All Absorbing Narrative and Confession of Edwin Winters*, 125; and Nat Turner, 39
Reynolds, George J., 89
Riqueti, Honoré Gabriel, Count of Mirabeau, 10
Robinson, Cedric, 10, 19, 46, 47, 62
Roediger, David, 186
Rogers, Carlton Holmes, 31, 38, 39, 43
Rogin, Michael, 116
Rohy, Valerie, 102
Rollin, Frances Anne, 93, 94
Rosenberg, Jordy, 131

Rosicrucianism. *See* Randolph, Paschal Beverly
Rosicrucian Club (Boston), 144, 145
Ruggles, David, 77
Rusert, Britt, 16, 29, 67, 71
Rusling, J. F., 31, 32
Russell, Charles Edward, 174

"safety valve" theory, 86
Sandusky, OH, 87, 89, 188
Schaack, Michael J., 174–77
Schuller, Kyla, 146
secrecy, 3, 66, 68, 79, 89, 95, 126, 147; and *Blake* (Delany), 60–62; and city mysteries, 124; and the IWPA, 171–74, 176, 183; and Marx on the commodity, 130, 131; versus mystery, 3, 68, 79; and Paschal Beverly Randolph, 137, 138, 143, 144, 150; and *The Secrets of the Twin Cities* (Averill), 111, 112, 197; and the underworld, 107. *See also* mystery
secret societies, 2, 19, 80, 87, 106, 125, 126, 142, 188, 203; and Paschal Beverly Randolph, 136, 146, 149, 152, 154, 157. *See also* African-American Mysteries; American Mysteries Secret U.G.R.R. Society; Anti-Man-Hunting League; Brotherhood of the Union; Camp of Israel; Order of Twelve
Sedgwick, Eve Kosofsky, 111, 193–95
settler colonialism, 41, 69
sex: and city mysteries, 117; and deviance, 105; and the erotic, 149; and Foucault, 147; and homosexuality, 193, 194; and the law, 150; and the paranormal, 146; and race, 148, 153; and Paschal Beverly Randolph, 20, 135, 136, 142, 144; and resistance, 46; and sexual freedom, 102, 108; and transgression, 107, 122; and the underworld, 16. *See also* sex magic; sex work; sexual violence
sex magic, 2, 3, 20, 135, 146–47, 148–50, 153
sex work, 108
sexual violence, 117, 155
Sharpe, Christina, 16, 49, 50, 66

Shockley, Evie, 12
Siebert, Wilbur H., 78, 86
Silliman, Benjamin, Jr., 30
Simpson, Audra, 23
Simpson, Joshua McCarter, 12, 76, 80–86, 87, 89, 95, 99, 100; *The Emancipation Car*, 80, 82, 84, 85–86; *Original Anti-Slavery Songs*, 80, 82, 84; and parody, 83; at Second U.G.R.R. Convention for the State of Ohio, 80, 87, 89
Sims, Thomas, 90
slavery, 9, 30, 41, 71, 116, 118; in "Afric-American Picture Gallery" (Wilson), 69, 70–71, 72, 73; anarchism and the history of, 184–91; in *Appeal to the Coloured Citizens of the World* (Walker), 51–53, 56; in *Blake* (Delany), 60–61, 63–64; and Cuba, 39, 60, 62, 63–64; and images of the underground, 48–49; in *Madge Vertner* (Griffith), 36–37; in *Moby-Dick* (Melville), 92; in *Peculiar Sam* (Hopkins), 98–99, 102, 164; in "Slavery, the Slumbering Volcano" (Douglass), 11, 18, 57–60; in *Winona* (Hopkins), 99–101; in *The Wonderful Story of Ravalette* (Randolph), 156–57. *See also* antislavery undergrounds; fugitivity; Knights of the Golden Circle; Mammoth Cave; "slumbering volcano," Underground Railroad
"slumbering volcano," 10–11, 12, 18, 47, 57–60, 63, 64, 100, 154, 175, 176
Smallwood, Elizabeth, 76
Smallwood, Thomas, 76
Smith, James McCune, 10
Smith, Joshua Bowen, 91
Somerville, Siobhan, 148
Spies, August: and the *Arbeiter-Zeitung*, 167, 185; as defendant in the Haymarket trial, 21, 167, 177–78; and revolutionary breath, 178; and "subterranean fire," 21, 169, 174, 191, 192, 197
Spillers, Hortense, 37, 49
Spires, Derrick, 68
spiritualism, 121, 134, 136–38, 140, 144, 148, 182, 183

Spivak, Gayatri Chakravorty, 131
Stadler, Gustavus, 31
Stallings, L. H., 134, 135–36
Stallybrass, Peter, 5, 129
"Stand Your Ground" laws, 58
Steele, Jeffrey, 123, 125
Stewart, David, 108
Still, William, 97
St. Louis, MO, 88
Streeby, Shelley, 108
subculture, 2, 3, 4, 11, 169, 198
Subculture: The Meaning of Style (Hebdige), 3
the sublime, 32, 68, 113; and the grotesque-sublime, 113–14
"subterranean fire," 11, 21; and *Billy Budd* (Melville), 191, 192–95, 197; and August Spies, 21, 169, 174, 191, 192, 197
Sue, Eugène, 105, 110, 130
Sundquist, Eric, 64
Supreme Grand Lodge of the Triple Order, 144
Surtees, W. E., 30, 37
Swank, Lizzie, 168, 173, 176–77, 178–79, 180, 188–89; "Election Day," 176–77, 187; "Two Stories in One," 188–89
Symmes, John Cleves, 44
Symmes Pit Branch, 44

Taney, Roger B., 70
Taylor, Bayard, 39
Taylor, Charles, 123
temperance, 137
The Terrible and All Absorbing Narrative and Confession of Edwin Winters, 106, 125–26, 128
Testut, Charles, 106
Theosophical Society, 135
Thompson, George, 111–13, 115, 117
Thoreau, Henry David, 94, 192
Tinsley, Omise'eke Natasha, 49
Tocsin of Liberty (newspaper), 76
Torok, Maria, 116, 128
Torrey, Charles Turner, 76
tramps, 21, 168, 179, 180, 186, 188, 240n51

trances, 118, 127, 134, 136–38, 154, 163. *See also* dreams; visions
Truth, Sojourner, 136
Tubman, Harriet, 199
Tucker, Benjamin, 181
tunnels, 8, 12, 18, 21, 101, 105, 133, 144, 176, 197, 200–202
Turner, Nat, 39, 40, 96, 99, 158

the unconscious, 21, 169, 194–95, 198
undercommons (Moten and Harney), 18, 50, 122
underground: in Black studies scholarship, 14–50; and the dead, 174, 180–83; and freedom, 19, 36, 39–40, 42–44, 76, 84–85, 100, 101–3, 105; methods for studying the, 13–17; racialization as Black, 4, 8–13, 18, 20, 26, 30–35, 44–45, 129, 133, 209n39; relations between literal and figurative, 4, 6–8, 11, 19, 26, 32, 44, 51, 52, 63, 69, 101, 105, 106, 110–13, 119, 120, 133, 175, 190; and unrecognizability, 3, 122–24, 128–29; versus resistance, 123; and Southern Hemisphere, 11, 60, 63–64; versus subculture, 2–4; temporalities of the, 17, 198; and the unconscious, 21, 169; 194–95
Underground, or Life Below the Surface (Knox), 6, 7
Underground Railroad, 71–77; in contemporary media, 198–202; and Henry "Box" Brown, 105; historiography of, 75; fantasies of, 19, 75, 76, 86, 93, 105; and Pauline Hopkins, 97–102; literalization of, 77–79; and maritime underground, 91, 92; media coverage of in the 1840s and 1850s, 74; and "safety valve" theory, 86; and secret societies, 87–89, 93; and Joshua McCarter Simpson, 76, 80, 82–86; and Subterranean Pass Way, 93–96, 100, 103
The Underground Railroad (Whitehead), 198–203
underlife (Wynter), 18, 48, 49
Urban, Hugh, 135
US Constitution, 55, 197

Vigilance Committee (Boston), 77, 90, 91, 104, 122
visions, 6, 99, 102, 118–19, 127, 154, 157–58. *See also* dreams; trances
volcanoes, 18, 47, 63, 100, 175, 176. *See also* "slumbering volcano"
Vose, John D., 110

Walker, David: *Appeal to the Coloured Citizens of the World*, 13, 15, 18, 47, 50–57, 59, 69, 88, 105, 160, 197; and citation, 55–56. *See also* abyss; footnotes; mines and mining
Wallace, Michelle, 38
Wallace, Robert K., 192
Wally, R. T., 106
Walsh, Mike, 107
War of 1812, 25
Washington, George, 118–21
Washington, Madison, 59–60
Weekly Anglo-African (magazine), 60, 134
Weeks, Kathi, 178
West, Peter, 26
What Is It (tavern), 108, 109, 110, 111
Wheatley, Phillis, 66
Whitehead, Colson, 198–203

whiteness, 33, 34, 41, 42, 186, 189, 211n58
Whitman, Walt, 107
Whittier, John Greenleaf, 64
Wilberforce, William, 57
Wilderson, Frank, 9, 49
Williams, George Washington, 86
Williams, Raymond, 14, 15
Pete Williams's dance hall, 122–23
Willis, N. P., 32, 35, 39, 40
Wilson, Ivy, 66, 71
Wilson, S. Robert, 181–83
Wilson, William J. ("Ethiop"): "Afric-American Picture Gallery," 3, 8, 18, 47, 50, 65–73, 74, 75, 134, 197, 203; column in *Frederick Douglass' Paper*, 65–66, 108; "What Shall We Do with the White People?" 216n79
Winters, Ben H., 198
Wong, Edlie, 108
Wood, Marcus, 97
Wright, Richard, 12, 46
Wynter, Sylvia, 8, 18, 48, 49

Yale University, 30
Yusoff, Kathryn, 5, 9, 51

Zabriskie, James C., 34

www.ingramcontent.com/pod-product-compliance
Lightning Source LLC
Chambersburg PA
CBHW020833160426
43192CB00007B/628